GENERAL ALBERT C. WEDEMEYER

GENERAL
ALBERT C. WEDEMEYER
AMERICA'S UNSUNG STRATEGIST IN WORLD WAR II

JOHN J. McLAUGHLIN

CASEMATE
Philadelphia & Oxford

Published in the United States of America and Great Britain in 2012 by
CASEMATE PUBLISHERS
908 Darby Road, Havertown, PA 19083
and
10 Hythe Bridge Street, Oxford, OX1 2EW

Copyright 2012 © John J. McLaughlin

ISBN 978-1-61200-069-5
Digital Edition: ISBN 978-1-61200-106-7

Cataloging-in-publication data is available from the Library of Congress
and the British Library.

10 9 8 7 6 5 4 3 2 1

Printed and bound in the United States of America.

For a complete list of Casemate titles please contact:

CASEMATE PUBLISHERS (US)
Telephone (610) 853-9131, Fax (610) 853-9146
E-mail: casemate@casematepublishing.com

CASEMATE PUBLISHERS (UK)
Telephone (01865) 241249, Fax (01865) 794449
E-mail: casemate-uk@casematepublishing.co.uk

MIX
Paper from
responsible sources
FSC
www.fsc.org FSC® C011935

CONTENTS

To Mary Jean McLaughlin

ACKNOWLEDGMENTS

In the four years that it has taken me to research and write this book, there have been a large number of people who have been tremendously generous to me, both with their time and their advice, and I would like to take this opportunity to thank them.

The idea for this book originated with my dissertation on General Albert C. Wedemeyer when I graduated from Drew University in 2005. My dissertation advisors William B. Rogers, Ph.D., and George Sirgiovanni, Ph.D., each encouraged me to expand the dissertation into book form. When I initially started my research I thought it would be a good idea to associate myself with a group of like-minded persons who had an interest in World War II, and the easiest way to do that would be to join a book club. The interaction with the members, I thought, would be a good opportunity to meet others interested in the Second World War and to expand my knowledge. To my astonishment I discovered that there was not a single WWII-oriented book club in the entire New York/New Jersey metropolitan area! More than one librarian told me that "there does not seem to be that much interest in that subject any more." This was very disturbing, and I decided to start one. We now hold monthly meetings at the Millburn, New Jersey Public Library, where we feature lectures by authors, historians, and others knowledgeable about World War II. We have about 100 members. The program has been a success, and Club members have been very supportive of my work. Many ideas in the book owe their origin to information supplied to me by these interested men and women, and, happily, some younger members! In particular, I single out my dear friend Rob Gagnon, a former Marine Captain and Vietnam veteran, the Book Club's first member and most ardent supporter. Rob's great interest in history generally, and World War II in particular has been very helpful both to me and the success of the Club. Rob was responsible for introducing me to the resources of the wonderful Brookdale College Center for World War II Studies, run by the indefatigable Paul Zigo, and the New York Military Affairs Symposium (NYMAS), which I attend regularly and where I often take the opportunity to engage some of their speakers. The Book Club's web address is ww2book-club.blogspot.com, and we get inquiries from interested people all over the world.

A General Wedemeyer website that my friend Brian Greer of Orillia, Ontario, a recognized internet expert, set up for me (www.general-wede-meyer.com) has put me in touch with many historians, authors, and others interested in the general's life. The site also allowed me to locate some of Wedemeyer's family. Through the internet I met Pamela Wedemeyer, who had a very close relationship with her grandfather, and she has been especially helpful, supplying me with a good deal of information about the General, including pictures and correspondence she maintained with him during his long life. Nicole W. Miller, a professional genealogist from Champaign, Illinois, has been helpful in giving me some information about the general's ancestors. My friend Frank Alexander has been an indispensable assistant in guiding me through the mysteries of the internet and the computer and has always been available for instant advice, when an inadvertent key stroke threatened to derail hours of labor. Dr. Steven Lomazow has been generous with his time reading, commenting, and editing many of the chapters, and I thank him especially for his efforts. One of my early supporters in the Book Club, Sharon Austin, our official photographer, has worked tirelessly with Nancy Webster, the brilliant videographer and CEO of White Horse Communications, who tapes all the lectures at the Book Club, and I thank them both.

Writing a book would be impossible without the unstinting support, assistance, and encouragement of the many archivists and librarians who labor in the shadows, but without whom a book like this would never be possible. In particular I want to thank the expert personnel at the National Archives, the Hoover Institution, the FDR Library in Hyde Park, the George C.

Marshall Library at Lexington, VA, the archivists at Carlisle Barracks, PA, and the local librarians at the New York, Newark and Millburn, NJ libraries who have been extremely helpful in locating rare, out-of-date books, documents, and newspapers. Especially helpful in locating many historical documents and government reports, was Beth Patterson at Drew University Library who deserves a special note of thanks. All these people deserve a lot of credit for their assistance to writers and historians, and I for one state that without their assistance a work like this would not be possible.

Finally, and most important of all, my devoted wife Mary Jean deserves a tremendous amount of credit for her unflagging support, advice, and encouragement throughout the entire period of writing this book. She has accompanied me to all of the places where I have done research and has sat patiently reading a book or magazine while I wrote, copied, or took digital images of literally hundreds of pages of photos, documents, and other material. She has helped me sort out this mass of paper and put it into some semblance of order this mass of paper so it would be useful. She has located numerous papers, books, documents and other items that I have misplaced or lost in the mountain of paper that accumulates in writing a book. She has also proofread every page of this work and made many excellent suggestions.

This work would not have been possible without her and it is dedicated to her with love.

John J. McLaughlin
Short Hills, New Jersey
March 2012

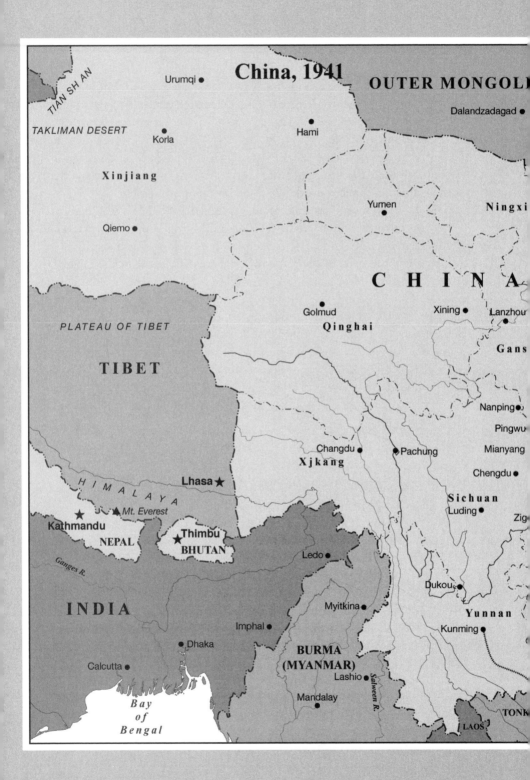

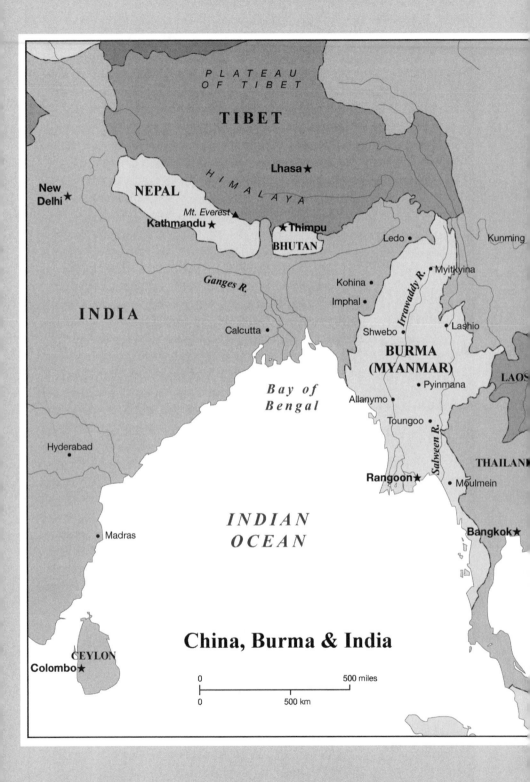

China, Burma & India

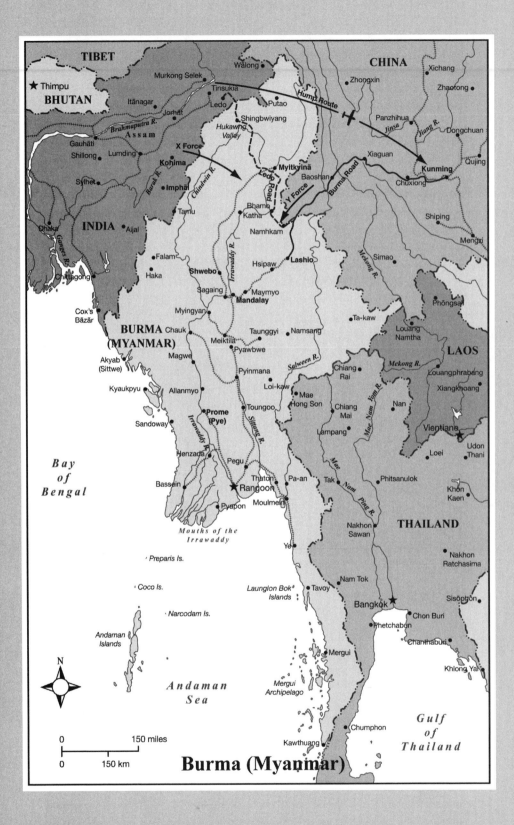

Burma (Myanmar)

PREFACE

If everyone is thinking alike, then someone isn't thinking.
—General George S. Patton

There are two types of military leaders. There are the swashbuckling battlefield commanders, highly adept at moving forces from point A to point B, whose bravery and guile are well suited for the unique circumstances presented in combat, often carrying flashy monikers like "Blood and Guts" "Rough and Ready" and "Vinegar Joe." Then there are those more cerebral types who function in lower profile roles, yet no less essentially. These "General's Generals" are those with an eye toward the more practical aspects of battle, the nuts and bolts planning, and even more rarely, a vision of the long term consequences of military action and its effect on world politics, so-called "grand strategy."

This work is devoted to Albert Coady Wedemeyer, one of America's finest military strategists, perhaps the finest of all, whose notable list of accomplishments and vision of the future of the world was clear, yet even today, greatly unappreciated. As historian Forest Pogue points out:

> Few officers in the large aggregation of faithful and anonymous "Staffs" that make the War and Navy Departments function are more faceless than those who "plan." Some of them—Marshall and Eisenhower are examples—find their way to high command, but during their period as planners they usually are overtired workhorses writing and rewriting hundreds of papers, produced often at

1

a moment's notice and at late hours, in which their contribution is often unrecognized. Their identifying initials, scrawled on thousands of pages of legal-sized documents, reveal little more than the amazing energy of the inscribers.[1]

Wedemeyer was one of those planners. After being "discovered" by one of America's greatest quiet generals, George Catlett Marshall, Wedemeyer's brilliance carried him rapidly from major to three-star general, the first in his West Point class to earn a star. His unique background and training in German battle tactics propelled him into the hub of the American planners of World War II strategy and, later, his political savvy and competence were highly respected, though grossly underutilized and characteristically sidetracked in the post-war geopolitical landscape. Had Wedemeyer's admonitions been followed more closely, the course of history would surely have been quite different.

My interest in Wedemeyer was spurred by my long-awaited trip to visit the D-Day battlefields of Normandy in the summer of 2005. As part of the preparation, the tour company suggested a list of a half-dozen titles to read. The one that made the greatest impression on me was John Keegan's *Six Armies in Normandy*, which begins with thumbnail sketches of eight men Keegan considered as having had the most significant impact on that momentous event. The list includes the obvious: Eisenhower, Marshall, Alanbrooke,[2] Montgomery, and Rommel; then the not so obvious like Soviet Foreign Minister Molotov, and the not obvious at all, Stilwell and Wedemeyer, the last two mentioned being the most remote. Stilwell appears to be included only as a contrast and segue to Wedemeyer.

Keegan portrays Wedemeyer as "one man who had foreseen what was to come, had taken its measure, and was ready with a plan for the American army to fight its way down the road back."[3] He credited him with authorship of the "Victory Program," a plan written *prior* to America's entry into the war, that called for a massive build-up of American military forces and armaments, with a plan for a cross-channel invasion of the European mainland, which Keegan called "one of the decisive acts of the Second World War."[4]

A decisive act? Then why hadn't any of the knowledgeable guides on the D-Day tour known anything about him, and why has he gone largely unnoticed in the history books? More importantly, if the Victory Program was so vital to success in the Normandy campaign, why was its author not part of it in 1944?[5]

Further research into this apparently underappreciated military genius led to the Hoover Institution at Stanford University in Palo Alto, California, the single largest repository of Wedemeyer's papers, where a remarkable and continuing record of vision and accomplishment was revealed. Not only had Wedemeyer been intimately involved in the planning of the European war, at the peak of his accomplishment he was mysteriously sent to a seemingly dead-end assignment in Asia, only to subsequently distinguish himself as the general primarily responsible for rescuing Nationalist China from the Japanese and rehabilitating a critical rapport with and respect for the taciturn Chiang Kai-shek, in direct contrast to the often outrageously inappropriate conduct of his predecessor, Joseph Stilwell. More questions arose. What brought about and who was responsible for his transfer to Asia? What aspects of his character led to his success? Why is so little written about him in the histories of World War II?

Immediately after the war, Wedemeyer, then in China as Commander of United States Forces, became a primary operative intent on enforcing the official American China policy of unification under Chiang. Wedemeyer had a prophetic understanding of the motives of Joseph Stalin and the Communist leader in China, Mao Zedong. In 1947, he led a fact-finding mission at the request of President Truman and wrote a comprehensive report outlining a specific course of action needed to avert a Communist takeover of mainland China, recognizing what the mainstream military and the State Department were loath to admit. The highly anticipated report was suppressed, and by the time his views were published in 1949, it was too late, setting the stage for the Cold War and conflicts in Korea, and later Vietnam that might have been avoided had his admonitions been heeded. Like the mythical Cassandra, Wedemeyer had been endowed with the ability to accurately forecast future events but unhappily cursed with the fate that his predictions would not be believed.

A modest and unassuming Nebraskan, Wedemeyer's character and intelligence were well known and respected by many of the giants of his time. Winston Churchill, Franklin Roosevelt, Harry Truman, and George Marshall top the list, yet his strong sense of duty to his country, his personal integrity and honor, which put principle ahead of personal gain, first imbued in him by his father and reinforced by his experience at West Point, often inhibited his professional career, and later his post-retirement civilian employment in industry.

Despite the seminal role Wedemeyer played at a time of cataclysmic change in world politics, his efforts remain grossly underappreciated. Most accounts of the Second World War in Europe do not include him. The vast majority of the volumes devoted to China do not give him the credit he is due. While historian Barbara Tuchman glorified Joseph Stilwell, Wedemeyer, the quiet hero of the China campaign is treated negatively. Although the supplying of China with arms and equipment over "The Hump" was fully functioning when Wedemeyer reported to China in October 1944, he completely familiarized himself with the operation, and after the war, while in Europe, he was consulted about the feasibility of airlifting food and supplies to Berlin when the Soviets shut down the land route. His knowledge and advice was accepted and partially responsible for the implementation of the operation. Still again, Wedemeyer's contribution has been overlooked. As recently as 2010, Richard Reeve's account of the Berlin Airlift[6] incorrectly characterized and grossly underestimated Wedemeyer's contributions.

Perhaps the most inaccurate and unfair assessment of Wedemeyer is how he is portrayed during the time he served in China after replacing General Stilwell. In order to fairly assess General Wedemeyer's role in China it will be necessary to take a closer look at the main players that lived, worked, and fought in that theatre during the war years, as well as what has been written about them.

This work will challenge the traditional view of the Joseph Stilwell–Theodore White–Barbara Tuchman paradigm that the Chiang Kai-shek regime failed because it was militarily incompetent, corrupt, and incompetent, and that Stilwell was the lone heroic figure valiantly fighting to defeat the Japanese against opposition from Chiang Kai-shek. This author believes that a closer look at the history of American and Chinese foreign relations will demonstrate that China, and Chiang up until shortly after Pearl Harbor, were viewed in the most positive light by United States political figures, as well as an overwhelming number of media commentators and writers. I will describe how that image changed dramatically, commencing in 1942 with the start of the Burma campaign.

During the period starting in 1937, China was depicted in the United States as the gallant and heroic resister of a cruel and aggressive Japanese invader. *Time* magazine in January 1938 pictured Chiang and Madam Chiang as Man and Wife of the Year on the cover. Newspapers and other periodicals followed the same story line. Immediately after Pearl Harbor, the Chinese were embraced as the ones who had gallantly fought our enemy, the Japanese, for four long years from 1937 to 1941. They were praised as a welcome ally. Early strategic views on how to fight the Japanese envisioned

China as a springboard from which to launch air attacks from the coast after the Chinese, with American assistance of arms and ammunition, dispatched the Japanese from the mainland. Both the strategic importance of China and the country's favorable image proved to be short lived.

Stilwell and the 1942 Burma campaign would erase this positive image. Now the picture presented to America was one of factionalism, poverty, filth, stench, greed, and corruption. Stilwell was the main purveyor of this new and disagreeable picture. He became a foil around which a story of corruption and incompetence of the Nationalist government was woven. And against this new picture, Stilwell stood as the only positive force that courageously stood up to the now inept Chiang and sought to engage the Japanese. Barbara Tuchman portrayed him as "quintessentially American": given to plain talk, against "phony propaganda," "too honest and outspoken" for his own good, and unsuited for the "Byzantine politics" of Nationalist China. The journalists focused on Stilwell and created a myth. America was hungry for news of anyone fighting the Japanese, and it would not do to disparage him. Brooks Atkinson, Jack Belden, Theodore White, and others all burnished Stilwell's image. Donovan Webster and Frank Dorn wrote glowing stories of Stilwell's retreat from Burma, and in the process found plenty of opportunities to criticize Chiang and the Chinese military. By comparison, the Chinese Communists were depicted in a positive light. This image carried overseas. Dorn, *The Stilwell Papers*, and Tuchman shaped the view set forth in Lloyd Eastman's *Cambridge History of China*.

In the Green Book Series, the official History of World War II, a three-volume set devoted to the China-Burma-India theatre by Romanus and Sunderland essentially supported Stilwell's view, and when Barbara Tuchman in her Pulitzer Prize–winning book on Stilwell built on both White and the official history, the story, as seen through Stilwell's cramped vision, assumed close to canonical proportions, and it was rare for historians to question it. The opposing view of two challengers, Joseph Alsop and General Claire Chennault, were drowned out by the avalanche of contrary opinion. Wedemeyer was intensely disliked by Stilwell, and the official history and many writers and commentators accepted much of what Stilwell said and wrote, including his negative comments about Wedemeyer. Of all the writers, Tuchman was the most influential, and her damaging and inaccurate assessment has impacted much of the story of General Wedemeyer.

It is time to take another look. This work affords a long overdue reassessment of one of America's most competent and unsung heroes.

INTRODUCTION

Genius is seldom recognized for what it is: a great capacity for hard work.
—Henry Ford

Late in the evening of June 21, 1942, Lieutenant Colonel Albert C. Wedemeyer received an unexpected phone call summoning him to report immediately to the White House. He was not told the reason or whether he would be called upon to speak. His orders were simple—to come as soon as possible. As he entered the meeting room, he found himself in the august company of Prime Minister Winston Churchill, President Roosevelt, their respective top military strategists, General Sir Alanbrooke and General George Marshall, together with a host of additional members of the military's top echelon. The meeting was for the purpose of making some major strategic decisions on the future course of the European war. Wedemeyer was not aware that both Churchill and Lord Louis Mountbatten had recently met privately with Roosevelt for the purpose of advocating their strategy for the European war. Earlier in the month Mountbatten arrived in Washington and had closeted with Roosevelt. A man of great charm, Mountbatten spent several hours at the White House reviewing all aspects of the war. He was there for the purpose of persuading the President to accept the British view of the correct military strategy to employ. During the course of this meeting, attended on the American side only by the President and Harry Hopkins, the President's advisor, the Admiral, in accordance with the British plan, communicated serious misgivings about portions of the American plan for the build-up of U.S. and British Forces in England in preparation for a 1943 cross-channel invasion into France (BOLERO and ROUNDUP). The misgivings centered on ROUNDUP, and a subsidiary plan, SLEDGEHAM-MER. The British were, of course, in favor of BOLERO, the build-up of American forces and supplies in England. Later in the month the second and most important stage of the British plan to undermine the American strategic objectives was put into action when Churchill himself arrived from London. He and Roosevelt first met in seclusion at Hyde Park; then the two heads of state journeyed to Washington for a crucial series of meetings, many of them one-on-one. Clearly, the British had done their homework and had ample opportunity to argue their case. Wedemeyer described the scene that June evening, Sunday, June 21, 1942:

> There was a large colored map of the European-Mediterranean area on the wall. The prime minister, wearing the one-piece jumpsuit for which he was famous, took the floor. Mustering all his eloquence, he stressed the importance of squeezing Rommel out of North Africa, regaining full control of the Mediterranean, getting Allied land forces into major action in 1942, and of meeting Soviet demands for a Second Front. I recall his making a sweeping gesture across the map, moving downward from the British Isles toward Gibraltar, eastward along the breadth of North Africa, back across the breadth of North Africa, back across the Mediterranean, and up through the Balkans into Central Europe. It was a stunning performance.
>
> President Roosevelt then turned to General Marshall. "George," he said to him, "what do you have to say?"
>
> "One of my planners is present," the general replied, "and with your permission I will ask him to comment."[1]

Since early 1941, after being "discovered" by Marshall by virtue of a hundred-page report he had written summarizing what he had learned as an exchange student in two years of study at the German War Academy in Berlin, Wedemeyer had been his top aide, intimately involved in the planning of American war strategy, and he was the primary architect of the "Victory Plan" to defeat America's potential enemies mandated by Roosevelt prior to Pearl Harbor. He had subsequently participated in various strategy conferences with the British and was well versed in the deep differences between the two allies concerning the proper strategy to be employed for the war in

Europe. The Americans advocated an early cross-channel invasion of France in 1943; the British position was less bold and recommended numerous actions at the periphery of the Axis.

Wedemeyer thought Roosevelt had a "mischievous twinkle in his eye" as he anticipated the confrontation. The President savored the drama of such a situation and was entirely comfortable in the midst of multiple conflicting opinions.[2] Here was Wedemeyer, a lowly Lieutenant Colonel at the epicenter of power, foisted into the spotlight in the presence of most of the major American and British military commanders and the two leaders of the free world!

He took a deep breath and began presenting his plan in detail, stressing all he had carefully thought and written about over the preceding year. He touched upon the major points one by one, assuring that at each stage there would be sufficient Allied strength, provided that it was not drained away by other military operations. He stressed the need to invade France in June of 1943 in a decisive action to ultimately paralyze Germany's industrial capacity in the Ruhr basin. He also very diplomatically pointed out the weaknesses of Churchill's peripheral approach, namely the difficulties involved in supplying and transporting troops thousands of miles across an ocean infested with Nazi submarines, and then through the straits of Gibraltar that could easily be blockaded by the Axis-friendly General Franco.[3] Most importantly, he discussed its effect on draining the resources needed for the Allied invasion force planned for 1943. While he did not mention it, Wedemeyer also knew that if we invaded North Africa, it would be only the first of many such peripheral operations, each with similar consequences of delaying the definitive cross-channel operation. Churchill could not have been pleased as the mid-level American officer categorically presented information that undermined his grand scheme. He sat silently through the presentation, afterward making no public comment. Occasionally stealing a glance in his direction, Wedemeyer thought he detected a faint hint of the famous Churchill scowl. While General Marshall later complimented him for a very creditable job, Wedemeyer had doubtlessly made a lasting and disagreeable impression on the British leader as the one who devised and was now the messenger of a plan that Churchill was dead set against. In perhaps the most important strategic planning session of the entire war, Churchill's position prevailed, but the British leader was not one to forget who had delivered this most disagreeable message. He later asserted in his memoir in a discussion of the Italian campaign that risks had been "needlessly sharpened" by "stern and strict priorities for "Overlord," which were *carried in the secondary ranks* (emphasis added) to a veritable pedantry." This comment is a dagger thrown directly at Wedemeyer, and there is considerable evidence that the Prime Minister later got his pound of flesh by dispatching his nemesis to a seemingly dead-end assignment in the China-Burma-India (CBI) theatre as a subordinate to Louis Mountbatten.

Fate again interceded in Wedemeyer's career. Despite the considerable plaudits due to him for his brilliance in his significant participation in planning the European war, his efforts might have been a mere footnote in history among the scores of highly competent yet unheralded administrators of the era. His removal in 1943 to the Asian theatre of operations set the stage for a far more high profile assignment—the replacement of the recalled General Joseph Stilwell as leader of the American forces, and Chief of Staff to Generalissimo Chiang Kai-Shek. Now a highly respected two-star general, Wedemeyer's experience in China defined his career, not only as a brilliant strategist but as a master diplomat and military commander of the highest competence. It also gave him a more authoritative voice to advocate the anti-Communist philosophy that he could previously only subtly imply as a junior officer.

Immediately after the end of hostilities in the Pacific, Wedemeyer was charged with assisting his mentor, Marshall, in a last-ditch and futile effort to achieve unification of China under Chiang. Again, in 1947, at the request of President Truman, he led a fact finding mission to China that reinforced his prophetic opinion that without more vigorous support for the Nationalists, China would ultimately come under Communist control. The report was suppressed by President Truman until 1949 by which time the die had already been cast.

The role the American State Department played in tipping the balance of power in China to Mao Zedong remains a subject of active debate. At the height of the post-war Communist paranoia, the notorious Senator Joseph McCarthy led the charge to implicate many high-level governmental officials for "losing" China and bringing about the conflict in Korea. Most notable on McCarthy's list was General Marshall. McCarthy, in his efforts to discredit Marshall as well as many operatives in the State Department, liberally cited Wedemeyer's suppressed 1947 report and the highly charged public outcries of former Ambassador to China Patrick Hurley as evidence. The exceedingly high-profile diatribe elevated Wedemeyer to the level of hero of the anti-Communists, though he did not actively participate in the sideshow and had merely been a loyal officer competently performing his assignment and rendering his honest opinion. In fact, Wedemeyer took pains to distance himself from the approach McCarthy took, especially his severe criticism of General Marshall:

> I emphatically disagreed with Senator McCarthy's attempt to represent him as having willingly associated himself with traitors, or as having been the tool of subversive, Communist-sympathizing elements in our Government.[4]

In 1958, long after McCarthy had been disgraced, Wedemeyer laid out his views in a remarkably intellectual and well thought-out memoir entitled *Wedemeyer Reports!* He succinctly outlined his philosophy and displayed his intelligence and heartfelt sense of duty in the Foreword:

> ... [M]y most strenuous battles were those of the mind—of trying, as we in Washington's planning echelon saw it, to establish a correct and meaningful Grand Strategy which would have resulted in a fruitful peace and a decent postwar world.[5]

In the conclusion he quoted Bismarck, the Iron Chancellor:

> "Fools learn by experience; the wise man learns by the experience of others."[6]

CHAPTER 1

BEGINNINGS

*Small opportunities are often the
beginning of great enterprises.*
—Demosthenes

Albert Coady Wedemeyer, of German-Irish descent, was born in Omaha, Nebraska on July 9, 1897 into a family with strong roots in the military. His father, Albert Anthony Wedemeyer, was born on November 29, 1859 at West Point, New York, where his grandfather, who had emigrated from Germany in 1848 and was soon to be a non-commissioned officer in the Confederate Army, was Army Bandmaster. Albert Anthony later served as a captain in the Quartermaster corps, retiring from active service in 1902 after serving again as a bandmaster at Fort Omaha after moving to Nebraska. He died of a heart attack on February 26, 1931, and was survived by his widow, Margaret Maggie (nee Coady), and his two sons, then-Lieutenant Albert C. Wedemeyer, who was stationed at the time in China and unable to attend the funeral, and the older son, Fred (1895–1968), who resided in Omaha. A female sibling had died in early childhood.

On the maternal side, Wedemeyer's grandfather Coady was born in Cashniel, Tipperary, Ireland, emigrated to America at the time of the potato famine, and served in the Union army during the Civil War as a non-commissioned officer. He was a well read man, raised Catholic, and left the Church to become a 33rd degree Mason. Albert C. speculated that his grandfather was a distant cousin of "Buffalo Bill" Cody, who often visited him in Omaha.[1]

War Department records still erroneously record that Albert C. was born in 1896, because in 1914, without the knowledge of his parents, he enlisted underage in the National Guard with hopes of seeing military service in Mexico in pursuit of the army of Pancho Villa.[2] His brother, whom he idolized, was already a Lieutenant in the Nebraska National Guard.

Wedemeyer's youth was spent in Omaha, where he attended two years at the Central High School, then two years at the Jesuit-sponsored Creighton Preparatory School. Though Albert's father was a Lutheran, he was brought up Catholic by his mother.[3] His brother Frederick remained a Catholic his entire life, but Albert became skeptical of the Jesuit priests in his late teenage years and joined the Protestant Episcopal Church.[4]

At the turn of the century, Omaha had a population of just over 100,000. A typical Midwestern community, most denizens had little interest in international developments, as they enjoyed the fruits of the industrial revolution that swept the country in the 1880's. The only other person of Wedemeyer's Omaha contemporaries who achieved worldwide distinction was Fred Astaire, and the two men's parents were friends.

Omahans were typically patriotic, energetic, and mostly Caucasian. The north side of town was residential and the south was predominantly industrial and commercial. Meatpacking was the principal industry, with bounding stockyards for the cattle raised in the Midwest. It was also a railroad center, boasting smelting works and a thriving dairy industry. After leaving home, Wedemeyer kept up on the hog receipts and the bank clearances in his hometown and was disappointed as they gradually fell behind its neighbor and rival to the southeast, Kansas City, Missouri.

Small town cultural opportunities were limited; however, the city did have the fine Mendelsohn Choir, made up of local musicians, created by and supported in no small measure by the senior Wedemeyer. A highly anticipated annual event was a visit by the renowned Thomas Orchestra of Chicago, which performed in conjunction with the local choir in the city auditorium. The city's public theater was modest in size, and there were two small art museums.

Music played a large role in Albert's childhood. His mother played the piano, his father the flute, and both children the violin. The family often played together. He was accomplished enough to give a solo performance of Dvorak's "Humoresque" at his grammar school graduation, but his musical pursuits soon took a back seat to his interest in athletics, where he "was not so good in football" but lettered as a pitcher on the baseball team, surely facilitated by his extremely tall and lanky six-foot-five-inch frame. He also took up boxing at the local YMCA and suffered a broken nose that intermittently caused him breathing difficulties in later life, especially during his China tour.

Wedemeyer recalled his upbringing in a happy "typical middle-class Christian home" in an attractive residential area, with an active social and athletic agenda, including tennis on the backyard court that his father had built, and skating in the winter when it was flooded and frozen over. There was plenty of outdoor recreation, and the family took long walks together. His father exercised strict supervision over both work and play. This often met with typical adolescent opposition, but in later life he described his father as a man of compassion and stature, and he fondly remembered him for his role in instilling an appreciation of history and honorable moral values.

The affluent Wedemeyers had a negro cook, who lived over the garage with her husband, the family chauffer. They were one of the few families in town to own an automobile.[5] Albert recalled the dusty roads that Eddie Rickenbacker, the famous racer and future World War I flying ace, competed on in races in the area. Years later, when Wedemeyer met Rickenbacker, he told him how he watched him in one particularly exciting race. Rickenbacker confided "Al, if I hadn't won that race, I would have been ridden out of town on a rail; I owed the boarding house lady, the mechanic and the grease monkeys who were taking care of my car. I didn't have a cent of money. I had to win."[6]

Albert took pride in the respect in which his parents were held in the community. He learned their lesson of fiscal responsibility and was indoctrinated with a strict sense of never purchasing anything he could not pay for in cash. Purchasing anything on credit was severely frowned upon. When he bought his first new car and financed the balance of four-hundred dollars, his parents expressed vigorous disapproval, and he never again bought anything on credit.[7] While in grammar school Wedemeyer took a job delivering papers after school and got an early lesson in human nature when he found that some of his customers did not pay him promptly. He recalls this as an "eye opener," learning how people pinched pennies by not paying the newspaper delivery boy while living in lovely homes. Wedemeyer later worked in the local bank as an assistant teller in the summer months. His spare time was devoted to reading, which was an early passion that stayed with him his entire life. "Rags to Riches" Horatio Alger stories were among his favorites.

Wedemeyer was always near the top of his high school class and originally aspired to follow in the footsteps of a number of his close relatives with a career in medicine, encouraged especially by his mother. While he loved the sciences in his early schooling, at an early age he was rooted in sophisticated intellectual thought by his father, who:

> ... first awaked my avid interest in history, which has remained my favorite study and has provided background for strategic thinking. Father's discussions with friends prior to our entrance into the First World War concerning its origins and German guilt had stimulated my thinking, made me immune to crude and unscrupulous war propaganda, and encouraged me to study what that mellow ironist, the historian Gibbon called "the record of follies, crimes and cruelties of mankind." Hence came my interest not only in military but also in political, economic and social theory.[8]

From high school on, Wedemeyer was keenly interested in military history. While studying the development of European empires, dukedoms, republics, and democracies, he was impressed by both the creative and destructive influences of the military and the remarkable degree of influence that religion played on it, observing that the Crusades and many other early European wars had strong religious overtones. With the understanding that the military was seemingly the most exciting experience at that time, he pondered the willingness to readily kill and be killed by cultures that hardly knew each other rather than by settling disputes through diplomatic negotiation and compromise.

Wedemeyer's first introduction to the formal military came when he joined the high school Reserve Officers Training Corps (ROTC) where he learned the manual of arms, developed deep pride in wearing the uniform, and became a cadet Captain. His interaction with the Regular Army officers sparked his interest in West Point.[9] One of his parent's friends had a son at the academy, George Wooley, who while home on a furlough saw Wedemeyer pitching for the local baseball team. Wooley suggested Wedemeyer apply to West Point, pointing out that his athletic prowess would be an asset to the application. Senator George W. Norris recommended Wedemeyer, who then sat for the competitive examination and was accepted.

WEST POINT
Although Wedemeyer's parents were justifiably proud of their son's accept-

ance into the United States Military Academy, as well as his military career, they harbored some disappointment in his decision to pursue a military career in lieu of medicine. Although he took a different path, he never lost his interest in the healing sciences and read widely, especially so after his oldest son became ill with lymphatic cancer.

In high school, prior to the time he expressed an interest in pursuing a military career, his course of study emphasized science, not mathematics. While at West Point, Wedemeyer realized that his poor mathematical skills put him at a disadvantage and he struggled mightily with math. He sought to mitigate it by stressing historical study but was admittedly less than highly motivated academically at the time. Consequently, he did not fare well in the class standings, a widely accepted standard of competence employed by superior officers that could potentially hamper his future military advancement.

At West Point, his athletic career was quite successful. As predicted by George Wooley, he became the pitcher for the West Point baseball team and had fond memories of the influence of his baseball coach, Hans Lobert, a former professional infielder. At West Point he played against future greats, including Lou Gehrig of Columbia, and Frankie Frish, the "Fordham Flash," carrying a scar on his ankle throughout his life from one of Frish's famous flying spikes.[10]

Wedemeyer was a man of undying principle and integrity, and he considered the Honor System the most important lesson he learned at West Point. By virtue of his strict adherence to the discipline, he was elected to the cadet committee empowered with enforcing the code of honor. While he wasn't a top student, his ethics were noted by the tactical officer and he was recommended for Cadet Corporal.

In his own words:

> Aside from technical instruction, the cadet is taught the importance of discipline, humility, and respect for others regardless of economic or social status. West Point training inculcates a sense of honor and personal integrity which in my judgment are the invisible guaranty of America's future.[11]

Wedemeyer's intolerance for those who "lie, steal, or cheat" was a guide he looked to for direction throughout his career in every important decision he made, and he later admitted that it sometimes caused him to alienate himself from some persons of high stature and influence, both military and civilian, often to his ultimate disadvantage. His own list included Harry Truman, Omar Bradley, Averill Harriman, and Henry Luce.[12] One he didn't cite, who clearly belongs near the top, was Winston Churchill.

The corps was small and intimate, numbering about 800. Student life at the academy was notably Spartan. The cadets lived in poverty and did not even have pockets on their uniforms, having to carry their handkerchiefs up their sleeves. Only under the most extreme circumstances were they permitted off the grounds, and a ledger was kept of their whereabouts and activities outside the barracks.[13]

Wedemeyer did passively object to some of the petty restrictions imposed. For instance, cadets were not permitted to receive packages of food from family or friends. His superiors would advise him when one arrived, "You are not authorized to get it. I will enjoy the candy or cookies or whatever just myself." With mature understanding, he blamed the system rather the "officers in charge" who were the beneficiaries of the rule.

Wedemeyer's class at West Point was unique. There were 383 cadets from all 48 states with a wide variety of backgrounds. They entered in June 1916, were graduated, and commissioned as 2nd Lieutenants, after only a year and a half of compressed study in anticipation of being mobilized for the European war to fight against the "terrible Hun." Newspapers incited their readers' anger by publishing lurid and provocative stories of alleged German atrocities, such as cutting off the hands of children in Belgium and France. After the war, Wedemeyer learned that the photographs in the *New York Times* were faked by a British major, who later admitted it in a book, much to the dismay of British authorities.[14] This experience fueled later skepticism of the pro-war factions in the United States after the outset of hostilities in Europe in September 1939, and had a marked influence on his sympathies for the isolationist movement in America prior to Pearl Harbor.

EARLY MILITARY CAREER

After the Treaty of Versailles ended hostilities on June 28, 1919, the former students were ordered back to West Point to complete the schooling cut short by the war. It was an awkward time for them, as well as the instructors and other underclassmen, being "neither fish nor fowl." Members of the faculty and administrative staff did not recognize them as officers, and they were not allowed to use the officers' club, yet as commissioned officers they were not permitted to fraternize with the cadets.[15] After completing the extra year at West Point, his class was sent back to Europe where they toured the battlefields and were lectured by the officers who had commanded the Allied Expeditionary Force.

Wedemeyer's most distinguished classmates were Al Gruenther, Chief of Staff to Dwight Eisenhower and later Supreme Allied Commander in Europe (1953–56); General Anthony "Nuts" McAuliffe, who stubbornly refused to surrender to the Nazis at Bastogne; and Nate Twining, who became Chairman of the Joint Chiefs of Staff. When he graduated, no one, least of all Wedemeyer himself, would have dreamed that he would be the first member of his class to achieve the rank of General. Peacetime promotions were rare, and quite typically it took over a quarter of a century of service to achieve that distinction.[16]

Long after retirement, Wedemeyer was appointed to the academy's President's Board of Visitors that included three college Presidents, four Senators, and six Congressmen, charged with annually inspecting the curriculum, quality of instruction, training methods, appropriations, and physical plant, and rendering a comprehensive report. At age 75, he lamented that the caliber of the corps was not "up to snuff," and that in too many instances students were coming from homes where there is "an environment of at least drug toleration—heroin, LSD and marijuana." The staid and conservative old soldier noted that "these were not problems at West Point years ago."[17]

Wedemeyer's first official assignment after the European tour was at Fort Benning, Georgia, an infantry training post where he spent three-and-a-half years primitively quartered in a tent. His tour in Georgia was unfortunately punctuated by a February 1921 disciplinary action for being drunk and disorderly and "conduct unbecoming an officer," especially in the age of prohibition! He pled guilty, was fined $50 a month for six months, and confined to base for a similar period. Viewing his military career as irreparably tainted, he submitted his resignation. Serendipitously, he was told it could not be accepted until his penalty was completed, during which time he obtained an offer for a civilian job, but some of his superiors dissuaded him from resigning and he withdrew the request.[18]

After Fort Benning, Wedemeyer spent most of the next ten years in the Philippines and China, the latter, in 1929, in lieu of a position as an instructor at West Point. On the trip to the Philippines in 1923 he met his future wife, Elizabeth Dade Embick. They were married on Corregidor in 1925 [pic. 4], and had two sons, Albert, in 1925 and Robert in 1928 [pic. 3]. The new Mrs. Wedemeyer also came from a military background, being the daughter of Colonel, later General, Stanley Dunbar Embick, a military scholar who loaned his son-in-law many books and had numerous discussions with him that broadened his knowledge of world events, history, and economics. Embick rose to prominence as a close confidante of General George Marshall and was one of the highest ranking pro-isolationists in the American military. His guidance and perspective had a profound influence on Wedemeyer's career and personal philosophy. The two men remained close and intimate friends their entire lives [pic. 10].

Wedemeyer spent ten years on his Asian tour of duty, serving for a time as an aide to General Charles Evans Kilbourne, a highly decorated World War I hero, interrupted for two years when he returned stateside to serve under General William Hood Simpson, later a four star general in charge of the 8th Army in Europe during World War II. While an aide in the Philippines on Corregidor, his duties included serving as Judge Advocate of General Courts Martial, where he was involved in a number of serious cases, most notably a 1924 case of murder by a West Point officer named Thompson of a girl with whom he was romantically involved. Thompson, the son of a minister from New Jersey, was found guilty and hanged. The President of the court was General Douglas MacArthur, and Wedemeyer had the opportunity to work closely with him, the beginning of a lifelong admiration.

While stationed on Corregidor between 1931 and 1933, he visited and inspected the Bataan Peninsula and carefully sketched out proposed defensive positions to be employed in the event of attack. This exercise gave Wedemeyer a good opportunity to demonstrate his tactical and strategic abilities. He was pleased to learn after the war from an officer who was in command of the Bataan defense that his work had been used to great effect.

In the Philippines Wedemeyer also developed a healthy respect for the native Scout Regiments while commanding and training a company of Filipino soldiers to become expert riflemen. He also was confronted with such issues as the epidemic of venereal disease among the American troops who frequently consorted with Filipino women, a firsthand lesson in the many problems associated with an occupation force that later influenced his recommendations as Deputy Chief of Staff in charge of operations in Europe.

Wedemeyer left Asia after being selected for the Army Command and General Staff School at Leavenworth, Kansas, which he attended between 1934 and 1936. This opportunity was not to be squandered. His class standing when he graduated tended to overcome his lower ranking at West Point and influenced his elevation up the ranks of the Army. This time there was no advanced mathematics in the curriculum, and the thirty-nine-year-old

Captain finished first in his class of 77 students. Toward the end of his schooling at Leavenworth, the Commandant informed him that that he had been selected to attend the *Kriegsakademie*, the German war college in Berlin, as an exchange student. Aside from his academic excellence, a working knowledge of German made him an ideal candidate.[19] Within eight years of graduation from Leavenworth he would be a three star General.

CHAPTER 2

THE EDUCATION OF A STRATEGIST

Learning is not attained by chance,
it must be sought for with ardor
and attended to with diligence.
—Abigail Adams, 1780

KRIEGSAKADEMIE 1936–1938

The two years Wedemeyer spent in Berlin at the *Kriegsakademie*, the German war academy, between 1936 and 1938,[1] were profoundly influential in both his career advancement and in molding and galvanizing his political ideology. The United States and Germany had entered into a reciprocal agreement in 1935 that allowed one member of their armies per class to be permitted to study in each other's military academy.[2] By virtue of his performance with honors and a working knowledge of the German language he had acquired in high school, Wedemeyer was selected on the recommendation of the staff of the United States Army Command and General Staff School at Leavenworth that he had been attending since 1934, completing a unique four-year curriculum that the career military officer had embarked upon at the age of 37.[3] Wedemeyer was only the second American to attend the German institution and the only one during the critical years prior to the outset of open hostilities. He was one of 129 students, of whom 120 were German officers, and the rest representatives from nine other nations, including China, Argentina, Bulgaria, Japan, and Turkey.[4]

His attendance during the critical pre-war years afforded him the opportunity to witness events that shortly would lead to global conflict. He watched members of the German youth movement march arrogantly through the streets, flags flying, wearing armbands prominently adorned with swastikas.[5] Storm troopers of the brown-shirted SA (*Sturmabteilung*) openly persecuted the Jewish people, the designated scapegoats of the National Socialist Party, and spread vitriolic Nazi doctrine.[6] Wedemeyer was in Vienna on March 12, 1939, at the time of the German annexation of Austria, the *Anschlus*, and was an eyewitness to troops goose-stepping between rows of exuberant onlookers.[7] It was obvious to him that Germany was preparing for war, and he marveled at the build-up of its armed forces at a dizzying pace. His classmates included many who would become prominent figures in the war, including his close friend, Colonel Claus von Stauffenberg, later famous for planting the bomb in the unsuccessful plot ("Valkyrie") to assassinate Hitler. His principal instructor was Ferdinand Jodl, brother of Alfred, the general who signed the instrument of Nazi surrender and was hanged as a war criminal at Nuremberg in 1946.[8]

Other than the rare occasion when foreigners were excluded on the grounds of military security,[9] Wedemeyer had wide access to every facility. The curriculum was radically different from that to which he had previously been exposed, in both method and content, and German strategy was uniquely integrated into a seamless web with a single defined goal: the advancement and prosperity of the nation.[10] Early on, he realized the superiority of what he was being taught compared to what he had learned at West Point and at Leavenworth, where, aside from more archaic and traditional use of tactics and strategy, mostly of World War I vintage, he had not at all been exposed to the importance of long-range strategic post-war objectives.[11]

The studies were arduous and the students had a prevailing sense of urgency. The instructors were of a consistently excellent quality that he had not previously been exposed to. The curriculum was designed to familiarize the students with all of the military equipment that the Nazis had recently developed and to educate them in battle tactics while in command of both large and small units. Practical exercises were introduced, and a good deal of instruction was outside the classroom. Students visited the battlefields of many of the previous European wars and debated the strategy and tactics of the great generals of the past.[12] The instructors encouraged creative problem solving with respect to conducting modern, mechanized, mobile warfare, both in terms of operations and the logistical arrangements necessary to support the operations. In one exercise, Wedemeyer was even given the opportunity to command a Panzer division in a practice maneuver. This particular exercise proved invaluable to him in understanding the capabilities of modern German armor, as well as the method of tank deployment in coordination with troops and aircraft. In addition to mock air and ground exercises, hypothetical battles were staged, including a practice "Czechoslo-vakia campaign" that turned out to be not at all so hypothetical in less than a year.[13]

Taught by the bitter lesson of the First World War, the Germans were determined to obviate future disappointments and not get bogged down once again in the stalemate of trench warfare. Everything the students were exposed to from the outset—the organization, doctrine, equipment and train-ing—was aimed at intensifying the tempo of the battlefield.[14] Blitzkrieg, literally "lightning war," a term actually coined in 1939 and widely credited to German strategist Heinz Guderian, encompassed the concept of *Schwer-punkt*, the concentration of enormous power at a single point of attack, in this case led by mechanized warfare integrated with air power, a strategy summarized by Guderian as *"Nicht kleckern, klotzen!"*[15] (Don't tap, smash!) The tactics of Britzkrieg were later utilized with stunning success as the Germans quickly overran Poland and France, and, in the early years of the war, the Soviet Union.[16]

At a time when the American Army and Air Corps were independently developing their strategies, earlier efforts at "cooperation" between air and ground forces were erratic, strained, and in numerous instances, particularly in the early stages of the war, actually harmful.[17] Upon his return from the *Kriegsakadamie* in 1938, Wedemeyer wrote a comprehensive 100-page report of his experience, providing a powerful tool for the American military that outlined German military capabilities and strategy, especially the integrated use of armor divisions, air power, and antitank units, none of which the American Army had knowledge of at the time.[18] Additionally, at the request of the Army he wrote of what he had learned about anti-tank defense in two articles for *The Field Artillery Journal* and *The Infantry Journal* in May 1941, both of which proved invaluable for training future tank officers.[19] It was not until the war was well under way that the United States begin to appreciate and apply this doctrine.

WEDEMEYER'S REPORT ON THE *KRIEGSADADEMIE*

It remains present-day military protocol that officers who attend a training exercise or school are compelled to write a report on completion of the program, with the intent of creating an archive of useful information for future study. However, like many military reports of this nature, they are often underutilized.[20] Wedemeyer's report in like manner lay largely unread by most military men until it crossed the desk of Brigadier General George C.

Marshall, newly appointed Chief of the War Plans Division and soon to be promoted to Chief of Staff, the most powerful military post in the nation.[21] Marshall carefully studied the report and realized that he was reading a document that for the first time not only provided accurate information on German equipment and tactics but also provided a strategy for defeating them.

Marshall reached out to Wedemeyer for several one-on-one talks, not only to discuss the contents of the report but also to get to know him on a more personal basis. When Wedemeyer appeared for the first of numerous meetings, Marshall had a copy of Wedemeyer's report on his desk.[22] Marshall marked him as someone he would be calling on for important assignments in the future, since he agreed with much of Wedemeyer's military philosophy, and he developed a strong faith in Wedemeyer's judgment and strategic ideas.[23] A true affection and mutual respect developed between them, clearly the most important factor in Wedemeyer's meteoric rise in the military hierarchy. Legend has it that Marshall was famous for his little "Black Book"[24] wherein he placed the names of those officers he determined to advance, and those unfortunate enough to be placed in the "don't advance" section.[25] Despite later differences, particularly over United States policy in China,[26] Wedemeyer never lost his profound admiration for his mentor.[27]

There is no doubt that Wedemeyer's experience at the German school and the impression his report made on General Marshall were the principal reasons why he was assigned to the War Plans Division of the General Staff in Washington in the spring of 1941, and ultimately, given the assignment of writing the Victory Program. General Eisenhower, who became chief of the War Plans Division in January 1942 *after* Wedemeyer had completed his original Victory Program report, quickly embraced the key points in the plan, the build-up of forces in England, followed by a cross-channel attack into France, and endorsed and upgraded them. This was the genesis of the final OVERLORD plan.[28]

Aside from the purely military analysis in his report, in Berlin Wedemeyer was "taught to consider the influence on strategy of geography, psychology, demography, economics, and politics," and he became cognizant of "Grand Strategy," which he later defined as "the art and science of employing all of a nation's resources to accomplish objectives defined by national policy." Wedemeyer's experience in Germany provided him with a deep understanding of international affairs and of the roots of world tensions, with a distinctly Germanic flavor, including the power of economic factors in

fueling the potential for war. Perhaps most importantly, the threat of Bol-
shevism, a major theme at the German school, made a deep and lasting impression on Wedemeyer,[29] one that would remain with him for the remainder
of his life, permeating a good deal of his later reports and recommendations
to his superiors.

In most Western nations, especially the United States, there was a long
tradition of sharp segregation of the military and the political, each having
its own distinct role, with politicians ultimately having the final say. In the
United States, American political leaders expected the military to check their
strategic concepts in the cloak room prior to entering the conference room.
The military, in their view, should take instruction from them! During the
years prior to World War II, the principle of civilian supremacy was so
dominant that not even the appearance of military dissent could be allowed.
Following Pearl Harbor, however, the urgency of full-scale war required close
daily consultation between the President and his military chiefs, such that
the separation between the two became blurred.[30]

WEDEMEYER DEVELOPS HIS VIEW ON "STRATEGY"

Before going to Germany, Wedemeyer had studied the "Heartland Theory"
first espoused in a 1904 paper, "The Geographical Pivot of History," by the
so-called Father of Geopolitics, Sir Halford John MacKinder, who argued
that control of Eastern Europe was vital to control of the world.[31] After his
arrival at the *Kriegsakademie*, Wedemeyer found that Germany's top military
strategist, Karl Haushofer, had adopted, then updated and modified
Mackinder's ideas for use in Nazi Germany in the late 1930's to one where
"the heartland consisted of enough of Eastern Europe to preclude an attack
from the East, if and when one were thinking of turning one's attention to
the West." Hitler readily adopted Mackinder's ideas for a step-by-step plan
of world conquest. As summarized in 1919:

> Conquer Eastern Europe and you dominate the Heartland (the
> core of Eurasia).
> Conquer the Heartland and you dominate the World Island (all
> of Europe and Asia).
> Conquer the World Island . . . and you dominate the World.[32]

Wedemeyer had MacKinder in mind when he advocated an early cross-
channel invasion and a drive to the Ruhr, Germany's industrial heart.

Winston Churchill, whose opinions dominated British planning, saw things differently, opposing a cross-channel invasion and a march toward Germany with a large force, instead advocating a series of relatively small simultaneous peripheral attacks on Nazi-held Europe, including, among others, France, the Balkans, and Norway.[33]

Until undermined by the British, Wedemeyer's views, which were in total accord with both Generals Marshall and Eisenhower, were the core of American strategic plans. Ironically, while Wedemeyer's strongest asset was a profound understanding of why long-range strategy was so critical to a nation, it was viewed by America's allies as his greatest weakness! When the American military presented their strategy to the British, Wedemeyer's contributions were recognized and rejected, very likely resulting in his eventual "promotion" and transfer to Asia. Ultimately, he was not afforded the opportunity to directly participate in the cross-channel invasion of the European mainland, for which he had played such a pivotal role in planning.

Wedemeyer's superior understanding of "Grand Strategy" led him to observe that most military men, as well as politicians, had a limited view of what "strategy" meant in the total context of war, and this stance was often a source of irritation to colleagues. His considerably broader knowledge than what was possessed by most other Western planners was often misunderstood and resented. Illustrative of this, as pointed out by Wedemeyer himself, was the often-quoted response of Winston Churchill to a question asked of him in Parliament in May 1940 as to what his strategy was. His response, to thunderous applause, was "You ask what is our aim? I can answer in one word: Victory—it is Victory at all costs."[34] This gallant yet shortsighted and narrow objective, defeat of the German Army, failed to take into account any postwar issues and was contrary to all that Wedemeyer had learned. Wedemeyer strongly believed that there was a lot more to "victory" than *winning the war*. As he knew from the lessons of the First World War, the structure of the peace that follows is far more important and longer lasting. The 50-year "Cold War" following World War II is attributed by many historians to a repetition of the mistakes of World War I in failing to give adequate thought to post-war problems. Wedemeyer was not guilty of this oversight, but he was in the minority among American planners.

Mention must be made that not every British planner was guilty of failing to take any long-range post-war planning into account. Sir John Kennedy, Director of Military Operations during most of the war, stood out from his British colleagues. But he was an exception. Kennedy points out in his excellent book, *The Business of War*, that long-range post-war problems were indeed an important subject, and some of his colleagues agreed with him, but not publically. The prevalent view was that if one entertained any long-range planning views which ran counter to those of the Prime Minister, or seemed to be in any way anti-Russian, they were better kept to oneself. Kennedy wrote:

> To us there seemed to be only one great power who could be re-garded as the potential enemy: Russia. . . . when it became known a few months later, that we [The Imperial General Staff] were think-ing along these lines, we received a stern rebuke, and were told to desist from mentioning possible tension with Russia, or from taking Russia into our calculations as a potential enemy.[35]

Wedemeyer's criticism of the British short-range strategy was centered primarily on Churchill, not the entire British Staff. When he wrote the "Victory Program," a key point was the importance of the Allied armies invading the heartland of Europe and reaching Poland and the Baltic countries prior to the Russians, thus denying them the opportunity to expand their territories.[36] Wedemeyer was in total agreement with Kennedy on this point, but the Americans had the same difficulty as the British Staff in bring-ing the political establishment over to their view. This was an understandably delicate point to address and could not be expressly set forth, since it was a "political" subject, considered to be beyond the scope of the military, let alone, in Wedemeyer's case, an officer of such a lowly rank. However, if Wedemeyer's plan had been adopted *in toto* and successfully implemented, the Allied armies would have had an excellent chance to beat the Russians to Eastern Europe and deny them the land grabs they acquired during and following the war. Wedemeyer was emphatic that it was critical to invade France in 1943 while the Russians were militarily occupied with the Germans, and the defensive Atlantic Wall had not been built up to the level attained in 1944. The likelihood of this plan succeeding remains to this day a hotly contested debate, though there is a credible minority opinion among historians that a 1943 invasion of France, though costly, would have been successful.[37] Plans for an early cross-channel invasion were not welcome in British military circles. Wedemeyer's plan to invade France in 1943 with massive force ran directly counter to the strategy envisioned by the powerful and influential Churchill.[38]

The cross-channel plan was not the only instance in which Wedemeyer and the British were in disagreement. The Prime Minister is widely credited for being one of the harbingers of the menace of Communism, but his famous Fulton College "Iron Curtain" speech,[39] delivered in 1946, was too little and too late. By then, the Soviets had already consolidated their presence in Eastern Europe, and it was becoming increasingly clear that their totalitarian ideology was more pernicious to American and British interests than Hitler's had been.

Churchill's inadequate understanding of the lurking danger of Communism is further evidenced by his response to the report submitted to him by Brigadier Fitzroy MacLean concerning the Communist threat in Yugoslavia. MacLean was sent on a mission to consult with Marshal Tito during the early years of the war. In his book, *Eastern Approaches*, MacLean recalled that the years he had spent in the Soviet Union had made him wary of the Communist menace, and he realized that Tito and his followers were determined to establish a Communist regime with close links to Moscow as soon as the war was over. MacLean told Churchill that he was concerned that British policy in Yugoslavia would lead to this outcome. Churchill replied that no consideration of long-term policy should deter MacLean from his task of "simply finding out who was killing the most Germans and suggesting means by which we could help them kill more."[40] British support of Marshall Tito with arms and other supplies was, in the view of some historians, largely responsible for the defeat of the anti-Communist Mihlovich, with disastrous consequences for all of Europe.

Wedemeyer was not the only American highly suspicious of Soviet intentions for the future of Eastern Europe. One who held similar views was George F. Kennan, author of the widely quoted "X" article,[41] and later briefly Ambassador to Russia and a prolific writer on subjects relating to the Soviet Union. After years of laboring in obscurity, he sprung into prominence with his article written at the outset of the Cold War, and he became an instant authority. Kennan and a group of prominent military personnel, with the enthusiastic backing of Secretary of War James Forrestal, formed the nucleus of the first National War College.[42] This was the first occasion that the curriculum of any American military teaching institute contained courses on the interrelationship of military and nonmilitary means in the promulgation of national policy, something which would have had the enthusiastic support of Wedemeyer. The students, all military personnel with the rank of Colonel or higher, read and discussed the philosophies of many of the same European theorists as Wedemeyer had been exposed to in Germany, in particular Karl von Clausewitz, who is widely recognized as one of the great military strategists of all time. His works were popularized in Germany and the Western world by Lieutenant General Freiherr von der Glotz, whose statement as to the precise goal of a military operation, a key theory of Clausewitz, made a deep impression on Wedemeyer:

> We already know its first objective, the enemy's main army. *Our first step will be to invade the theatre of war occupied by this army, seek it out, and to force it to a battle under the most favorable conditions possible.*[43] (emphasis added)

Translated into a strategy to defeat the Germans in World War II, this meant an early invasion into France followed by engagement with the German Army, with the goal of destroying the enemy's industrial centers in the Ruhr at the earliest possible time, the essence of what Wedemeyer was advocating.

With the notable exception of their widely differing views on America's foreign policy toward China (Kennan was very Euro-centered), Wedemeyer and Kennan had very similar ideas about dealing with the threat of Communism. There is no evidence that they ever met, and neither ever mentions the other in his writings. Kennan's attempt to incorporate a different level of thinking into American foreign affairs undoubtedly influenced the attitude of the students attending the War College but does not seem to have made a lasting impression on the political scene. As he lamented in another portion of his *Memoirs*, "Our actions in the field of foreign affairs are the convulsive reactions of politicians to an internal political life dominated by vocal minorities."[44]

Wedemeyer expounded his well-grounded geopolitical philosophy throughout his 1958 treatise, *Wedemeyer Reports!* In one remarkable paragraph, he concisely spelled out his entire understanding of strategy, the strategic failures of the Allies, as well as the role of the chief civilian leaders and the utter failure of the doctrine of "Unconditional Surrender":

> War is, or should be, the last means resorted to for the accomplishment of an aim. It cannot be a substitute for a policy, yet Roosevelt and Churchill—as well as the other Western 'architects of victory' —seem to have regarded it as such. They confused means with ends,

substituting total victory for a policy. They demanded the unconditional surrender of our enemies instead of defining civilized war
aims and seeking to attain them at the least possible cost and with
due regard to our future security vis-a-vis our temporary and reluctant ally, the Soviet Union.[45]

Noting Clausewitz' dictum that "war is the extension of political
processes by the employment of military force" in the same source, he liberally
cited the Chinese philosopher Sun Tze Wu who, over two millennia ago,
wrote "to fight and conquer in all your battles is not supreme excellence.
Supreme excellence consists in breaking the enemy's resistance without
fighting," adding the Roman philosophy adapted by Clausewitz that war is
but the *final* argument between states "*ultima ratio dictum.*"

Throughout his long life, Wedemeyer carried with him these notions of
strategy, national policy, dread of Communism, and the imperative to have a
clear national policy, all of which stemmed not only from his deep study and
understanding but from the teachings to which he was exposed at the
German school.

No record exists of whether the Germans charged any tuition for the
two years of intensive course of study they dispensed to Wedemeyer, but if
there was, no price would have been too much to pay.

CHAPTER 3

WRITING THE VICTORY PROGRAM

―――――――――

Two roads diverged in a wood, and I –
I took the one less traveled by.
And that has made all the difference.
— Robert Frost

If General Wedemeyer could be asked in retrospect what the most significant year in his professional life was, without a doubt he would have chosen 1941. For it was in May of that year that the obscure Major was appointed by General George Marshall to the War Plans Division and then in July selected to lead the committee charged with one of the most important assignments of the war, the formulation of a document incorporating specific strategic recommendations that laid out how the United States should prepare to wage a war that it might soon be involved in. At first saddled with the unwieldy moniker "The Joint Board Estimate of United States Over-All Production Requirements," it came to be known as "The Victory Program." Before we discuss the selection of Wedemeyer as the chief architect of this program, it is useful to outline the events that preceded his selection.

Planning for a *possible* war had been a function of the War Plans Division since prior to World War I. Hypothetical contingency plans were continually being updated to reflect new information and changes in conditions.[1] Until recently, the conventional wisdom of virtually all military historians was that between the two World Wars, the activity of the War Plans Division was casual, informal, and conducted in a purely academic atmosphere with no sense of urgency and little or no direction from the high-level military or political establishments.[2] This view, though widely held, is not entirely accurate. In 2003, Henry G. Gole reported that in 1957 a lost cache of twenty-five footlockers of documents compiled by the Army War College between 1919 and 1941 had been discovered. Presently located at Carlisle Barracks, PA, these documents reveal a substantial body of work devoted to strategic planning for a possible war with both Germany and Japan. Clearly, this research would have been a valuable foundation for the War Plans Division in the spring of 1941. In his well researched and documented study, Gole concludes: "American strategic planning may have come of age in 1939–41, but the 'spade work' done by students and faculty during the period 1934–40 at the U.S. Army War College was very important to the maturation process."[3]

At the time Roosevelt and Churchill first came face to face on the battleship HMS *Prince of Wales* in Newfoundland in August 1941[4] to form the Atlantic Charter, America was precariously balanced on the edge of a national and world political crisis. The international situation was volatile, and the fears of the American public about entering the raging conflict in the Far East, and especially in Europe, polarized domestic politics. The crux of the issue was the role the United States should and would play in the world. On one side were the isolationists, hell bent to keep America out of the conflict.[5] The opposing view came to be championed by President Roosevelt, who envisioned America as a world power required to be involved in a role greater than that of a passive observer,[6] though because of strong opposition to any move that would draw the United States into war, he had to proceed with extreme caution. Any policy he endorsed that even came close to supporting hostilities, let alone outright involvement in war, was viewed with great suspicion.

Events in Europe and the Pacific at this time elevated the War Plans Division to an urgent and critical role as top leaders of the administration and military were confronted with increased urgency to make serious preparations for a likely conflict. Roosevelt had already decided to assist England in every way possible,[7] and the War Plans Division was secretly assigned top priority to devise a workable strategy.

THE BRITISH/AMERICAN ABC-1 CONFERENCE, JANUARY 29–MARCH 29, 1941

Despite more than a year of conflict raging in Europe, most Americans were remarkably detached from the events. German armies held the continent from the Atlantic coast of France in the west to the doors of Leningrad, the Ukraine, and the shores of the Black Sea in the east. Only Spain, Sweden, Portugal, and Switzerland remained outside the Axis camp, though Franco's

Spain was extremely friendly to it, and the perilous prospect of his coming into the conflict on their side and shutting the straits of Gibraltar would later haunt the planners of the North African campaign in November 1942. Germany also held the Mediterranean island of Crete, menaced Cyprus and Malta, threatened the Middle East and Egypt, and appeared on the verge of knocking the Soviets out of the war. Nonetheless, the majority of Americans continued to rely on President Roosevelt's earlier promises to keep the United States a non-combatant, though after the fall of France on June 22, 1940 and the debacle at Dunkirk, Roosevelt was convinced that it was inevitable that America would be drawn into the war and that it was crucial to come to the aid of Great Britain and develop a joint strategic approach to defeating Germany.[8] It was time for America and Great Britain to plan for the coming war.

Representatives of Great Britain and the United States met for the first time to devise a set of specific proposals to meet the world crisis at the ABC-1 Staff Conference in Washington, held between January 29th and March 29th, 1941.[9] Since America was still technically neutral, elaborate steps had to be instituted to keep the meetings highly secret and avoid any suggestion of commitment to war.[10] The participants wore civilian clothes, masquerading as advisors for a British purchasing company, and attendance was limited to only a few key American and British planners.[11] Admiral Harold Stark, Chief of Naval Operations, and General Marshall appeared briefly at the opening session, leaving the balance of the work to low and mid-level subordinates in an effort to insulate themselves from the charge, later leveled at them despite these precautions, that they had worked with the President to bring the United States into the war through the back door.[12]

Even at this early stage, important differences over strategy between the future allies surfaced that would persist throughout the war. Marshall expressed his view that the battle in Europe could be won only with a large ground force. A contrary position was held by the British, who argued that a blockade, support of resistance forces in occupied countries, a series of attacks at perimeter points, and a powerful air offensive were the necessary ingredients for the defeat of Germany, or at least to soften their defenses prior to a land attack.[13]

Although the American representatives during these meetings had made no pledge to enter the war alongside the British, according to Roosevelt insider Robert Sherwood: "These staff talks, and the complete interchange of expert opinions as well as facts that they produced, provided the highest degree of *strategic preparedness* that the United States, or probably any other non-aggressor nation, has ever had before entry into war."[14] During the time that these surreptitious joint negotiations for war preparation were being conducted, anxious Congressmen, unaware of the meetings, were being assured that the Lend-Lease bill then being debated[15] was designed to *avoid* war.[16]

The overwhelming American public opinion was that we should remain neutral,[17] fueled by cynicism about the "War to End All Wars," as World War I was once called, the ineptitude of the League of Nations, in which America declined to participate, and the abject failure of collective security rendered impotent by the aggressive actions of Hitler. On May 22, 1941, a rally of the isolationist America First group at Madison Square Garden in New York City attracted an overflow crowd of 22,000, with the great American hero and paragon of isolationism Charles A. Lindbergh as the keynote speaker.[18]

Following the ABC-1 conference, consultations between representatives of Great Britain and the United States continued, both in the United States and in England. Concurrently, President Roosevelt supported the British in every possible way short of declaring war by providing escort conveys, gathering and reporting information on German submarine activity, and continuing Lend-Lease assistance.[19] The Lend-Lease Act was only the most transparent indication of Roosevelt's intentions. In September of 1940, he had approved a plan to provide fifty American World War I-vintage destroyers to the British for protection against German submarines.[20]

The problem with Lend-Lease, apart from the fact that it was clearly pushing America closer to war, was the haphazard system of allocation of equipment to forces engaged in opposition to Nazi Germany.[21] Long before Pearl Harbor, American industry was rushing to fill the urgent orders of the French, British, Chinese, and, after June 1941, the Soviets. As long as the allocation lacked specificity, every claimant to U.S. resources swallowed up production that potentially attenuated America's own war preparedness;[22] it was a chaotic situation that clamored for resolution.

THE ORIGIN OF THE VICTORY PROGRAM

Fortunately, the savvy Under Secretary of War Robert P. Patterson understood the consequences of such a disorganized course and was in a position to do something to rectify the situation. On April 18th,[23] he sent a memo to Secretary of War Henry L. Stimson urgently requesting the creation of a clear-cut directive based on our accepted strategy toward our own armed forces, coordinated with our commitment to all of the countries receiving military aid.[24] This was the first effort to bring order out of chaos and right the ship. Stimson, provoked by Patterson's memo, then convinced Roosevelt to issue an order on July 9, 1941 directing the Secretaries of War and the Navy to prepare a mobilization plan that would be needed to ensure the defeat of our potential enemies, paving the way for the formulation of the Victory Program. The President's response to Stimson read in part: "I wish that you or appropriate representatives designated by you would join with the Secretary of the Navy and his representatives in exploring at once the overall production requirements[25] required to defeat our potential enemies. I realize that this report involves the making of appropriate assumptions as to our probable friends and enemies and to the conceivable theaters of operation which will be required."[26] Clearly, Roosevelt's order, precipitated by Stimson's memorandum, was the impetus to start the program that led to the implementation of strategic plans to defeat Germany and Japan.

Enactment of the plan fell upon George Marshall, who instructed General Leonard T. Gerow, chair of the War Plans Division, to designate Wedemeyer as head of the team to write the Victory Program. The choice of Wedemeyer was logical,[27] since he had already been assigned to the War Plans Division, had familiarized himself with the existing plans prepared by the department, and had amply demonstrated his competence and leadership ability. Gerow explained to Wedemeyer that they had a mere ninety days to devise a comprehensive plan for all of the requirements necessary for America to engage in a war with its "potential enemies" that included providing for supplies and equipment necessary for the job. Additionally, they were instructed to factor in all existing and future Lend-Lease requirements for America's allies.

In a different time, Wedemeyer's selection would have been regarded by most military men as a dead end, since planning and staff work was not the preferred formula for advancement and recognition. But these were not normal times, and Wedemeyer was to be the beneficiary of a combination of circumstances that propelled him to the top of his profession. Doubtless, Marshall had originally appointed Wedemeyer to the War Plans division in May because of Wedemeyer's experience at the *Kriegsakademie*, the favorable impression he had made during their numerous conversations, and the report submitted after his two-year experience in Germany.

Although Wedemeyer had the benefit of the work of his predecessors and months of prior study, the time frame he was given to produce the document and the scope of the assignment made the project a daunting challenge. The 44-year-old Wedemeyer and his small staff set up shop in the cramped, hot, and humid offices of the War Plans Division, located in the Munitions Building in Washington.[28] The importance of the project afforded him the luxury of his own private office and secretary, highly unusual for a man of his rank. The office was adjacent to those of Generals Gerow and Marshall, who were constant visitors.[29] Although Wedemeyer's staff included eight other planners to whom he parceled out discrete portions of the program, he was the chief architect, personally reviewing and approving everything that was submitted for consideration. Other members of the committee included Colonels Thomas Handy, Franklin A. Kibler, C.W. Bundy, and Lieutenant Colonel Leven C. Allen. Military protocol was turned upside down by placing the lowest ranking officer in charge, but these were special circumstances, and the order came directly from the top.[30]

Wedemeyer and his staff met with scores of political and military leaders and industrialists, carefully framing their questions so that the secrecy of the project would not be compromised. In his 1983 interview with Keith Eiler, he discussed the pitfalls of the interviewing process: "Needless to say, at a time when merely discussing such things [preparations for war] was often interpreted as plotting war, few of the harassed senior officials in Washington were in a position to offer much guidance."[31]

The strategic hub of the Victory Program was to bolster Allied forces in England (later codenamed BOLERO) in preparation for a cross-channel invasion of France in the summer of 1943, followed by a massive strike at the industrial heart of Germany in the Ruhr basin, the source of her war making potential. American strategy in favor of a 1943 invasion was based on the conviction that the Germans had not had adequate time to strengthen their Atlantic Wall since they were still heavily engaged in the east with the Soviets after their invasion that began on June 22, 1941. A large portion of German military capability would thus be unavailable to oppose a full-scale invasion on a second front.[32]

Wedemeyer and his staff had to provide answers to a number of complex problems, including where the fighting would take place, how many troops would be required, how and where they would be trained, and where they would land. He then needed to calculate the number of ships required to transport and support the vast numbers of troops to the staging areas and battlefields, followed by estimates of the types and quantity of the airplanes and tanks needed, and then construct a plan to mobilize the country's industrial power to produce equipment to properly supply the fighting forces.[33]

The planners carefully scrutinized mobilization plans from previous wars. One of their first conclusions was that approximately ten percent of a nation's population was the maximum that could be placed under arms while still leaving sufficient manpower to produce weapons and food and to administer the affairs of government while still satisfying all the domestic requirements of a wartime economy. The population of the United States was 140 million in 1940, leading to an initial proposal of an armed force of 14 million.[34] The actual figure later arrived at was ten million, and this proved remarkably close to the number that were actually inducted.[35] The size of each of the individual armed forces was also determined after consultation with the senior heads of the various branches.

Although the Victory Program provided estimates of the total size of military forces necessary to defeat both Germany and Japan, the emphasis, even after Pearl Harbor, was primarily on Germany. The Pacific was relegated in the early years of the war to a more defensive posture. This decision was later officially endorsed at the first Anglo-American wartime conference, ARCADIA, in Washington in January, 1942.[36]

Although given *carte blanche* authority to complete the critical assignment, there were still constraints that were sometimes difficult to overcome. With the top level of secrecy assigned to the job, Wedemeyer had to be careful in framing his questions and requests for information so as to mask the ultimate objective of the plan, to some extent limiting the value of his authority to call on officials and agencies of the government and civilian contractors for information and advice. For example, in order to provide full support to accommodate the ten million soldiers to be outfitted, the planners had to deal with civilian production chiefs and ask relevant questions. Any contractor involved in the production of large quantities of rifles, tanks, ships, helmets, binoculars, blankets, airplanes, and the myriad of other items required to equip, train, transport, and maintain a huge modern fighting force could make a pretty good guess as to what the questioner was driving at and deduce a fairly good estimate of the size of the projected army. It would also undoubtedly be evident that these armaments were not being produced for a peacetime army.[37] One of many anecdotes demonstrating the enormity of the problem of security was the knowledge gained by members of the press that an order had been placed with a civilian contractor for 4 million dog tags. George Marshall's public explanation of each soldier requiring two seemed wanting, considering the size of the army at that time was a mere quarter of a million men![38] Surprisingly, this glaring inconsistency never appeared in print.

Comparisons with World War I were only partially helpful. Although American industry expanded in 1917 to meet military requirements, the country was never converted to a full-blown war economy on anything near the scale needed for the crisis at hand. Furthermore, as Kirkpatrick notes, inadequate records were maintained and preserved.[39]

The genius of Wedemeyer was not so much in the act of coordinating, editing, and drafting the document, but in the intellectual force he brought to bear in focusing on the subject and framing the precise questions that needed to be addressed. In order to determine the ultimate production requirements, he had to compute the size of the military force necessary to meet the threat, but a precondition to making this estimate was *knowledge of the mission that the military was to undertake.* This, in turn, depended on *overall strategy*, and this meant *he had to know the national objectives in the event of war.* Moreover, current and projected Lend-Lease requirements needed to be factored in. No American military planner had ever approached war plans in this fashion. The difficulty was magnified since it was not Wedemeyer's assignment, as such, to independently articulate overall American strategic objectives, this being the responsibility of the top military and political leaders. Kirpatrick takes the reasoning process discussed in *Wedemeyer Reports!* to its logical conclusion by posing the four questions that framed the overall project:

1. What is the national objective of the United States?
2. What military strategy will be devised to accomplish that national objective?
3. What military forces must be raised in order to execute that military strategy?
4. How will those military forces be constituted, equipped, and trained?[40]

What is intriguing is that Wedemeyer had to address and answer the first three questions before he could answer the fourth, but in addressing the problems related to the first question he was clearly, in a strict military sense, exceeding the bounds of anything conventional wisdom would have deemed appropriate for a military planner, let alone a mere junior officer. It is highly unlikely that anyone without Wedemeyer's background and fund of knowledge would have even included question number one on the list, but Wedemeyer was capable of seeing the big picture and did not limit his inquiry to a simple catalogue of armaments and supplies. In drafting the Victory Program, he drew on all he had learned about military history, geography, economics, and science, and amalgamated this experience with concepts he learned in the *Kriegsakadamie* from the teachings of Clausewitz, Mackinder, and Fuller. Marshall had chosen wisely. No other person in the United States military was better equipped for the job at hand.

It is also a certainty that if, in drafting the overall American strategic plan, Wedemeyer had incorporated the imperative which to his thinking was essential, namely including efforts to limit Russian expansion and the spread of Communism, he would have been immediately relieved of his position. Yet this is precisely what he intended to accomplish, but he was coy enough to disguise this objective with the indefinite language of *strategy to defeat the Nazis*, never overtly stating that the Victory Program incorporated overall grand strategic war aims. The proposals, however, clearly envisioned these goals. Wedemeyer was deeply concerned about how the world would emerge from the cataclysm of war and what sort of peace the country was willing to enforce, but he cleverly made these objectives implicit in his Victory Program rather than literal.

With the knowledge that determining the correct governmental policy for the war was an essential precursor, he found the task of gathering that information and stating that policy "almost as elusive as the philosopher's stone."[41] Despite difficulty in information gathering, Wedemeyer did not rush to conclusions constrained by the use only of his own ideas, but was largely unsuccessful in finding other authoritative sources of information. Working from dawn until late into the night, and with the clear understanding that it was beyond his mandate as a military planner to set national policy, he studied intensely and often sought guidance on the question of the military objectives of the United States from his two most knowledgeable superiors, Marshall and Stimson. Though immensely helpful, even these two top-level officials were in no position to tell Wedemeyer "with any authority what the nation intended," and he had even less luck with other senior governmental officials he approached.[42] Thus, a lowly Lieutenant Colonel, not the heads of government, was at the forefront of the task of formulating the objectives of the United States in the coming conflict!

Eventually, a limited amount of guidance came from Stimson after Wedemeyer sent him a cleverly drafted proposal which, in a very general sense, carefully disguised his real intent. Wedemeyer suggested that America's national purpose was *to eliminate totalitarianism from Europe* and, in the process, to be *an ally of Great Britain* and, in addition, to deny the Japanese undisputed control of the western Pacific"[43] (emphasis added). Stimson quickly approved the proposal, and this policy became the backbone of the Victory Program from which all other determinations and recommendations flowed.

Two critical points are noteworthy. First, the phrase "to eliminate totalitarianism" is deliberately vague. There were *two* totalitarian rulers in Europe, but one was destined to become our ally. Ideally, Wedemeyer would have preferred to include not only Nazism but also include language to limit or contain Communism, but adding this in the submission to Stimson would have been viewed by President Roosevelt as overtly and dangerously hostile to America's new strategic bedfellow, the Soviet Union. With an understanding of this sensitivity, though he personally believed it to be important, Wedemeyer eliminated any reference to the Soviets from the final report, though he did express his fears about Communism off the record on more than one occasion, not only to Marshall but to several others with whom he was associated.[44]

Perhaps in a calculated act of passive aggression, the Soviets were never referred to as an ally. Only Great Britain was mentioned in the report. It is hard to understand how this escaped attention, and Wedemeyer must have been pleased since he understood the potential for the Soviets to be an enemy after the war and truly believed that resistance to Communism should be an essential tenet of America's long-term strategy. He was a careful and exacting wordsmith, and it was no accident that he chose the precise language that he submitted to Stimson, which was then approved.

On several occasions prior to completion of the Victory Program and thereafter, Wedemeyer accompanied Marshall to see Roosevelt for the purpose of personally discussing his work. Wedemeyer was justifiably proud of his efforts and relieved to have finally completed the 147-page document on September 25, 1941,[45] whereupon it was personally presented to Roosevelt by Marshall and tentatively approved. Shortly after completion of the program, Wedemeyer went with Secretary Simpson to the White House to discuss the Victory Program with the President.[46] Going into their first encounter with British planners in early 1942, the two soldiers believed that they had the President's tentative support for the recommendations contained in the plan, including, most importantly, a 1943 invasion of France.[47] The timing was fortunate, since only a few months after its completion, the United States was engaged in a very real war on two fronts.

Much of the Victory Program, except for some specific strategic proposals that grew out of it dealing with the European conflict, was entirely consistent with the strategic aims of the British. For example, language such as suggesting military activity "wherever soft spots arise in Europe or adjacent areas," and the use of "blockade, propaganda, subversive activities, air superiority, and the establishment of effective military bases, encircling the Nazi citadel . . ." were entirely consistent with British strategic military policy. This language undoubtedly arose from study of the joint meetings at ABC-1 and was quite clearly included to gain the support of our future ally.

However, one provision in particular, general in nature as it was, later assumed enormous importance and was to define a sharp division of opinion with the British, who were close readers, and immediately focused on language which stated that the Allies must prepare to fight Germany *by actually coming to grips with and defeating her ground forces* and definitely breaking her will to combat"[48] (emphasis added). The British must have paused and contemplated the import of this ominous phrase when they read the report. They would soon learn what the Americans meant when they used that language. Although Maurice Matloff and Edwin M. Snell in their 1980 treatise, *Strategic Planning for Coalition Warfare 1941–1942,* acknowledge that this language seemed "vague" as to the precise manner in which the Allies had to "*come to grips,*"[49] it was not long before it was transformed into a specific American proposal to invade France in 1943 and became the centerpiece of the strategic portion of the Victory Program. The significance of this provision became a serious bone of contention, epitomizing in a single sentence the difference between American strategy to invade France in force early, and the British concept of nibbling around the edges.

"THE BIG LEAK"

Aside from these differences, another major crisis was soon to arise. When Wedemeyer reported to his office on the morning of December 5th, he was stunned to find the entire staff in a state of shock and bewilderment. In a sensational development, the entire contents of the Victory Program had been disclosed on the front pages of both the *Chicago Tribune* and the *Washington Post* of December 4th, under the byline of reporter Chesley Manley.[50] [pic. 12] A copy of the front pages of these newspapers was on almost every desk with three-inch headlines blaring "F.D.R.'s WAR PLANS!" Virtually every important feature of the Victory Program was spelled out in detail. It was obvious that Manley had had access to the entire document. The impact of this incredible breach of confidentiality was blunted only by the monumental events of December 7th, the day that would "live in infamy."

The identity of the person(s) who leaked the story was never established with certainty, though substantial circumstantial evidence suggests that Senator Burton K. Wheeler, a staunch isolationist, transmitted the document to Manley.[51] Historian Thomas Fleming astutely hypothesizes that the actual source of the leak was Roosevelt himself who, in the weeks prior to Pearl Harbor, knew from intercepted Japanese messages that war with Japan was imminent. Wedemeyer told Fleming in 1986 that he was convinced that Roosevelt was the source.[52] It was war with Germany that Roosevelt really wanted, and he knew that the release of the secret war plans would push Hitler closer to declaring war on the United States, which indeed happened on December 11th, relieving the President of the unenviable task of convincing a reluctant Congress to declare war on Germany.

A full FBI investigation of the leak followed, and Wedemeyer initially was a prime suspect. The report of the investigation is now available at the National Archives, and the contents make it clear that shortly after the commencement of the probe, the FBI did not believe Wedemeyer was culpable and eliminated him as a suspect. Secretary of War Stimson, another of Wedemeyer's chief supporters, was convinced of his innocence. In a letter to President Roosevelt dated March 2, 1942, he said he had been advised by the FBI that their investigation "ran in quite a different direction from that of Colonel Wedemeyer."[53] However, in the chaos following Pearl Harbor, Wedemeyer, and for that matter anyone else outside the inner circle of the FBI, was not informed of this. General Marshall also immediately declared Wedemeyer completely innocent of any complicity in the leak, and because of this support his military career was saved. In retrospect, knowing what we do today of Wedemeyer's impeccable moral standards and devotion to duty, it is easy to surmise that it would have been completely out of character for him to violate the confidentiality of his task.

Although it is remarkable that the Victory Plan remained secret, at least until December 4th, it is even more notable that despite dealing with countless civilian production managers and dozens of military chiefs, with the clear implication that America was gearing up for war, the leak most probably came from a governmental source.

On December 12, 1941, Dwight Eisenhower was reassigned by General Marshall to Washington for the purpose of utilizing his tactical skills in the War Plans Division. Until this time Eisenhower's focus had been in the Pacific theatre.[54] Shortly after his appointment, Eisenhower was designated to replace Gerow as Chief of War Plans, immediately expanding his scope to a more global perspective. In a March 25, 1942 memorandum to Marshall on the strategic goals of the Allies, Eisenhower endorsed virtually all the recommendations of the Victory Plan, precisely echoing the earlier recommendations of Wedemeyer, *including the need for an early cross-channel attack against Germany*.[55] Over time, Wedemeyer's recommendation evolved into a cardinal portion of what came to be called the Marshall Memorandum or, alternatively, the Eisenhower Doctrine, which set forth the military view on how the war should be waged. Only *after* the war did Eisenhower express any doubts about the success of a 1943 invasion.

The drafting of the Victory Program was Wedemeyer's first major effort in his lifelong passion to define national objectives. In his later years he continued to be a vigorous advocate of the necessity for a nation to have long-term strategic objectives, and in his writings and speeches he urged American policy makers to follow this course. At the age of 84 he set forth his idea of what a nation's goals should be in a "Memorandum on a National Strategy Council":

> ... [A] journey can be charted only with a destination in mind, and STRATEGY can be plotted only with goals or aims in mind. I accordingly set out to discover what the objectives of U.S. involvement might be—other than the physical destruction of the forces which might be then arrayed against us. What were our country's true interests? How could those interests best be protected and advanced? What kind of world did we wish to emerge from the cataclysm of another terrible war?[56]

When he wrote this memorandum in 1983, the now well-respected Lt. General was thinking back to 1941 and must have wondered how different things might have been had the American leadership addressed these issues at the time that his own influence did not officially extend beyond that of a mid-level officer.

It is always difficult to mount a convincing counter-factual argument, and admittedly, it is entirely hypothetical whether a 1943 cross-channel invasion would have been more successful than the one on June 6, 1944. Furthermore, the weight of authority has assumed almost canonical proportions that a 1943 invasion would have miserably failed.[57] Hanson W. Baldwin, the distinguished military critic of the *New York Times*, contended in 1950:

In retrospect it is now obvious that our concept of invading Western Europe in 1943 was fantastic; our deficiencies in North Africa, which was a much-needed training school for our troops, proved that. The British objection to a 1943 cross-channel operation was also soundly taken militarily; we would have had in that year neither the trained divisions, the equipment, the planes, the experience, nor (particularly) the landing craft to have invaded the most strongly held part of the Continent against an enemy whose strength was far greater than it was a year later.[58]

Wedemeyer would not have agreed with Baldwin, especially the statement that the Normandy coast was stronger in 1943 than in 1944. In 1979, in a foreword to Walter Scott Dunn's book *Second Front Now 1943*, Wedemeyer, referring to his recommendations for a 1943 cross-channel attack, avowed, "I have never changed my earlier views of these matters."[59]

There are at least two American historians who later argued that not only would such a plan have been successful, but that the capture of Eastern Europe from an invasion launched from the west would also have denied the Russians the lands they eventually annexed.[60] Additionally, no less an athority than the Chief of Staff of the German Army during the early years of the war, General Franz Halder, as well as other senior German officers, confirmed to Wedemeyer in 1946 that the Atlantic coast was indeed vulnerable in 1943, and in his opinion an invasion at that time would have succeeded.[61] Additional support came from the highly regarded Field-Marshall von Rundstedt, who had been in command of the western sector (including northern France) since early 1942. In a post-war conversation with British historian B. H. Liddell Hart,[62] von Rundstedt expressed concern about the stretching of German forces in the east and revealed he expected a 1943 invasion.[63] Likewise, surviving members of General Rommel's staff told Hart of the feverish efforts made in the spring of 1944 to hasten the construction of underwater obstacles, bomb-proof bunkers, and minefields along the entire Normandy coast after their commander correctly surmised the invasion would come there. In the few months before D-Day, Rommel also increased the number of mines installed along the coast three-fold.[64] Clearly, Rommel's last-minute efforts made the invasion in 1944 far more arduous.

Unfortunately, in 1942 the opposing strategic philosophies of the Americans and the British created a rocky path for the enactment of the Victory Program as a whole. Even though it ultimately was not implemented in its entirety, its importance in energizing the mobilization of our armed forces cannot be overestimated. In a note to the President shortly after Pearl Harbor, Secretary of War Stimson praised Wedemeyer, stating that without the timely analysis of blitzkrieg that was provided "we should be badly off indeed."[65] The head of the War Production Board, Donald Nelson, noted that the Plan "revolutionized our production and may well have been a decisive turning point."[66] General Marshall always appreciated the enormous contribution Wedemeyer had made in heading the group which prepared the Victory Program. In a letter to Wedemeyer dated December 23, 1942, Marshall said he was deeply appreciative of:

> ... the tremendous burden you have carried during the past year. As head of the Strategy and Policy Group of Operations Division and as the Army representative on the combined British-American Planners, you have rendered an outstanding service.
>
> The assistance you gave me in London last April [the London British American Planners Meeting] was of vital importance to Allied strategy in this year.[67]

There is little other contemporary praise for Wedemeyer's efforts. The influential and widely respected Forrest Pogue did not share Stimson's or Nelson's positive appraisal. In his biography of General Marshall, *Ordeal and Hope*, Pogue spends little time discussing the details of how the Victory Program was constructed, the contents of the plan, or its importance to the war effort, and fails to mention Marshall's and Roosevelt's endorsement of it.[68] Pogue seemed reluctant to give much credit to Wedemeyer at all in his references to the War Plans Division, strongly contributing to a diminished historical perspective of the degree and importance of Wedemeyer's participation.[69] Two recent books on the major military architects of World War II also barely give Wedemeyer any recognition whatsoever, crediting the plan to Eisenhower and Marshall.[70]

On the other hand, it was John Keegan's brilliant and succinct assessment of Wedemeyer's demeanor and contribution that spurred this author's interest in Wedemeyer without which this book would never have been written:

> ... [W]hile Stilwell was weather-worn, uncouth and angular, Wedemeyer was handsome, graceful and smooth ... and his inclination was to win arguments by determining beforehand the terms on

which they would be debated rather than trusting to the cutting-edge of the tongue in the duel itself. It was this intellectuality which had recommended him to Marshall; that and the particular circumstances in which he had refined his mind. For Wedemeyer was that rare bird in an Anglo-Saxon Army, a graduate of the German Staff College, class of 1936–1938. . . . The *Kriegsakadamie*, by a stroke of supreme irony[71] had unwittingly planted in the machinery's control centre someone to whom it had taught a philosophy of war exactly complementary to its own, . . . a strategist with no thought but that of bringing the Wehrmacht face to face with its mirror-image. . . . It thereby determined that the coming struggle between Germany and the United States must inevitably take the form of a great land battle between their two armies on the land mass of Western Europe. Presciently, Wedemeyers's plan . . . *Its conception and delivery was to be one of the decisive acts of the Second World War.*[72] (emphasis added)

Israeli academic Tuvia Ben-Moshe singles out Wedemeyer as the major influence in the writing of the report, quite correctly noting that Eisenhower, who was appointed head of the War Plans Division *after* the report was completed, subsequently adopted and endorsed the entire program.[73]

Others who fully credit Wedemeyer include Major Charles E. Kirpatrick, stating:

. . . [T]he (Victory Program) took shape under the direction of a single officer who developed the conceptual framework, outlined and allocated specific tasks for subordinate planners, guided the many different parts of the plan into a coherent whole. . . . This intellectual tour de force was the accomplishment of Albert C. Wedemeyer . . .[74]

Historian Mark Stoler also appreciated the contribution of Wedemeyer,[75] but aside from Keith Eiler's abortive biography, Wedemeyer's contribution has otherwise been largely underappreciated.[76] Marshall never wavered in crediting Wedemeyer for his enormous contribution to the planning of the cross-channel invasion, telegraphing his protégé in India shortly after a beachhead had been established in Normandy with the news that "your plan has succeeded."[77]

CHAPTER 4

UNDERMINING THE VICTORY PROGRAM: RATTLESNAKE OR BOA CONSTRICTOR

There is at least one thing worse than fighting with allies—
And that is to fight without them.
—Sir Winston S. Churchill

The Victory Program was finished in late September 1941, and the provisions relating to the construction of the armed forces and the civilian industrial complex to feed the war effort were implemented almost immediately. The strategic plans calling for the build-up and utilization of American forces and where and when they were to be employed were to await events as they developed. Robert Sherwood, referring to the completed plan, called it "One of the most remarkable documents of American history, for it set down the basic strategy of a global war before this country was involved in it."[1]

A key two-step component of the American plan, codenamed BOLERO and ROUNDUP, contemplated the gathering of a large number of American troops in England and supplying them with arms and equipment in preparation for a 1943 cross-channel invasion. In September 1941, the drafters of the plan had no indication of how this particular proposal might be received by the British. Yet had they known of Harry Hopkins' visit to London in January 1941 and his numerous meetings with Winston Churchill, they might have been forewarned that the British had other ideas about how to conduct the European conflict.

HARRY HOPKINS IN LONDON WITH CHURCHILL, JANUARY 1941

Jean Monnet, the highly influential French leader and businessman who worked during World War II as a supply coordinator and economic liaison to the United States, has been credited with the first use of the phrase "arsenal of democracy" (later co-opted by Roosevelt in one of his famous "Fireside Chats"). Drawing upon his personal insights, the Frenchman forewarned Hopkins, who made a special trip to London in January 1941 to confer with Churchill. He advised him to talk to no one but Churchill for "[he] is the British War Cabinet, and no one else matters."[2] Echoing this sentiment after his first meeting with Churchill, Hopkins wrote Roosevelt:

> Churchill is the gov't [sic] in every sense of the word—he controls the grand strategy and often the details—labor trusts him—the army, navy, air force are behind him to a man. The politicians and upper crust *pretend* to like him. *I cannot emphasize too strongly that he is the one and only person over here with whom you need to have a full meeting of minds*[3] (emphasis added).

In noting that the politicians and upper crust "pretend" to like Churchill, Hopkins was only hinting at the consequences of challenging the Prime Minister. For any British military person or political figure, opposing Churchill was a courageous act that could be a career-ending event, and even in the case of Wedemeyer, who was not under Churchill's direct command, one fraught with potentially serious consequences. The powerful Prime Minister did not take kindly to anyone standing in his way, and blocking the American plan for a cross-channel attack was uppermost in his mind.

Churchill's opposition to any large-scale battle with Germany long preceded America's entry into the war. During Hopkins' January 1941 visit to London he and Churchill engaged in numerous far-ranging discussions about the war, and in the course of one of the discussions Churchill revealed in one sentence his concept of the proper strategy, which did not include anything resembling a cross-channel invasion followed by a march overland to Germany. Churchill told Hopkins that air power would be the key to winning the war, not armies, and that ". . . this war will never see great forces massed against one another."[4] This stance was repeated and continually stressed in later military conferences, and the same message, albeit sometimes in a different form, was heard in many of Churchill's speeches in the months preceding America's entry into the war. On February 9, 1941, Hopkins, on his way home from London, had a short stopover in Lisbon after his nearly three-week visit to England. That evening he listened to a radio address of the Prime Minister broadcast to the world. It was the inspiring "Give us the tools and we will finish the job" speech. Again, Churchill revealed at this early date his overall strategic war aims when he pronounced: "But this is not a war of vast armies, firing immense masses of shells at one another."[5] In each of the statements, one to Hopkins directly and the one in the radio address heard by Hopkins while in Lisbon, Churchill echoed the horror of the trenches of the First World War and its enormous casualties, which were uppermost in his mind. He was determined to not repeat the mistakes of that conflict, and as events would disclose, a cross-channel invasion, in Churchill's mind, would repeat the mistakes of the Great War.

A few months later, the British military advisors used the occasion of the first major pre-war Anglo-American conference (ARGENTIA, August 1941) at Newfoundland, to reiterate this view, stressing the argument that they were employing bombings, blockades, and propaganda as the means to weaken and ultimately defeat the Nazis. They believed that even if some penetration into Europe was necessary, armed "local resistance groups" would rise up against their occupiers and obviate the need for a large-scale invasion.[6] The British were merely reiterating Churchill's position. Of course, ultimately, at the Teheran Summit in November/December 1943, Churchill finally had to give in, and he agreed to a spring 1944 date, but this agreement was the result of considerable arm-twisting from Roosevelt and Stalin.[7]

THE ARCADIA CONFERENCE—WASHINGTON, D.C., DECEMBER 22, 1941–JANUARY 14, 1942

Within weeks after Pearl Harbor, Churchill hurried to Washington for the Arcadia conference,[8] his first wartime meeting with Roosevelt, conducted between December 22, 1941 and January 14, 1942, in order to solidify a "Germany First" strategy and head off what he feared might be a U.S. concentration against the Japanese, which would mean a diversion of Lend-Lease material to the Pacific.[9] His concerns were fueled by a War Department act that had interrupted the shipment of all war material from American ports, pending a reassessment of the point of allocation.[10] Churchill feared this act signaled a move to concentrate on the Pacific. It would soon be evident that the Prime Minister would espouse the same positions at ARGENTIA that he had related to Hopkins in January 1941 and in his radio broadcast.

Roosevelt and his military advisors, including Marshall, were reluctant to meet Churchill so early into the hostilities. They were not yet sufficiently prepared to deal with the British chiefs in discussions of world strategy. By contrast, the British were already well versed in the ways of war and anxious to bring the Americans around to their view of how it should be conducted. As American Major General Thomas Handy put it: "After Pearl Harbor the Prime Minister descended on Washington with a whole gang of people. . . . We were more or less babes in the woods on this planning and joint business with the British. They'd been doing it for years. They were experts at it and we were just starting."[11] To the British, the Americans appeared hopelessly inept. British Colonel Ian Jacob was shocked at the informal way the Americans did business at the first meeting, describing one conference in the Oval Office attended by Roosevelt and Churchill with no tables, just chairs, no prepared agenda, no maps, and a very informal atmosphere. Jacob was dumbfounded when Roosevelt's dog Fala began barking during one of Churchill's orations.[12] As Andrew Robert's observed, "This country club atmosphere . . . could not survive the rigors of a global war."[13]

The Americans felt that the proper time for Churchill to come to Washington was after they "had settled its basic war strategy and decided its production and shipping priorities, and not have Churchill meddling in the making of those decisions."[14] At first Roosevelt was in agreement with this view. In an unsent telegram and a written note, also never sent,[15] the President intended suggesting a delay in the meeting. However, the Prime Minister persuaded Roosevelt to change his mind and approve an early meeting.[16] Though overjoyed that the United States was finally in the war, especially since the catastrophic prospect of unilaterally fighting a war on two fronts was now averted, Churchill's elation was tempered by a pressing uneasiness that in their zeal for revenge for Pearl Harbor, the Americans would make the Pacific their principal interest. This prompted him to suggest an immediate conference in order to champion his own strategic vision and ensure that Europe would still have first priority.[17]

The American concerns about not being ready to deal with the British were justified. Churchill and his military advisors came with a well thought-out and elaborate presentation at the first meeting, along with multiple proposals:

(i) Allied occupation, with French cooperation [if possible], of North Africa, eastward all the way to the Turkish border.

(ii) Multiple measures to regain control of the Pacific, though at this

time Churchill had little appreciation of the extent of damage
to the American fleet at Pearl Harbor.

(iii) An "invasion" at some location on the European continent in
1943, though not a cross-channel expedition into France[18]

These arguments were the core of a "Europe First" strategy that had
previously been agreed on in principle, but because of the recent Japanese
attack, Churchill felt he needed confirmation that this strategy had not been
eroded.

It is interesting to note the not so subtle shift in Churchill's negotiating
tactics. Prior to Pearl Harbor, the Prime Minister was persistent but somewhat deferential in his requests for aid. Immediately afterwards, his efforts
to control the war and obtain approval of his plans took on an increased sense
of urgency, and he was no longer shy about pushing his weight around with
American planners. For example, at a British staff meeting on December 8,
1941, in response to one of his aids who diplomatically suggested a somewhat
cautious approach to the Americans on some specific point under discussion,
he remarked to his staff ". . . with a wicked leer in his eye: 'Oh that is the way
we talked to her while we were wooing her; now that she is in the harem, we
talk to her quite differently',"[19] a stance he never abandoned throughout the
years of conflict.[20] Accordingly, Churchill planned to push his plan for the
Mediterranean theatre more vigorously.

The Victory Program's strategic recommendations with respect to operations in Europe first required the approval of President Roosevelt, and then
collaboration with and approval by America's chief ally, Great Britain,
following America's entry into the war after December 7, 1941. The critical
recommendation codenamed BOLERO called for a build-up of American
forces in England in anticipation of a cross-channel invasion into France in
the summer of 1943. This proposal was met with qualified but not wholehearted approval when it was first introduced to the British. The opposition
to the American plan focused not on the build-up of American forces and
the supplying of large amounts of military equipment and supplies to England, but on that feature of the American proposal which incorporated a subsidiary "emergency" plan, SLEDGEHAMMER, to land a small force in
France in the summer or fall of 1942, only *under the dire circumstance* of (i)
having to divert German forces away from collapsing Soviet resistance in the
east, or (ii) a total collapse of Germany. More will be said about this shortly.

While the build-up of American arms and the expansion of the military and civilian industrial production were never in doubt, getting approval by the President for the Victory Program's recommendation for a cross-channel invasion in the summer of 1943 was another story, first with President Roosevelt and next with Great Britain, since from an early stage Churchill's opposition had to be overcome.

There were several reasons for British resistance to a cross-channel attack: the British had a different longstanding strategic viewpoint due primarily to their belief in the superiority of the tactics they had developed over many centuries, including against Napoleon-held Europe, and more recently, the nightmarish memories of their casualties in the First World War. Then again, when we say "British resistance," what is primarily meant is Churchill's resistance. As British military historian General J.F.C. "Boney" Fuller so correctly stated: the decision to create a Combined Chiefs of Staff to direct the war was sound, but ". . . throughout the war unanimity was frequently impeded by the systems of control adopted by the two heads of state. While Churchill looked upon his Chiefs of Staff as the instruments of his will, Roosevelt treated his as free agents."[21] The British position was Churchill's position. Not surprisingly, Churchill never viewed himself as autocratic in his relations with his war ministers, but aware of critics who thought otherwise, in his war memoirs he took pains to tone down the perception: "I cannot say that we never differed among ourselves even at home, but a kind of understanding grew up between me and the British Chiefs of Staff that we should convince and persuade rather than try to over-rule each other."[22]

The Prime Minister favored a Mediterranean campaign, code-named GYMNAST for several reasons. It would satisfy the President's desire to get American troops into action quickly, allay the diversion of arms and equipment that would otherwise go the Pacific, and most importantly, provide a launching pad for additional expeditions in Sicily and Italy and North Africa. Not wanting to tip his hand, Churchill did not stress the last two points.

Other British recommendations favored by Churchill called for sending American divisions to the Southwest Pacific to shore up the shaky British forces there; providing American ships to transport British reinforcements to the Indian Ocean area; opening of air offensives against the Japanese from China, northeast India, and the Aleutians; and finally, massively increasing military supplies to England. However, with regard to the build-up of forces and supplies in England, Churchill was walking a delicate tightrope; yes, he wanted all the American armaments, but he was concerned that if the supply grew too large in England, it would be difficult to divert them to the other location he had in mind, namely the Mediterranean. On the other hand, if he protested too strongly, he was concerned that the war material might be moved to the Pacific. All these recommendations and proposals were now coming from America's new "junior partner," which had now nominated itself as senior partner immediately following Pearl Harbor.

Churchill demanded a strong voice in the allocation of armaments as well as the placement of troops, and, in particular, he favored an approach different from the Americans: implementation of strategic initiatives, consisting in large measure of multiple offensives initiated by the Allies on the periphery of the Axis stronghold. This approach was not favored by the Americans. Marshall and the other U.S. planners were alarmed by what they were hearing and looked on the British concept as a piecemeal scattering of Allied forces, vividly described by Stimson as the stopping up of "urgent rat holes" and a dangerous dispersion of resources. The American opposition to the British approach was summarized in January 1942 by Eisenhower, whose view represented the consensus of American war planners' thinking as well as the War Department's, and even at this early stage President Roosevelt's, when he stated:

> We've got to go to Europe and fight—and we've got to quit wasting resources all over the world—and still worse—wasting time. If we're to keep Russia in, save the Middle East, India, and Burma, we've got to begin slugging with air at West Europe; to be followed by a land attack as soon as possible.[23]

The American planners felt it important to move quickly, since the war was not going well in any theatre. The President was under enormous pressure to produce some good news. The key strategic feature of the Victory Plan focused Allied efforts on an offensive in Europe with a decisive cross-channel expedition concentrated at a single point. All of this, of course, would be preceded by a massive build-up in England of material, arms, and equipment, troops, construction of airfields, and naval craft needed to invade France. As devised by Wedemeyer and endorsed by Marshall and Eisenhower, it recommended that America take all measures to implement and:

> . . . develop, in conjunction with the British, a definite plan for operations against Northwest Europe. It should be sufficiently

extensive in scale as to engage, from the middle of May [1943] onward, an increasing portion of the German Air Force, and by late summer an increasing amount of his ground forces.[24]

MARSHALL PERSUADES ROOSEVELT TO ADOPT AMERICAN APPROACH

General Marshall knew the influence of the Prime Minister on the President. The Arcadia meeting left a cloud hovering over the question relating to the President's support for the American position. Out of concern that Roosevelt might change course under Churchill's influence, Marshall deviated from his characteristic posture of restraint. He arranged for his proposals to be presented to the President on March 25, 1942 at a luncheon in Washington attended by Secretary of War Henry Stimson, Naval Secretary Frank Knox, Air Corps chief General Henry Harley "Hap" Arnold, Admiral Ernest J. King, and close presidential advisor Harry Hopkins. At the luncheon, Marshall outlined in an abbreviated fashion the picture of an operation focusing on the shipment of troops and huge stores of munitions to England in preparation for hostilities, codenamed BOLERO. Until the concept of BOLERO was approved, discussion of the specifics of a plan for a cross-channel invasion was premature. Roosevelt gave his approval for BOLERO.

The conference then turned to plans for an attack launched from England using the most direct sea route to France, the protection of shipping using the shortest possible Atlantic crossing from the United States, the location and construction of airfields in England needed for close ground support, and a discussion of the importance of continued engagement of Hitler's forces on the Eastern Front. Marshall was relieved to gain acceptance by the President of his entire program at this luncheon but later said he feared it was not a wholehearted endorsement. More than once, the President added to Marshall's discomfort by his "cigarette holder gesture," body language described by the general as a jaunty upward tilt, implying a disregard for either unpleasant facts or a disagreement with a point presented.[25]

Ultimately, although approving Marshall's proposals, Roosevelt demanded additional details, especially of the proposed cross-channel invasion, and he ordered Marshall to return in a week with a more specific plan. Marshall did so on April 1, 1942, outlining a cross-channel attack at the narrowest point of the English Channel, the Pas-de-Calais, prospectively to be launched in the spring of 1943.

Cognizant of Roosevelt's desire to employ American troops sometime in 1942, as well as his assurances to Soviet Ambassador Molotov that a second front would soon be opened (FDR's commitment to Stalin was a continual factor in his strategic considerations), Marshall also included in the proposals a subsidiary plan called SLEDGEHAMMER, an operation that, if launched, would encompass an attack across the Pas-de-Calais in September 1942, a mere five months in the future. SLEDGEHAMMER, though, was seriously flawed, since there would of necessity be inadequate air support and far too few American troops available in England for the operation. Even if the initial attack was successful, there would not be sufficient forces to support a follow-up full-scale invasion. The British were to find out the consequences of this kind of limited foray in their disastrous venture at Dieppe in August 1942.[26] Most importantly, since America would have relatively few troops in England, it would be substantially a British operation, thus subject to their veto. This last point was its fatal weakness. We will shortly see how the British exploited the weakness of SLEDGE-HAMMER to derail the entire 1943 cross-channel proposal.

On the face of it, the April 1, 1942 meeting at the White House[27] was another success for Marshall. The President gave his approval, subject to the British acceptance of the plan, and he ordered Marshall to fly immediately to London, present it to the British and secure their endorsement. At the suggestion of Hopkins, the President ordered all those present to say nothing of the plan to Sir John Greer Dill,[28] Chief of the British Joint Staff Mission in Washington and Senior British Representative on the Combined Chiefs of Staff, whose duty it would have been to report it to London. Hopkins feared that if the British learned in advance of the American proposals that "it would simply be pulled to pieces and emasculated." Hopkins was correct. As Andrew Roberts put it, if the British had known of the proposals in advance, they would have:

> ... put the proposals through their stringent analytical process before Churchill and the Chiefs had a chance to view them. Indeed, had the British been forewarned of the details of Eisenhower's proposals, they would have had their refutations prepared even before Marshall's plane touched down.[29]

In spite of these precautions, Roberts says British Brigadier General Vivian Dykes came into possession of a document outlining the American objectives and forewarned his counterparts in London, eliminating any element of surprise that Marshall and his team had hoped to have when they presented their plans for a cross-channel invasion to Churchill and the British War Cabinet.[30]

The roots of the schism between strategies were deep, traceable in some measure to the different experiences of Britain and the United States in the last war. Unlike their British allies, America had emerged from the First World War relatively unscathed, without the vivid memories of the combined one-and-a-half million casualties at the Somme, the years of trench warfare, and the abject failure at Gallipoli, for which then First Lord of the Admiralty Churchill had taken the brunt of the blame. As in the prior conflict, the Americans were entering late in the game, after the British homeland had endured a devastating Blitz and the humiliations at Dunkirk, Greece, and Crete. Despite this, the British maintained their hubris about their military capabilities, though clearly the duration and degree of their involvement and the fury of their previous engagements had rendered them gun-shy for a campaign with the potential for bloodletting that a full-scale cross-channel invasion would entail.

On the other hand, the Americans, literally oceans apart from the escalating hostilities, were imbued with a World War I "Over There" mentality and a widespread belief that their entry into the conflict in Europe would, as they perceived it in World War I, tip the balance of power and rescue Britain from the German aggressor. While Roosevelt understood that defeating Germany should be the top priority, the American public appeared to be more hungry for vengeance against the Japanese, an enemy that could be easily identified and segregated in the homeland, that had perpetrated a dastardly sneak attack on Pearl Harbor on December 7, 1941. As Paul Fussel so aptly put it: "For most Americans, the war was about revenge against the Japanese, and the reason the European part had to be finished first was so the maximum attention could be devoted to the real business . . . destruction of the Japanese. The slogan was . . . *Remember Pearl Harbor*. No one ever shouted . . . *Remember Poland!*"[31]

APRIL 1942 IN LONDON

The British were first officially presented with the Presidentially sanctioned Victory Program when General Marshall, including Wedemeyer as his *aide de camp*, along with a small group of key American planners left Baltimore for London on April 4, 1942 for a secret conference, code named MODICUM. The Americans were neophytes in the world of international diplomacy and were about to be taught a valuable lesson by their more experienced counterparts. What they were about to witness was diplomatic skill honed over centuries.

The group arrived in London on April 8, and Churchill attended every important session. The Americans presented their proposals. The British at first were quiet and non-committal, politely listening to the American presentation, but as Wedemeyer astutely observed, their true intentions were revealed by the form and substance of their subtle questions directed to the timing and potential obstacles to implementation of the plan. Nothing complimentary about the plans was forthcoming; however "courtesy," not to mention deference to their then-dependent status as an ally, demanded that the British not bluntly tell the Americans that their talk of an early invasion was, in their opinion, wrong-headed.

It was clear that the British were well prepared and they were ultimately very effective in pressing their views. Invariably, as was their custom, they spoke in a unified voice. Much like their battle strategy, they never attacked the American plan directly; instead, they returned over and again with calm measured tones to revisit the concept of "scatterization," or periphery pecking, designed to wear down and weaken the enemy to a point that would eventually permit an unimpeded cross-channel invasion at an appropriate time. Their presentation was well rehearsed and almost theatrical. Whenever a controversial point arose, especially the cross-channel argument, they produced in unison, almost as a chorus, numerous richly bound, embossed, red leather dispatch cases, then snapped them open, revealing "wondrously precise studies and statistics. . . ." Their subtle persistence in quietly returning over and over again to their carefully rehearsed talking points had the effect, as Pulitzer Prize-winner Rick Atkinson so vividly describes, of "the dripping of water on stone."[32] For example, they would mention that their meticulous research revealed that the Germans had forty-five divisions in France or the Low Countries and another eleven available in Germany that could be swiftly deployed, or that a particular location was fortified in such a manner as to make it almost impregnable. The red folders held a seemingly innumerable cache of unimpeachable statistics about roads, railways, canals, and weather. (It would have been extremely helpful if these wonderful dispatch cases had contained useful information about the infamous "hedgerows" that bedeviled the Americans who landed on Omaha beach shortly after their invasion on D-Day.) The Americans, by comparison, had compiled their information in three beat-up loose-leaf binders that contained little to supplement or contradict the mountain of information the British had compiled. The same regimented presentation was later witnessed at Casablanca in January 1943 when, again as described by Atkinson, a disputed point arose and Chief of the Imperial Staff Lord Alanbrooke solemnly produced his trusty red leather folder with which he thoroughly demolished an American argument:

> Out came the red folders [that described the strength of German forces]. (Alanbrooke) said in a monotone that implied exasperation 'That is sufficient strength to overwhelm us on the ground and perhaps hem us in with wire or concrete . . . we cannot go into the Continent in force until Germany weakens'[33]

Then, as if to put an exclamation point on the argument, the folders were synchronously snapped shut.[34] To the slack-jawed Americans, disagreement seemed out of the question.

BOLERO outlined the staging of troops, equipment, and supplies in England in support of a cross-channel invasion (in Wedemeyer's words, a "sitzkrieg"). Churchill knew that once that unending stream of material and troops reached a critical level, it would be increasingly difficult to mount a convincing argument that they should be shifted to another sector. Withholding his strategy from the Americans, he still endorsed the mobilization but wanted to slow its concentration in England so that it could be utilized in areas *he* had anticipated, i.e. North Africa or the Mediterranean. Churchill was well aware of the strength of the American economy, and of Britain's almost complete dependence on America for its supply of war material. He also knew that the Victory Program envisioned the building of a ten-million-man American army that ". . . would absorb most of the weapons and supplies the British would need for the next two years."[35] A huge arsenal of equipment and ammunition stockpiled in England would have made any argument for a Mediterranean campaign more difficult, if not impossible. At the same time he knew that if he discouraged the build-up, there was the danger that it might go to the Pacific, something Churchill was determined to avoid. The genius of a Churchill was needed to walk this delicate tight rope, and he was up to the task.

The British argued ceaselessly for an Allied invasion of North Africa as opposed to the more direct invasion of Europe recommended in the Victory Program, leading Marshall and Eisenhower to believe that they were haunted by the ghosts of their military setbacks, those in the First World War and their more recent ones at the hands of the Nazis. Marine Corps strategist Joseph L. Strange believes that the British rejection of SLEDGEHAMMER and opposition to ROUNDUP had as much to do with the recent military defeats, pointing out that by mid-1942, the British had sustained devastating losses in Crete, Tobruk, and Singapore, and in the latter two had surrendered to enemy forces considerably smaller in size using inferior equipment. At Tobruk, the Germans captured 33,000 British soldiers, and at Singapore 85,000 British troops surrendered to a Japanese force less than half their size. The crux of Strange's argument is that the Prime Minister had serious doubts about the morale and stamina of his soldiers and had lost confidence in the British army.[36] Whatever their motive for the rejection of the American plan, by mid-1942, the British maintained an almost obsessive apprehension of anything resembling a cross-channel operation and were determined to oppose it.

Marshall and Eisenhower resisted the British position. They felt it violated their most fundamental military belief: that they should *find the enemy, fight him, and defeat him*. In their mind, peripheral battles such as a North African invasion were nothing more than a postponement of the final definitive engagement. The American generals envisioned a great battle with "blood and guts" General George Patton's tanks sweeping through France. This was in keeping with the American tradition, dating from the days of Ulysses S. Grant, of concentrating power at a decisive point at the earliest possible moment, and then delivering a devastating blow to the heart of the enemy.

The British continued to argue in favor of a strategy that contemplated encircling and progressively strangling the enemy. It is no coincidence that Churchill entitled Volume 5 of his history of World War II, "Closing the Ring," envisioning ever decreasing concentric circles of pressure on the German forces, like a boa constrictor squeezing the life out of its victim. The British plan also advocated strong support of the Soviets' Red Army to engage the German Wehrmacht on the Eastern Front, coincident with the bombing of German and Italian cities, supporting resistance in occupied countries, and jabbing through the "ring" whenever an opportunity presented itself. This tightening would continue to increase until the enemy was so strangled and bleeding that the final offensive needed only be a *coup de grace*. The essence of the difference between the positions of the two allies for defeating the Germans was the American rattlesnake versus the British boa constrictor.

Leading the British charge was Churchill, whose personal opposition was the single most important factor in finally undermining an early cross-channel invasion, and there were few influential British who chose to oppose him. One exception was the highly influential Lord Beaverbrook, probably the most prominent British opponent of Churchill's strategic plans. He argued continually for an early cross-channel attack.[37] Other key members of his planning group occasionally discretely disagreed with his grandiose strategic vision,[38] but the Prime Minister's view easily predominated.

Both Marshall and Wedemeyer left the April 1942 meeting with the British planners impressed with the skill of their counterparts, as well as with an uneasy suspicion that they were not fully in support of the plan. Despite these misgivings, when the conference adjourned it seemed that the Americans had carried the day, and they returned to America with what could best be described as a halfhearted British endorsement of a cross-channel plan for 1943, but with a deep concern that British opposition had not been fully squelched.[39]

Marshall seemed more optimistic than Wedemeyer. On April 11, 1942, he telephoned his deputy in Washington, Major General Joseph T. McNarney, and told him that the Prime Minister had accepted virtually *in toto* the proposals that had been submitted: "... and that the British War Cabinet Defense Committee would undoubtedly approve. I regard this as acquiescence in principle."[40] On April 14, Churchill followed with his own statement that evening at a meeting of the committee which was attended by both Marshall and Hopkins. Churchill spoke eloquently in his famous style of "two nations marching ahead in the noble brotherhood of arms,"[41] and this statement provided the Americans with some reassurance, but even then they remained suspicious of the sincerity of the British endorsement. Characteristically, both Lord Alanbrooke and the Prime Minister, when they gave their "approval" of the plans, had managed to insert ingenious conditions and/or qualifications that, if necessary, could be interposed as an escape hatch if one were needed in the future. This was typical of British negotiating tactics, learned over centuries of dealing with the vagaries of European politics, and reflected in some fashion in virtually every agreement the British made during the conflict. Looking at the "agreements" reached between the two allies, it did appear as though the British would be able to veto any cross-channel operation until they were satisfied that both the Indian Ocean and the Middle East were safe from Japanese and German aggression, and that the United States was fully committed to bringing about that seemingly utopian state of affairs. Notwithstanding, in the end Churchill "gave [Marshall] a solemn assurance that the British would support the great enterprise energetically and unreservedly."[42] As Roberts astutely surmises,

> Perhaps the very extravagance of Churchill's remarks, especially as no dates were given and there was no indication of whether he was referring to SLEDGEHAMMER, BOLERO or ROUNDUP, ought to have given Marshall pause for thought. What he could not fail to spot, however, were the implications that British support for European attacks depended upon America protecting British positions in the Indian Ocean, and the Middle East.[43]

Was the British assurance of support for the Americans' strategy sincere? Were the British being deceptive and intentionally evasive? Maurice Matloff and Edwin M. Snell, authors of the Official History of the United States Army in World War II, answer these questions affirmatively. They say in the "Green Book" series that Churchill's "acceptance" of the American plan was a deception designed to head off American efforts to concentrate on the defeat of Japan:

> The Prime Minister has since recorded that . . . his satisfaction in receiving General Marshall's proposal and his readiness to accept it grew out his anxiety lest the United States continue to direct its main efforts to the Pacific.[44]

It was not long before whatever qualms the Americans had about the sincerity of the British were verified.[45] In mid-April 1942, Soviet ambassador Molotov came to Washington to meet with Roosevelt, stopping in London on the way, and then had a second meeting in London on the return leg. Shortly after Molotov left London to return to Moscow, Churchill cabled Roosevelt, "We must never let GYMNAST pass from our minds," conveying the first concrete suggestion that the British were hedging their approval of the American position and now suggesting diversionary operations. Australian war correspondent Chester Wilmot, after two 1948 interviews with Ian Jacob, went further in stating that " [the British] . . . went a long way towards admitting that [they] had deliberately misled the Americans six years earlier."[46]

EISENHOWER'S TRIP TO LONDON MAY 1942

British reservations were made explicit when General Eisenhower, newly appointed Chief of War Plans, accompanied by Generals "Hap" Arnold, Brehon B. Somervell, and Mark Clark, traveled to London in late-May 1942 for what they thought would be implementation of the plans. This was the second trip to London for the American Planners to work out details for what they expected to be a cross-channel attack in 1943. Wedemeyer was not included in this trip. Eisenhower immediately detected a lack of enthusiasm for the American plan. Clark was more emphatic, recalling that the Prime Minister lost no time in stating "that he was in favor of postponing the cross-channel operation" and substituting a North African one.[47] With the 1943 cross-channel plan still seemingly intact, though now under severe and critical examination, the Americans sensed that it would not be long before the British made a full-fledged affirmative attack on it. When Eisenhower returned on June 3, he reported his concerns. Furthermore, British Admiral Louis Mountbatten, who had returned with Eisenhower, added to the uncertainty when he conveyed to the American Chiefs of Staff the news that there might be some question of revision of the ROUNDUP/ SLEDGEHAMMER agreements made in London six weeks previously. It was the consensus of the American planners that Mountbatten was expressing not his own personal view, but that of the British staff, and there would be more to the story in the very near future.[48]

ROUNDUP was a viable strategy. Wedemeyer and his team had meticulously gone over the plan and considered every eventuality. The British were assured that by June 1943 the training and availability of all other necessary material, in particular landing craft, the sticking point of British concerns, would be ready.[49] However, ROUNDUP did have an Achilles heel. It was joined at the hip to SLEDGEHAMMER, a smaller cross-channel invasion, to be launched in late 1942, *contingent* as an emergency plan to be employed only if such an expedition was deemed necessary to stave off a Russian collapse, or in the highly unlikely event of a Nazi collapse. It was to be a much smaller expedition, entirely severable from the main plan for 1943 and, of necessity, almost entirely British.

No American planner believed that SLEDGEHAMMER would ever provide a sufficient lodgment in France to support an attacking force large enough to defeat Germany. If the British had been intellectually honest with the Americans and endorsed the 1943 invasion program *on condition that SLEDGEHAMMER was scrapped*, the Americans would likely have acceded to this demand, and the discussions concerning the cross-channel 1943 invasion could have proceeded strictly on the merits. But this was not the tactic employed by the British, who used the weakness of SLEDGEHAMMER as a ploy to scrap the entire concept of a cross-channel invasion. Accordingly, they linked the two programs together as inseparable, discrediting the admitted shortcomings of SLEDGEHAMMER in an effort to undermine ROUNDUP.[50]

In truth, ROUNDUP was contaminated by the flawed SLEDGE-HAMMER and should have been separated, but the British were quite content to deal with them as a package, as a means to an end, the military equivalent of the legal reasoning of *falsus in uno, falsus in omnibus*, [false in one, false in all]. The Americans probably should have agreed to drop SLEDGEHAMMER when they realized it was tainting their primary objective; however, they did not have that option.

Historian Gordon A. Harrison points out that the War Department's original memo to the President made in preparation for the trip anticipated this very issue and expressly provided for a partition by recommending that if the American planners were compelled to sacrifice SLEDGEHAMMER they should do so and concentrate on ROUNDUP. To the American planners, SLEDGEHAMMER was a "throw away" plan, to be ditched in favor of the more important cross-channel operation for 1943. However, this option was deliberately *removed* by Roosevelt, who instructed the planners to insist on *both* operations. Indeed, the President's instructions stated that SLEDGEHAMMER be strongly urged as the most important and imperative task for 1942.[51] The President's directions "explicitly ruled that the main issue was to decide upon some positive action for 1942, to be undertaken regardless of the course of events on the Soviet front."[52] Of the final three-page directive, Robert Sherwood noted, "Of all the instructions given by Roosevelt to Hopkins and the Chiefs of Staff, the most important—and, indeed, the ultimate determining factor—was this: 'If SLEDGEHAMMER is finally and definitely out of the picture, I want you to consider the world situation as it exists at that time, *and determine upon another place for U.S. Troops to fight in 1942*'[53] [emphasis added]." The single plan the Americans had with them for U.S. ground forces to be put into action in 1942 at the time of the May meeting in London was SLEDGEHAMMER, and this plan had no chance of passing British scrutiny. The fix was in. If SLEDGE-HAMMER went down, as it surely would, ROUNDUP went down with it! American forces, Roosevelt said, had to be put into action in 1942 in "another place," and the only other option that was available was the Mediterranean.

The President's directive to get U.S. armed forces into action in 1942 was grounded on political, not strategic motives, which goes a long way toward explaining why he later so readily endorsed the Prime Minister's plan for the Mediterranean campaign. Is it possible that the shrewd Roosevelt deliberately planted this "poison pill" in his instructions, anticipating the British veto, thereby sabotaging his own generals? If true, it certainly was a brilliant, if diabolical, move by the President. Regardless, it certainly served his needs, and arguably, his motive was more to put American troops in action in 1942 than to undermine his military advisors. As American historians Richard Leighton and Robert Coakley point out, "...what had been regarded as the best argument for SLEDGEHAMMER, a strike near the heart of German power, was now turned against it as involving great risks not balanced by possible gains."[54]

The British succeeded in making substantial progress in jettisoning the 1943 invasion. All that was required to finalize it was to receive Roosevelt's endorsement, and the war effort would be diverted in another direction. Andrew Roberts admits that "Marshall had indeed been misled, by Churchill if not by Brooke, and he understandably came to resent it."[55] Lord Ismay also later admitted that the British should have "come clean" with their plan to torpedo ROUNDUP at the next meeting but characterized it as "unintentional."[56] According to historian Ben Moshe, throughout the negotiations, the British were under strict instructions never to admit the Prime Minister's plan for substituting GYMNAST for ROUNDUP, and most importantly, if the Mediterranean campaign was approved it would effectively gut any plans for a 1943 cross-channel attack, and possibly any other future time.[57] If the British were aware of the President's earlier directive to the planners about the necessity for an early mobilization and insistence on a 1942 campaign, i.e. that "the fix was in," their preparations would have been a lot less anxiety-provoking. Not knowing this, they made careful and elaborate preparations for the next meeting.

THE CRITICAL JUNE 1942 MEETING IN WASHINGTON

The next meeting of the British and American planners was scheduled for June 1942 in Washington. The British intended to come with guns blazing in order to effectively gut ROUNDUP and install a substitute plan. Prior to the meeting, there had been many telephone calls between Churchill and Roosevelt dealing with overall war strategy. Though there is no record of these critical communications,[58] Churchill undoubtedly used them to promote his agenda. During this same period, British and American planners were in constant communication, and the British were instructed by the Prime Minister to stress and exploit problems with ROUNDUP and to suggest alternative courses of action. The British once again trained heavily for the next round of negotiations that they considered crucial for forcing their will on the Americans.

Militarily, the British were on the ropes in 1942. It was only the strength of American economic and military support that would enable them to survive. Conversely, things were looking up for the Americans, as evidenced by their first success against the Japanese at Midway in June. America was in a position to dictate the entire wartime program, with the British having no choice but to acquiesce, but Churchill never felt in any way inferior or bashful about the position of the British, and his bulldog determination permeated the British delegation. As Wedemeyer aptly noted, Churchill was the virtuoso who ". . . led the orchestra, although America furnished practically all the instruments and most of the musicians."[59] Churchill also maintained a much closer relationship with his generals than Roosevelt. Marshall contrasted this to his own relationship with the President: Churchill, he said, "was very intense when he got a certain idea and he did business with [his own military advisor] every day, where sometimes I didn't see the President for a month."[60]

Until the battle of Midway, America had sustained a steady stream of military disasters in the Pacific. *Time* magazine acidly observed that in the first six months of the war, the United States had "not taken a single inch of enemy territory, not yet beaten the enemy in a major battle on land, nor opened an offensive campaign."[61] The American public was not aware of the perilously depleted state of the American fleet after Pearl Harbor and were hungry for vengeance. Reminiscent of the overconfident northern sentiment at the outset of the Civil War, Sam Rayburn, the powerful Speaker of the House, told the President of the public's disappointment that the U.S. had failed to thrash Japan in six weeks! It is likely the American public would have both welcomed and preferred a strong push in the Pacific. Certainly the American naval chiefs would have.

Churchill was aware of America's eagerness to fight and was determined to exploit his advantage by encouraging action, so long as it served *his* needs. He conceived a plan which, with one brilliant stroke, would not only achieve his true objective of sidetracking or perhaps even permanently cancelling the planned invasion of France in June 1943 but would also satisfy Roosevelt's desire to put American boys into battle before that date. It was to be unveiled at the upcoming meeting.

How remarkably effective the British were in presenting their plans was described by Wedemeyer in an interview with Keith Eiler long after his retirement.[62] The first step in the elaborate plan was a preliminary "softening up" meeting between Roosevelt and Lord Louis Mountbatten, with no American military advisors present. Mountbatten had previously been instructed by Churchill to discourage a cross-channel invasion and to suggest a substitute Mediterranean campaign. He arrived in Washington on June 2, 1942 and went directly to the White House. With only the President and Harry Hopkins present, Mountbatten stressed the problems that an early invasion of France would encounter, including heavy German opposition and an insufficient number of landing craft. It was important for him to phrase his objections delicately so as not to disparage all the hard work of the American planners. Accordingly, in the usual method of British indirection, he suggested that that the cross-channel idea be put off, and that instead it would be more important to get American and British troops engaged earlier against the Nazis in North Africa. He observed that this would be a better move militarily as well as *politically*.[63] Ever the politician, this naturally piqued Roosevelt's thinking about how he could capitalize on a North African invasion so that it would be in the headlines just before the mid-term elections scheduled for November 3rd. This proposal, of course, was readily agreed to by the British. General Marshall recalled that when he first broached the subject of a North African campaign with the President, Roosevelt gestured with his hands as if to pray and pleaded: "Please make it before Election Day!"[64] Roosevelt did not wish an encore of the disastrous consequences of losing control of the Congress that had befallen Woodrow Wilson's administration, in which Roosevelt had served as Assistant Secretary of the Navy shortly before the end of World War I. As it turned out, it was not possible to satisfy the President's wish to stage the operation before the mid-term election. Planning problems delayed the launch of the North African campaign until five days after the election, but there were plenty of headlines in the leading papers heralding the operation and praising the President.

Mountbatten did not directly attack the cross-channel invasion. Instead he subtly outlined "obstacles" to SLEDGEHAMMER/ROUNDUP. His motive was to sidetrack the American plan with the hope that future events would make the invasion either unnecessary or too dangerous. Churchill used Mountbatten as an opening act before his star performance and arranged for another private meeting with himself and the President in advance of the full-scale conference. On June 18, Churchill arrived in Washington and went directly to Hyde Park for a top-secret meeting, again out of view of the potentially critical ears of Roosevelt's military advisors or State Department personnel. No written record exists of Mountbatten's previous encounter or Churchill's private meeting with the President, though the latter included talk of development of the atomic bomb and a hefty dose of consolation by the President for the disastrous and demoralizing British defeat at Tobruk.[65] However, there could be little doubt that the main thrust of Churchill's arguments centered on pressing the North African campaign.

The final Washington meeting took place on the evening of June 21 at the White House and was attended by most of the Combined Chiefs of Staff.[66] The feature presentation of the evening was to be a cameo performance by Churchill outlining his plans for the war with special attention to a North African campaign. Wedemeyer was not informed of the meeting, nor was he even aware at the time of the two previous meetings that Roosevelt had had with Mountbatten and Churchill.

In the dramatic confrontation between Wedemeyer and Churchill previously described in the Introduction, Wedemeyer and Marshall lost the argument.[67] The die was cast and the invasion of North Africa, codenamed TORCH, was slated to be the next major military campaign, the first in the theatre for the Americans. At Churchill's brilliant suggestion, the operation was publicly attributed to Roosevelt. It was the end result of seven months of sparring between the two allies, much of which was conducted by one-on-one communication between the two leaders without the benefit, or perhaps more accurately, the hindrance, of high-level planners who might have raised some sticky points or expressed reservations.

The next day the *New York Times* ran a front page article headlined "Leaders in Accord." It was the first report since the highly secret meetings had begun several days previously. The story was carefully worded so as not to reveal any military plans, and references to future offensive actions were especially guarded. A formal statement by the President and the Prime Minister revealed for the first time that conferences were being held in Washington and that Mr. Churchill was at the White House. The report also included a list of the British and American representatives who participated.[68] Wedemeyer was not mentioned in any of the accounts.

Operation Torch commenced on November 8, 1942, and the press gave all the credit for originating the idea to Roosevelt. There were several potentially catastrophic problems that Churchill had never dwelled on, the most frightening of which was the potential closure of the Mediterranean strait at Gibraltar. A sudden German occupation of Spain and the seizure of Gibraltar would have required Allied forces in North Africa to be supplied by a long overland route.[69] That Franco did not make an arrangement with Hitler to allow the closure of the Mediterranean strait is now simply a footnote in history that had dangerous possibilities at the time of becoming a whole chapter. Other serious risks to the success of the operation included the prospect of prolonged opposition by the Vichy French in North Africa.

Fortunately for the Allies, none of the possible recipes for disaster eventuated and the operation was a success. Though fighting did occur between Allied and Vichy units in Morocco and Algeria, it was for the most part short-lived, if not half-hearted on the part of the French. A German counter-move via Spain did not transpire, and the weather was unusually good; and the feared shipping losses to German bombers and submarines did not materialize. Stimson, who was never in favor of the operation, "always believed Torch to be the luckiest operation of the war . . ." and this seems to have been the case.[70]

British plans, however, entailed a great deal more military activity in the Mediterranean than the North African campaign. Andrew Roberts has contended that the British fully intended to conceal their long-range plans from the Americans. "If the Americans had suspected that the British wanted to attack Sicily and Italy after North Africa, rather than land in France, they would not have looked favorably on attacking North Africa in the first place,"[71] also adding that if Brooke had initially proposed North Africa as a stepping stone to mainland Italy and the Balkans, the Americans would never have agreed to undertake TORCH.[72] General Marshall also suspected that North Africa would be followed by other military expeditions in areas that he characterized as "suction pumps" draining Allied strength from the main objective of carrying the fight to German soil.[73]

In fairness to the President, political decisions, though playing a part, were not the only factors considered, and his decision was not an easy one. As Robert Sherwood wrote:

> One can only guess at the extent of the conflicts that went on in Roosevelt's mind and heart and soul when he had to decide whether to follow the advice of his own most trusted advisers or Churchill's warnings that the Channel would be 'a river of blood'.[74]

The decision for the Mediterranean was a total victory for the Prime Minister, who planted the seed for a North African expedition and then stood back and allowed Roosevelt to expand upon the idea as if it was his from the beginning. To Wedemeyer's way of thinking, it was a real setback. Disappointment about the Torch decision was so pronounced among the American Chiefs of Staff that they seriously considered recommending a radical revision of the Europe First strategy to the President. Whether or not this was a bluff is open to debate, but Sherwood did not think it was.[75]

Plans for a 1943 cross-channel invasion were shelved in favor of TORCH, but the dying embers of BOLERO/ROUNDUP continued to be fanned by both Marshall and Eisenhower. The persistence of the Americans, assisted by a final hard shove by Stalin at the Teheran conference in December 1943, forced the decision to invade France to go forward, and the cross-channel attack, now codenamed OVERLORD, was set for May 1944.

When the 1944 invasion of France proved successful, Churchill was ever alert to ward off criticism that he had opposed the venture. Never one to disassociate himself from a successful venture, he was even more determined to deflect criticism leveled at him for opposing the invasion. He hastened to write in his own defense, "I trust [I will] finally dispose of the many American legends that I was inveterately hostile to the plan of a large-scale Channel crossing in 1943 . . ."[76] However, the letter to Roosevelt to which he was referring merely gave lukewarm endorsement to the plan while simultaneously attaching so many conditions that it amounted to a rebuff. In Volume 3, Chapter 18, of his six-volume history of the Second World War, "Second Front Now, April 1942" Churchill attempts to convince the reader that he was always supportive of the 1943 cross-channel attack. A close reading of this chapter would satisfy any fair-minded reader otherwise. Churchill admits that there were several conditions to his endorsement of the plan. There is no way to read these "conditions" except in the sense that they amounted to an option to reject the plan. Even more importantly, nowhere in the chapter is there any hint that after North Africa, Churchill contemplated invading both Sicily and Italy, and perhaps even the Balkans. Any intimation that this was his ultimate plan would have doomed operation TORCH.

Wedemeyer continued with his duties as a chief war planner with a significant role in the next three important conferences, but he now had a bull's eye on his back. He was at Casablanca in January 1943, where British preparation and persistence resulted in a continuation of operations in the Mediterranean. Despite the opposition of all the American planners,[77]

Churchill succeeded in convincing Roosevelt to invade Sicily, and Italy immediately followed. Stalled by fierce German resistance atop rugged terrain, the Allied forces did not finally enter Rome until June 5, 1944, the day before D-Day. Unhappy at the decisions reached at this conference, Wedemeyer lamented that "We lost our shirts. . . . we came, we listened and we were conquered."[78]

The manner in which Churchill was able to forestall the planned 1943 invasion, and his near-success in eliminating the invasion entirely, is a tribute to his powerful personality, if not his character, and his remarkable access and storied friendship with Roosevelt. It is no secret that North Africa was only the first step in the Prime Minister's plan to stall the cross-channel operation with further expeditions in the Mediterranean. Two months prior to the January 1943 Casablanca Conference he ". . . toyed joyously with all sorts of Mediterranean projects to follow the expected victory in Tunisia."

He came well prepared for the January 1943 Casablanca conference with a substantial contingent of British Planners, where he first announced his desire to "strike at the soft underbelly of the Axis,"[79] setting the stage for his well-prepared plan for the invasion of Sicily. Disingenuously, he insisted that his strategy ". . . need not rule out a cross-Channel invasion in the late summer of 1943," but his support was predicated on the unlikely possibility of a "marked deterioration in German morale and capacity for resistance."[80] This was vintage Churchill, in effect "agreeing" to a plan of operation, to which he had attached such unrealistic expectations that his agreement actually amounted to a veto: incredibly supporting a 1943 invasion of France on the condition that there was no German army on the beaches to oppose the landings!

American endorsement of military campaigns in the Mediterranean effectively cancelled the cross-channel plans for 1943,[81] though Churchill's vigorous and undying opposition to it was not universal in higher British military circles. To his embarrassment, the powerful Lord Beaverbrook was an early and vigorous proponent of an early Second Front in France.[82]

In fairness, criticism of the Americans' attempt to forestall further Mediterranean operations was not all British. In 1995, Leighton and Coakley weighed in on Wedemeyer's "We lost our shirts" comment, not only in support of Churchill's Mediterranean strategy but also to take another critical shot at the original BOLERO/ROUNDUP plan:

But given the American insistence upon an augmented effort in the

Pacific, the implication that a decisive cross-Channel invasion could have been mounted in 1943 under any reasonable allotment of resources to other theaters was not borne out by the best available estimates. In early 1943 it was all too easy to forget how flimsy had been the logistical basis of the original BOLERO-ROUNDUP plans of March and April 1942. The logistical estimates of the Casablanca planners, it almost immediately appeared, were just as flimsy.[83]

By 1995, conventional wisdom about the 1944 cross-channel invasion had been heavily influenced by the endorsement of General Eisenhower, who had flip-flopped in his own memoirs,[84] and so many historians had fallen in line with Churchill's writings that it was rare for anyone to deviate from that position. It had become the equivalent of military canon, not subject to review or criticism.

Wedemeyer maintained his steadfast support for the 1943 invasion for the same reasons he had advanced during the war, noting forty years after the fact with his Grand Strategy in mind: "If the plan had been followed . . . the Western Allies would have gained control of European areas taken by the Soviet Union."[85]

As an indication of the high esteem in which Wedemeyer was held, shortly following Casablanca, the President personally informed General Marshall that he would like Wedemeyer, accompanied by Generals Arnold and Somerville and chief British planner Sir John Dill, to tour the Middle East, India, Australia, China, and the South Pacific and report back with their observations. It was also the intention to send the group, along with Marshall, to meet Stalin, but the Soviet leader sent word that he could "see no purpose" in having them come. The tour consumed a full two months, and Wedemeyer returned to Washington on March 10, 1943. On the trip Wedemeyer consulted with Generals Douglas MacArthur, Joseph Stilwell, Chiang Kai-shek, and many other major military figures in each sector. Every encounter broadened his knowledge of world affairs.

Upon his return, Wedemeyer participated in the May 1943 Trident Conference in Washington and the August 1943 Quadrant conference in Quebec, but soon thereafter was assigned to Asia. The decision to move him out of the hair of the British had likely been made following the June 1942 meeting in Washington. Only the appropriate time of implementation remained. That opportunity arose at the Quebec conference.

After the war in the book he quickly rushed into print, Churchill claimed to always be of the opinion that a decisive assault on the German-occupied countries on the largest scale possible was the only way to defeat Germany, saying that his sole concern was the "timing" of the invasion.[86] British historians, well aware of Churchill's sensitivity to the criticism leveled at him by numerous historians that he was unalterably opposed to the cross-channel plan, rummaged the war records in search of evidence to counter the charge, such as Churchill's May 1942 instructions for the "Mulberry" harbors (floating harbors effectively used in the first days of the 1944 invasion) and his ordering plans for tanks capable of being transported over water for use on beaches, immediately after Dunkirk.[87] However, evidence indicating Churchill's support for any cross-channel invasion is severely undermined by the fact that as late as October 19, 1943, long after his many earlier commitments to the May 1944 date for the invasion, he convened an emergency top-level staff conference with the intention of putting "political muscle" behind a push for the Balkans instead of France. This went unmentioned in his war memoirs, ". . . probably because he did not want readers to appreciate how doubtful he still was about Overlord."[88] Even more persuasive, from the same source: "On April 18, 1944, shortly before D-Day Churchill once again expressed his severe doubts about OVERLORD itself, writing to the Foreign Office: 'This battle has been forced upon us by the Russians and the United States military authorities." Although he quoted from other parts of the minute in his war memoirs, *that sentence and others like it were excised.* Indeed, it is nearly impossible for a reader of "Closing the Ring" to surmise any doubts that Churchill had about the success of OVERLORD six weeks before it was launched."[89]

If there is any doubt that Churchill harbored ill feelings toward Wedemeyer for his recommendation in support of a contrary military operation, it is resolved in his history of the Second World War where he wrote, commenting on the North African/Italy campaign:

> Great credit is due to General Eisenhower for his support of this *brief and spirited campaign.* Although the *execution fell to Alexander,* the Supreme Commander had really taken the British view of the strategy, and had been prepared to accept to accept the ultimate responsibility for an enterprise the *risks of which had been needlessly sharpened* by his *own military chiefs in their rigid adherence to the plans for Burma,* and by their stern and strict priorities for "Overlord,"

which were *carried in the secondary ranks to a veritable pedantry.* There can be no doubt at all that Italy was the greatest prize open to us at this stage, and that a generous provision for it could have been made without causing any delay to the main cross-Channel plan of 1944.[90] (emphasis added)

Aside from the many glaring inaccuracies, the "support" of General Eisenhower, the length of the campaign,[91] the relegation of the Americans to a secondary support role behind Alexander, the statement that the risks of the Italian campaign had been: "... *needlessly sharpened by his ... military chiefs in their rigid and strict priorities for "Overlord" which were carried in the secondary ranks to a veritable pedantry"* is a criticism of Wedemeyer, the only American planner in the "secondary ranks" who stood up to Churchill.

In commenting at the age of 88 on the Italian campaign, Wedemeyer still smarted from what he felt was Churchill's cavalier selection and/or omission of facts in his version of the war, especially the suggestion that the Italian campaign was an easy undertaking. Wedemeyer angrily noted that: "history will record the Allies took terrible losses as they advanced northward in that difficult terrain to reach unremunerative goals in the north,"[92] and there is no doubt that American servicemen who fought at Salerno, Cassino, and Anzio would agree. The 608-day campaign to liberate Italy would cost 312,000 Allied casualties, equivalent to 40 percent of Allied losses in the decisive campaign for northwest Europe that began at Normandy. Among the three-quarters of a million American troops to serve in Italy, total battle casualties would reach 120,000, including 23,501 dead.

While in his earlier writings Wedemeyer was quite restrained in his criticism of Churchill's wartime strategy, he was much more open and critical in later life, describing it once in his unfinished book as "cockeyed." With historical astuteness, he noted that the Prime Minister's penchant for "plunging into the cauldron," as evidenced by his unfulfilled guarantee of the territorial integrity of Poland, made in 1939 "with such fanfare and aplomb,"[93] was contrary to the more tempered tradition set by his predecessors Palmerston, Pitt, Castleraegh, and Disraeli.

Despite being overruled by the cunning and powerful Churchill, Wedemeyer's value as a master strategist had now been recognized. New and important challenges for America lay elsewhere, and Roosevelt called upon him once again to solve them, now not as a mid-level subordinate, but in the leadership role he had so deservedly earned.

Wedemeyer himself points out the greatest irony of his involvement in the European campaign:

> It was paradoxical that I, a military man, had political objectives in view while the politicians, Churchill and Roosevelt, had narrowed their vision to purely military objectives. While political leaders were telling the soldiers how to win the war, soldiers were suggesting how to win the peace.[94]

WESTERN INFLUENCE ON CHINA

Take up the white man's burden.
—Rudyard Kipling

Up to now in this study of Wedemeyer, little attention has been given to the other war in the Pacific, on the far side of the world. In order to best appreciate the political and military environment encountered by Americans in China during World War II, it is essential to understand the history and consequences of the malignancy of Western imperialism in the region. It is no surprise that longstanding abuse poisoned the Chinese attitude toward Westerners, whom they referred to as "foreign devils."

For this reason, we must look back in time and briefly review events in Asia, especially China, where both Wedemeyer and his predecessor, General Joseph Stilwell, were to serve. American relations with China rarely followed a straight line. Instead, as Michael Schaller so aptly points out, they have often been:

> . . . confused and contradictory, exhibiting bizarre shifts in policy that reflect drastic differences in national interest and superficial knowledge of each other. Examples of this abound. Americans sent missionaries to save Chinese souls, but participated in the opium trade that ravaged the population. Americans promoted Chinese immigration to the United States when they needed low-cost labor to construct the railroads, then barred Oriental immigration because Asians were considered racially inferior. Americans encouraged the

establishment of democratic institutions in China, then supported and maintained a dictatorship in power.[1]

Schaller could have added the complete reversal of attitude of many Americans about their view of Chiang Kai-shek from his valiant "Man of the Year" image on the cover of *Time* Magazine in 1937 to a "corrupt dictator," at least as portrayed by many in the liberal media in the last years of World War II and up to 1949.

America was not alone in intruding into Chinese society with untoward results; in fact, in terms of degrees of fault, America would not be the major player in this enterprise. Great Britain deserves first place. The incursions of Western imperialism which transpired over a period of two centuries initiated a malignancy which immensely complicated the mission of American commanders. For this reason, a review of American and Western foreign policy with China must, of necessity, examine events not only pre-World War II but actions of America and Western nations toward China in the nineteenth century which created a profound and lasting negative impression that even today, has not totally dissipated. The actions of the Western nations were of long standing, but first we review those of China's contentious neighbor, whose more recent actions ultimately brought the United States into the war.

JAPAN'S AGGRESSIONS AGAINST CHINA

In 1931, elements of the Japanese Kwantung Army, stationed in Manchuria since the early twentieth century, fabricated an incident and staged an uprising, quickly driving Chinese troops out of the province. Japan hastily installed Henry Pu Yi, last head of the 300-year-old Mancho dynasty, as "boy emperor" and head of the puppet state of "Manchukuo." United States reaction was tepid. The headline in a leading Hearst newspaper put it simply: "We Sympathize. But It Is Not Our Concern." Formal United States reaction was hardly more forceful. Secretary of State Henry L. Stimson responded by declaring that the United States "would not recognize the legal existence" of Manchukuo.

Japan, realizing that its aggression in Manchuria was essentially ignored, upped the ante. On July 7, 1937 the Japanese staged another incident, this time at the Marco Polo Bridge in Peking. China rushed troops in to counter the attack and the incident escalated. Just as Japan had planned, both sides mobilized, and China and Japan found themselves in a massive undeclared war. Japan quickly occupied the entire southern and eastern coasts, taking control of all the major ports, cities, and rivers. It took little more than a year for Japan to hold all the major rivers and the entire coast of China *(China maps, pp. x–xiii)*. Again, while sympathetic to the Chinese plight, America provided little assistance beyond verbal protests to the world community. President Roosevelt's fruitless call for a "quarantine" of the Japanese in an October 5, 1937 speech in Chicago served no purpose: "When an epidemic of physical disease starts to spread, the community approves and joins in a quarantine of the patients in order to protect the health of the community against the spread of the disease."[2] Despite this public disapproval of Japanese actions, it was a toothless stance and was ignored by the Japanese. America took no direct or positive action to deter the Japanese until a few months prior to Pearl Harbor. Oil and steel had been exported to Japan in large quantities, which was being used to support its war against China. Necessity brought about a shift in American policy after December 7, 1941. China was now embraced not only as an ally but, far more importantly from the American strategic perspective, a geographically important launching point for an attack on Japan. America was now ready to change its course.

OTHER EARLIER WESTERN INFLUENCES ON CHINA WHICH POISONED RELATIONS

China viewed America's new efforts at diplomatic courtship after Pearl Harbor with a wary eye, and with good reason. Their Chinese distrust of outsiders was deep and eminently justifiable. Western overtures, especially in the nineteenth century, were a self-interested amalgam of commercialism and missionary zeal, both efforts initiated without invitation. The missionary efforts were not necessarily in the best interests of the Chinese, and some profit-making ventures, especially the importation of opium, produced grave harm.[3] The British imported vast quantities of Indian opium into China, generating huge profits and wreaking untold havoc on Chinese society. At one point, the revenues from the opium trade represented one seventh of the revenues of British India. Americans sold their own special brand of Turkish opium, accounting for a ten percent market share. The missionary efforts had mixed results, and this intrusion into China's society actually resulted in a major civil war during the years 1850–1864, the "Taiping Rebellion" in which 20 million Chinese lost their lives.

THE OPIUM WARS

During the first of two Opium Wars between 1839 and 1842, the British completely overpowered weak Chinese resistance as the Americans stood on the sidelines and watched carefully with approval.[4] In 1842 the conflict was settled to the enormous advantage of the British with the heavy-handed, one-sided Treaty of Nanking, enforced by British Gunboats on the Yangtze that threatened to destroy the city if Chinese officials refused to knuckle under. Thus began what the Chinese justifiably called the "100 years of disgrace."

Traffic in Opium had been illegal in China since 1729, and in 1800 additional prohibitions were placed on cultivation and importation.[5] Chinese laws relative to importing opium were ignored by the West. Native Chinese reformers looked on in horror at what was occurring in their country and rebelled in 1839, instituting tough, no-nonsense reforms in an effort to enforce the ban. The opium warehouses in Canton were seized, and 20,000 chests were burned in the Chinese equivalent of the Boston Tea Party. While an "explanation" for the seizure was offered in a letter to Queen Victoria,[6] the British were not placated and their response was quick and severe. The British government avenged the "wrong" done to their citizens by launching a punitive military campaign against China. The campaign was far more successful and vengeful than the one with their former American colonists!

In addition to huge monetary penalties, far worse indignities were imposed by the British. The island of Hong Kong was declared a British colony "in perpetuity."[7] The Chinese were compelled to purchase Western goods and to permit the construction of several dozen "treaty ports" (eventually expanded to about 80), which were privileged gated sanctuaries in the best areas of cities with signs at the entrance that often read "No Chinese or dogs allowed!"[8] Foreign citizens living in the treaty ports were accorded the extraordinary privilege of "extraterritoriality," a grotesque legal fiction and a euphemism for a license to kill, steal, or commit other acts of barbarism without fear of being subject to Chinese law. All foreigners in China were, under this law, deemed "not to be residing in China" for the purpose of determining guilt or innocence in criminal matters, but rather to be treated as if at home. All offenses, no matter the severity, were adjudicated under the law of the country of which the foreigner was a citizen. Even in rare cases of conviction for criminal acts, since there were no "suitable" jails in China (it would have been unthinkable to house them with Chinese), perpetrators were sent home free.

As if this were not enough, British and French imperialists perpetrated a second war in 1856 in retaliation for the Chinese seizure of a ship they suspected was being used for smuggling and piracy. Now supported by the

Americans and Russians as well, even greater indignities ensued as a result of the 1858 Treaty of Tianjin.

WESTERN MISSIONARY PURSUITS

Missionary efforts added insult to injury. Westerners entertained the self-righteous conviction that missionary work was a benign and obligatory task to save the souls of heathens. As iconic political scientist John W. Burgess sanctimoniously proclaimed:

> The larger part of the surface of the globe is inhabited by populations which have not succeeded in establishing civilized states. There is no human right to the status of barbarism. The civilized states have a claim upon them, and that claim is that they shall become civilized.[9]

The "White Man's Burden" was enthusiastically embraced by the missionaries. In their devout regard for the heathen, however, they did not overlook their own welfare. Jealously observing the benefits enjoyed by the inhabitants of the treaty ports, they sought the extension of extraterritoriality to their church property and converts. All this, of course, was piously proclaimed as the spreading God's gospel! Is it any wonder that when Mao gained power in 1949, expulsion of the missionaries was one of his earliest priorities.

Although the British led the charge, the Americans benefited as silent partners to the outrages. They carefully monitored events and profited by the terms of the British-negotiated 1844 Treaty of Wanghia, by which Americans automatically were afforded all the privileges that the British had won, sort of an early version of "legislative earmarks."[10] By taking a back seat to the active hostilities, the Americans deflected any slight criticism in the West that might have been directed toward the British. At the same time in the United States, Chinese immigrants suffered incredible hardship and oppression, as well as intolerable working conditions in the building of the transcontinental railroad. In an earlier version of the Mexican "bracero" program of the 1950's, Secretary of State William Seward inserted a provision into the 1868 "Burlingame Treaty" to allow Chinese contract laborers to enter the country. Having served its purpose, in 1882 the shameful Chinese Exclusion Act repealed this immigration provision, resulting in total exclusion of all Chinese. This provision was only cosmetically "repealed" in 1943, when

Congress changed total exclusion to a token one hundred and five Chinese being permitted per year. Congress finally passed meaningful immigration reform in 1965.

Undoubtedly most missionaries were dedicated men and women, and they were responsible for the building of many schools, hospitals, and orphanages. But Christianity was not entirely compatible with longstanding Chinese social customs. Spreading religion, therefore, meant encouraging an entirely new way of life for the Chinese and a gnawing away of the centuries old Confucian ideals. Not surprisingly, many Chinese viewed the missionaries' efforts as just another form of Western imperialism. The "threat" of Christianity as a foreign ideology was met by the massive Taiping Rebellion in central China during the 1850s and 1860s. Hung Hjsiu-ch'uan, greatly influenced by Christian religious tracts and having received "visions," saw himself as the younger brother of Jesus Christ, destined to convert the Chinese to a perverted version of Christianity. He converted several million Chinese to his cause and sought to overthrow the ruling Manchu-led Qing dynasty, but his efforts were met with massive official resistance. Before this rebellion was suppressed by the ruling dynasty, assisted by French and British forces, almost 20 million Chinese had died and entire regions of the country were devastated.

The "Boxer Rebellion" at the turn of the 20th century was just the most recent manifestation of Chinese resentment of foreign influences. Partly a "grass roots" anti-foreign, anti-Christian movement, it is more widely known, probably because no foreigners were killed in the Taiping Rebellion while several hundred Westerners were killed by the Boxers. Both uprisings had roots in the response to European "spheres of influence," with grievances ranging from opium trading, political invasion and economic manipulation to missionary evangelism. The Boxers' 55-day siege of Peking [Beijing], especially of the foreign legations, finally brought the armed forces of eight nations, including 20,000 troops, some from the United States, which finally quelled the rebellion. Again, severe penalties and indemnity to the eight nations were imposed. The political and military ramifications were wide-ranging and severe. On September 7, 1901, the "Boxer Protocol" was instituted, mandating numerous other draconian sanctions and execution of the leaders of the rebellion. Rape and pillage was both physical and economic. Reparations that lasted until 1939 were paid in silver, including seven percent to the United States, that totaled the equivalent of sixty billion present-day dollars.[11] But even more importantly, the political landscape of China and the Far East was forever altered. The Boxer Rebellion hastened the end of the dynastic system and laid the groundwork for the 1911 revolution led by Sun-Yat-Sen that established a nationalist government. Post-rebellion Russian incursions into the Japanese sphere of influence in Manchuria led to the 1905 Russo-Japanese War that established Japan as a world military power.

These longstanding abuses poisoned the Chinese attitude toward Westerners, to whom they referred as "foreign devils." Treatment such as the Westerners imposed on the Chinese during this period is not easily forgotten or forgiven, even by those Chinese favorably disposed toward the West. Even after Pearl Harbor, the bitter taste of a century of foreign imperialism remained. In 1942, Chiang-Kai-shek wrote a scathing anti-Western diatribe, *China's Destiny*, blaming foreigners for warlordism, prostitution, gun-running, opium smoking, gangsterism, and all of the bloody chaos incurred at the birth of the Chinese Republic; he also bewailed the influence of foreign missionaries and their universities on Chinese culture. This book sold half a million copies before it was "withdrawn for revision," probably at the insistence of Madame Chiang. No foreign correspondent was permitted to quote from it.[12] With this background of mistreatment, it is little wonder that Westerners in China were resented if not hated. Thus, it should not come as a surprise that both Stilwell and Wedemeyer had enormous difficulty in securing the trust of the Chinese. When the United States became allied with China in World War II, a keen awareness of its history, politics, and culture was necessary to maximize the productivity of their working relationship. Two generals would lead American forces and act as liaison to China's taciturn leader, Chiang Kai-Shek. One became a hero to the American press through the force of his personality, and he ultimately failed. The other did his homework and succeeded.

CHAPTER 6

STILWELL'S WAR

When the facts conflict with the myth, go with the myth.
—Liberty Valance

George Marshall called the command of the Asia sector the most impossible job of the war.[1] As *Time* Magazine reporter Theodore White
later commented about the China-Burma-India (CBI) Theatre: "Americans
used to say you needed a crystal ball and a copy of *Alice in Wonderland* to
understand it."

> It had everything—maharajas, dancing girls, warlords, head hunters,
> jungles, deserts, racketeers, secret agents ... American pilots strafed
> enemy elephants ... Chinese warlords introduced American army of-
> ficers to the delights of the opium pipe; ... Leopards and tigers killed
> American soldiers, and GI's hunted them down with Garands.[2]

Despite being near the bottom of the pecking order for supplies throughout the entire war, the strategic importance of the CBI, especially in the early
years, was to prevent a Japanese advance into India and southeast Asia,
to engage as many Japanese forces as possible to divert them from the Pacific,
and, most importantly, to establish American air bases within reach of the
Japanese home islands. Its leader would have the challenge of supplying and
commanding a heterogeneous mixture of Chinese, Indian, Nepalese, Gurkha,
British, and American forces and working with the taciturn and unpre-
dictable Chiang-Kai-shek.

SELECTION OF GENERAL STILWELL

No story about General Wedemeyer would be complete without a discussion of his popular and colorful predecessor, the first commander of the CBI, General Joseph Warren ("Vinegar Joe") Stilwell and his triumphs, failures, and tribulations, all of which he bequeathed General Wedemeyer when he was relieved by President Roosevelt in October 1944. Leadership of the CBI required a person of remarkable stamina, determination, and tact. Stilwell was the personification of the first two but failed miserably with the third.

A 1904 graduate of West Point, Stilwell placed 32nd in a class of 124. He served with distinction in the First World War, followed by assignments that shuttled him between the United States and China for the next twenty years. He possessed unusual leadership qualities that first came to Marshall's attention when they served together in China between the First and Second World Wars. He was fluent in the Chinese language and was considered an expert on Chinese military affairs. In addition, while commander at Fort Benning, Georgia in 1929, Stilwell displayed curious and often unconventional "screwball" tactical skills that earned him a reputation as one of the top War Game commanders in the Army. Thus, in 1939, when Marshall was directed by President Roosevelt to revamp the Army, he remembered Stilwell from both China and the Fort Benning maneuvers and promoted him to Brigadier General, jumping him ahead of more senior officers. When the opportunity arose to appoint an officer to command American forces in China after Pearl Harbor, Stilwell was high on the list.

It is probable that no one wanted the assignment, and Stilwell was not the first choice. Secretary of War Stimson preferred Lieutenant General Hugh Aloysius Drum (1879–1951), a well-worn veteran whose service dated back to the Spanish-American War and who had been Assistant Chief of Staff to Supreme Commander John J. "Black Jack" Pershing during the First World War. When offered the job, Drum considered it beneath him and was so condescending that Stimson withdrew the offer, effectively ending his military career.[3, 4]

After Drum's refusal, Marshall called on his old friend and contemporary. He did not directly order Stilwell to accept the assignment but rather asked him out of courtesy, "Will you go?" To a loyal soldier like Stilwell, who was rumored to have been slated to lead the far more glamorous and high-profile American invasion of North Africa, a "request" from his ardent supporter and superior was tantamount to an order, and he dutifully, yet with disappointment and trepidation, responded, "I'll go where I'm sent."

In retrospect, the qualifications for Stilwell to assume this command would have to be questioned. One of his most important responsibilities was command of troops in combat. Stilwell had never commanded troops in battle, had not even attended the Fort Leavenworth Command and General Staff School, and had absolutely no experience in Combined Operations or working with forces of two other nations, in this case Britain and China.[5] Admittedly, it was not a popular assignment, and Marshall was working with a short list. Undoubtedly, factors that favored Stilwell were his personal loyalty and the fact that Marshall knew he could count on him for some offensive operations, although as will be seen, this turned out not to be a positive. Stilwell's request for some American troops was refused by Marshall.

Only one Chinese representative, Ambassador to the United States T. V. Soong, Chiang's brother-in-law, had been "consulted" in the selection process, but he could do little more than rubber stamp Marshall's directive.[6] This was the regular protocol for decisions that impacted China throughout the war, dating back to Arcadia,[7] the first American/British war council held just two weeks after Pearl Harbor in Washington, where the first order of business was to establish a unified Allied high command that resulted in the creation of a Combined Chiefs of Staff's Council to coordinate the war effort and a Munitions Assignment Board to allocate Lend-Lease material.[8] The seven members, four Americans and three Britons, had authority and influence that was exceeded only by the President and the Prime Minister. China was not consulted (nor were the Soviets), and neither was granted a place on these critical boards. China's leader, Generalissimo Chiang-Kai-shek, was asked to endorse the proposals and was then soothed by Roosevelt, who asked him to assume command of allied land and air forces in the China Theatre. The CBI was not officially formed until June 1942.

Chiang did not anticipate the arrival of an outsider to take command of his troops and weaken his authority.[9] He did not want a powerful interloper whose opinions about policy and strategy could sharply differ from his own. Rather, he had hoped for someone who would function merely as a strong advocate for the allocation of Lend-Lease supplies. Soong had earlier made a suggestion to the War Department that the American commander "need not be an expert on the Far East," and even better if he were totally unfamiliar with China's military and political system. Too much knowledge, Soong asserted, would only confuse him! This advice fell upon deaf ears. The Chinese disappointment over Stilwell's selection was the first in a series of events that eventuated in the contentious relationship that would characterize his tour of duty.

Stilwell had an awesome list of responsibilities, including commanding American forces in the CBI, acting as Chief of Staff to Chiang-Kai-shek (an inherently contradictory assignment),[10] serving as American representative on any war council in the theatre, and assuming responsibility for training the Chinese army in allied tactics. He was also charged with maintaining the Burma Road, the only land supply route to China, which had been constructed between 1937 and 1938 by 200,000 Chinese laborers. The road extended 712 miles from Lashio, a major air terminus in Burma, to Kunming in China, and was linked to a rail connection from Rangoon *(Burma map, p. xiv)*. Stilwell's duties were later expanded when the Burma Road was cut by the Japanese, leaving the treacherous air route from India over the Himalayas, "the Hump," as China's sole source of supply. He was further delegated the additional task of building a new land-based supply route, the Ledo Road, to bypass the captured area and reopen the overland supply line from India to China through Burma.[11] All of this was expected to be accomplished on a shoestring, the consequence, of course, of the "Europe First" strategy adopted at the first Allied War Conference, Arcadia, in January 1942.

Stilwell's task was complicated by lukewarm cooperation from the British, who were essential to maintaining his air- and land-based supply routes. British military leaders and politicians considered Burma a backwater in their huge empire. They were unprepared for the frontier warfare necessary to fight the Japanese in Burma and were far more devoted to their imperialist interests of maintaining their presence in India and retaking Singapore and Sumatra.[12] Although two British divisions were stationed in Burma, they were led by the ineffective and soon-to-retire Major General M.N. McLeod, who had prepared no useful plan for defense, and who received little direction from London or Delhi.

Stilwell was incensed by the knowledge that the British opposed his proposals for Burma's defense, a policy that came directly from Churchill, who never looked favorably on any operations in Burma. Churchill did not conceal his negative attitude toward military operations there, and on more than one occasion spoke openly about it. When he sent Harold Alexander to take command of British forces in Burma, he commented, "Never have I taken the responsibility of sending a general on a more forlorn hope."[13] During his voyage to attend the Trident conference in May of 1943, Churchill again expressed his disdain for any Burma operations and likened fighting the Japanese in jungles to "going into the water to fight a shark. It is better to entice him into a trap or catch him on a hook and then demolish him ... after hauling onto dry land."[14]

STILWELL AND "THE RASHAMON EFFECT"

Up to this juncture of the war, few would be likely to disagree with this author's portrayal of the Stilwell story. From this point on, however, the many historical accounts of Stilwell's mission in China, his failed effort to hold off the Japanese in Burma in the spring of 1942, his refusal to listen to Chiang's instructions to employ delaying defensive measures at Myitkyina and Mandalay, insisting instead on what turned out to be a failed offensive effort at Tonggoo, his famous retreat from Burma, his stormy disputes with Chiang Kai-shek, the building of the Ledo Road, the retaking of Burma in 1944, and finally, his removal from command in October 1944, are in sharp disagreement. Until comparatively recent times, the conventional wisdom and the weight of authority portrayed Stilwell as a lone heroic warrior, properly lionized by the press, magazine writers, and historians, struggling to build a unified military force consisting of Nationalist and Communist forces with the laudable single minded purpose of defeating the Japanese. Chiang Kai-shek and his regime were seen as hopelessly corrupt and continually thwarting Stilwell's valiant efforts. Finally, Stilwell was unwisely removed from command by Roosevelt, and replaced by General Albert C. Wedemeyer. The consensus of the vast majority of Americans concurred with this view and considered Stilwell to have been treated unfairly and wrongly removed. When General Hurley first arrived in China on November 7, 1943, he told Stilwell that he was viewed as "the savior of China." As time went on, a few contrary opinions surfaced, questioning the majority view, but for the most part these dissents were drowned out by the major news writers, authors, and commentators.

Akira Kurosawa would have explained these divergent views with his famous "Rashamon effect," one view offered by Stilwell himself, one by his many supporters and admirers in the media and government who commented so favorably on his exploits, and the third by a small group of objective contemporary reviewers of the history of United States and China policy. The reader can make his or her own choice, but no one has put the issue more sharply into focus than historian Hans J. van de Ven in his book, *War and Nationalism in China, 1925–1945*:

To a graduate student at a time when the USA repeatedly backed nasty governments, when the Nationalists imposed a harsh martial law in Taiwan, and when Communist rule still retained the vestiges of promise, Tuchman's *Sand Against the Wind: The Stilwell Papers*, and Theodore White and Annalee Jacob's *Thunder Out of China* were convincing and confirmed that the Nationalists had deserved their fate.

As I read what I then still thought of as the Pacific War, initially with the restricted aim of providing a short synopsis, *it became clear that the Stilwell story could not stand up.* I concluded that a new presentation of Stilwell's activities, placed in the context of Allied strategy, was unavoidable.[15] (emphasis supplied)

As Kurosawa reveals in "Rashamon," each account is filtered through the subjective perception of the narrator, and each account seems equally plausible. This author's account of the story, albeit with every effort to be fair and accurate, tends to follow the line of van de Ven, who presents an exhaustive and impressive historiographical and contextual overview that is clear, direct, and rich in detail. Van de Ven reached two major conclusions about Stilwell in his book: [1] The Stilwell picture as a great war hero cannot stand up to careful scrutiny; and [2] in fairness to Stilwell, he cannot be held responsible for all that went wrong in Burma.

One important observation is that few individuals, and certainly not this author, have any criticism of Stilwell's immense popularity with his troops or his personal courage, integrity, and bravery. The soldiers under his command worshiped him. Criticism centers on the strategy he employed while in Burma, including his insistence on aggressive offensive operations in 1942 when he first arrived, instead of employing a defensive posture as recommended [actually ordered] by Chiang Kai-shek, his disgraceful treatment of Chiang, and more importantly, his failure to understand his major responsibility as Theatre Commander, which encompassed a good deal more than his solitary campaign in Burma. While in Burma, first in 1942 and later in 1944 when he defeated the Japanese, he was many times exposed to enemy fire and spent a good deal of his time on the front line, sometimes in direct sight and the line of fire of the enemy. Chinese officers, not used to seeing their commander in the front line, continually but unsuccessfully attempted to dissuade him from this practice. They were terrified that if anything happened to Stilwell, they would be held personally accountable.

Regarding the high esteem in which Stilwell was held personally by troops under his command, one incident will serve to demonstrate their affection as well as his operating style, and at the same time reveal the difference in his leadership style and that of his replacement, the reserved and disciplined Wedemeyer. While training his troops in India, General Stilwell responded to complaints from the American soldiers about the quality of their food. He showed up unannounced at one mess hall, as was his custom. Stilwell then went through the line with the GI's and found the food inedible. He stood up on the mess table and announced, "All right boys, let 'em have it," and the troops enthusiastically responded by overturning the tables and throwing food all over the mess hall. When the melee ended, Stilwell summoned the distraught mess commander, told him to clean it up, and, if he did not make an immediate improvement in the quality of the food, he would be relieved and shipped home.[16]

STILWELL ARRIVES IN BURMA—CONDITION OF THE CHINESE ARMY

On Friday the 13th of February, 1942, Stilwell left for India, the first stop on his itinerary in Burma, to assume command of a rapidly deteriorating state of affairs.[17] The Japanese had invaded Burma shortly after Pearl Harbor, and by the time of Stilwell's arrival, 80,000 British troops had surrendered at Singapore, on February 15th, and eight days later the British-Indian brigades in Burma were crushed in the Battle of the Sittang Bridge, leaving the Japanese an unimpeded path to the country's capital and primary port, Rangoon. Stilwell had been assigned to take over a crumbling military situation.

Upon his arrival in India, Stilwell met with the British to discuss strategy and was immediately confronted with the daunting task of stemming the Japanese advance. To most historians the outcome was a foregone conclusion, and this view is probably correct, although a case can be made that the Japanese could have been substantially delayed if other tactics had been employed. This will be discussed shortly. Such a delay would have had other beneficial consequences, but Stilwell did not actually get involved in the Burma defense until about March 21, when he took over the local forces. Rangoon had fallen on March 7th.

According to Christopher Thorne, a good deal of the blame for the loss of Rangoon rightly belongs in the lap of the British. He relates that on March 2nd, with a week to prepare the defense, Chiang Kai-shek made the suggestion to Archibald Wavell, commander-in-chief of the British forces, that he should gather his forces at Pegu, just north of Rangoon, and await the arrival of the Chinese 5th Army, which was on its way, and together the forces could mount a counteroffensive. (A Chinese army is approximately the size of an American division.) Thorne says Wavell refused this help and actually radioed a message to Churchill saying that it was better for British forces to defend Rangoon, and that the Governor had asked him not to use any more Chinese forces than actually necessary.[18] Supposedly he did not want Chinese help. If this story is true, it would have to rank high on the scale of ill-advised political as well as military decisions.[19]

Although Rangoon was gone, there was a lot more territory to deal with. Given his tactical skills, Stilwell might have been able to mount an effective contest with the Japanese if he had had a properly trained and motivated army, but too many obstacles stood in his way to make that a realistic option.

STILWELL'S PROBLEMS WITH THE CHINESE ARMY

Rehabilitating the dire situation required that he immediately reorganize and revamp the Chinese forces under his command. He quickly set out to accomplish this by starting to eliminate ineffective elements of the Chinese military leadership, but this proved impossible within the limited time frame and constraints under which he worked. Major changes in the structure of the Chinese army required approval from Chiang-Kai-shek that were slow in coming. The Generalissimo had risen to power by forming alliances with warlords, powerful business interests, and Chinese generals, and was deeply loyal to many of them, including some incompetent and corrupt officers and officials who had supported him. Admittedly, this was a serious impediment to any significant reform of the Chinese army. Wedemeyer would later face the same problem, but approach it differently and with greater success.

Corruption in the Chinese military was rampant. Many division commanders, who were in charge of paying their soldiers, padded the muster rolls with fictitious names in order to receive a larger amount and pocketed the difference. The Chunking government, considering "loyalty" uppermost, looked the other way.[20]

Even more disheartening to Stilwell, Chinese Generals gave him little attention and less compliance.[21] He had been assured by Soong[22] that he would have the same power to hire and fire as a commanding general in the American army. However, it soon became quite clear that "while Soong proposed, Chiang disposed," and the Generalissimo was reluctant to delegate powers that included dismissal of officers to an American." In his attempts to reorganize and redirect the troops of the Chinese Fifth and Sixth armies in Burma, Stilwell discovered that the prior assurances of power were only "nominal," necessitating an urgent trip to Chunking to confer with Chiang Kai-shek to garner support for his authority. To make the point crystal clear, Stilwell insisted that both Chiang and his wife return with him to face the Chinese generals, who were informed in no uncertain terms that Stillwell was to have ultimate authority over the army, enforceable with the power of execution over those who would not obey.[23] Another problem was an overestimate of the size of the Chinese army that was loyal to the Nationalist cause. On paper, the aggregate size was four million, comprised of three hundred divisions. Not only was this figure grossly inflated, but of those divisions that did exist, only a small percentage were truly loyal to Chiang.[24] The rest were kept in line through bribery.

Stilwell had similar problems with Chinese governmental officials. He was never able to blend his military skills with the political necessities of the assignment. While supposedly an expert on Chinese culture and manners, he generally treated Chiang respectfully while in his presence in public but refused to acknowledge the deeply inbred Chinese etiquette of "loss of face" and continually scraped the sensitivity of the proud and pompous leader like sandpaper. Chinese officials were offended by the way he bluntly dismissed their ideas. This cultural *faux pas*, as well as widely divergent views on how to run the army, was a recipe for disaster.[25] The tactless Stilwell did not hide his attitude and made little effort to instruct his subordinates to treat the Chinese with respect. Consequently, his demeanor was mirrored by his close associates and advisors and hamstrung any real possibility of developing a harmonious working relationship.

But Stilwell's greatest stumbling point was his ignorance of and refusal to deal with the deeply conflicting political goals and convoluted motives of the two major Chinese political factions, Chiang's Nationalists and Mao's Communists, whom he mistakenly believed had put aside their differences to harmoniously defend their homeland against the Japanese. There was no place in his thinking for consideration of their intense mutual distrust and rivalry for the ultimate control of their country after the war. Two wars were being waged simultaneously in China, and the divided loyalty of both factions, fighting the Japanese and each other, would be an ongoing and festering problem for any American commander in China. Stilwell wanted to hear nothing of fratricidal squabbles, and he met with constant opposition from Chiang with respect to his desire to supply Lend-Lease arms, ammunition, and supplies to the Communists with expectations they would be used solely against the Japanese. This serious disagreement created a standoff that was a continuous source of friction.

Accustomed to the American military tradition of immediate response and respect for orders, Stilwell was frustrated when his commands to Chinese officers and men were not followed. His orders to Chinese troops to stand and fight were ignored. He met with their officers, presented them with clear and unambiguous commands for troop movements, and found few of them obeyed.[26] On one occasion, he was flabbergasted when an entire Chinese division deserted and disappeared into the jungle, never to be seen again. "There's no trace of it," Stilwell told Jack Belden of *Life* Magazine. "It's the God-damnedest thing I ever saw. Last night I had a division. Today, there isn't any."[27]

STILWELL'S COUNTERATTACK AT TOUNGOO

Stilwell's first serious strategic error, which occurred almost immediately after he took command of the rapidly worsening situation in Burma in March of 1942, was to insist on a counterattack at Toungoo. In an effort to stem the Japanese advance, Stilwell planned for an aggressive counterattack to oppose the advancing Japanese forces. This plan was directly contrary to what Chiang wanted, so the two discussed the issue at their Chunking meeting on March 9 and 10. Chiang's position was that since Rangoon had already fallen, all plans for a counteroffensive should be scrapped. Intelligence indicated that the next objective of the Japanese was Toungoo, some 50 kilometers to the north. Chiang wanted a defensive ring constructed around Mandalay with several strongpoints south in concentric circles, and his argument made sense. The allies had no air force to speak of. Mounting a counteroffensive would take several weeks. Everything was in the Japanese favor at the moment, since they had their air force, artillery and naval support and firm supply lines. Stilwell was downright deceitful in dealing with Chiang regarding this strategy. He listened, made little comment, and pursued his own course, planning and then implementing an aggressive counterattack intended to retake Rangoon. In his diary, Stilwell characterized his discussions with Chiang contemptuously as "a session of amateur tactics . . . backed up by a stooge staff . . . he [Chiang] gave me a long lecture on the situation . . . I showed him the solution, but the stooge jumped in . . . I let them rant."[28] Stilwell left the March meeting without letting Chiang know that he intended to do just the opposite of what the Chinese leader wanted.

On or about March 21, when Stilwell first arrived at the front, he ordered the Chinese 55th and 22nd divisions south to Pyawnbwe and Pyinnama and instructed them to advance and engage the advancing Japanese. It turned into a rout. Within four days, Japanese troops encircled Toungoo, and Stilwell's forces had to beat a hasty retreat. One of the unfortunate consequences of his strategic blunder is that it immediately led to further reverses. The Japanese, who had initially not intended to extend their supply lines too far and would have likely slowed their advances, found documents when they captured Toungoo showing that Chinese forces were far south of Mandalay. With this unexpected and welcome news, the Japanese decided to immediately push further north and, in the process, turned the allied flanks and divided the British and Chinese forces. On April 20 they captured Lashio, and the Burma Road was severed. Confusion reigned in the British and Chinese command centers. The logistical and supply lines broke down, and Stilwell decided to withdraw to India. He never informed Chiang Kai-shek of this decision. During all this time Chiang was sending orders to Stilwell to set up a defensive perimeter at Myitkyina, but if Stilwell received these instructions, he ignored them. He instructed the Chinese 5th Army to retreat to India, and decided to do the same himself. Stillwell obviously did not consider it his responsibility to personally see that his troops were safely evacuated. He just gave instructions to the highest-ranking Chinese general to move his troops to India. His brief report to Washington and to Chiang said that the Chinese divisions had broken into small parties that would make their way to India, so "his further command would be unnecessary."[29] Chiang was outraged when he heard this and commented, "This is contrary to my order to concentrate the entire army at Myitkyina; isn't Stilwell losing his nerve?" Van de Ven, one of the first historians to fault Stilwell for his aggressive and failed counterattack, commented on this turn of events:

> The inexperienced Stilwell could not see the defeat as the result of overwhelming Japanese advantages and the consequences of a very risky move that had gone horribly wrong. He blamed Chinese stupidity and backward preference for the defense.[30]

Taylor also criticizes Stilwell for his decision to ignore Chiang's advice.[31] Both Taylor and van de Ven point out that the monsoon season commences at the end of April, so for five months any offensive actions would likely have been halted, and the allies should have been able to hold the important airfield at Myitkyina almost 200 kilometers north of Lashio, at least until the fall. Stilwell's decision to leave effectively surrendered all of Burma to the Japanese.

Burma fell in 1942 for a variety of reasons, many of them not attributable to Stilwell: inadequate air force; indifferent Burmese who believed the Japanese promise of a grant of independence; failed coordination between the British and Chinese; lack of maps; flawed intelligence; inability of the British to maneuver their armour; and finally, not the least, British and Chinese inexperience in jungle warfare. While no historian believes that Stilwell could have prevented the loss of Burma in 1942, and Taylor's and van de Ven's criticism is that he could have delayed the conquest for at least five months, clearly, Stilwell's actions at Toungoo contributed to the early loss.

In Washington, senior officials were alarmed at the developments. T.V. Soong passed on to Chiang a request from the Department of the Army asking for an assessment of Stilwell's handling of the situation. Doubtless this message originated from General Marshall. Chiang had lost confidence in Stillwell and was presented with his first chance to be relieved of him. Instead, on advice of his wife, and fearful of causing a rift in United States–China relations, he told T.V. Soong to advise that he had "full confidence in Stilwell."[32] Stilwell had dodged a bullet, but it would not be the last.

STILWELL'S FAMOUS RETREAT

An incident during the evacuation was to become the most talked about event of the entire Asian war. A C-47 transport was sent to return Stilwell and his staff to India. After loading the plane with officers and headquarters personnel, Stilwell refused to get on the plane, informing the pilot that "he preferred to walk."[33] He then gathered a group of 114 Americans, British, Indians, and Burmese civilians and soldiers to join him on a march to India. William J. Slim, the general in charge of British troops, led another group of approximately twenty-five thousand who retreated on foot on a roughly parallel course.

With the Japanese in close pursuit, Generals Stilwell and Slim would have to hack their way to safety across 140 miles of virtually impassable bamboo jungles and steep mountainsides, all the while fighting vicious biting ants, flies, leaches, dehydration, hunger, thick vines, deep muddy rivers, withering sun, and bouts of food poisoning and malaria. The spindly-legged fifty-nine year old Stilwell, nearly blind in one eye from an accident during a training exercise years previously,[34] led the retreat. A three-star general, he wore no insignias or badge of rank. Younger men in far better physical condition found it difficult to keep up with him, and he was compelled to give in to requests for frequent breaks to allow for rest. He took no special privileges for himself, taking the same meager rations as the lowliest private.

Stilwell's drive and fierce determination were an inspiration to every member of his party. Air drops resupplied the marchers. The journey lasted two weeks, and Stilwell's last jaunty message to Headquarters in India on May 6, 1942 concluded, "This is probably last message for awhile, Cheerio!"[35] Incredibly, Stilwell did not lose a single person of the 141 who accompanied him, while the group under the command of General Slim lost 13,000 of the original 25,000 to encounters with the Japanese, disease, and desertion.[36] The retreat was closely followed in the world press and generated enormous interest.[37] When Stilwell finally reached Delhi, he was mobbed by a swarm of over a hundred newsmen and photographers. Not mincing words, he admitted that the Allies had taken ". . . a hell of a beating. The Japs ran us out of Burma."[38i] With a dearth of favorable war news in America, the "walk out" and his promise to retake Burma landed him on the cover of major newspapers and magazines.[39] No mention was made of Toungoo.

Never one for paperwork, Stilwell submitted a confidential 50-page report to the War Department on the Burma campaign,[40] excoriating the British and Chinese for their bungling and inept command, and reserving his harshest criticism for Chiang Kai-shek for interfering with his efforts to command Chinese troops.[41] A highly sanitized version of the report was personally presented by Stilwell to Chiang upon his next visit to Chungking. Nonetheless, it only worsened their already fragile relationship. Everything that Stilwell did or said confirmed Chiang's worst suspicions about Stilwell's motives.[42] The downward slide quickened, without a doubt exacerbated by Stilwell's iron-fisted control over Lend-Lease material that he used to enforce his insistence on commanding the military.

STILWELL'S RETAKING OF BURMA

Stilwell's next move was to plan for a return to Burma. He was determined to smash the Japanese sea blockade of China and retake Burma, despite less than enthusiastic support by the British,[43] who felt that removing the Japanese from China was an American problem. Stilwell vented his anger in his diary: "What a break for the Limeys. Just what they wanted. Now they will quit and the Chinese will quit, and the God damn Americans can go ahead and fight. . . . Unless we get tough and nail the G-mo [Generalissimo Chiang] down now, he'll get out of hand for good."[44]

At Casablanca in January 1943, the Combined Chiefs of Staff (CCS) approved a three-pronged plan to retake Burma, codenamed ANAKIM. An "X" force of Chinese troops in India that had fled from Burma, then personally trained by Stilwell, would attack Burma from the north. Ultimately, this force grew to number 33,000. A "Y" force, commanded by Chinese but trained and guided by Americans in China, would enter Burma from the east. When the two armies met, the Japanese blockade of the Burma Road would be lifted. A "Z" force was also to be trained in China and used as a back up for the "Y" force. The third element was an amphibious assault on Rangoon by the British to cut the Japanese supply line. After retaking Burma, X, Y, and Z would then combine to drive the Japanese from China.

Never enthusiastic about the plan, Chiang shrewdly endorsed it, attaching conditions that gave him a clear-cut escape hatch, stating his intention to go forward with ANAKIM if the British agreed to supply the men, ships, and material necessary to handle the attack on Rangoon. Chiang withdrew his support after the British announced they could not supply the naval force or landing craft necessary to go forward. At the Quadrant conference in August 1943, plans were finally approved for a modified campaign to commence January 1944, subject to further confirmation at the Cairo conference in November. This plan included British participation without the previously promised naval attack on Rangoon.

Stilwell personally oversaw the training of the "X" force, and for the first time Chinese troops were well fed, well trained, and properly equipped for combat. Anticipating approval and wanting to get a jump on the Japanese, he secretly ordered the Chinese 38th Division to commence moving into Burma in late October. The original plan also called for the "Y" force of 115,000 troops to simultaneously enter Burma from the east, but Chiang stalled.

The epic five-month, 200-mile jungle campaign to retake Burma was as terrifying as any in World War II. Clad in khakis and a floppy campaign hat, Stilwell personally led his troops, often from the front line. With the help of effective air support they were immediately successful in driving the Japanese back. For the first time, the supposedly invincible Japanese Imperial Army was being beaten at its own game. The confidence of the Chinese troops soared. Additional support came from a fierce and gallant 3,000-man ranger battalion led by Brigadier General Frank Merrill, nicknamed Merrill's Marauders, and the Chindits, a force of 20,000 British and Commonwealth soldiers formed and led by the brilliant and unconventional British Major General Orde Wingate.[45]

From late December 1943 to May 1944, Stilwell's troops made good progress down the Hukwang Valley that was to be the path of the Ledo Road. By February, they had pushed the Japanese nearly 75 miles to the south. All along, Stilwell continued to press for release of the "Y" forces, but to no avail. Chiang first promised to release them on January 1, then changed the date to mid-April. He was continually urged to release these troops. Under threats from President Roosevelt, Chiang finally ceded control "without strings."[46] The *coup de grâce* came on April 10, 1944, when General Marshall informed Chiang that all Lend-lease support would be cut off unless the "Y" force was released to Burma with Stilwell in complete command. Finally, on May 11, the Generalissimo gave the order for the first contingent of 32,000 troops to move into Burma. The monsoon season was soon upon them, however, and the force was not fully effective until the fall of 1944.

As the Burma campaign progressed, priority for a backdoor operation in China was diminishing due to the success of the island-hopping campaign and the Soviet promise to enter the war three months after defeat of the Nazis. An October 1943 War Department position paper, *Re-Analysis of Our Strategic Policy in Asia*, signaled a shift in American China policy from that of establishing air bases from which to bomb Japan to the alternative of simply tying up Japanese forces to prevent them from being used elsewhere.[47] The central message in the report was: expend as little money and resources as possible, just enough to keep China in the war!

The reduced priority translated into reduced supply. Chiang now found a request for a large loan refused. Additionally, Roosevelt pressured him to allow an American mission to Communist headquarters in Ya'nan in the belief, supported by the State Department, that this would eventually further the goal of unifying Chinese Communist and Nationalist forces against the Japanese. The mission, officially known as the "Military Observers Mission," was dubbed "The Dixie Mission," and ran from July 1944 to March 1947.

JAPAN'S LAST OFFENSIVE IN CHINA, "ICHI-GO"

A second aspect of Stilwell's judgment not often addressed is whether it was good military strategy for a three-star general and Theatre Commander to be nearly out of communication from his headquarters in China while on the front lines in Burma for a period in excess of five months. While Stilwell was otherwise occupied in Burma, the Japanese mounted their last massive attack on western China, ICHI-GO, fought from April to December 1944. While the two primary goals of ICHI-GO were to open a land route to capture air bases in southeast China from which American bombers were attacking the Japanese homeland and shipping, it also badly weakened the strategic position of the Nationalist government and created a tangible threat to capture Kunming, the terminus of the Burma Road and the only remaining airfield that could accommodate supplies coming over the Hump.

This was the final effort of the Japanese to bring China to terms. If Kunming was lost, Chiang's most vital supply line would have been eliminated and he would have had no choice but to surrender. Stilwell's potentially disastrous oversight of ignoring the risks of losing China while personally directing his troops on the front line in Burma led his detractors to label him "the best three-star battalion commander in the United States Army."[48]

STILWELL'S RECALL BY PRESIDENT ROOSEVELT

Stilwell continued to make no attempt to hide his contempt for Chiang. As he confided to his diary:

> I have brought all the deficiencies to his notice. I have warned him about the condition of his army. I have demonstrated to him how these things can be corrected. All of this he ignores and shuts his eyes to the deplorable condition of his army, which is a terrible indictment of him, his War Ministry and his General Staff.[49]

He openly referred to the Chinese leader as "peanut," a "lily livered chink," a "slant–eyed snake," and worse. This was not the kind of language a Chief of Staff should use about his direct superior. It is no surprise that this attitude permeated his entire command. The friction between Stilwell and Chiang grew from almost the first day of their relationship. Although he was not relieved until October 1944, Stilwell came perilously close to losing his job in November 1943, and earlier, in the fall of 1942 after his loss in Burma, his strategy came under close and disapproving scrutiny in Washington. Even as Stilwell was beating back the Japanese Imperial Army in Burma, Chiang Kai-shek instructed Ambassador Soong to again lobby for his removal. After conferring with Roosevelt, Marshall met with Soong on July 14th and informed him that Stilwell still had the complete support of the President and would not be removed,[50] though the administration had to balance this decision against Chiang's thinly veiled threats that the Chinese would make a separate peace with Japan.[51] Roosevelt now authorized his removal if Chiang insisted. The removal was only obviated after Stilwell was persuaded to "apologize" to Chiang by Madam Chiang, whose intercession was no doubt assisted by the gift of a bejeweled compact presented to her by Louis Mountbatten, who also interceded with her husband to change his mind.[52]

Although Stilwell's reputation was enhanced by the media, he still had a few detractors, including one individual who spoke with unique authority. In 1948, General Claire Chennault went public with his criticism of Stilwell and his attitude toward the Chinese:

> As if by calculated design, official American estimates of the Chinese Central Government and its armed forces became common conversational stock wherever Americans gathered in Chungking. While American servicemen were ostensibly admonished to refrain from a discussion of the Chinese Government it appeared to be approved practice among American offices in Chunking to recite all the Government's real or fancied short-comings on the slightest cue.[53]

Chennault had many opportunities to observe Stillwell. He bore witness to one particularly shocking example of Stilwell's public indiscretion:

> In the spring of 1943 in the presence of President Roosevelt, the Combined Chiefs of Staff, and the Prime Minister, President Roosevelt asked Stilwell his impression of CKS: Stilwell rose and belabored Generalissimo Chiang at length. He accused the Generalissimo of being undependable, ungrateful, dishonest, and untruthful. President Roosevelt interrupted the tirade to ask: 'Chennault, what do you think about this?' I told them that in all my years in China the Generalissimo had never broken his word to me in any manner, that I considered him a great man, the only leader capable of holding China together.[54]

Chennault and Stilwell detested each other [pic. 16, 24]. For one thing, Stilwell resented Chennault's status as a general who had not come from the United States Military Academy. Their approach toward military strategy was also markedly different. Stilwell had no appreciation for the use of air power and barely gave Chennault enough critical supplies to keep his meager air force flying. Ultimately, Stilwell's truculent and defiant personality brought about his own removal, despite his personal courage and the renowned leadership abilities recognized by his soldiers and promoted by the top American military establishment, the American public, and the press.

The incident that finally tipped the scales occurred after Roosevelt sent Chiang a sharply worded telegram on September 19, 1944 that virtually ordered him to turn over command of all Chinese forces. The message was so critical that the American Ambassador, Major General Patrick J. Hurley, recommended that it be toned down through an interpreter.[55] Fluent in Chinese, Stilwell refused, and relished the opportunity to personally hand the unexpurgated version directly to Chiang. Stilwell crowed about it in his diary:

> Mark this day in red on the calendar of life. At long, at very long last, F.D.R. has finally spoken plain words and plenty of them, with a firecracker in every sentence: 'Get busy or else.' A hot firecracker. I handed this bundle of paprika to the Peanut and then sank back with a sigh. The harpoon hit the little bugger right in the solar plexus, and went right through him ... [B]eyond turning green and losing the power of speech, he did not bat an eye. He just said to me, "I understand." And sat in silence, jiggling one foot ... at last F.D.R's eyes have been opened and he has thrown a good hefty punch.[56]

This was the last straw. Chiang demanded Stilwell's recall, and this time rebuffed all efforts to change his mind. Even an October 5 offer by Roosevelt to modify the previous demands in order to preserve Stilwell was refused. This time Stilwell's removal was supported by Hurley, who had been drafting Chiang's communications.[57] In his last message Hurley informed Roosevelt that he must choose between an "expendable general" and "the leader in China." Facing a fourth term election and fearing the consequences of what might be a political firestorm, Roosevelt ordered Stilwell's recall, framing it as a "case of personalities."[58]

The recall of the popular General triggered a furious anti-Chiang backlash in the American media. Perhaps the most noteworthy was a long multi-column front page story in *The New York Times* by the Mao-sympathizing theater critic turned temporary war correspondent Brooks Atkinson that reported: "Inside China [the relief of Stilwell] represents the political triumph of a moribund anti-democratic regime which is more concerned with maintaining its political supremacy than in driving the Japanese out of China."[59]

The article went on to assert that Chiang had demanded the recall and refused to be "coerced" by Americans into making terms with the Communists, that he insisted on control of Lend-Lease material, and if the American government would not agree to these demands, that China would go on to fight the Japanese alone.

Upon Stilwell's return to America at the end of October, 1944, it fell upon Marshall to personally muzzle him because the President was concerned about the upcoming election. The conduct of the war was a major issue in the campaign, and Roosevelt was losing ground to Dewey. Secretary of War Stimson admitted to his diary that Stilwell had been treated poorly, but nonetheless that he should be kept "out of reach of all newsmen" and not give them the opportunity to catch and distort any unwary word just before the election.[60]

Later, Stilwell revealed his sentiments in a report to the War Department:

> Nowhere does Clausewitz's dictum that war is only the continuation of politics by other methods apply with more force than it did in CBI. In handling such an uncertain situation as existed in that theater of war, the Americans would have done well to avoid committing themselves unalterably to Chiang, and adopted a more realistic attitude toward China itself. We could have gained much by exerting pressure on Chiang to cooperate and achieve national unity, and if he proved unable to do this then *in supporting those elements in China which gave promise of such development.* (emphasis added)[61]

Stilwell's astounding commentary failed to take into account the utter impossibility of the Communists' ever cooperating with any other political group. Wedemeyer must have winced at Stilwell's lack of comprehension of the nature of Chinese politics as well as his complete misreading of Clausewitz's military strategy.

A PLOT TO ASSASSINATE CHIANG

If one intriguing anecdote is true, circumstances might have taken a different turn. As told by Stilwell's close friend Colonel (later Brigadier General) Frank Dorn in his compelling 1970 firsthand account, *Walkout with Stilwell in Burma,*[62] Stillwell returned to Burma after meeting in Cairo with President Roosevelt and Harry Hopkins, where he was given confidential instructions. He summoned Dorn to his quarters, secretly informing him that he had been instructed "on the highest authority" to "make preparations for the assassination of Chiang Kai-shek"[63] In accordance with the order, Dorn formulated a plan whereupon Chiang and his wife were to fly to India to inspect the troops that were training there under Stilwell's command. The plane would develop engine trouble, and Chiang and his wife, whose parachutes had been sabotaged, would bail out and fall to their deaths. To disguise the plot, at least two of the American officers on board would meet with a similar fate.[64] Nothing was to happen until Stilwell received the final go-ahead from the "higher authority."[65] No such instruction was ever received.

The story of the plot was reiterated in a 2007 book that cites Dorn and also references a 1985 story published in *The Chicago Tribune* in 1985.[66] Stilwell would not have mourned Chiang's loss. His September 9, 1944 diary entry opined: "What they ought to do is shoot the G-Mo [Chiang] and the rest of the gang." Stilwell had both the motive and the opportunity. Dorn's apparently credible story of at least "preparations" for a proposed political assassination is by no means unique in the annals of American history.

To Stillwell's credit, the retaking of Burma in 1944 stands out as the only major combat victory won by Chinese troops over the Japanese in eight years of fighting. Yet one significant event which occurred earlier, during Stilwell's first foray in Burma in 1942, arising out of his unilateral decision to retreat from Burma when Lashio was captured by the Japanese, stands out as a near disaster for China and her allies.

THE SALWEEN RIVER BATTLE

It is inevitable in every war that certain battles and events are given considerable publicity, and the participants, usually the commanders, receive commensurate praise or condemnation, sometimes richly deserved and sometimes the product of other forces like luck, weather, surprise, or the fortuitous presence of journalists to record the event. Occasionally the deliberate self-promotion of commanders can play a significant role. It is equally true that sometimes really important contests take place in a war, the outcome of which could determine whether victory or defeat of the nation will be the result, and these battles for one reason or another receive little or no recognition in the history books.

The Salween River Battle, which took place in Burma between May 6 and May 18, 1942, fits the description of a little-known battle that, had it turned out otherwise, would very probably have resulted in the Japanese Army's forcing China to capitulate and sue for peace. A settlement of the Japanese/Chinese conflict would have had profound consequences for the

Allies, the most important of which would have been the availability of well over another million soldiers to contest American forces in the Pacific, which in early 1942 were faring very poorly.

Shortly after Pearl Harbor, the Japanese attacked Burma in force. Their original intent was to rapidly advance northward and eventually sever the Burma Road, the only land route available for China to receive Lend-Lease materials from the Allies. It did not take them long to achieve this goal. When the Japanese took Lashio on April 29, 1942, the Burma Road was severed. Burma was lost, and General Stilwell made the decision to retreat to India.

The Japanese could not believe their good fortune. Their supply lines were grievously overextended, but they had been fortunate to capture large quantities of food, ammunition, and much else by way of military supplies due to their rapid and unimpeded advance. From Lashio they had a clear shot over the Burma Road which would eventually lead them to China. The only impediment standing in their way was the deep and fast-moving Salween River, the last natural obstacle. The bridge over the river had been destroyed by the retreating Chinese, but Japanese engineers could quickly erect a pontoon bridge in a matter of no more than a day. Then the Japanese could have poured into China unimpeded and gone directly on to Kunming, the last and most important air terminal in China for receiving Lend-Lease material over the "Hump." There would have been no other practical way to supply China with war material. And the Japanese would have been successful but for the efforts of General Claire Chennault, who had come up with a way to block their advance.

As it approaches the Salween River, the Burma Road is a twisting, one-lane serpentine track chiseled out of the solid rock of the mountains which rise a thousand feet above the deep gorges a mile below. The rapid Japanese advance caused the road to be backed up for many miles with Japanese trucks, tanks, supply vehicles, infantry, and the inevitable thousands of innocent refugees fleeing the battle area and seeking refuge in China. Included in the refugees were many innocent Chinese civilians and their families who, once the bridge was repaired, would pour unimpeded back to their homeland. Chennault, head of the American Volunteer Group (AVG), more famously known as the "Flying Tigers," immediately understood the seriousness of the threat and decided that if he could quickly make some modifications to his fighter planes which would allow them to carry heavy bombs, they might drop them on the cliffs overlooking the road which, he hoped, would cause huge rock landslides that would block the Japanese passage into China. With the assistance of his engineers, in a matter of hours, he made the necessary modifications to the planes. Since he knew that he could not accomplish this mission without sacrificing the lives of many innocent civilians, he sought and received permission from Chiang Kai-shek to commence the operation. For twelve straight days his planes strafed and bombed the hapless Japanese, inflicting many casualties. Huge landslides completely blocked the passage, destroying many Japanese vehicles and tanks, and killing thousands of soldiers who were trapped, unable to go forward or retreat. Chennault's planes strafed the almost defenseless Japanese relentlessly over the entire 12 day period. Eventually, they realized the futility of trying to proceed and completely withdrew. Chennault and his heroic men have never been officially recognized for this remarkable mission. Meanwhile his superior, General Joseph Stilwell, had no intention of seeing any recognition afforded to his bitter rival. These two men intensely disliked each other.

Except for the half-dozen pages which Chennault devotes to it in his 1949 biography, *Way of A Fighter*, the battle is scarcely mentioned in any of the many books on the Burma campaign. It is briefly mentioned, without any explanation of its true significance, by Martha Byrd in her *Chennault Giving Wings to the Tiger*. Louis Allen, in his comprehensive and detailed study *Burma: The Longest War, 1941–45*, laconically referencing Romanus & Sunderland, dismissed the episode by suggesting that [Japanese commander] Iida made the decision to halt the advance on his own:

> Had they wished to push on into Yunnan there is no doubt nothing could have stopped the Japanese, but Iida ordered them on 26 April to halt on the line of the Salween, a resolution simplified by Chennault's AVG pilots who bombed 56 Division's supply convoys.[67]

Oddly, research has uncovered only one instance where a military historian has reviewed this significant battle for long-term strategic consequences. Major Reagan E. Schupp, USAF, did a comprehensive Research Report on the Salween Gorge Battle in 2006. The subject of his report was "Effect-Based Operations." Schupp lists three major battles of World War II which occurred in 1942 which he called "turning points" in the war: the Battle of Midway; the British breakout from El Alamein; and the Soviet counteroffensive at Stalingrad. Further, in a very careful and detailed analysis of the Salween River Gorge battle, Schupp equates this battle's importance as the same as the other three, giving full credit to Chennault's "Flying Tigers." He does not, however, suggest that Stilwell purposefully suppressed information about the event.[68] One might logically suspect, moreover, that if this battle was to be given recognition it would most likely be the result of an Air Force research project.

Even after his removal in November 1944, Stilwell remained a favorite of Marshall. After a short rest, he was reassigned to command the Tenth Army on Okinawa after its commander, General Simon Bolivar Buckner, was killed by artillery fire. This critical command included participation in the anticipated invasion of the Japanese homeland. Of course, the dropping of the Atom Bomb obviated the need for an invasion. Stilwell was in poor health during the last months of 1945 and returned to his beloved home in Carmel, California shortly afterward. He died of stomach cancer on October 12, 1946. The Combat Infantry Badge, the most coveted military decoration of the infantry, was at the time awarded only to enlisted men and officers up to a rank which did not include generals. However, just prior to his death, an exception was made, and Stilwell's great wish to be awarded the Combat Infantry Badge was honored. It was pinned to his pillow as he lay dying.

After the war, Congressman Walter Judd acknowledged the impossible predicament into which Stilwell had been placed, characterizing him as "one of the most tragic American figures in the last war ... He was a magnificent combat soldier, a good field commander, but it was his misfortune to be given a job which required more political and diplomatic skill than strictly military."[69] As John Eisenhower wrote: "As an organizer and combat leader of Chiang's armies, Stilwell would be a master; as a diplomat in pretentious New Delhi or corrupt Chungking, he would be a misfit."[70]

The "Vinegar" was gone from China, and the Americans now needed to heal the open wounds brought about by nearly three years of bitter contention. A more diplomatic and cerebral envoy was required. Albert Wedemeyer was off to China.

CHAPTER 7

EASED OUT TO ASIA

Disappointment is as good as success;
for it supplies as many images to the mind,
and as many topics to the tongue.
—Samuel Johnson

At the highly secret Quadrant meeting at Quebec in August 1943, a detailed plan for OVERLORD was presented to Roosevelt and Churchill
by British Lieutenant General Sir Frederick Morgan, Chief of Staff to
Supreme Allied Commander in Europe Dwight Eisenhower.[1] This permitted the Allies to apportion the proper amount of resources necessary between
the cross-channel invasion of France and additional operations in the
Mediterranean. Sicily had been taken and plans were being made for a campaign in Italy, the next objective in Churchill's "soft underbelly" of Europe.
For Brigadier General Wedemeyer, now Chief of the War Plans Division,
Quadrant was a career-changing event, as British Admiral Louis Mountbatten, who had just been appointed to head the newly created Southeast
Asia Command (SEAC) that had been carved out from CBI, informed him
that he had requested that General Marshall assign Wedemeyer to New
Delhi as his second in command.[2]

When Wedemeyer approached his mentor, he was amazed to discover
that his assignment had been discussed at the top levels of the American and
British staffs. Since Mountbatten was related to the King, it undoubtedly
had been the subject of discussion between Roosevelt and the Prime Minister.
Marshall informed Wedemeyer that President Roosevelt was in favor of
the transfer because of his belief that he could "bring about better cooperation in a complex area." In the code of military-speak, the offer was not

negotiable. The new job carried with it a second star, though Wedemeyer would clearly have preferred a combat command or a continued role as a strategic planner. His zeal for a combat assignment was such that while in North Africa with General Patton a few months earlier, he had volunteered for a demotion to Colonel in order to take command of a regiment. Patton was duly impressed.[3]

Wedemeyer immediately speculated about whether the move to Asia might somehow be related to his advocacy of the early cross-channel invasion he had presented at the White House in June 1942. Years later, columnist Drew Pearson confirmed his suspicions, reporting that it was indeed a consequence of his role in the longstanding disagreement between the Americans and British over European strategy:

> At times the argument among Roosevelt advisers was bitter, especially over Churchill's opposition to the second front across the English Channel. This reached a crisis at Casablanca in 1943, when the U.S. General Staff argued that the way to win the war in a hurry was by a direct attack on Germany across the Channel. Churchill was opposed, finally stipulated that if such a second front was undertaken the troop ratio would have to be 70 per cent American to 30 percent British. "We cannot squander the seed of the Empire," he said, referring to expected loss of manpower. However, it would have taken one year to transport enough American troops to England to carry out this ratio, and in this case the second front could be started in the summer of 1943. *Churchill was quite irked at Wedemeyer....* After Casablanca, *Churchill suggested that Lord Louis Mountbatten needed an expert liaison officer for his campaign in India, and specifically asked that General Wedemeyer be attached to him.* Wedemeyer was an expert on German tactics, knew nothing about the Far East, but was transferred to India anyway. (emphasis added)[4]

Over time, bits and pieces of additional evidence confirming British involvement began to surface. Shortly after Quadrant, Wedemeyer's secretary, Betty Lutz, told him of a conversation she had overheard outside his office in the Pentagon. Several British officers waiting to see him were talking about his "new assignment" and speculating about who his replacement might be and how that person would be "much more acceptable."[5] Occasionally a historian would weigh in. William Stueck observed that Wedemeyer's "adamancy [on the cross-channel invasion] probably led to his transfer to the Southeast Asia Command later in the year."[6]

Based in Kandy, Ceylon (present day Sri Lanka) at SEAC, Wedemeyer would be far out of the sight of the Prime Minister. On the trip to join Mountbatten, he could not shake the suspicion that both he and his new superior were both being "kicked upstairs" for a similar readiness to speak their minds and feared they were facing "a vegetative state in a remote and relatively unimportant sphere." Mountbatten had a reputation for bluntness and often got in the hair of the British Chiefs of Staff.[7] A number of planners had a dim view of Mountbatten's strategic acumen,[8] but his blood relationship to the King insulated him from direct criticism.[9] As time passed, Wedemeyer changed his view about the importance of the Asian theatre but never changed his belief about the reasons for the move. Indeed, Wedemeyer entitled chapter six of *Wedemeyer Reports!* "Eased Out to Asia."

GENERAL STANLEY DUNBAR EMBICK

Any discussion of the reasons for Wedemeyer's transfer must take into account his close relationship with his father-in-law, General Stanley Dunbar Embick, whose deep personal enmity towards Churchill dated back to the First World War, when he noted that "a close up observation of Churchill [then serving as First Lord of the Admiralty] during the war and at the [Versailles] Peace Conference left me with no respect whatever for his character."[10] [pic. 10]

Wedemeyer and Embick's views about the British did not endear them to either Churchill or President Roosevelt.[11, 12] Prior to Pearl Harbor, they were vigorously opposed to furnishing aid to Britain and were convinced that America had been "propagandized" into the First World War,[13] sharing the viewpoint of a substantial number of Americans, championed in Congress by Montana Senator Burton K. Wheeler who supported "America First," the influential isolationist organization. Wedemeyer had befriended America First's highest profile spokesman, Charles Lindbergh, while acting as his guide during a tour of Germany in 1937.[14]

Embick had been appointed by George Marshall as a representative to the British/American ABC1 planning sessions held in early 1941, where the main order of business was discussion of a possible war against the Axis. At a meeting out of the presence of the British, Marshall consulted with his group to solicit their opinion about whether or not he should recommend to President Roosevelt that America join England in the war against Germany, and, if so, was it necessary to make this decision immediately? Embick responded that not only was he adamantly opposed to America's entry, but that he was against giving substantial military or economic aid to England at all. He did not view their situation as precarious and believed that even if it was and if the current crisis led to the fall of the Churchill government, so much the better for the British.[15]

Despite this, Embick never lost Marshall's confidence as a valued member of strategy groups throughout the war. Mark Stoler praises him as "an officer who was playing and would continue to play a pivotal role in U.S. strategic and policy planning" and "one of the most senior, highly respected strategic thinkers within the army."[16] The most highly respected Marshall biographer, Forest Pogue, speaks approvingly of him, reporting that Embick made his views known through his son-in-law while he was an important member of the War Planning Board.[17] Along with Wedemeyer, Marshall and Embick shared the common belief that British strategic recommendations were often grounded on purely Imperialist interests, and together, they lobbied unsuccessfully against plans for TORCH, the November 1942 landings in North Africa.

During the long ABC1 meetings, there were few secrets between the British and American planners. Churchill must have been infuriated when he learned of Embick's remarks and most certainly would have associated Wedemeyer with them. Like most powerful political figures, he held a dim view of those who opposed him, especially when the criticism was directed against what he considered to be his infallible military stratagems.

UNTOWARD CONSEQUENCES OF HARBORING ANTI-RUSSIAN SENTIMENTS

Yet another factor that probably influenced Roosevelt and Churchill was an awareness of Wedemeyer's strong anti-Bolshevist sentiments. They wanted a close and harmonious relationship with Stalin and were dismissive of those who warned about the dangers of Communism. On June 12, 1951, in testimony before the Senate Committee on Armed Services and the Committee on Foreign Relations, Wedemeyer revealed that:

> I enjoyed a very close relationship with the General [Marshall] and I talked to him very confidentially . . . about my concern with reference to communism; I also . . . talked with Harry Hopkins and to Averell Harriman back in 1941 and 1942 about what I believed to

be the dangers of communism; there were similar or equal dangers with fascism and nazism.[18]

The advice was largely ignored, but if Wedemeyer's strong antipathy for Stalin was relayed to the President by these close advisors, and it almost certainly was, it would have been a cause for concern. The President harbored some unease about Wedemeyer following the leak of the Victory Program to Chesley Manley. On February 26, 1942 he sent a letter to War Secretary Henry Stimson about the possibility of his [Wedemeyer's] leaking this program.[19] Although Stimson replied on March 2[20] that Wedemeyer "is one of the very best officers we have in the General staff," that he was the "right hand man of the chief of the War Plans Division," and that he would "bet his hat that he had nothing to do with the leak," it is clear that the President was keeping a close eye on him.

Roosevelt, ever vigilant, kept his eye on other issues. He was intent on supporting his ally in Moscow and had little tolerance for anyone casting aspersions on Stalin or his ideology. When Congressman Martin Dies, the Chairman of the House Committee on Un-American Activities, became insistent on digging Communists out of the Roosevelt administration, he was summoned to the White House where the President told him, "Several of the best friends I've got are Communists. You're all wrong about this thing"[21] Roosevelt's attitude towards the Soviets was echoed by his closest advisor, Harry Hopkins, a staunch Stalin advocate. In the summer of 1942, Major General James H. Burns, head of the Army Ordnance Department, sent Hopkins a detailed three-page memo containing his suggestions for better relations with Russia. Perhaps the most significant passage in the memo resulted in the transfer of numerous officials deemed "not friendly" to Russia: "Establish the general policy throughout all U.S. departments and agencies that Russia must be considered as a real friend and be treated accordingly and that *personnel must be assigned to Russian contacts that are loyal to this concept.*"[22] (emphasis added)

Roosevelt's interest in maintaining good relations with Russia had many consequences. Historian Thomas Fleming relates the incredible story of how this policy of being "good to Russia" translated into actual operation. It enabled Soviet Ambassador Maxim Litvinov to single-handedly engineer the removal from the State Department of an entire group of men he deemed not to be "cooperative" with Russia. They were replaced with individuals who actively worked to advance anti-Chiang policies.[23]

FDR was infuriated by the opposition of the isolationists to his efforts to assist Britain and the Soviets, and their characterization of him as a "war monger." When Lindbergh spoke at Fort Wayne, Indiana in the summer of 1941, he charged Roosevelt with contemplating action to limit freedom of speech so as to cut off the anti-war talk of the isolationists. The President was so outraged that he summoned Attorney General Francis Biddle and ordered him to look into the possibility of a Grand Jury investigation, and possible indictment, of Lindbergh and America First on the grounds of treason. The Attorney General quickly responded that there was no basis in fact or law to look into the situation, and that no laws were being violated.[24]

A telling incident which illustrates the lengths to which Roosevelt would go to suppress information he deemed detrimental to his policies is related by Laurence Rees in *Behind Closed Doors*, in which he describes an absorbing account of a behind-the-scenes conversation between Roosevelt and George Howard Earle III, former governor of Pennsylvania and friend of the President during the 1930s. During the war, Earle had been serving as American diplomatic minister in Bulgaria, and later the President's special emissary for Balkan affairs. He returned to Washington in 1944 to give Roosevelt his views on the infamous Katyn massacre, in which the Russians had murdered some 10,000 Polish officers and buried them in the Katyn Forest. When the massacre was discovered, the Russians blamed the act on the Nazis, and both Roosevelt and Churchill, in their desperation to maintain good relations with Russia, fully accepted the Kremlin's claims. Earle, now in the White House alone with Roosevelt, had proof positive in the form of affidavits, pictures, statements, and other documentation. The Bulgarian and White Russian agents indicated they were willing to have the Red Cross go in as an independent agency, investigate the crime and make a report. The evidence was overwhelming, but Roosevelt refused to accept it, replying to Earle: "George, they could have rigged things up." Roosevelt was adamant that "this is entirely German propaganda and a German plot." In the same meeting, Earle condemned *Mission to Moscow*, the "dreadful book of Joe Davies" (first American Ambassador to Russia during World War II), that made Stalin out to be a benign Santa Claus. Earle said, "We never recovered from that. It made such an impression on the American people."

Frustrated in his unsuccessful efforts to convince Roosevelt of Soviet guilt for the Katyn massacre, Earle decided on his own to tell the world the true facts. As a loyal friend of the President, he first asked for permission. Almost immediately, Roosevelt sent a letter to Earle specifically forbidding him to make the disclosure [appendix vi]. As if the letter were not sufficient deterrent, Earle soon learned how determined Roosevelt was to keep him quiet. While fishing in a remote lake in Maryland a few days later, Earle was surprised by another boat which approached. On board were two FBI agents who advised Earle that they had a letter from the President which advised that, effective immediately, Earle had been appointed assistant head of the Samoan Defense Group and had to leave immediately. He remained more or less isolated there in the Pacific until "rescued" by President Truman after the war.[25]

Churchill took no back seat to Roosevelt in dealing with, dispatching, or eliminating political problems or people who stood in the way of their agenda. The infamous case of Tyler Kent is a good example. In 1940, a young United States State Department code clerk working in London, accumulated information that severely compromised Roosevelt's longstanding deception that he had been in compliance with the Neutrality Laws. Kent was swiftly scooped up by the British authorities and imprisoned in London. His diplomatic immunity was waived by the United States, and he spent five years in a British prison, incommunicado.[26]

The Earle, Lindbergh, and Tyler cases are mentioned solely to illustrate the lengths to which powerful politicians will go to hide or suppress information *or people* they deem inimical to their agenda. Wedemeyer would also be a victim of this technique. Churchill, ever on the alert to neutralize his adversaries and advance his agenda, carefully nursed his own intent for dealing with the one leading American planner who might stand in the way of his grand strategic objectives. The ideal opportunity for Churchill to settle the score with Wedemeyer presented itself in Quebec with the formation of SEAC. Here was a golden opportunity to send him to Asia. Roosevelt undoubtedly would have been consulted, and he himself was well acquainted with the stratagem of getting "rid of problems." And transferring problematic diplomats to remote outposts was only one way of solving a problem.[27] In the case of a loyal officer, a "promotion" associated with a transfer to a distant theatre of operations would appear to be an ideal solution. This was the American solution to a problem: "Up and Out."

It was not until the publication of *Wedemeyer Reports!* in 1958 that the dutiful soldier gave any public hint of his disappointment about his transfer to Asia or leveled any criticism at the military and civilian leadership:[28]

> I pondered how fate had now decreed that I should be pitted against the Japanese instead of the Germans. Often when working in the

War Plans Division back in Washington I had hoped that one day I would be given an assignment in Europe. Having studied German tactics, I hardly expected to fight the war in the Far East.[29]

If the Washington press corps and the political establishment are considered the ultimate "rumor mills," the military runs a close second, and the gossip of how and why Wedemeyer was mysteriously transferred to Asia in 1943 was rampant; yet hard information was slow in leaking out to the average American. The first public notice of Wedemeyer's shift to Asia was reported by Hanson W. Baldwin in *The New York Times* on October 30, 1944, in an article entitled "Behind the Removal of General Stilwell," in which he expressed surprise about the move and opined that it would likely be some time before the full story was revealed. He was equally dumbfounded as to why a man was selected as his replacement with a "background of experience more associated with Germany than with China."[30] The same seeming lack of interest or lack of knowledge permeated the academic community, and the transfer, though thoroughly reported, was not explored in detail. Perhaps the first academic to raise a question was Captain Alexander H. Von Plinsky, III who, in a compelling 1991 Master's thesis, concluded that the transfer "was a decision made by President Roosevelt that begs further explanation."[31] No one seemed to have picked up on Von Plinsky's suggestion.

Just before leaving for Asia, Wedemeyer was asked by Harry Hopkins, with Marshall's approval, to brief former President Herbert Hoover on American war strategy (with the notable exception of the Atomic Bomb). Wedemeyer greatly respected Hoover and was entirely comfortable sharing with him some very private thoughts that few others would have heard. He told Hoover about his new assignment, stating:

> I explained also that I respected the British viewpoint [about an early cross-channel invasion] but couldn't, as an American, agree with it. Obviously they wanted to adopt a strategy that would favor their empire—but I was interested in protecting American interests. This brought me to cross-purposes with the British. I explained that *I felt that the British were doing what they could to undermine me in the War Department, and probably would ultimately have me sent out to the field, away from planning responsibilities in Washington.* Mr. Hoover understood and agreed that the British could brook no interference with the realization of their policies.[32] (emphasis added)

Otherwise, Wedemeyer kept his opinion to himself, though he did confide privately in letters to his former close associate, Colonel Ivan D. Yeaton.[33]

In 1965, Wedemeyer was asked whether the chapter in *Wedemeyer Reports!* that he titled "Eased Out to Asia" was indicative of his belief that his attendance at the German War College, his knowledge of German, and his friendship with many of the German Generals was responsible for the transfer. Wedemeyer responded that he did not believe that this entered into the situation at all, asserting his consistent position that it was "policy differences," especially with the British, that were the cause.[34] Twenty-five years after the war, he admitted openly that he was confident the British wanted him removed from the Planning Group.[35] In 1983 he expanded his thoughts to Eiler in a published article:

> There were rumors in Washington to that effect [that he was sent to Asia because of his stance on the 1943 cross-channel operation] at the time. I discounted them because I could not believe that Mr. Churchill would attempt to influence Allied strategy in such a manner. Since the war, however, much evidence has come to light suggesting he was indeed capable of such maneuvers.[36]

Wedemeyer never implicated Roosevelt and, unlike his father-in-law, personally held Churchill in high regard. *Wedemeyer Reports!* recounts numerous cordial encounters, both public and private, including a number *after* his assignment to Asia. Not once did Wedemeyer relate any unpleasantness, except when the subject of European strategy arose, and that seemed to incite the Prime Minister to "mental and emotional fits."[37]

OTHER EVIDENCE SURFACES

Wedemeyer received a remarkable letter dated December 27, 1968 from Col. Orren L. Jones, USAF Res. (Ret.) which gave him even more reason to suspect the British had conspired to have him removed to Asia (letter Appendix III). During the period 1943–1945, Jones was an alternate on the Joint Logistics Committee of the Joint Chiefs of Staff and privy to many secret and classified documents. Jones attended the Cairo Conference and became a close associate of General Patrick Tansey, then the Army member of the Joint Logistics Committee, who went on to become Deputy Director of the CIA. As Jones says, "General Tansey would frequently call for me to discuss many sensitive and important items on the Agenda. . . . He told me that

General Wedemeyer was one of the few officers on duty who was well versed in the politics of many nations . . . spoke many languages, *and was always a threat to the British because of his vast knowledge as to their methods of operations and intent. . . .* General Tansey told me that Sir John Dill and Lt. General Freddie Morgan . . . *were intent on getting Wedemeyer out of Washington, and into a place where he could have little impact upon the operations and objectives of the British.*" (emphasis added)

Jones further said that General Morgan made his views and recommendations known to Churchill, "who . . . on a political level, appealed to Roosevelt for a special assignment . . ." Wedemeyer acknowledged the letter from Jones and agreed with his conclusions.[38]

Another convincing and perhaps even more telling bit of evidence supporting a calculated British effort to move Wedemeyer to Asia comes from a 1971 letter to him from Air Force historian Dr. Murray Green, discussing the testimony of General Sam Anderson, who later served as Wedemeyer's Air Deputy.[39] Anderson made it quite clear that Churchill decided to have Wedemeyer moved out after Trident, a meeting in Washington in June 1943, where the British at last agreed to OVERLORD. It appears that Wedemeyer strongly threatened that if Churchill did not support a cross-channel invasion, the Americans would send supplies earmarked for England to the Pacific, and spoke with such authority that the Prime Minister had him transferred:

[Churchill] didn't want Arnold and Marshall to go to the Pacific. He was afraid if they did, that the materiel and personnel that he wanted to come to England and eventually go to Europe, would instead go to the Pacific . . . *And Wedemeyer did so well in that meeting that Churchill got him sent to India after the meeting was over.* (emphasis added)[40]

As it turned out, Wedemeyer indeed played a pivotal role in getting the invasion enacted. For his efforts he was "rewarded" with a second star and transfer to Asia. In the end, Wedemeyer's transfer was a net loss for the European theater, depriving a brilliant strategist from participating in the final planning stages of the invasion that he had originally conceived.

WEDEMEYER MOVES TO ASIA

Wedemeyer joined Mountbatten in Asia in October 1943 and found him intelligent, personable, and cooperative. The deteriorating relationship between Stilwell and Chiang that exacerbated an already serious situation of lack of coordination among the Americans, Chinese, and British was a continuing problem. Efforts by Mountbatten to heal the rift were unsuccessful. Another source of conflict was the debate over the completion of the Ledo Road, a central mission of CBI.[41] Wedemeyer had serious reservations about the basic premise, that construction of the road allegedly could facilitate the delivery of 100,000 tons of supplies to China a month. In his opinion it was an impractical and costly operation on a route beset by landslides, washouts, and monsoons that necessitated prohibitive amounts of time, labor, and materiel to keep the road in operation. This is one question on which Wedemeyer and Churchill both agreed. Churchill, who was negative about every operation in Burma, opined that by the time the road was finished the need for it would have passed.[42] However, the construction was Stilwell's pet project and, since it was supported by Marshall, the Combined Chiefs of Staff, Roosevelt, and Churchill, Wedemeyer had no choice but to dutifully support the effort.

During his time under Mountbatten, Wedemeyer drew up plans for several military operations involving the coordination of British and Chinese forces that never came to fruition. These included AXIOM,[43] an amphibious assault on Burma, and CULVERIN, an attack against Sumatra, followed by a push against Singapore, then northward along the coast of China.

Wedemeyer also made several trips outside the theatre as liaison to the Combined Chiefs of Staff. In December 1943, he accompanied Mountbatten to Cairo to attend the SEXTANT summit, where the only decision that directly affected SEAC was a short-lived commitment to dedicate additional forces and shipping to support AXIOM. Chiang Kai-shek and Madame Chiang were in attendance and returned to China highly pleased. After SEXTANT, the remaining members of the conference departed for Teheran to meet with Stalin, who refused to include the Chinese leaders, giving the excuse that he was technically neutral. This was the first summit that the Soviet leader attended, ironically invoking issues of health to justify a location near the Soviet Union that forced the frail Roosevelt to travel seven thousand miles. To Churchill's chagrin, Stalin was vehement that OVERLORD be undertaken in the spring of 1944. Roosevelt concurred, and Churchill, still clinging to hopes of an alternative operation in the Balkans, was grudgingly compelled to go along.

As a consequence of the decisions made at Teheran, equipment and supplies that had been earmarked for Burma would now be sent to England.

Commitments to Chiang made at Cairo were withdrawn, and Wedemeyer was designated to deliver the bad news, fully aware of the terrible sacrifices Chiang had been making since 1937.[44]

In February 1944, Wedemeyer went to London to present the plans for CULVERIN to the British Chiefs of Staff. He learned ahead of time that although Churchill favored the operation, the British planners did not. He was given a polite but cool reception and the operation was cancelled.

Stilwell bore a deep resentment for Wedemeyer as a result of his contrary views about retaking Burma and his opposition to construction of the Ledo Road. In fact, the visionary Wedemeyer's doubts about the ultimate utility of the Ledo Road proved accurate. As General Chennault had predicted, supplies carried over the Ledo Road at no time approached tonnage levels of supplies airlifted monthly into China over the Hump. In July 1945, the last full month before the end of the war, 71,000 tons of supplies were flown over the Hump, compared to only 6,000 tons using the Ledo Road.

As his recall was being pressed in the spring and summer of 1944, Stilwell did not want to be replaced by a man he characterized as "the world's most pompous prick,"[45] exclaiming just before the ax fell: "Good God—to be ousted in favor of Wedemeyer—that would be a disgrace."[46]

In October 1944, Wedemeyer received orders to replace Stilwell as commander of United States forces in China, where he would have his hands full between rehabilitating both the precarious military situation and the relationship with Generalissimo Chiang Kai-shek that his predecessor had torpedoed. He was replaced as deputy to Mountbatten by Lieutenant General Raymond Albert Wheeler. Burma operations were returned to British command.[47]

Writing to Roosevelt on November 20, 1944, in a friendly letter signed "Dickie," Mountbatten praised Stilwell for his leadership in coordinating American, British, and Chinese forces on the Ledo front and bemoaned "because it meant I lost my beloved Al Wedemeyer, who has been such a tower of strength to me during the last year."[48] Roosevelt responded on December 9th that "Wedemeyer has inherited a tough problem."[49] The new China commander was up to the task.

CHAPTER 8

CHINA COMMANDER

*What lies behind us and what lies before us are tiny
matters compared to what lies within us.*
—Ralph Waldo Emerson

After Wedemeyer received a telegram on October 27, 1944 from George Marshall directing him to assume command of the China theatre, his immediate reaction was that he was once again being shoved in the wrong direction. Many, including Wedemeyer at this point, believed that "China was a graveyard for American officials, military and diplomatic . . . nothing could be done with the Chinese, they just wouldn't cooperate; they led you into difficulties with your own government as well as theirs." Stilwell had played no small part in creating and reinforcing that attitude, not only to his own subordinates but to the American diplomats who lived in China, the journalists who worked there, and in his many communications to the War Department and especially General Marshall. Accordingly, Wedemeyer approached his new assignment very much influenced by the only source of information available about the situation in China: that supplied by his predecessor and reported in the press.

There was no shortage of claimants who professed to be responsible for Wedemeyer's new assignment. Ambassador Patrick J. Hurley and Vice President Wallace topped the list.[1] Captain Joseph Alsop, a distant Roosevelt relative and brother of a prominent Washington columnist, then serving in China as part of General Chennault's command, also claimed responsibility for making the recommendation.[2]

The new commander entered into his assignment with trepidation. Not only the military, but columnists and political pundits in America shared Wedemeyer's assessment that China was a dead end. Drew Pearson ridiculed the new assignment in the *Washington Times*, describing the General as spending his time "reading Carl Sandburg's Abraham Lincoln ... foisted into a comic opera Hollywood setting with liveried servants at [his] beck and call while the foot soldier was slogging it out in the steaming jungles of Burma."[3]

At the time of Stilwell's removal, China had been on the strategic back burner for at least twelve months.[4] By October of 1944, American forces had effectively put the Japanese navy and air force out of business with victories at the Battle of Leyte Gulf and in the Philippines. Continuing advances from island to island contributed to the reduction of China's strategic role in the war to simply maintaining a second front to prevent Japanese troops from being diverted to the Pacific.

Wedemeyer barely had time to place the message in his dispatch case in preparation for his flight to China before a second telegram arrived informing him that the China-Burma-India Theatre had been divided into two and that he was to assume the dual role of commander of the new China theatre and Chief of Staff to Chiang Kai-shek, while his friend Mountbatten was to remain in command of India and Burma. Despite the bifurcation there would still be some overlap.

Stilwell's recall was very unpopular in the American press. Just after returning from Chunking, *New York Times* foreign correspondent Brooks Atkinson commented:

> The decision to relieve General Stillwell represents the political triumph of a moribund, anti-democratic regime that is more concerned with maintaining its political supremacy than in driving the Japanese out of China. America is now committed ... to support a regime that has become increasingly unpopular and distrusted in China, that maintains three secret police services and concentration camps for political prisoners, that stifles free speech and resists democratic forces ... [T]he Chinese communists ... have good armies that are now fighting guerrilla warfare against the Japanese in North China.... The Generalissimo regards these armies as the chief threat to his supremacy ... has made no sincere attempt to arrange at least a truce with them for the duration of the war.... [N]o diplomatic genius could have overcome the Generalissimo's basic unwillingness to risk his armies in battle with the Japanese.[5]

There were many others who agreed that Chiang was resisting the "democratic forces" of the Chinese Communists. The prevailing atmosphere in Washington was far more sympathetic to Stilwell and Mao Zedong than Chiang. The pro-Communist viewpoint had been gradually taking hold in America, and Atkinson mirrored the viewpoint of many others. Edgar Snow, a writer embedded for months with Mao Zedong, was thoroughly propagandized during interviews with senior Communists and provided with highly selective documents, all decidedly complimentary to the Communists, which he trumpeted in his glowing 1939 testimonial,[6] *Red Star Over China.*[7] Agnes Smedly wrote a similarly complimentary account.[8] Both books received glowing reports in the American press that was fed rave reviews by the Communist-infiltrated Institute of Pacific Relations. The books were widely read in the United States and added immeasurably to the false public perception that the Chinese Communists were the true hope for China's future.

One of the few American journalists who opposed this viewpoint was ironically a former Communist, Whittaker Chambers,[9] a senior editor of *Time,* who understood the motives of Mao Zedong and had the full support of his powerful publisher, Henry Luce, a strong advocate of Chiang. In a prophetic 1944 *Time* essay highly critical of the Atkinson article, he wrote:

If the rift in the U.S.-Chinese relations were not quickly repaired, both China and the U.S. would be the losers. For China, the loss would be great. For the U.S. it might be catastrophic. For if Chiang Kai-shek were compelled to collaborate with [the Communists] on Yenan's terms, or if he were forced to lift his military blockade of the Chinese Communist area, a Communist China might soon replace Chunking. And unlike Chunking, a Communist China (with its 450 million people) would turn to Russia (with its 200 million people) rather than to the U.S. (with its 130 million) as an international collaborator.[10]

WEDEMEYER'S ARRIVAL IN CHINA

The Nationalists were overjoyed to be rid of Stilwell and planned an elaborate reception for Wedemeyer upon his arrival from India at the Kunming airport, but their welcome met with an unanticipated comic wrinkle:

The top Chinese officials in Kunming and the ranking Chinese and American army officers went in an imposing cavalcade of staff cars to the airport to greet the new American army commander with due dignity and ceremony. They watched the skies for a plane with an escort of fighters. When a lone transport barged in, the control tower waved it off to a far corner where it wouldn't interfere with the imminent ceremonies.

A tall, spare man in a uniform bare of decorations emerged from the transport. A truck full of Chinese laborers came by, and the soldier thumbed a ride across the field. Alighting, he walked over to the flustered bevy of frock coats and brass hats and with outstretched hand and genial smile announced, "My name's Wedemeyer. Glad to be here."[11]

This unassuming and unconventional approach to command typified Wedemeyer. The same article continued:

[Wedemeyer] shunned pomp and circumstance, kept his headquarters simple. If nobody else had beer or Coca-Cola, neither did headquarters. The General announced that he would go out to dinner only once a week. He soon found that the Generalissimo shared his simple tastes, and they passed the word that they wished official dinners limited to four courses—a mere snack in Chungking.[12]

One cannot imagine how a pompous MacArthur, Patton, or Montgomery would have responded to being transported without escort in a modest plane and reduced to hitching a ride on a truck full of Chinese coolies!

Wedemeyer admitted that when he first arrived in China he did not fully understand the dilemma facing the Nationalists[13] and that, like Marshall, he had been influenced by Stilwell's negative assessment of both Chiang and the military situation.[14] However, he had never accepted Stilwell's point of view that the Communists were China's last best hope, and it did not take Wedemeyer long to make a new assessment of the situation which differed markedly from Stilwell's.[15]

When Wedemeyer arrived at Stilwell's headquarters, he was dismayed to discover that his predecessor had departed without seeing him and had not left a single briefing paper for his guidance. He met with staff officers but learned little, since Stilwell had apparently kept everything in his "hip pocket."[16] There were no written plans or records of prior or anticipated operations,[17] nor any insights into any problems that Wedemeyer might confront. This was not surprising given the fact that Stilwell had spent the last five months in Burma in the jungle fighting the Japanese, nearly incommunicado with his headquarters.

Wedemeyer was commencing his new assignment with a *tabula rasa,* and it seemed evident to him that Stilwell had deliberately made his job more difficult. Wedemeyer was justifiably chagrined at the egregious violation of military protocol but kept his views to himself, except for a few intimate confidants, until he published *Wedemeyer Reports!* where he leveled his first harsh public criticism at his predecessor for this breach.[18] No less than General Douglas MacArthur was on record in agreement. After his recall from Korea by President Truman in the Spring of 1951, he testified before the Joint Senate Committee on Armed Services and Foreign Relations, and was asked by Senator Henry Styles Bridges (R-New Hampshire) as to whether "...it is customary in the recall ... of a commander, to do it in such a manner that he will be able to turn over his command to his successor and brief him upon the current status of the operation?" MacArthur succinctly replied: "Unquestionably!"[19]

Unlike Stilwell, the diplomatic Wedemeyer was not one to publicly disparage another commander. However, it did not take him long to confidentially vent his anger in a letter to his father-in-law three months later:

> My overall estimate of American assistance here the past two years indicates that my predecessor made a botch of the job. He spent so much time in the jungles in Upper Burma commanding a few battalions and acquiring a great deal of publicity as a great tactician that he neglected sorely the responsibilities inherent in his position as Chief of Staff to the Generalissimo and as Commanding General of American Forces in the China Theater. General Chennault explained to me that he never received any directives from Theater Headquarters and [he] was practically operating a private army wholly uncoordinated with the ground effort. When I tried to determine where all of the Americans were in China, and what they were doing, it was such a jumbled mess that even today, over one month later I have not yet received that information.[20]

He reiterated his frustration in 1972 in a letter to Colonel Ivan Downes Yeaton, his close associate while in China, urging him to write his own book and offering to give him all the assistance he needed. Undoubtedly Wedemeyer was upset by the very negative manner in which Barbara Tuchman had portrayed him in her just published *Sand Against the Wind*. (Also known as *Stilwell and the American Experience in China*.) Wedemeyer could be forgiven if in urging his close friend and associate to write a book he hoped and expected to get some support:

> To be absolutely frank, Ivan, I cannot bring myself to stating factually the conditions that I found in the China Theater, for they were so terrible, not only as to organization, assignment of responsibility and delegating authority but also spiritually. It would be interpreted as self-serving, and perhaps rightfully, if I were to outline the conditions that my staff and I found. Practically no one would interpret my writing as constructive, particularly in the light of Barbara Tuchman's book, Brig. General Dorn's book, and the contributions made by Barrett and Service.[21]

Stillwell's biggest concern as he left his command seemed to be "whether he would be made a scapegoat for the fracas that followed." His fears were allayed when he was universally greeted as a hero, and he was even more gratified to find that Wedemeyer was the butt of criticism. The historians deified Stilwell for his "walk out" and retaking of Burma, placing him on a high pedestal. Conversely, Wedemeyer suffered by comparison.

One of Wedemeyer's first observations was the growing strength of the Communist forces in China. He would have liked to lend as much assistance as possible to the Nationalists, but his orders specifically enjoined him from using United States resources "for suppression of civil strife." In other words, he was not to get involved in the conflict between Chiang and Mao Zedong.[22] Fighting Communism was not on the radar screen of American policymakers.

Militarily, it was China's darkest hour. The capital at Chungking was in serious danger of being lost. The mauled and malnourished Chinese Army seemed to have little fight left. With the exception of the campaign in Burma, they had not defeated the Japanese in any battle. While Stilwell was off in Burma, the Japanese had concentrated twelve divisions south of Changsha intending to overrun Kunming, the only remaining terminus available to receive the trickle of supplies coming in over the Hump. Preventing this catastrophe was of the utmost importance, for if the air supply route to China was lost there would be no point in maintaining troops in Burma, since their main function was to protect the supply route from the south against an advance by the Japanese. The Ledo Road was not yet complete and there was no other source of supply.

Recognizing the impending disaster, and with Chiang's blessing, Wedemeyer placed the protection of the air depot at Kunming above the defense of the capital. Although Mountbatten was not happy about it, two of his American-trained Chinese divisions in Burma were urgently commandeered and flown to China to prevent the loss of Kunming. Meantime, serious consideration was given to evacuating Chunking.[23] The situation was so perilous that in early December 1944, the American Embassy received repeated warnings that American civilians should make preparations to leave China.[24] Under Wedemeyer's direction, however, and with the assistance of the reinforcements, the Japanese advance was stopped.

Stilwell had left relations between the American military and the Chinese in tatters, and Wedemeyer took the reins to exert the strong leadership needed to reverse the prevailing atmosphere of mutual distrust that permeated the entire command. Ambassador Clarence Gauss astounded him when he declared, "We should pull up the plug and let the whole Chinese Government go down the drain."[25] Stilwell's Chief of Staff, Major General Thomas Hearn, shared this negative attitude, viewing the Chinese as "noncommittal and deceitful." Wedemeyer learned from Hearn that there were regular Thursday meetings at the Chinese headquarters to discuss operations, but Stilwell had rarely attended, sending a subordinate in his place because he considered them a "tea drinking, time consuming farce."[26] To Wedemeyer's mind, Hearn, or any other officer who shared this view, was an impediment to the command and had to be removed. Little time was lost in finding appropriate replacements. In an effort to build bridges, he instituted a new program at his headquarters with compulsory attendance for all senior Chinese and American officers.[27] After a few weeks, a noticeably more cooperative attitude was evident, and soon the Generalissimo, getting positive feedback about the meetings, began to attend [pic. 29].

Wedemeyer wrote Marshall shortly after his arrival:

My approach to the Generalissimo has been friendly, direct and firm. I believe that he likes and respects me now. . . . I have been uniformly careful not to take action that conflicts with agreed plans. I have been uniformly careful to massage his ego and place myself in an advisory position so that he will not lose face.[28]

In time, Chiang came to rely even more heavily on his American chief of staff:

> The Generalissimo often asks advice concerning political matters involving other countries as well as China's internal affairs. I have emphasized tactfully to him that advice under such circumstances is given no official cognizance. At times his trust and dependence are almost childlike.[29]

Wedemeyer found himself immediately and singularly responsible for the conduct of military operations far from supply sources and with the lowest priority of all the theatres of war. To make matters worse, he was dismayed to discover that Chiang, who considered himself an effective military strategist, had no effective plans for either attack or defense.[30] Wedemeyer next took a hard look at Stilwell's staff and the condition of the Chinese army. He found the staff's morale at low ebb, and he was shocked at the condition of the Chinese troops. Aside from military supplies, the army was in desperate need of food and medical care. Over half of the soldiers were undernourished and seventy percent were ill. Stilwell had left his troops in a deplorable state of affairs. Wedemeyer vividly recounted the events in 1976:

> I went to China with high hopes. . . . I was determined to do everything in my power to weld the Chinese into a strong combined effort which would defeat the common enemy and lay the foundations of a better world for all. Much to my concern, I found on my arrival . . . that relations between the Americans and Chinese . . . were even worse than I had been told. . . . I had no doubt that the time had come for a fresh start.[31]

According to Theodore White, in 1938 the Chinese army on paper consisted of four million men. For the next six years the government allegedly conscripted a million and a half men per year. By 1944 that would theoretically have meant there were 12,000,000 on their roster, but there were still only 4,000,000! The eight million "missing" had simply vanished through sickness, hunger, or desertion, either to their home or to the enemy.[32] Conscription was brutal and corrupt. "Press gangs" roamed the country seizing any man they spotted.[33] The pervasiveness of corruption permitted those with sufficient resources to purchase exemptions. Wedemeyer also realized that the Chinese soldiers needed respect from the American military. He was appalled by the disdain of the Americans and announced that lack of friendliness would be cause for dismissal. This, among other reasons, caused him to immediately relieve two Major Generals, four Brigadiers, and twelve Colonels.

The new commander's sensitivity to Chinese culture dictated that, as a first order of business, in order to optimize performance, the unique problem of "saving face" of the commanders of the Chinese army had to be addressed. Wedemeyer installed a plan whereby each division was led by a Chinese general with an American military advisor attached. Procedures were implemented to tactfully take into account the eventuality that the Chinese commander might disagree with the advice of the American. Stilwell's "solution" was to compel obedience upon the delivery of an "order" to the Chinese officer, from whom he expected immediate compliance, such as he could expect in the American army. This had proved not only ineffective, but a source of immense friction and resentment. Wedemeyer's innovative solution was for the American commander to accept the disagreement without rancor, and for the two commanders to jointly institute a rapid oral appeal process going up the line of command, if necessary all the way to the Generalissimo, and then back down again to the local commander. The command then would have the appearance of the full force of the Chinese army. There was nothing comparable in the American army. The solution wasn't perfect, and there were occasions when Wedemeyer had to give orders "in the name of Chiang Kai-shek," but it was probably the most novel and positive step that had been instituted since the arrival of the Americans, and it went a long way toward establishing harmony.

There were about 350 Chinese divisions of 10,000 men each (compared with 15,000 in an American division) when Wedemeyer assumed command. Knowing he would never be able to obtain sufficient equipment and supplies for all of them, he decided to focus on about forty, satisfied that with this number of well trained and equipped divisions he would be able to drive the Japanese from China.[34] By the spring of 1945, thirty-nine newly trained, well supplied Chinese divisions were combat ready. The new "War Room" was fully equipped with easels and maps and accurately depicted troop dispositions. But for the end of the war in August 1945, Wedemeyer would likely have succeeded not only in being able to command his first combat operation but, if successful, the plan would have opened Chinese seaports for the first time since hostilities commenced in 1937. As Keith Eiler noted:

Observers have generally agreed that the results of these initiatives were outstandingly positive. The Generalissimo, strengthened and genuinely appreciative, sought earnestly to cooperate. The Chinese staffs responded with enthusiasm. A sense of common purpose was achieved . . . the effectiveness of the Chinese army improved; the Japanese offensive was contained; plans were laid for further operations.[35]

Among the other areas where Wedemeyer felt Stilwell had been deficient was his lack of attention to military decorations. Recommendations for promotions and medals sat unread on his desk. Suggestions for an oak-leaf cluster for Merrill's Marauders' heroic stand at Nhpum Ga were dismissed with a curt "spend more time fighting and less time worrying about promotions and awards." (Eventually, each and every member of the unit received the Bronze Star for gallantry.)[36] Realizing their immense morale-building value, Wedemeyer immediately facilitated a host of decorations and promotions that had been ignored by his predecessor. He also held weekly press conferences that were usually attended by about 50 reporters. To modestly de-emphasize his own name, reports were issued as "China Theatre Communiqués."[37]

With full knowledge of the true objectives of the Communists to take over China and destroy the Nationalist forces, Wedemeyer viewed the American policy of extorting collaboration from Chiang in exchange for aid as short-sighted and fraught with danger. He encouraged both military and economic aid to the Nationalists, as well as strong measures to curb corruption.

The extent to which the Communists fought the Japanese has been a source of disagreement among historians. Mao always claimed that he did the most fighting, and Chiang did little. Wedemeyer held a different view, maintaining that the Communists did little fighting against the Japanese and were no help to him. "No Chinese Communist forces," he wrote, "fought in any major battles of the Sino-Japanese war," adding: "I knew that Mao Zedong, Zhou Enlai, and the other Chinese Communists were not interested in fighting the Japanese because their main concern was to occupy the territory which the Nationalist forces evacuated in their retreat."[38]

Far from viewing the Japanese as "enemies," the Communists saw in them a real opportunity to defeat Chiang. Years after the defeat of the Nationalists, when some Japanese visitors apologized to Mao Zedong for starting a war with China, Mao instead of accepting the apology, *thanked* the

1. General Wedemeyer with sons Robert, Albert and Mrs. Wedemeyer. *Hoover Institution, Stanford, California*

2. Wedemeyer's mother and father, Margaret Coady Wedemeyer and Albert Anthony Wedemeyer (undated). *Hoover Institution, Stanford, California*

3. *Left:* General Wedemeyer's sons Albert and Robert, 1951. *Hoover Institution, Stanford, California*

4. *Below:* General Wedemeyer's wedding, Corregidor, Philippine Islands, February 5, 1925. *Front row, left to right:* Miss Cecil Hart, Miss Barbara King, Miss Peggy Embick, the bride and groom, General and Mrs Wedemeyer, Miss Dorothy Rosenstock, Miss Nora Hero, Miss Adeline Kendall; *rear row, left to right:* Lt. C.R. Gross, Lt. J.H. Warren, Capt. A.J. McFarland, Lt. R.P. Ovenshine, Mrs. S.D. Embick, Lt. C.E. O'Connor, Colonel Stanley D. Embick, Chaplin E.W. Weber, Mr. G.L. Byroade, and Capt. F.H. Hastings; *foreground:* flower girl Betty Lou Dingley. *Hoover Institution, Stanford, California*

5. Wedemeyer and some of his classmates at the German Kriegsakademia, September 3, 1937. Picture taken at maneuver grounds, Grafenwohr (near Bayreuth). *Left to Right:* Major Amano, Japan; Capt. Fusano, Italy; Major Gonzales, Argentina; Major Asim, Turkey; Colonel Poppoff, Bulgaria; Major Speth, Germany; Major Lopez, Argentina; Major Chou, China; Major Avalos, Argentina; Major Chung, China; Capt. Wedemeyer, United States; Major Weinstein, Argentina.

Hoover Institution, Stanford, California

6. United States and British meet at Casablanca, December 1942. *Left to right:* Admiral Ernest King, USN; General George Marshall, USA; General Henry Arnold, USAF; General J.R. Deane, USA; Brig. Vivian Dykes, Br.; General Wedemeyer, USA; General Hastings Ismay, Br; Admiral Lord Louis Mountbatten, Royal Navy; Sir Dudley Pound, Br, 1st Sea Lord; Sir Alan Brooke, Br.; Sir Charles Portal, RAF.
Hoover Institution, Stanford, California

7. Allied War Conference, Quebec, Canada, August 1943. *Left to right:* Maj General T.T. Handy, Operations Division; Brig. General Wedemeyer, United States Joint Planner; Maj. General M.S. Fairchild; and Vice Admiral Russell William, Strategic Survey Committee. *Hoover Institution, Stanford, California*

8. General Patrick Hurley, United States Ambassador to China, a close friend and confidant of General Wedemeyer. *Hoover Institution, Stanford, California*

9. Colonel Ivan D. Yeaton, United States representative at the Dixie Mission to Yenan China, designated by General Wedemeyer. *Hoover Institution, Stanford, California*

10. General Stanley Dunbar Embick. (undated). *Hoover Institution, Stanford, California*

11. Allied Conference, Quebec, Canada August 23, 1943. *Seated left to right*: United States Combined Chiefs of Staff—General George C. Marshall, USA; General H.H. Arnold, USAF; Brig General J.R. Deane, sect to Chiefs of Staff; Admiral Ernest King, USN; Admiral William Leahy, USN (British officers not named). *Hoover Institution, Stanford, California*

12. Chicago Daily Tribune, December 4, 1941, front page. Courtesy Chicago Daily Tribune

13. Combined Chiefs of Staff meeting, Casablanca Conference, December 1942. *Left to right:* General George Marshall, General Henry Arnold, General J.R. Dean, General Albert Wedemeyer, General Hastings Ismay, Admiral Dudley Pound, General Alan Brooke, and Sir John Dill. *Hoover Institution, Stanford, California*

14. General Albert Wedemeyer and General Hastings Ismay, Br. at Combined Chiefs of Staff meeting, Casablanca, January 1943. *Hoover Institution, Stanford, California*

TIME

THE WEEKLY NEWSMAGAZINE

Boris Chaliapin

GENERAL WEDEMEYER, U.S. COMMANDER IN CHINA
One road to Tokyo runs through the mainland of Asia.

15. Cover *Time* magazine—General Wedemeyer, June 4, 1945. *Courtesy Time magazine*

Japanese for "lending a big hand," commenting, "I would rather thank the Japanese warlords." Without them occupying much of China, "we would still be in the mountains today."[39] Wedemeyer was convinced that the Nationalists, unlike the Communists, were sincere in their desire to fight the Japanese. They had been doing so almost single-handedly since 1937 with no more than a trickle of aid.

While Stillwell went to great lengths to disparage Wedemeyer in the widely circulated *Stilwell Papers* edited by Theodore White and published posthumously, his more tactful successor never returned the criticism during his active service. Years later, Wedemeyer revealed in a book published exclusively for veterans of the CBI that he had telegrammed General Marshall to recommend Stilwell for his fourth star for his performance in Burma, particularly the recapture of Myitkyina.[40] The book *Where I Came In* is a rare, beautifully embossed, imitation leather-bound limited edition (1500 copies) edited by Lt. Colonel Robert T. Kadel, U.S. Army Air Force. Almost 400 pages in length, the book contains many color photographs and short biographies of many of the men and women who served in the CBI, as well as histories of the various campaigns and much more. It is a remarkable, loving tribute by one former service man who pays honor to all his former comrades. Naturally, General Stilwell is lavishly praised. General Wedemeyer is also prominently mentioned, and since he was still alive at the time of publication, he was asked to make some comments. What Wedemeyer said is a masterpiece of indirection: Here is his inscription in the book:

> It was difficult to succeed General Stilwell . . . I could understand, after serving there two years and after having intimate contact with Chinese officials, that General Stilwell's complete disinterest in diplomatic niceties and his innate desire "to get the job done" would bring about conflicts with certain Chinese.[41]

Given Stilwell's enormous personal popularity among his officers and enlisted men, as well as civilians who served in the area, this would not be the proper forum for Wedemeyer to let his hair down and speak his mind about Stilwell; yet Wedemeyer was no hypocrite and could not bring himself to lie about his feelings and heap praise on the man who spent so much time disparaging him. Hence, his very careful and guarded compliments on getting "the job done" and a half-hearted compliment (or is it a criticism?) on his disregard of "diplomatic niceties."[42] This is Wedemeyer at his best as a superb craftsman of words. To describe a Theatre Commander, the representative of his country in a foreign land, one whose primary mission is to relate to and interact with foreign leaders, as disregarding the most important part of his job, *i.e.* the "diplomatic niceties," is not likely to be intended as a compliment. Yet a quick reading would not pick up this carefully nuanced meaning. It is likely that Wedemeyer thought carefully before he submitted the statement.

Until his negative assessment of Stilwell in *Wedemeyer Reports!* Wedemeyer never publically disparaged Stilwell. However, in a private December 1944 letter to General Embick, shortly after his arrival in China, he did not hold back his true feelings:

> When I reported here the first week of November, I expected to find a headquarters at least fairly efficient. Actually, it was terrible. . . . I am sorry to tell you that [Stilwell], in my opinion had neither the character nor the ability to be a good regimental commander, yet the powers that be saw fit to make him a four-star general and to heroize him in the press. *One day the facts may be known, and he will be the most deflated hero in the history of our fine army.*[43] (emphasis added)

While a junior in the War Plans Division, Wedemeyer had to temper his anti-Communist agenda, but in China, now with three stars on his shoulders, there was less of a need to pull punches. He held the strong opinion that a Communist takeover of China would be the worst possible outcome, and he sought to prevent it by recommending constructive measures to aid the Nationalists. In order to keep tabs on the Communists, he appointed his close friend Colonel Ivan Yeaton, formerly a military attaché in Moscow, to the United States Observation Group in Yenan, the primary Communist outpost in the north. In turn, Yeaton supplied Wedemeyer with detailed reports of subversive activities. Wedemeyer also made a point of conferring with Mao Zedong and Zhou Enlai in their headquarters in Chunking, and in his numerous conversations with the Communist rulers he confirmed and reinforced his belief that the Chinese Communists had as their principle objective converting China to Communism with all the available help they could obtain from the Soviets. Destruction of the Nationalists was their most important objective.[44] These conversations were often brutally frank and heated. Hostility between Wedemeyer and Mao[45] flared up on more than one occasion. Most notably, after the Japanese surrender, the American general bluntly confronted Mao and Zhou over the pretense of "agrarian reform" they had put forth as a means to end poverty and advance humanitarian principles, accusing them of using it as subterfuge to achieve power, deny freedom of speech, religion, and governmental self-determination, and to imprison and torture dissenters. Directly to their faces he charged Mao Zedong, Zhou Enlai and their troops with the murder and mutilation of John Birch, an American officer, and "with more than a hint of a threat" warned them that the United States was considering bringing atomic bombs and up to a half-million troops into China.[46] Of course, Wedemeyer had no authority to make such provocative declarations, and it can only be "explained" as a rare lapse of judgment from an otherwise extremely careful wordsmith. But the statement did have its intended effect. Unaccustomed to being spoken to in such an accusatory tone, the Communist leaders were dumbstruck. They excitedly sought to deny the charges, but in their rebuttal fell into the rhetorical error of actually *admitting* the charge by seeking to justify their conduct as necessary in their struggle against the Nationalists, and in the process, directly contradicting the propaganda of "democracy" and "non-violence" they had been advocating to American politicians and journalists.

The effectiveness of the Chinese Communist propaganda campaign in swaying the American public is evidenced by an article written by the influential columnist Drew Pearson in June 1945, after the arrest of three pro-Communist activists who were charged with stealing secret government documents and giving them to the editors of the pro-Communist *Amerasia* magazine. Amazingly, Pearson justified the treasonous theft of the secret documents on the grounds that the United States was "backing the wrong horse":

> There is a lot more than meets the eye behind the arrest of two State Department officials and one Naval officer on a charge of passing out secret documents to magazine writers. Chief factor behind it is the intense cut-throat rivalry between two Chinese factions— Chiang Kai-shek's War Lords in the South of China, and the *so-called Chinese Communists, actually an agrarian party*, in the north. Mixed up in all this is the action of the Chinese Secret Service operating under cover in the USA against anyone opposed to Chiang Kai-shek. . . . It so happens that all three of the young Far Eastern experts arrested . . . feel ardently that the USA is *backing the wrong horse* in China. They feel that the northern Chinese Government [*sic*] is much more representative of the Chinese people, has done

more fighting against Japan and that Chiang Kai-shek is chiefly an important prisoner of his own southern War Lords. Moreover, these three are not alone in this belief. General Stilwell emphatically believed it and was *ousted from China as a result.* John R. Davies, Secretary of the American Embassy, also believed it and was ousted ... Also John Service, another Secretary of the Embassy, believed it, and was fired ... Finally, US military men solely concerned with winning the war quickly feel that the Northern Chinese can be a vitally important factor in defeating Japan ...[47] (emphasis added)

It was not until years after the war, when the die had already been cast, that the Communists' intentions became abundantly clear to the outside world, although the evidence had been present earlier for those who chose to examine it. As early as 1937, Mao, the superb politician, had recognized the unique opportunity the Sino-Japanese war afforded him to advance his cause. Recognizing the chance the war presented, he issued written instructions to his followers who were ordered to conceal their real intentions, pretending support for the Nationalists while dividing their efforts 70% toward expansion, 20% against the Kuomintang, and 10% in resisting Japan.[48] This astonishing document surfaced many years later, though Wedemeyer intuitively realized that this was the core of their plan, and its disclosure merely confirmed what he had long known to be true.

Wedemeyer also came to realize that the American interest in China was limited and self-serving. China was expected to exert an unqualified effort to assist the United States in the defeat of Japan, while little consideration was given to the value of the tremendous sacrifices China had made in unilaterally resisting the Japanese between 1937 and Pearl Harbor. The country was exhausted. Few Americans were aware of how anxious the Japanese were to settle the Chinese war that tied up more than a million of their troops. Chiang had rejected numerous Japanese peace overtures. Had he accepted them, a vast number of veteran Japanese troops would have been freed up for deployment elsewhere, and the consequences to U.S. fighting forces in the Pacific would have been catastrophic. If the Chinese conflict had been settled prior to 1941, an amphibious assault on the virtually defenseless Hawaiian Islands would undoubtedly have succeeded.

Furthermore, if Chiang had made peace earlier with the Japanese, it is highly probable that his superior forces would easily have defeated the Chinese Communists. By late 1943 there was little dispute that American forces would prevail against the Japanese. If Chiang had accepted the Japanese overtures and turned his forces to defeat the Communists it would be a very different world today.

Wedemeyer's record of achievement in China was remarkable and underappreciated. As Leonard Mosley put it:

> His military-cum-diplomatic activities, exercised with a great deal of tact, had done much to restore good relations between the Chinese and U.S. administrations, both of which had suffered from the xenophobic blunders of previous American commanders.[49]

By the end of the war, Wedemeyer had made himself an expert on Sino-American affairs and won the respect of Chiang and the few American pundits with the vision to recognize the Communist strategy. The only place in China where he was not popular was Yenan. It is no surprise that in today's Communist-run China, there is a museum devoted to Stilwell but no evidence whatsoever of Wedemeyer's existence.[50]

TUCHMAN'S STILWELL AND THE AMERICAN EXPERIENCE IN CHINA

Brief mention was made earlier in this chapter about Wedemeyer's irritation at Barbara Tuchman's treatment of him in her book, *Stilwell and the American Experience in China*. Given Tuchman's immense influence and popularity, it is easy to see how a very negative assessment of Wedemeyer, coupled with a lionizing of Stilwell, would have enormous impact on the perception of both men in the press, the public eye, and the view of other historians. For this reason, we will take a close look at exactly what Tuchman said about Wedemeyer in this influential, Pulitizer prize-winning book.

Wedemeyer is mentioned 16 times in the work, seven times in a negative light, several of which could be called highly negative, sarcastic, or demeaning. He is mentioned nine other times in a neutral way. There was not a single complimentary or positive comment about him in the Tuchman book. Her description of Wedemeyer on page 429 is demeaning in the highest degree:

> Enjoying, unlike Chennault, the favor of the War Department, Wedemeyer, aged forty-six, was *the new candidate of Stilwell's opponents*. He was an *ornament* of the General Staff who had served with 15th Infantry at Tientsin in 1930–32. After graduating with honors from Leavenworth he took another General Staff course at the

Kriegsakademie (the German War College) in 1936–38 under the Nazi regime, returning from the experience, according to one observer, "with a suggestion of the *monocled apomb* which distinguishes the best of the German General Staff." Tall and imposing, smooth, able and ambitious, he went on to an impressive career in the Planning Division of the War Department and was making an equal impression at SEAC. *Not given*, as he climbed, *to reticence about his virtues*, he subsequently vindicated his career in a book which bore his own name and an *exclamation point in the title*. "Thinks well of himself, that young man," Stilwell had noted mildly once or twice, feeling as yet no need for a caustic nickname, although inspiration did not fail when the time came.[51] (emphasis supplied)

On page 516 Tuchman says, "According to reports, Wedemeyer and his staff 'are making a case that we [Stilwell] messed it up so badly that even they will have trouble putting it straight'." No citation of authority is cited for this claim and it is entirely at odds with every historical document available for review. On the next page Tuchman faults Wedemeyer for withdrawing two American-trained Chinese divisions from Burma to halt the ICHI-GO offensive which, in Wedemeyer's opinion, had the real potential to overrun both Chunking and Kunming. Tuchman, who had no military training, lacks convincing standing to make the statement that the withdrawal of the troops was "unnecessary."

Tuchman's treatment of Chiang Kai-shek is troubling, and in one particular instance clearly inaccurate. On page 404 she makes much of Chiang's supposed ignorance of "monsoons," and from this one inaccurate claim leaps to the conclusion that Chiang, since he does not know what a "monsoon" is, has no ability to understand, let alone direct a military campaign in Burma. It is additional proof, Tuchman says, of "some of Stilwell's difficulties with the G-mo" [one of Stilwell's disparaging nicknames for Chiang]. Here is how Tuchman reaches these conclusions. She relates a story told to her by Mountbatten that during the Cairo conference of November 23–26, 1943, during a discussion of strategy with Mountbatten, an issue arose concerning the impact a "monsoon" would have on a particular strategy. Mountbatten told Tuchman: " . . . the Generalissimo evidently had not understood the term 'monsoon,' and that Madame Chiang had explained that the Generalissimo 'does not know about monsoons'."

Taylor scoffs at this egregious error:

But Chiang's memos, letters, and diaries on many occasions refer to the "rainy season" *(yu ji)* in Burma and its obvious military implications. It seems that he was simply not familiar with the Portuguese-origin word "monsoon." In such a manner do seemingly revealing but totally misunderstood statements become part of a historic legend if they fit a preconceived stereotype.[52] (emphasis supplied)

Thus, out of this misreading and inaccurate historical detail, large and damaging conclusions are cemented and reputations either enhanced or demolished, all the more so depending on the reputation of the writer.

With the Japanese surrender on August 14, 1945, Wedemeyer's mission in China turned to preventing the Communists from wresting control of the government, while still staying in compliance with the limitations imposed upon him.[53] He immediately initiated a series of measures designed not only to contain Maoist influence but to assist the Nationalist government in regaining territories formerly occupied by the Japanese by stepping up calls for American intervention to "preclude the movement of Communist troops to occupy critical points" in northern China and Manchuria. Vigorous support came from an unlikely source, British General Sir Carton de Wiart, Churchill's special representative to Chiang Kai-shek, who knew a bit about the Communists:

There was only one answer to the Communists and that was defeat. To me the right time for negotiations is after a victory when, backed by force, words seem to attain a meaning not so well understood before.[54]

There was little or no support from other sources. Wedemeyer's request for seven American divisions to insulate Manchuria against occupation by Soviet troops was denied.[55] This would have provided a serious check on the poorly supplied Chinese Communist expansion,[56] but it obviously ran afoul of the secret arrangements that Roosevelt had made with Stalin at Yalta, whereupon he signed off on Stalin's plan to transfer a million Soviet troops to the Manchurian border and ceded control of critical rail lines and ports without the consent, or even the knowledge, of Wedemeyer, Hurley, or Chiang Kai-shek!

At the same time, Wedemeyer developed plans for an increase in the flow of military aid to the Nationalist government with partial success. American military brass instructed him to exclude the Chinese Communists from participating in the surrender of the Japanese[57] but severely limited his ability to enforce this edict by admonishing him not to become involved in "fratricidal warfare."[58] As a practical matter, then, the instruction was toothless and meaningless. On August 17, 1945, *General Order Number One*, written by the American and Joint Chiefs of Staff, was approved by President Truman and designated to whom various elements of the Japanese military should surrender:

> The senior Japanese commanders and all ground, sea, air and military forces within China (excluding Manchuria), Formosa and French Indo-China north of 16 degrees north latitude shall surrender to Generalissimo Chiang Kai-shek.
>
> The Senior Japanese commanders and all ground, sea, air and auxiliary forces within Manchuria, Korea north of 38 degrees north latitude and Karafuto shall surrender to the Commander in Chief of Soviet Forces in the Far East.

Quite obviously, this language was crafted to be concordant with the then-secret agreements made at Yalta in February, in essence creating the spheres of influence that Roosevelt had been hesitant to admit to the American public in his address to Congress on March 1.[59] But it also followed the stated American policy that Chiang was the leader of China.[60] This was something that Mao and the Soviets had little intention of honoring. Under direct instructions from Yenan, through General Chu Teh, the Communists took immediate steps to occupy as much territory *within China* as possible, in an effort to seize as many abandoned Japanese supplies and munitions as possible. They were well aware that their actions would not be opposed by force. Chiang's objections fell on deaf ears, and Wedemeyer was powerless to commit troops to an action that was contrary to his orders from Washington.[61] A November 20, 1945 directive from the State Department reiterated the prior American policy of non-intervention in the Chinese domestic political rivalry.

COMMUNIST ACTIVITIES IN EUROPE SUGGEST SIMILAR PROBLEMS IN ASIA

There were now, at long last, rumblings of suspicion of Communist motives in Asia appearing in the American press, in no small measure influenced by the post-war seizure of the Balkans by the Soviets. The slumbering political establishment was slowly awakening. An editorial in the *New York Times* on August 17, 1945 denounced the Maoists for instigating civil war, colluding with the Russians, and delaying the surrender and repatriation of Japanese troops.[62] There was now an enhanced sentiment within the Truman administration for continuation of aid to China. An ominous scenario was emerging that threatened to nullify many of the geopolitical achievements America had gained in nearly four years of war. Urgent measures were in order to stem the tide of Communist expansion. President Truman was about to take action that would bring Wedemeyer to center stage.

CHAPTER 9

GENERAL MARSHALL'S
FAILED MISSION IN CHINA

The great mass of people . . . will more easily fall victim
to a big lie than to a small one.
—Mein Kampf

RESIGNATION OF AMBASSADOR HURLEY

On November 27, 1945, Ambassador to China Patrick J. Hurley submitted a scathing letter of resignation to President Truman, lambasting the American State Department for its lack of focus in its policy toward China and for its support of the imperialist European powers in the area. Citing a betrayal of the principals of the Atlantic Charter,[1] he openly criticized his colleagues for sabotaging America's pro-Chiang policy in favor of the Communists, initiating the first stage of a contentious and highly charged debate that would in a few short years provide cannon fodder for the red-baiting ramblings of Wisconsin Senator Joseph McCarthy.

In August 1944, Hurley had been assigned the task of preventing the collapse of the Chinese government and unifying it in the war against the Japanese. Shortly after his arrival, he had been responsible for the removal of American officials in China, in particular George Atcheson, Jr. and John W. Service, in the belief that they were undermining his efforts by virtue of their sympathies to Mao.[2] He ultimately discovered that they had been reassigned to even higher positions in the State Department and as advisors to General Douglas MacArthur, where they continued to assert a viewpoint that was directly contrary to his philosophy of how to accomplish his mission.

Hurley's resignation kicked off a Senate investigation. In a stormy three-hour session on December 5th before the Senate Foreign Relations Committee, Hurley launched into a diatribe against what he viewed as pro-Communist and divisive elements in the State Department led by John Carter Vincent, head of the Far East desk. After a particularly contentious interchange with Chairman Tom Connally of Texas, the white-haired former Secretary of War in the Hoover administration, trembling with anger, added: "I want my government to say what its policy is in China and stop pussyfooting and running away from the truth!" The hearing room broke out in thunderous applause. Hurley went on to exclaim that he was "left naked to my enemies and the enemies of America," and "I decided I would commence firing and I did."

It fell upon Secretary of State James "Jimmy" Byrnes to respond to Hurley's pronouncements. A few days later he claimed that "there was no indication that Mr. Atcheson or Mr. Service had failed to adhere to the American policy of submitting their views directly to the State Department, and that there was nothing to support the charge that either had been guilty of "the slightest disloyalty to his superior officers." Byrnes cited a number of documents that Hurley had been barred from referring to, even those that he had written!

The Secretary did admit that the Generalissimo's government "affords the most satisfactory base for a developing democracy," but added that the government must be broadened to include representatives of large and well-organized groups that were not represented, and that it would be necessary to encourage concessions by the Central Government, by the "*so-called* Communists" (the usual terminology for those opposing the Nationalists), and by other factions.

Byrnes' position was something relatively new. Between 1937 and 1946, America exhibited little interest in being involved in Chinese internal political problems.[3] While strategists were aware of the growing power of the Communists in China, it was viewed only through the lens of any impact it might have on the American war effort. No serious thought was given to the potential deadly consequences of Russian involvement; the focus was on defeating the Japanese, and if the Communists could assist in that effort, so much the better. Little thought was given to the welfare of China. In fact, until almost a year prior to Pearl Harbor, America was supplying aid to the Japanese that was being used in its war *against* China, turning a blind eye to the massive and brutal suffering the Japanese were inflicting.[4]

In the early stages of World War II, the Americans saw the Nationalists and Communists as a potentially powerful "United Front" against the Japanese (this was the mantra repeated by military as well as civilian leaders). The warnings of Wedemeyer that growing Communist power posed a threat not only to China and Asia, but to the United States, fell on deaf ears. Likewise, admonitions about the unlikely prospect of effectively combining both forces to create a unified force against Japan were dismissed. Only as World War II ended, when the Truman administration woke up to the reality of Soviet domination of Eastern Europe, did they begin to take notice of the potential danger of the growing Communist power in Asia.

By virtue of Hurley's bombshell, the Republicans, now in the majority in Congress and thirsting for a new political issue, sensed a ripe opportunity to gain further political ground. To neutralize this prospect, President Truman appointed the highly-respected George Marshall as his Special Envoy to China on December 20, 1945. He was simplistically charged with "bringing China's warring factions together, ending the fighting, integrating the armed forces of the several parties, and engineering a coalition government."[5] The decision to select Marshall appears to have originated with a suggestion by Secretary of Agriculture Clinton Anderson at a Cabinet meeting on November 27th.[6]

APPOINTMENT OF GENERAL MARSHALL AS MEDIATOR

Marshall's appointment was popular. Chiang was conferring with General Wedemeyer when he learned of it and immediately began making preparations for his arrival.[7] Even in Yenan the announcement was received with cautious optimism.[8] Marshall was considered the principal architect of the Allied military victory in World War II and was described by Truman as "the greatest military man this nation has ever produced."[9] War weary and badly in need of a rest, Marshall accepted Truman's assignment with reluctance.[10] Critics of the assignment regarded it as the original "mission impossible." Within a short time, it would become clear that this assessment was correct.

Marshall's briefing by pro-Communist members of the State Department included heavy doses of the premise that the Chinese Communists were merely "agrarian reformers" who would willingly come to a rapprochement with the Nationalists and assist in forming a stable government.[11] Wedemeyer was not consulted and had mixed emotions about his old boss coming to China; on one hand, Wedemeyer was delighted to renew his longstanding friendship but on the other, apprehensive about the success of his mission and about what role Marshall would expect him to play in its implementation.[12] Despite his great respect for Marshall, he viewed the appointment as a poor choice since, in Wedemeyer's view:

> Marshall had neither the time, inclination or opportunity to study
> the methods of Communism; and he implicitly believed the reports
> of his old friend General Stilwell, who ascribed all ills of China to
> the government of Chiang Kai-shek. . . . Moreover, by the time he
> arrived in China on his fatal mission, George Marshall was physi-
> cally too worn out to appraise the situation correctly.[13]

In theory, the task seemed straightforward: demanding an immediate
cease-fire, then unifying the warring groups into a single force and persuading
the political leaders to agree to a coalition government.[14] Wedemeyer had
been in his new assignment in China fourteen months, and extensive personal
interaction with the leaders of both factions convinced him of the impossibility of reconciling the differences between them. He had been laboring hard
to cultivate a good working relationship with Chiang Kai-shek and had an
intimate understanding of how far the Generalissimo would bend. He knew
that Chiang was in an extremely difficult position. He was dead set against
any close working relationship with the Communists, yet he desperately
needed American assistance, making him susceptible to pressure that Wedemeyer feared would undermine his efforts to keep the Communists at bay.

Wedemeyer had previously conveyed to his superiors his real concern
about the growing Communist influence, but he saw little to indicate that
his messages had been taken seriously. Washington was not accustomed, and
generally did not welcome, dispatches from military commanders that dealt
with long-range global political goals, considering them to be out of their
field of responsibility. An insightful dispatch sent to the War Department
Chief of Staff on August 15, 1945, four months prior to Marshall's arrival in
China, outlined his apprehensions:

> I view Asia as an enormous pot, seething and boiling, the fumes of
> which may readily snuff out the advantages gained by Allied sacri-
> fices the past several years and may also definitely preclude realiza-
> tion of the objectives of the Atlantic Charter, and the Teheran, Yalta
> and Potsdam agreements.[15]

Fully conversant with the proceedings of the Atlantic Charter and the
other named agreements, and armed with the knowledge he had gained from

his participation in many important wartime conferences, Wedemeyer weighed the issues raised in those meetings, the promises made, and the decisions reached at those conferences against his own understanding of what America's long-range strategic goals should be. He perceived a great disparity between the lofty aims proclaimed at those meetings and the reality he was experiencing in Asia. Wedemeyer never lost sight of the principles for which America had gone to war. However, from long experience with U.S. diplomats, politicians, and State Department representatives, he was well aware that his personal views on global strategy were at variance with views generally considered acceptable for a military figure. And more importantly, his dispatches to Washington had to be filtered through the screen of what is now termed "political correctness." He desperately wanted to make the administration aware of the dangers he saw in China, but he also realized the need for discretion in articulating his views. This discretion is clearly demonstrated by examining a message which he drafted, but after serious consideration, never submitted. In it he said:

> America has unwittingly contributed to the trend of events in Europe which facilitate the substitution of Communism for Nazism, yet it is accepted that both forms of ism are equally abhorrent to Americans and diametrically opposed to the ideologies of democracy; both forms of ism abrogate the very principles for which we have made unstinted, astronomical sacrifices in lives and resources. The situation in Europe is a *fait accompli*; however, we may still provide a framework [in Asia] for realization of ideas and ideals for which I feel we are fighting.[16]

In one paragraph Wedemeyer had synthesized the entire problem, and history has proved him correct. The Communists had succeeded in taking over a large part of Eastern Europe and stood poised to do the same in Asia. Historians continue to dispute who is at fault for allowing this to happen, and Wedemeyer was enough of a pragmatist to now look beyond this question and deal with the present, the situation in Asia. To Wedemeyer's mind, halting the spread of Communism in Asia meant that the United States needed to vigorously support regimes that resisted it, despite their shortcomings. In China this meant Chiang Kai-shek. While American policy makers had become highly sensitized to matters European, with respect to Asia they were still wearing blinders. Even George Kennan, the most outstanding contemporary scholar on Communism, was Euro-centered and did not view events in Asia with concern. The vaunted and highly successful Marshall Plan had no Asian counterpart. Congressman Walter Judd, perhaps the most vocal anti-Communist in Congress, succinctly epitomized the disparity: "In Europe we insisted that in order to get our help the governments must keep the Communists out; but in China we insisted that in order to get our help the government must take the Communists in."[17]

MARSHALL ARRIVES IN CHINA

Upon his arrival, Marshall met Wedemeyer at the famed Cathay Hotel[18] in Shanghai.[19] He had little idea how difficult his mission to broker a deal between the Nationalists and the Communists would be. Nevertheless, he was not accustomed to failure and optimistically plunged into his task. Like the President and most American political leaders, he assumed the job was a straightforward question of sincere debate and compromise, akin to negotiations between management and unions. He was to have a rude awakening.

Marshall arrived in China exhausted from his wartime duties and a grueling examination from hostile Senators during the recent Congressional investigation to explore the Pearl Harbor attack.[20] Uncharacteristically, he had made little preparation for the negotiations[21] and insisted, as had been his standard wartime directive, that his briefing paper be reduced to a single typewritten page.[22] To think that the titanic struggle in China might be summarized so succinctly was ludicrous.

Wedemeyer understood Communist negotiating tactics, having observed them firsthand for the previous fourteen months. He knew they would never willingly share power, and that any concessions they made at the bargaining table would only be temporary expedients for the purpose of gaining a foothold, in order to allow them to infiltrate the government and undermine the opposition in preparation for a final takeover.[23] He hoped that he would be able to convey this insight to General Marshall. In the past Marshall had insisted on forthrightness from his subordinates, so when Wedemeyer reported his pessimistic assessment of the prospects of success, Marshall uncharacteristically exploded, his face flushed with anger: "It *is* going to work! I am going to do it and what's more, *you* are going to help me do it!"[24] Wedemeyer was upset at the unexpected admonishment from his respected mentor but hastened to reassure him "that there was no question of his desire to give him every possible help; that all the resources of the China Theatre would be placed at his disposal and that he had already assigned him two of the ablest officers on his staff to assist him."[25,26] For the remainder of the briefing, Wedemeyer sensed a hostility he had never witnessed from his mentor, and he could never surmise the reason. A good guess is that Marshall had been poisoned by the vitriol of his old friend Stilwell. The confrontation with Wedemeyer must also have also been a troubling experience for Marshall, for there is no evidence that he ever mentioned it to his biographer Forrest Pogue.[27]

The following day Marshall and Wedemeyer flew to Nanking to confer with the Generalissimo and Madame Chiang.[28] Wedemeyer was pleased with the mood of cooperation that he witnessed. Marshall then went on to Chungking to meet Mao. Wedemeyer stayed behind, well aware that he "was anathema to the Communists," and it would be better if Marshall went without him.[29]

Marshall was gratified to find that his first efforts at reconciliation were surprisingly successful; at least so it seemed.[30] Within two months he was able to obtain an agreement, initialed by both Zhou Enlai and Chiang Kai-shek, designating Chiang as Commander in Chief of the combined Nationalist and Communist armies.[31] Wedemeyer was both astounded and pleased at this remarkable accomplishment.[32] Congratulations flooded in from all sources, and confidence abounded in Washington that the nagging problem had finally been solved.[33] Marshall returned home in March to report on the next phase to an overjoyed President Truman,[34] who had already decided to name Marshall to replace Jimmy Byrnes as Secretary of State, citing his success in reconciling the two opposing factions in China as his crowning achievement. Arrangements were made for Marshall's return to China, accompanied by his wife, to put a ribbon on the package with a formal signing. At this juncture, Marshall believed that all that remained was to tie up a few loose ends.[35]

Was Marshall's success illusory? Retrospectively, Suzanne Pepper sensed an intentional deception on the part of both sides:

> [The negotiations between the CCP and the Nationalists] appear rather to have been a cynical maneuver entered into by both parties in order to pacify Chinese public opinion and the American ally, while buying time for the most advantageous possible deployment of their mutual armed forces.[36]

Pepper is partially correct, but it is the Communists who benefited most from the delay while negotiations continued. Indeed, the Communists needed more time to regroup and strengthen their forces and clearly were the chief beneficiaries of the attenuation of active hostilities brought about by the negotiations. The Nationalists appeared to be somewhat more sincere.

While Marshall was still in Washington, the first inkling surfaced that something had gone awry when the Communists announced that they were refusing to sign the formal document.[37] This was par for the course. A lesson in Chinese culture and manners goes a long way toward explaining this apparent contradiction. In Marshall's absence, he had left the highly regarded General Alvan C. Gillem in charge of the negotiations. Gillem had attended all the previous meetings and was well acquainted with the intricate formal protocol required, and opened the meeting precisely as Marshall would have. Picking up where Marshall had left off, even before he had even finished his first sentence, Gillem was astonished to be told that both sides had retracted virtually every point that had previously been settled. When the flabbergasted Gillem asked for an explanation, he was told by one side, "We love General Marshall, and we respect him," and "We would do anything that was required to keep from hurting him." The other party added, "Yes, that is right. *And* General Gillem, we don't owe *you* anything."[38] (emphasis added)

Marshall was understandably incensed. Members of his staff urged him not to return to China at all, but as Henry A. Byroade, a China expert who accompanied him to China, remarked, the General "was not a type that could accept defeat. It was foreign to his nature."[39] With his standing inexplicably deteriorated, Marshall was more determined than ever to get the matter back on track, so he made plans to return in late April.[40] He had experienced his first taste of the Communist and Nationalist antics that were so familiar to Wedemeyer. It would not be his last.

A rumor was circulating among the Nationalists that Marshall was blaming them for the Communist change of heart, and that he intended to return and pressure them to make reforms in order to demonstrate that the Communists were "worthy partners."[41] The Communists' reversal of their promises was more likely their usual negotiating tactic.

The changing mood in China was casting a cloud not only on the appointment of Wedemeyer but on Marshall's entire mission. Marshall was beginning to suspect that further negotiations with the Communists and Nationalists were pointless, and that Wedemeyer had indeed been correct in his assertion that no deal was possible between the two warring factions.

Ultimately, Marshall's mission was a failure. His efforts in China are a tale of earnest perseverance and ultimate disillusionment. Marshall is not to blame, and it is unlikely that anyone else would have succeeded. In Wedemeyer's view, it was a "tragic tale of false hopes and mistaken assumptions."[42] In the view of historian Jung Chang, Marshall, like most Americans, did not understand Mao Zedong or the Communists. He was taken in by the blandishments of Zhou Enlai and seemed to accept the sweet talk that they desired nothing more than democracy in China. It is also crystal clear that he, as well as many of his State Department advisors, were not cognizant of Mao Zedong's relationship with Stalin.[43] Anthony Kubek agrees: "From the start, Marshall, long influenced by the views of General Stilwell, appeared to have been captivated by Zhou Enlai, who represented the Communists as "agrarian reformers" and the Chunking government as 'despotic' and 'reactionary'."[44]

In Wedemeyer's view, this was the ultimate tragedy—Marshall's being thrust unwillingly into a situation that was beyond his powers and abilities to control. Wedemeyer strongly professed a belief in the sincerity of General Marshall's motives in his assessment of the China policy but thought he had arrived at the wrong conclusions and remained ignorant of their ultimate effect on the long-range interests of the United States. Wedemeyer cited a number of factors that led him to this conclusion, including Marshall's "getting on in years," and his implicit faith in the reports of his old friend General Stilwell, who ascribed all the problems in China to the government of Chiang Kai-shek.[45] Furthermore, although both he and Marshall were career military men, Wedemeyer thought *his* experience, training, study, and particularly his exposure to Communism both in Germany and then in China, better equipped him to perceive the reality of the situation:

> General Marshall was primarily a military man who had little knowledge of the complexities of the world conflict and no conception of the skill with which the Communists pervert great and noble aspirations for social justice into support of their own diabolic purposes. Moreover, by the time he arrived in China on his fatal mission, George Marshall was physically and mentally too worn out to appraise the situation correctly. Finally, as I hate to admit because I never revered anyone more than General Marshall, he was not immune from the besetting sin of most human beings who rise to the heights of power or influence.[46]

Wedemeyer might have been correct in this assessment, but to some this particular passage must have seemed a bit pretentious, even if it was his honest, if blunt, assessment. However, if he intended the passage to be constructive criticism with a silken glove, this writer would have to disagree and suspect that Marshall, the architect of the "Marshall Plan," the Chief of Staff during the greatest war we have ever fought, probably the best soldier to ever wear an American uniform, was justifiably a proud and ambitious man, and surely would have been furious on seeing Wedemeyer's words. In charging Marshall with "little knowledge" of the complexities, "no conception" of the skill of the Communists, "too worn out" to deal with them, and worst of all "not immune" from the "sin"—by which he meant arrogance—of those who rise to power, Wedemeyer might have gone a bit too far. In fact, in the next passage, he may have poured salt into the wound by mentioning Lord Acton's famous dictum about absolute power corrupting absolutely!

General Marshall never had absolute power; but his reputation at war's end was so great, and his political influence consequently so overpowering, that he might have thought he could accomplish the impossible. Thus he became prey to the crypto-Communists, or Communist-sympathizing syco-phants who played on his vanity to achieve their own ends. Otherwise he never would have believed that he could mix oil and water by reconciling the basically antagonistic aims of the Nationalists and the Moscow-supported Chinese Communists. When Marshall read Wedemeyer's assessment of his efforts to reconcile the Communists and Nationalists in *Wedemeyer Reports!* he was probably livid. The retirement of general officers, just like the 1947 Indian Constitution which "abolished" the caste system, does not erase human memory of who was the superior officer and who was the subordinate. It might have been better for Wedemeyer to have left this passage out of his book. In a conversation Wedemeyer had with Eiler just before or after Marshall's death (it is not clear from the passage), he said he was sorry he had been so hard on Marshall.[47]

After a few years as Secretary of State, Marshall finally abandoned his incredibly naïve position that "in China we have no concrete evidence that the Communist Party is supported by Communists from the outside."[48]

By the end of 1946, Wedemeyer had become quite concerned about the likelihood of any solution to the China problem and feared that the United States would simply wash its hands and withdraw, predicting that "all of Asia, in less than a generation, will come under Soviet domination by means short of war."[49] In an August 10, 1946 memorandum entitled "Chinese Problem," he laid out his fears concerning the future of China with uncanny foresight, charging that the State Department and the administration were either unaware of what Communism would produce in China, or worse, were indifferent to either outcome:

Some people, perhaps even in responsible positions [e.g. the State Department], may feel that China is best regenerated by first permitting the destruction of the old order. On the bedrock remaining, a new order would then arise. This is Marxian [*sic*] doctrine [as] applied in Russia. Another solution is to recognize that China will be troubled for a long while, that Soviet Communism will be the force moving into the vacuum created by the fall of the Central government.[50]

As he explained in August 1946, Wedemeyer believed that the primary obstacle to the United States effort to mediate a truce was the impossibility of having a representative government in China that involved the Communists:

I am not suggesting that the ultimate objective of China should not be a truly representative government. However, conditions ... would indicate that the time is not propitious for such a coalition. . . . We advocate multiparty government for China yet I have the conviction that as Communist strength increases in that country, multiparty government will become more remote. In no area under Communist influence in the world do we find representative government.[51]

The misreading of the political situation in China by the Truman administration started at the top. In a policy statement in December 1945, Truman exclaimed that: *it was the duty* of the United States' representatives in China to assist in creating a "unified, democratic, and peaceful nation" only to be achievable through cessation of hostilities and a negotiated *broadening* of the government. Truman went on to proclaim support for the national government while being critical of its domination by a single political party, and concluded with a pledge of economic aid *if the Chinese parties followed his prescription for peace and unity.*[52] (emphasis added)

Just as it largely governed his instructions to his new Special Ambassador to China, Truman's goal to export our vision of government remains a permanent feature of United States foreign policy, wielded with favors, promises, and money given and withheld. This example of flawed "carrot and stick" American foreign policy in 1945 continues to have repercussions to the present day.

CHAPTER 10

WEDEMEYER'S 1947 MISSION TO CHINA

All that is necessary for evil to triumph
is for good men to do nothing.
—Edmund Burke

WEDEMEYER'S "APPOINTMENT" AS AMBASSADOR

While in China on his mediation mission in March 1946, Marshall approached Wedemeyer to inquire whether he had any interest in becoming the next Ambassador to China,[1] since no one had as yet been appointed to replace Hurley. President Truman had earlier informed Marshall that he would appoint whomever Marshall favored.[2] So Marshall presented his offer in Chungking shortly before Wedemeyer was due to depart for the United States to take care of an old medical problem. Immensely flattered, Wedemeyer believed he could make a contribution, and though he had some reluctance to leave the Army, he remained dutifully obedient to his boss and indicated that he would accept the position if offered.[3]

In the several months following Wedemeyer's tentative appointment as Ambassador to China, a series of events would not only derail the appointment but would also cause a serious impairment in his close personal relationship with his mentor. In May 1946 Wedemeyer returned stateside for surgery on his nose to correct a breathing problem that he suffered from an injury received while on the boxing team at West Point. After the surgery, he was assigned to temporary duty in the War Department in anticipation of his move to China. In preparation for his ambassadorial appointment, he spent eight hundred dollars for an appropriate wardrobe.

In early July, Wedemeyer was summoned to the office of Undersecretary of State Dean Acheson, who informed him that news of his prospective appointment had leaked to the Communists, who had complained to Marshall that Wedemeyer was biased in favor of Chiang Kai-shek, to whom he had served as Chief of Staff. In addition, they charged that Wedemeyer had been responsible for moving Chinese troops into northern China to accept the surrender of Japanese forces which, to the Communists' thinking, showed favoritism towards the Nationalists.

Wedemeyer was then informed that General Marshall had caved in to the Communists' specious claims and had sent an urgent radiogram to President Truman withdrawing his recommendation of Wedemeyer as Ambassador. At this time, Marshall still held the mistaken notion that he could bring about an accord and was willing to sacrifice Wedemeyer's appointment to that cause. Wedemeyer was more disappointed that General Marshall and the President would allow a diplomatic appointment to be vetoed by the Communists than by losing the ambassadorship, since he had only accepted it in the first place out of a sense of duty to Marshall and his country.

It was not entirely clear exactly how the leak occurred, or who pressured Marshall to cancel the nomination. Diplomat and China expert Henry Byroade at first suspected that it was the work of the Soviets, who were monitoring the situation far closer than the State Department believed. Later he concluded that it was Mao Zedong, who independently ordered Zhou Enlai to withdraw his consent.[4] The Communists were not interested in fairness or impartiality; they simply wanted someone who was sympathetic to them. Wedemeyer shared Byroade's view, later quoting the radiogram Acheson read him that laid out the Communists' objections. Indeed, after all he had witnessed, Wedemeyer probably *was* incapable of being impartial.[5]

Perhaps Marshall's change of heart arose out of a series of letters Wedemeyer wrote that were critical of the State Department's China advisors and the Secretary's reliance on empty Communist promises. More likely, Marshall's military training dictated that the mission was more important than any individual. It is unlikely it was based on any personal animosity towards Wedemeyer.

Following the withdrawal of the appointment, Wedemeyer was given a number of choices for his next assignment, ultimately choosing to assume command of the Second Army based at Fort Meade, Maryland. On leaving Washington, Secretary of Defense James V. Forrestal asked him to write a memorandum setting forth his views about the course the United States was following toward China. With typical candor, Wedemeyer was not only critical of American policy, but in particular General Marshall:

There is a question as to whether Marshall realizes the delicate situation revolving around the peace conference in Paris and the necessity for keeping our political policies and relationships on a very even keel at the present time.

There is a question that Secretary of State Marshall is fully aware of all the implications of the present world situation as it concerns the Soviet Union and the vital place China (good or bad) plays in maintaining some sort of world equilibrium. It is unfortunate that General Marshall does not have available the clear and forceful studies on the Russian situation which have been prepared at the request of President Truman.[6]

Wedemeyer went on to fault Marshall for a lack of preparation in dealing with the problem and having an inadequate understanding of the long-term ramifications of the course he was directing, especially the failure to support Chiang Kai-shek. Wedemeyer accused his former mentor of failing to read, or worse yet, to fully understand critical information in documents contained "in the Secretary of War's files . . . indicating the U.S. had to continue to support the Chinese Nationalist Government as a basic element of U.S. policy." He was particularly upset by Marshall's statement that "there is and will continue to be civil war in China" and for ignoring vital information readily available to the Secretary of State, most notably that: "The Army Intelligence Division of the General Staff (G-2) had irrefutable evidence proving that the Chinese Communists were directly linked with Moscow."[7] Although the 1946 memorandum to Secretary Forrestal was written specifically for him, it is a certainty that like all government documents, it swiftly made the rounds, and surely Marshall was aware of it, although no mention of it is made in Pogue's biography or the extensive oral interviews Pogue conducted. Wedemeyer later regretted penning that memorandum which, he realized, "widened the rift with my esteemed chief . . . who I fear has never forgiven me for opposing his China policy."[8]

In a speech at the National War College on November 13, 1946, Wedemeyer summed up his views on the Chinese problem, commenting on the progress he had personally witnessed between November 1944 and the end of the war. Although not mentioning Stilwell by name, it was clear that he had him in mind when he referred to progress being made when the Chinese had the benefit of "friendly and concrete American advice":

These experiences taught me that the Chinese situation was capable of rapid improvement. The great gains made, and the lessons learned in 1945, were too late to contribute much to final victory; we learned that the Generalissimo and his associates can and will co-operate. They can and did improve the condition of their armies and people. They made rapid strides when they had the benefit of friendly and concrete American advice.[9]

Wedemeyer firmly believed that it was not too late to reverse the slide toward Communist control, and what China needed most was concrete assistance. He again forcefully and directly criticized Marshall's limited understanding of the situation, especially his failure to understand the ultimate goals of the Communists and their ties to Moscow:

The question is often asked: Are the Chinese Communists real followers of the doctrines of Karl Marx? I am certain that the Chinese Communist movement follows the Moscow line from week to week, insofar as conditions permit. . . . The fundamental philosophy and aims of the Chinese Communists differ very little if at all from their Communist brethren the world over. There is no real difference in ultimate objectives. I have talked with the Chinese Communist leaders, Mao Tse-tung and Chou En-lai, particularly with the latter. . . . Their loyalties are first in the interest of Stalin and his program and then in the welfare of their own countrymen.[10]

Wedemeyer told his audience that the Kuomintang's ultimate aim was the "establishment of a constitutional republic, whereas the Communists wanted to establish a totalitarian dictatorship on the Soviet pattern." He also took issue with the constant criticism of Chiang Kai-shek and the portrayal of his regime as totalitarian, noting: "In my two years of close contact with Chang Kai-shek I had become convinced that he personally was a straightforward, selfless leader, keenly interested in the welfare of his people, and desirous of establishing a constitutional government according to the precepts of Sun Yat-sen." He acknowledged that the Generalissimo did indeed have weaknesses, but that the main one was unqualified loyalty to friends and supporters, many of whom were not deserving of support.[11] Wedemeyer was especially concerned about the Marshall-imposed embargo and the harmful impact it had on the Nationalists. He voiced strong criticism of Marshall's decision to impose the embargo (begun in August 1946 and ended in October 1947), warning that it would eventually cripple the Nationalists' military campaign,[12] and concluded by asserting that: "The Nationalist Government has the capacity to defeat, to crush militarily, the Communist forces right now."

By 1947, Wedemeyer had said and done all he could, and he left the fate of China in the hands of the Truman administration. He knew that the Forrestal memorandum and the speech at the National War College had, in effect, been his "crossing of the Rubicon" in his relations with Marshall[13] and feared that he had permanently put himself out of the loop as far as any other connection with the Truman administration was concerned. The future of his military career was unclear.

In the spring of 1947, Wedemeyer was in England delivering a lecture to the Imperial War College when he was surprised to hear from Secretary Marshall, who asked him to assess the conditions in several countries in Europe and make a report to him upon his return in July. After completing his tour, Wedemeyer was informed that the administration wanted him to lead a fact-finding mission to China. Two years had passed since the Japanese surrender, a vacuum had developed in the Far East, and an increasing number of American officials were expressing concern that the Communists were moving to fill it.[14] Wedemeyer was surprised by the request but heartened by the belief that it was grounded on a desire to understand the true conditions in China. With the hope of assisting in the creation of an American policy more sympathetic to Chiang Kai-shek, he accepted the assignment.

A directive written by Wedemeyer and approved by President Truman on July 9, 1947 called for Wedemeyer to make "an appraisal of the political, economic, psychological and military situations" in China and Korea and to make it clear that the United States would participate in a rehabilitation program "only if the Chinese government presents satisfactory evidence of effective measures looking towards Chinese recovery." The directive further directed Wedemeyer to make a prediction of "the probable consequences of assistance, and the probable consequence in the event that assistance is not given."[15] The directive also called for a trip to Korea for the same purposes.

In drafting the memorandum of instructions, Wedemeyer was careful not to include any requirement for a coalition government. Given his dim view of that prospect, he probably would have rejected the assignment if he was saddled with that condition, and it is interesting to speculate on why it was omitted. Understandably, the Nationalists were overjoyed at his selection to head the mission, anticipating economic and military assistance. The Communists pulled no punches in their opposition. They were not happy to see their old nemesis reappear. A July 16, 1947 broadcast from North Shensi Province[16] revealed their angst, in part:

> By sending the infamous General Wedemeyer back to China, American imperialists hope to carry out aggression in China with a free hand and to prop up Chiang Kai-shek's moribund rule. The Chinese people are all too familiar with Wedemeyer, American imperialist educated in Prussian militarism.[17]

Wedemeyer wrote a series of letters to publishing magnate Henry Luce, a strong supporter of Chiang, in which he expressed no illusions about the difficulty of the assignment and revealed his apprehension about what he might find in China in the face of a hostile press and partisan opposition after an absence of almost a year-and-a-half. He noted that the situation in China was far more perilous than in the fall of 1945,[18] candidly chastising America's "stupid policies and lack of moral courage," yet voicing guarded optimism that his efforts might assist in bringing China out of the abyss of political chaos:

> I do not feel that we can stop the Chinese snowball in its headlong dash to the bottom. But I am convinced that we can evolve a philosophy supported by a realistic plan of action that will preclude the complete disintegration of China in the bottom of the valley and permit the Chinese snowball to begin the arduous but definite advance up the other bank of the valley toward the objectives of happiness, prosperity and stability.[19]

Wedemeyer arrived in Nanking on July 16, 1947 with a hand-picked group of eight assistants, including military, engineering, economic, and political advisors, an aide-de-camp, an interpreter, and Mark S. Watson, an extremely valuable press liaison. During his two-month stay, he traveled widely and met with both American and Chinese officials.[20] On August 22nd, he was asked by Chiang to speak before a joint meeting of the State Council and the ministers of the National Government. Encouraged by the Generalissimo to speak frankly,[21] he brilliantly linked a framework for success to addressing the malignant atmosphere of inefficiency and corruption: "The

Central Government can defeat the Chinese Communists by the employment of force, but can only win the loyal, enthusiastic support of the people by improving the political and economic situation immediately."[22]

Wedemeyer had taken the pulse of the Chinese people and observed that the Communists were winning the battle for their hearts and minds with acerbic criticism of the central government and promises of reform. While Wedemeyer's remarks were challenged by representatives of the Nationalist officials, the Communists were much less diplomatic, labeling him a "bloodthirsty butcher" and a "hypocrite," adding, "It is very possible that he will urge Washington for further aid to Chiang to prop up the Kuomintang government from imminent collapse."

Wedemeyer pulled no punches in the comprehensive report he submitted to President Truman on September 18th.[23] (See Appendix II.) In a scathing indictment of Communism, he characterized it as "a force presenting even greater dangers to world peace than did the Nazi militarists and the Japanese jingoists." He focused on how China's efforts at reform had been sabotaged and

> jeopardized by forces as sinister as those that operated in Europe and Asia leading to World War II. The pattern is familiar— employment of subversive agents; infiltration tactics; incitement of disorder and chaos to undermine popular confidence in government and leaders.

With respect to Soviet policy in the Far East:

> Events of the past two years demonstrate the futility of appeasement based on the hope that the strongly consolidated forces of the Soviet Union will adopt either a conciliatory or a cooperative attitude except as tactical expedients. Soviet practice in the countries already occupied or dominated completes the mosaic of aggressive expansion ... far exceeding that of Nazism in its ambitious scope and dangerous implications . . . Therefore in attempting a solution to the problem presented in the Far East. . . . every possible opportunity must be used to seize the initiative in order to create and maintain bulwarks of freedom.

Wedemeyer further noted that "notwithstanding the corruption . . . in China, it is a certainty that the bulk of the people are not disposed to a Communist structure," and he critically alluded to the secret giveaways by President Roosevelt at Yalta that opened the door to Soviet domination of Manchuria. He opined that China's difficulties were compounded by the withholding of economic assistance to the Nationalist government, citing the supreme irony of the Marshall Plan that supplied substantial aid to Greece and Turkey in 1947 to protect them from Communist takeover while refusing to render similar assistance to China, a policy he viewed as having even more dire consequences for the future of America and the world.

Wedemeyer recommended that China immediately request the assistance of the United Nations for material and advisory assistance and called for a cessation of hostilities in Manchuria. He recommended that Manchuria be placed in a guardianship, accept American military advisors, and present evidence that political and military reforms were being initiated.

Wedemeyer "held himself in readiness" to be called by the administration or Congress to a public forum to defend and expound upon his viewpoints.[24] Instead, he was summoned by Marshall to meet him in New York to discuss the matter. After superficially complimenting him for his efforts, Marshall claimed he had not studied the report thoroughly and cautioned that *under no circumstances was he to discuss the contents with anyone.*[25] Wedemeyer was also informed that similar constraints applied to all other members of the commission that had accompanied him. Wedemeyer was puzzled by Marshall's instructions, which seemed strange since, if he had not carefully studied the report, then how could he have legitimate concerns about the contents? The injunction was obviously disconcerting and also difficult to comply with since the media, members of Congress, and governmental officials had already expressed a keen interest in the contents of the report.

A representative of the State Department informed Wedemeyer that if he agreed to delete certain portions of the report, Marshall might agree to its publication. Wedemeyer refused,[26] reluctantly and sadly concluding that he had been naïve to believe that the State Department would change its attitude toward the internal political struggle in China. He was certain that if his report had been supportive of the policies of the State Department, it would have been published with great fanfare. Wedemeyer was outraged at the administration and equally disappointed in Marshall as their vehicle. Only later did he come to realize that had he been chosen "to allay doubts in Congress and in the country and to provide justification for continuance of the old disastrous China policy." If he had known that he would not be able to make his views public unless they comported with the administration's view, he most certainly would not have accepted the assignment. The "official" explanation for suppression of the report was that it contained "confidential material the publication of which might cause embarrassment to the nations concerned."[27] Marshall accepted full responsibility for the decision.[28] He later testified before the Senate Committee on Appropriations in December 1947, and upon being asked why he "joined in the suppression" of the report, he replied curtly: "I did not *join* in the suppression of the report. I personally suppressed it."[29]

In mid-December 1947, Wedemeyer testified before the same Senate Appropriations Committee on a bill to approve aid of sixty million dollars to China. As part of a worldwide plan to contain Communist expansion, he urged that all possible assistance be extended, including military supplies and advisors similar to what had been approved for Greece and Turkey.[30] As always he was careful to protect American interests when advocating aid to foreign countries. Wedemeyer was not in favor of assistance to China without supervision. Assistance should be extended, according to Wedemeyer, on a scale commensurate with the ability of the United States to give it, and subject to China's making "effective use of it." He paid tribute to Chiang Kai-shek's character, his sincerity in fighting Communism, and his resistance to the Japanese for seven years, characterizing him as a loyal ally who was worthy of American support. His testimony was supported by other witnesses, including William C. Bullitt, former Ambassador to the Soviet Union. Bullitt was especially critical of the State Department for placing an embargo on the shipment of arms and ammunition to China the previous year. Congressman Walter H. Judd echoed similar concerns. The committee was interested in hearing about the report Wedemeyer rendered to President Truman but backed off after being informed that he had been cautioned not to disclose its contents. The administration's lid of secrecy was so tight that subsequent requests that the contents be shown to a select group of the committee in secret executive session were denied.

On August 13, 1948, shortly before the Communist takeover, Marshall finally abandoned his efforts to resolve the China issue, declaring: "I wash my hands of the problem which has passed altogether beyond my power to make a difference." By the time the report finally became public in 1949, the Communists had already seized power, and even then it was buried in a 1,000-plus-page White Paper written by Dean Acheson that few people read in its entirety.[31] In 1951, when the notorious Joseph McCarthy virtually accused Marshall of treason, based partly on his suppression of Wedemeyer's report, Wedemeyer loyally came to the defense of his mentor, stating: "I emphatically disagree with Senator McCarthy's attempt to represent [Marshall] as having willfully associated himself with traitors, or as having been the tool of subversive Communist-sympathizing elements in our Government."

At a Congressional hearing on May 3, 1951 (the famous "MacArthur Hearings"), General Douglas MacArthur echoed Wedemeyer's views on Communism and the political situation in China:

> SENATOR WILEY: What would you have done . . . advised . . . [in China] back there in 1945?
> GENERAL MacARTHUR: I would have given such assistance to [Chiang] as to have checked the growing tide of Communism. A very little assistance in my belief, at that time would have accomplished that purpose.
> SENATOR WILEY: Would you have sought to have amalgamated the Communists and Nationalists?
> GENERAL MacARTHUR: Just about as much chance of getting them together as that oil and water will mix.[32]

While Wedemeyer contemplated resignation in order to publicly speak his mind and bring home the truth to the American people, ultimately his deeply ingrained sense of loyalty to his country won out, and he remained silent until he published *Wedemeyer Reports!* in 1958. Is it any wonder that when he finally went public, he included an exclamation mark in the title?

CHAPTER 11

THE ROLE OF THE RUSSIAN BEAR

Soviet Union foreign policy is a puzzle inside a riddle wrapped in an enigma and is the key to Russian foreign policy.
—Winston Churchill

RUSSIA'S ROLE IN THE COMMUNIST TAKEOVER OF CHINA

While four previous presidents had refused to recognize the Soviet Union, soon after his inauguration in 1933, Franklin Roosevelt was persuaded by Commissar of Foreign Affairs Maxim Litvinov that Moscow would never promote armed revolution in the United States. In a letter dated November 16, 1933 and signed by Litvinov, Russia, in order to gain recognition promised, among other things, "Not to permit the formation . . . [of any group] having the aim of armed struggle against the United States . . . and to prevent the recruiting [of] such organizations and groups . . . and not to permit the formation . . . [of any group] which has as an aim the overthrow . . . or the bringing about by force . . . a change in, the political or social order . . . of the United States."[1] This commitment, along with almost every other one made, was never honored, thus establishing a pattern of Soviet subversion and American blind-eyed appeasement that permeated American foreign policy for a decade and a half.

During the first two terms of the Roosevelt administration, activities of the American Communist party were of secondary concern to the State Department. At the outset of hostilities in September 1939, America functionally forgot the shocking non-aggression pact between Hitler and Stalin. Historian William Henry Chamberlin notes that a more frightening scenario was the potential of a satisfactory agreement to divide the loot. Had Molotov's demands for an additional cut in the spoils of Poland not gone beyond what Hitler was prepared to concede,[2] Stalin was quite ready to pledge eternal friendship to Hitler and join the Axis, despite the Nazis' deeply entrenched fear of Communism. In the fateful turnabout after Hitler invaded Russia on June 22, 1941, the Soviet Union became America's new friend to be embraced. The agile Communist press, which up to that time had bitterly condemned Britain for its anti-Soviet stance, turned on a dime and reversed its course. Likewise, The United States developed amnesia when Russia turned the corner in its fight against the Nazis.

Even in the early days after Germany invaded Russia, there was philosophical support in Moscow for the Chinese Communists, but it had to remain just that, moral support. As long as the Soviet Union was locked in a life-threatening struggle with Nazi Germany, she was unable to provide substantial material assistance to Mao Zedong and his People's Liberation Army (PLA). A trickle of aid got through to the United Fronts, but only enough to keep the Japanese occupied and ward off a feared Japanese invasion of Manchuria, Stalin's greatest concern at the time. After VJ Day on August 14, 1945, Stalin signed the Sino-Soviet Treaty with Chiang, ostensibly to mitigate the insults perpetrated against China by the concessions to Russia made at Cairo and Teheran (but not those made secretly at Yalta), and to encourage Chiang in bringing the Chinese Communists into a unified government under his control. The treaty stipulated that only the Nationalists would be the beneficiary of Russian assistance, but Chiang had every right to be suspicious of Stalin's motives. Before the ink was dry, virtually every provision of the treaty was violated. The real Soviet goal was to expand their sphere of influence in the east by assisting Mao Zedong's takeover of China. The empty treaty was no more than a ploy to buy time.

Stalin declared war against Japan on August 8, 1945, immediately after the dropping of the second Atomic Bomb on Nagasaki, rushing to occupy Manchuria in order to grab huge quantities of abandoned Japanese arms and equipment. In complete violation of the treaty, the Soviets timed their withdrawal from Manchuria to essentially allow a transfer of control to Maoist forces. The spoils of the Japanese Kwantung Army yielded a bonanza of more than 3,700 artillery pieces and mortars, 600 tanks, 861 aircraft, and nearly 680 military depots. Chiang's efforts to enter Manchurian ports and prevent the takeover were forcibly blocked by the Soviets for a crucial five weeks, during which time Mao's forces were able to consolidate their positions. Mao's ultimate booty was sufficient to arm fifteen divisions. In addition to the seized Japanese materiel, Stalin also provided the Chinese Communists with an additional 369 tanks as well as artillery that was no longer needed after the end of active hostilities, thereby erasing Nationalist superiority in equipment. Additionally, Russia lent substantial assistance to train a Communist army of 800,000 that eventually routed the Kuomintang. All of this was accomplished as America stood quietly on the sidelines, articulating perhaps the most tragic manifestation of its policy of appeasement.

The armaments seized in Manchuria would also play a decisive role during the Korean War, enabling Chinese Communist forces to rout Douglas MacArthur's forces in a surprise winter offensive across the Yalu River with 300,000 well-supplied troops. Soviet-made tanks supplied to the Chinese overran American forces sent to Korea shortly after the outbreak of hostilities in June of 1950.

Wedemeyer's uncompleted book, parts of which are in the Wedemeyer files at the Hoover Institution,[3] outlines his meetings with President Roosevelt and the limited understanding the president had about Communism. Wedemeyer wryly observes that he was informed by Roosevelt's intimates that the president was not much of a student of history (indeed he was, but not as it applied to Asia) but rather a devotee of mystery novels. Wedemeyer was deeply disturbed by the supreme irony of the leader of the free world, charged with the need to understand the motives of his allies and his enemies, neglecting historical precedent and favoring fiction!

Wedemeyer noted that "It is regrettable that he [Roosevelt] did not read a book by William Z. Foster, National Chair of the Communist party, *Toward Soviet America*."[4] Published in 1932, this treatise laid out in precise detail the reasons why a Communist revolution was inevitable and vividly described their plan to take over America and destroy capitalism. Foster's outline was so candid in laying out the Party's secrets that it greatly troubled Communist leadership, leading them to halt the book's publication. The appalled party leaders instructed their members to steal all existing copies from libraries. The few remaining copies are now valuable collector's items.

Any Roosevelt administration officials who found pro-Soviet policies not to their liking and were bold enough to voice their view might soon be looking for other employment or find themselves transferred to less influential positions. Within the State Department, in the early years of the war there was an extremely capable and informed group in the Division of Eastern European Affairs that dealt with the Soviet Union and relied on an extensive library of documents and books on the subject. The division was headed by the scholarly and decidedly anti-Communist Robert F. Kelly. With his skepticism about Stalin's motives being completely out of tune with Roosevelt's policy of appeasement, he was summarily "transferred" to a post in Turkey and shortly thereafter retired. The library was dismantled and the unit incorporated into the larger Western European Section, where a closer watch could be imposed on the personnel.[5] An invaluable resource was forever lost. One of the largely forgotten sentinels of anti-Communism in America, Congressman Walter Judd, commented on the lamentable state of affairs that permitted the ouster of key personnel from the State Department:

> I urge our Government to call back into emergency service statesmen like Grew, Hornbeck, Dooman, Berle, and others. Men who are real experts on Asia or on communism, men whom the left wing boys pushed out of the Department. You will recall that Alger Hiss was a key man in the Far Eastern Office from 1939 to 1944 when the pattern of building up the Chinese Communists and building down the Chinese Government was established.[6]

Journalists who wrote articles critical of the Soviets were marginalized. However, those who wrote favorably were given special access to the administration. Forrest Davis, editor of the prestigious *Washington Post*, traveled to Teheran with the American delegation for the meeting in November 1943 and wrote a two-part article for the *Saturday Evening Post* in May 1944 entitled "What Really Happened at Teheran." The articles were submitted to Roosevelt and "approved" by him before publication.[7] Davis laid out the President's views on foreign policy, his impressions of Stalin, his understanding of Communism, and how it factored into post-war planning. In portraying a highly positive opinion, Davis reported that in one of his conversations with the President, Roosevelt said that Stalin avowed that he had no desire to acquire vast territory in Europe, and that Roosevelt believed him. He further reported that the President chose not to seek commitments from Russia, not only because he *trusted* Stalin, but because he was deferring potential political problems to military success, and, most importantly, seeking a commitment from Stalin to support the United Nations, a dream that Roosevelt believed would be a panacea in solving the problems of the post-war world.

Without the strong post-war world peace organization that required Stalin's support, Roosevelt feared that his legacy would be closely linked with that of Woodrow Wilson. As Assistant Secretary of the Navy in the Wilson

Administration, Roosevelt had witnessed both the deterioration of Wilson's health in his campaign to gain acceptance of the League of Nations and the disastrous consequences of its failure that laid the groundwork for the rise of Adolph Hitler. It was Roosevelt's belief that the best way to avoid a repetition was to establish close relations with the Soviets in order to gain their commitment to democratic ideals. Sadly, this approach ultimately defeated its own purpose.

Appeasement of Russia started early and continued through the hostilities. At QUADRANT, the first Quebec conference, held between August 11 and 24, 1943, appeasement was institutionalized. Harry Hopkins carried with him a document entitled "Russia's Position," that opined:

> Russia's postwar position in Europe will be a dominant one. . . . Since Russia is the decisive factor in the war, she must be given every assistance and every effort must be made to obtain her friendship. Likewise, *since without question she will dominate Europe on the defeat of the Axis,* [emphasis added] it is even more essential to develop and maintain the most friendly relations with Russia. . . . The most important factor the United State has to consider in relation to Russia is the prosecution of the war in the Pacific. . . . Should the war in the Pacific have to be carried on with an unfriendly or a negative attitude on the part of Russia, the difficulties will be immeasurably increased and operations might become abortive.[8]

Robert Sherwood points out that this document "was obviously of great importance as indicating the policy which guided the making of decisions at Teheran and, much later, at Yalta."[9]

At the time of QUADRANT, it is reasonable to understand how policymakers could have assumed that Russia's assistance would be needed to defeat Japan, but it is less understandable why they conceded Russian domination of post-war Europe at so early a date. American foreign policy was now geared to permit Russia an unobstructed free hand in Europe, with little consideration of how Soviet domination of East Asia might ultimately be harmful to American interests.

Nowhere was Roosevelt's inclination toward Stalin to "give him everything," and brook no interference manifested more graphically than as it applied to Lend-Lease. In 1943, General John R. Deane, head of the American Mission in Moscow, recorded that the Russians were requesting large shipments of diesel engines, which were in short supply in the United States. As Dean tried to evaluate the situation on a comparative need basis, he was rebuffed when he attempted to ascertain from the Russians the justification for their demands. When the matter was broached with Soviet Commissar of Foreign Trade, Anastasius Mikoyan, Deane was bluntly informed: "It should not be necessary to go behind a request made by the Soviet Government since it was axiomatic that such a request would not be made unless the need was great."

Mikoyan also implied that even if Deane objected to the request, the Soviets would have no trouble obtaining the material despite his views. Dean decided to test the Russian claim, telegramming to the Joint Chiefs of Staff in Washington on January 16, 1944 to suggest that the allocation be made only on the recommendation of the American Military Mission. General Marshall concurred. Shortly thereafter, Deane received authoritative word from Harry Hopkins to *attach no strings to our aid to Russia*. As Mikoyan had forecasted, the extra supplies were sent as requested.[10]

William C. Bullitt, former Ambassador to the Soviet Union and to France, was one of Roosevelt's most trusted advisors. In an article entitled "How We Won the War and Lost the Peace" that he wrote for the August 30, 1948 issue of *Life* magazine, Bullitt described how, acting on the advice of Harry Hopkins, the President hoped to convert Stalin from imperialism to democratic collaboration by giving him, without stint or limit, everything he asked for in the prosecution of the war, and to refrain from asking anything in return. According to Bullitt, Roosevelt actually hoped to entice "Uncle Joe" into an acceptance of "Christian values and democratic principles," and persuade him to adhere to the principles of the Atlantic Charter by informing him that the influence of the White House was being used to encourage the American public to take a favorable view of the Soviet Union.

Bullitt wrote a memorandum critical of Roosevelt's policy and, shortly thereafter, had a three-hour meeting in which the President accepted as accurate all of his charges, yet still opined:

> Bill, I don't dispute your facts; they are accurate. I don't dispute the logic of your reasoning. *I just have a hunch that Stalin is not that kind of a man.* Harry [Hopkins] says he's not and that he doesn't want anything but security for his country. And I think that if I give him everything I possibly can and ask for nothing from him in return, *noblesse oblige*, he won't try to annex anything and will work

with me for a world of democracy and peace. [emphasis added][11]

On a hunch and Hopkins' endorsement, America's leader mobilized the military production capability of the United States to support his decision and set out on a course destined to end in diplomatic bankruptcy.

Bullitt's experience was not unique. Secretary of Labor and longtime Roosevelt stalwart Francis Perkins reported that after his return from Teheran the President told her:

> I really think the Russians will go along with me about having no spheres of influence and about agreements for free ports all over the world. That is ports which can be used freely at all times by all the allies. I think that is going to be the answer.[12]

Shortly after his first meeting with Stalin at Teheran, in his fireside chat on Christmas Eve, 1943, Roosevelt attempted to put the country's mind at rest about the Soviet leader:

> To use an American and ungrammatical colloquialism, I may say that I got on well with Marshal Stalin. . . . I believe that we are going to get on well with him and the Russian people, very well indeed. . . . The rights of every nation, large and small, must be respected and guarded as jealously as are the rights of every individual in our republic. The doctrine that the strong shall dominate the weak is the doctrine of our enemies, and we reject it.

The President also enlisted Secretary of State Cordell Hull in his crusade. Making an unprecedented appearance before a Joint Session of Congress on November 19, 1943 after a visit to the Soviet Union, Hull characterized Stalin as "one of the great statesmen and leaders of this age," adding:

> As the provisions of the Four Nations Declaration are carried into effect, there will no longer be need for spheres of influence, for alliances, for balance of power, or any other of the special arrangements through which, in the unhappy past, the nations strove to safeguard their security or to promote their interests.[13]

Hull's comments gave notice that any criticism of Russia or its leader at this time was considered to be the height of political incorrectness. It is sadly ironic that at a time of euphoric approval of all things Russian, the Soviet armies, fueled by the support of American Lend-Lease, were overrunning the German army on their way to Berlin, leaving in their wake a trail of murder, rape, and pillage worthy of the hordes of Attila the Hun, carving out for Stalin a mightier empire than any Tsar had ever imagined.

Tragically, the American people were propagandized into a love affair with Russia by their President, aided and abetted by a willing and enthusiastic media. The March 29, 1943 edition of Henry Luce's *Life* magazine featured a full-page cover portrait of Joseph Stalin on a "Special USSR Issue" that included many photographs depicting Lend-Lease aid to Russia. The first page naïvely yet prophetically announced that: "*LIFE* has ... used every effort to present a true picture of the country whose power and greatness is the greatest political fact to emerge from this war." This fairy tale of Russia and its policies would again be replicated with respect to the Far East. China would be served up in similar fashion.

According to "assistant President" and future Secretary of State James Byrnes, Roosevelt made minimal or no preparation for the Yalta Conference in February 1945, writing that the extensive State Department file prepared for the commander-in-chief had never been read.[14] Roosevelt's blind spot for Communist intentions infected his entire administration. His closest advisor, Harry Hopkins, said after the Yalta Conference:

> We really believed in our hearts that this was the dawn of the new day we had all been praying for and talking about for so many years. We were absolutely certain that we had won the first great victory of the peace—and, by 'we' I mean *all* of us, the whole civilized human race. The Russians proved they could be reasonable and farseeing and there wasn't any doubt in the minds of the President or any of us that we could live with them and get along with them peacefully for as far into the future as any of us could imagine.[15]

During the later stages of the war, the tenuous state of President Franklin Roosevelt's health needs to be factored into the equation of American foreign policy. From April 1944 onward, Roosevelt was restricted to a four-hour workday and his autocratic reign over the State Department clearly suffered. Likewise, the infirmity of Secretary of State Cordell Hull and the selection of a hopelessly weak replacement, Edward Stettinius, compounded the problem. A healthy President would have kept a closer eye on State Department operatives that were functioning counter to the stated American policy of support for a unified government under Chiang. At Yalta, the diplomatic shots in large part were called by Alger Hiss and Harry Hopkins, both with well documented Stalinist sympathies. Unbeknownst to either Wedemeyer, then head of American forces in China and chief liaison aide to Chiang's Nationalist government, and Patrick Hurley, American Ambassador to China, Roosevelt secretly agreed to permit Stalin to transfer ten divisions to the Manchurian border, in addition to restoring all of the territories lost by Russia to the Japanese in 1905, giving Stalin control of the Manchurian railroad and unfettered access to the warm water port at Dairen. All of these concessions were made without the consent, let along the knowledge, of Chiang Kai-shek.

With the remarkable secret concessions to the Soviets concerning Manchuria, the die was cast, and Roosevelt's rapidly declining mental capabilities and determination to establish the United Nations at virtually any cost precluded a change of course. In March 1945, when Wedemeyer came to the White House to warn his commander-in chief of the dangers of a Communist takeover, he was unable to penetrate Roosevelt's addled brain, writing in *Wedemeyer Reports!* that he "was shocked at his physical appearance. His color was ashen, his face drawn, and his jaw drooping. I had difficulty in conveying information to him because he seemed in a daze. Several times I repeated the same idea because his mind did not seem to retain or register"[16] (Roosevelt died several weeks later, on April 12, 1945.)

The combination of factors that ultimately permitted the Soviets to ensure that the vast cache of captured Japanese armaments fell into the hands of the Maoist forces was an enormous factor in their ultimate success in 1949. Even such staunch Roosevelt supporters as Robert Sherwood cast severe criticism on these secret Yalta agreements as being the most important negative result of the Conference.[17]

The dire consequences of America's appeasement policy toward Russia were not long in surfacing. On February 5, 1946, an emboldened Stalin predicted that it was both inevitable and proximate that there would be war between the USSR and USA.[18] While Soviet behavior after the war is often viewed with resentful disillusionment, there is no need for surprise or indignation. With their long history of subversion it could and should have been predictable by anyone with a reasonable background in Soviet history, let alone the so-called "experts" in the State Department. Thus, it became apparent that many of Roosevelt's policy decisions regarding Russia were flawed, inconsistent, and sometimes downright contradictory.

The reasons for the meltdown continue to be debated. Many faulted the policies of President Roosevelt, which they now began to see in a different light. Many of his former policies were seen as contradictions, and they could not reconcile them. How to understand these contradictions puzzles many historians. One explanation offered by a man who devoted 30 years of his life to the study of President Roosevelt seems to be as good as any explanation offered. "History, Warren F. Kimball says, is a series of contradictions, and historians spend years, even careers, trying to reconcile those contradictions, seeming to make the presumption that everything that someone does must fit neatly into a fixed pattern of purpose and action." This is a useless exercise. He illustrates his thesis with a quotation from Walt Whitman:

> Do I contradict myself?
> Very well then I contradict myself
> (I am large, and I contain multitudes)[19]

CHAPTER 12

HOW THE COMMUNISTS TOOK CHINA

Political power grows out of the barrel of a gun.
—Mao Zedong

On October 1, 1949, a beaming Mao Zedong and his second-in-command, Zhou Enlai, stood atop Tien An Men, the Gate of Heavenly Peace at the center of the old Forbidden City of Peking, and triumphantly proclaimed the birth of the People's Republic of China. A host of newly installed Communist political operatives and nearly half a million jubilant followers who had jammed into the massive square joined in celebration. Chiang Kai-shek and two million of his followers had been exiled to the island of Taiwan. Formal diplomatic recognition of Communist China by the Soviet Union came on the very next day. Five months later, the two countries signed a Treaty of Friendship.

Debated to this day is whether the United States, as a consequence of its actions (or inaction) failed China or, as Barbara Tuchman opined at the end of her Pulitzer Prize-winning treatise, *Stilwell and The American Experience In China*, that "China went her own way as if the Americans had never come."[1] The issue has been posed pejoratively by conservative historians as "How Did We Lose China?" Liberal pundits correctly and dismissively counter that "China Was Not Ours to Lose." Clearly though, the perfect storm of military, political, economic, and social circumstances that brought about the transition of power in China has exerted a monumental and lasting influence on the history and geopolitical climate of the world.

There is no shortage of opinions as to the reasons China went Communist. In *The Man Who Lost China*, Brian Crozier, as the title of his book suggests, lays the blame squarely on the personal deficiencies of Chiang Kai-shek and of his administration.[2] Conservatives, especially in the early years of the Cold War, invoked the influence of elements within the administrations of Presidents Roosevelt and Truman. Indeed, China's government fell for a complex variety of reasons, many of which had been percolating for decades. But clearly, American diplomacy played a longstanding and critical role. The main causes will be examined.

THE "CHINA HANDS"

American State Department China policy was largely the product of the so-called "China Hands," principally John Stuart Service, John Paton Davies, and John Carter Vincent. Their defenders claim that the stance they took was sincere yet ultimately misguided, stemming from a pragmatic desire to defeat Japan which they felt could only be done with a United Front. This view is championed by historian Peter Rand:

> It seems in retrospect that U.S. advisers in China, and Stilwell himself, were determined to believe the best of the Communists in their zeal to achieve their war goal of defeating Japan. John Paton Davies has admitted as much.[3]

Others contend that they were loyal patriots who well understood the problems of China and proposed solutions in good faith, but that their reputations subsequently suffered principally as a result of the accusations of Senator Joseph McCarthy and his followers. E.H. Kahn, author of *The China Hands: America's Foreign Service Officers and What Befell Them*, champions this opinion,[4] characterizing them as scapegoats who were hung out to dry by the State Department. Another more benign view is that of historian Jay Taylor who says that these officers were very much "the product of their times," but even so, "Their generally black-and-white views of Chinese politics seem curiously devoid of perspective or nuance . . ."[5]

On the other hand, their critics, most notably Anthony Kubek, feel they were disloyal at best and blatantly pro-Communist at worst.[6] Early in his tenure as Ambassador to China, Patrick Hurley recognized their pervasive influence in opposition to the stated American policy of support of a coalition government headed by Chiang Kai-Shek. Even after he removed them from China, they continued to exert a dominant influence upon American China Policy.

A more moderate viewpoint is that, rather than being intentionally disloyal, they simply did not do their homework and acted from a position of ignorance. It is difficult, though, to understand how such a group could not fathom how basic Communist doctrine ran counter to the overall interests of the future of their country, and how the aims of the Chinese Communist Party (CCP) were no different from those of their Soviet brethren. The critical position of the China Hands in shaping American policy demanded a thorough understanding of the aims of Marx, Lenin, Stalin, and Mao. This was lacking. A telling indictment is supplied by Acheson's successor as Secretary of State, John Foster Dulles, who felt no firm personal commitment to the left-leaning Foreign Service Officers. Dulles showed John Carter Vincent, former head of the China desk at the State Department, a copy of Stalin's *Problems of Leninism*, and asked if he had read it. After Vincent said he had not, Dulles replied, "If you *had* read it, you would not have advocated the policies you did in China!"[7]

The China Hands should not have mistaken the CCP for anything resembling democracy. There was plenty in the available literature which should have been examined by these men. In 1934, Stalin announced in *Problems of Leninism*:

> It is inconceivable that the Soviet Republic should continue to exist for a long period side by side with imperialist states. Ultimately one or the other must conquer. Meanwhile a number of terrible clashes between the Soviet Republic and the bourgeois states are inevitable.

In 1939, he reiterated in *Foundations of Leninism*:

> The victory of socialism in one country is not an end in itself; it must be looked upon as a support, as a means for hastening the proletarian victory in every other land. For the victory of the revolution in one country (in Russia, for the present) is not only the result of the unequal development and the progressive decay of imperialism, it is likewise the beginning and the continuation of the world revolution.

Anthony Kubek dates the genesis of their opinions to the time they served with General Stilwell:

> There can be no doubt that the Foreign Service Officers in General

Stilwell's staff were determined to destroy the Nationalist Government and remove Chiang Kai-shek as head of state. They were very explicit in their advocacy of this change and argued it repeatedly and forcefully. The Roosevelt Administration formulated its policies largely on the information reported by these men. Now and then Harry Hopkins would call the attention of the President to what they wrote.[8]

Diplomatic dispatches from China intended to guide American superiors consistently reflected a decidedly pro-Communist sentiment:

John Patton Davies, June 24, 1943:
The Kuomintang and Chiang Kai-shek recognize that the Communists, with the popular support which they enjoy and their reputation for administrative reform and honesty, represent a challenge to the Central Government and its spoils system.[9]

John Stuart Service, July 30, 1944:
... the Communists base their policy toward the Kuomintang on a real desire for democracy in China under which there can be orderly economic growth through a stage of private enterprise to eventual socialism without the need of violent upheaval and revolution.[10]

And on August 3, 1944:

... the Communist party becomes a party seeking orderly democratic growth toward socialism—as it is being attained, for instance, in a country like England—rather than a party fomenting an immediate and violent revolution.[11]

The most notorious and most quoted was John Service's report number forty, dated October 10, 1944, which read in part:

Our dealing with Chiang Kai-shek apparently continues on the basis of the unrealistic assumption that he is China and that he is necessary to our cause. It is time, for the sake of the war and also for our future interest in China, that we take a more realistic line. In the present circumstances, the Kuomintang is dependent on

American support for survival. But we are in no way [dependent] on the Kuomintang. We need not fear Kuomintang surrender or opposition. The party and Chiang will stick to us because our victory is certain and is their only hope for continued power....All the other groups in China want to defend themselves and fight Japan. Any new government under any other than the present reactionary control will be more cooperative and better able to mobilize the country....We need not support Chiang in the belief that he represents pro-American or democratic China. All the people and all other political groups of importance in China are friendly to the United States and look to it for the salvation of the country, now and after the war. . . . we must, for instance, plan an eventual use of the Communist armies and this cannot be purely on Kuomintang terms.[12]

These dispatches weighed heavily in the decision of the State Department to include a provision in the December 1945 orders to General Marshall that required a coalition government be installed as a condition of continued United States support—a poison pill that doomed the negotiations and ultimately the Nationalist government. As George Creel pointed out in a criticism of General Marshall's inadequate preparation and understanding of the situation in China when he undertook the mission in 1945, he "could have been under no delusions as to the result of his mission . . . as shown by the bitter experience of Poland, Rumania, Bulgaria and Yougoslavia, so called 'coalition governments' had paved the way for complete Communist control."[13] Yet the China Hands pressed for insertion into Marshall's instructions a requirement of a coalition government. John Carter Vincent wrote Secretary of State Byrnes just prior to Marshall's departure, strongly underscoring the importance of "broadening of the base of the Chinese government" to include so-called Communists.[14]

Persuasive evidence against the China Hands comes directly from an admission made by Davies himself in 1962. After having been exiled to Peru following his dismissal from the Foreign Service as a security risk, in an interview with Leonard Gross, European editor of *Look* magazine, he admitted: "My mistake in 1944 was in saying that the Chinese Communists were democratic . . . I confused the popularity of the Communists with democracy . . . they had a democratic facade . . . [but] the leadership betrayed the people."[15]

THE ROLE OF THE JAPANESE

The Nationalists' best window to consolidate their hold on the Chinese government was the ten-year period between 1927 and 1937, often referred to as "China's Golden Age." During this decade, Chiang put down regional separatists and developed the nucleus of a strong army with central control. China reformed its currency, developed a central bank, developed markets for exporting its goods, and was in the process of improving its transportation system and instituting "agrarian reforms," the moniker later subverted by Mao Zedong. Chiang's reforms gained him recognition in the West. In 1937, *Time* magazine proclaimed Generalissimo and Madame Chiang Kai-shek "Man and Wife of the Year" for their valiant efforts to resist the Japanese.

The growing power and unity of their neighbor did not escape the notice of the Japanese, who elected to invade Manchuria in 1931 and initiate a full-scale war in 1937. The Japanese concluded that the longer they delayed their attack, the stronger Chiang Kai-shek would become and the more difficult it would be to subdue the Nationalists. The hostilities achieved their aim, bringing Chiang's efforts at internal reform to a grinding halt. The Japanese onslaught was devastating. Every major city was bombed, and twenty million soldiers and civilians perished in the decade between 1931 and Pearl Harbor. The entire eastern coast, including every major port, was occupied, resulting in a complete blockade intended to bring China to its knees. The only remaining source of supply was the soon to be closed Burma Road, leaving only the treacherous "Hump" air route over the Himalayas. The net effect of the strangling of China was to make her totally dependent on foreign aid.

With bitter memories of their defeat in the Russo-Japanese War, the Soviet Union stood nervously on the sidelines and embraced a strategy of surreptitious assistance to the Chinese Communists in order to insure that Chiang would not be able to subdue them. Since Chiang's forces were far superior at the time, it was the Soviet goal to walk a delicate tightrope, keeping the Chinese forces engaged and just strong enough to protect the Russian eastern flank against the Japanese, yet not strong enough to crush the CCP. The plan was to just keep the pot boiling and the struggle between the Chinese Communists and the Nationalists brewing, with neither side prevailing. This explains why Stalin intervened to save Chiang's life in 1937, after he was treacherously betrayed and captured by the CCP in the city of Sian in 1937.[16] Stalin ordered Mao Zedong to release Chiang on the condition that the KMT and the Chinese Communists join forces in a "United Front" against Japan. Accordingly, the first of three tenuous alliances between

16. General Joseph W. Stilwell and General Clair Chennault confer at Kunming China (these guys do not like each other; note the body language).
Hoover Institution, Stanford, California

17. General Wedemeyer and General George C. Marshall review troops in China, December 1945. *Hoover Institution, Stanford, California*

18. General Wedemeyer with General Clair Chennault and Chinese General Lung
in China, 1945. *Hoover Institution, Stanford, California*

19. General Wedemeyer with T.V. Soong, China's Ambassador to the United States,
1945. *Hoover Institution, Stanford, California*

20. General Wedemeyer along with General Patrick Hurley, U.S. Ambassador to China, and Generalissimo Chiang Kai-Shek after conference at Wedemeyer's headquarters, Chunking China, December 1945. *Hoover Institution, Stanford, California*

21. General Wedemeyer with California Governor Earl Warren and General MacArthur in San Francisco on the political trail, April 1951. *Hoover Institution, Stanford, California*

22. Chiang Kai-shek in full military regalia, 1940. *Hoover Institution, Stanford, California*

23. Kungming China, February 1943. *Left to right:* Field Marshall Sir John Dill, Br; Major General Clayton Bissell, Commander U.S.A. X Air Force, India; Major General Claire Chennault, Commander USA XIV Air Force China; Brig. General Wedemeyer. *Hoover Institution, Stanford, California*

24. General Joseph W. "Vinegar Joe" Stilwell and General Claire Chennault in China, 1944. *Hoover Institution, Stanford, California*

25. General Wedemeyer with wife Elizabeth and sons, Robert D. and Albert D. at the Presidio, San Francisco, California, 1950. *Hoover Institution, Stanford, California*

26. General Albert Wedemeyer and family in China, 1931. *Hoover Institution, Stanford, California*

27. General Albert Wedemeyer with wife Elizabeth and son Albert, 1951.
Hoover Institution, Stanford, California

28. Wedemeyer cover,
U.S. News and World Report,
September 15, 1951.
*Courtesy US News and
World Report*

29. General Wedemeyer at Chunking staff meeting, May 1945.
Hoover Institution, Stanford, California

these bitter fratricidal rivals was cobbled together for the sole purpose of holding Japan at bay, all to the ultimate benefit of the Soviet Union. At the time, Stalin knew that Mao and his followers were not yet prepared to take over the nation and provide an effective buffer against Japanese aggression. Any further attenuation of Chiang's power would very likely have brought China closer to making peace with the invaders, increasing the risk to the Soviet heartland.

It was a brilliant move on Stalin's part, yet as insurance, he still was obliged to maintain twenty divisions of troops in Siberia to forestall potential Japanese aggression in the region. He was subsequently able to remove a substantial number of these troops from Siberia after receiving information through the infamous Sorge Spy Ring that the Japanese military had ordered summer uniforms instead of cold weather gear, thus indicating a push in a southerly direction instead of into the Soviet Union.

In an effort to obviate the threat of hostilities on an eastern front, the Soviets entered into a five-year non-aggression pact with Japan on April 13, 1941. The pact had other tangible benefits, permitting Stalin to commit a greater number of troops to defend against Operation Barbarossa, the Nazi invasion of the Soviet Union which was launched that June. In the later stages of the war, the pact also allowed him to piously decline to enter the war against the Japanese because of his need to honor his "commitments."[17]

Mao Zedong benefited from the United Front far more than Chiang. He had always been a more effective propagandist than his rival and capitalized on this advantage by capturing the lion's share of favorable publicity in the Western press, despite being vastly outnumbered and far less involved in fighting the Japanese. By necessity, Chiang developed a strategy during the war of surrendering territory to the Japanese and launching counterattacks. Never at a loss to exploit a propaganda advantage, the strategy was denounced by Mao as "proof" that the Nationalists lacked the will to fight, a flagrant untruth that was readily bought by a majority of Western journalists.

In 1937, Mao Zedong secretly instructed his forces to use seventy percent of their effort on Communist expansion, twenty percent fighting *against* the Nationalists, and only ten percent against the Japanese. CCP military efforts were largely confined to small commando-like raids designed more to capture arms and ammunition than to engage the enemy. In 1941, the CCP's Central Revolutionary Committee affirmed that the party's main emphasis was a "political offensive" against the Japanese and consequently reduced the size of the Communist army by twenty percent.[18] Mao Zedong used the war as a training ground to battle-harden his troops, develop border regions as proving grounds for his administrative techniques, and indoctrinate peasants with propaganda hostile to the Nationalist government in his continually expanding area of influence in the north. He was in no hurry to defeat the invader; the war abetted his ultimate goal of wresting control of China. Mao Zedong knew that if the Japanese were defeated or a cease fire negotiated at a time when his forces were not at sufficient strength, Chiang would then return to devote all his efforts against the CCP. After the war, Mao Zedong admitted that but for Chiang's need to engage the Japanese, he would not have been able to defeat the Nationalist forces.

The CCP ran a brilliant campaign to capture public opinion in the areas they controlled by instituting selected "land reforms." This involved confiscating large land holdings, then executing the former owners after mock trials and redistributing ten-acre parcels to tenants, thereby creating immense good will among the formerly landless sharecroppers who were the beneficiaries. Of course the new "land owners" were not informed that the grants were only temporary and the land would ultimately be taken back and be incorporated into huge collectives. In America, only a few anti-Communist journalists saw through the deception.[19] Mao Zedong also instituted a propaganda campaign describing how he would remedy oppressive land taxation and other ills attributed to the National government. His popularity and influence soared, and many were recruited to his ranks.

THE ROLE OF CHIANG KAI-SHEK

Although Chiang was not personally corrupt,[20] far too many officials in his government and military were. The rich and privileged were able to avoid conscription, and taxes were not honestly collected. Treatment of draftees was deplorable; soldiers rarely had enough to eat, and their pay was stolen by officers. Loyalty to Chiang was the key factor in promotions. While Wedemeyer as his chief-of-staff had recommended reforms, and some were instituted, Chiang feared that pressing too many reforms, especially those that impinged on his "loyal supporters," would weaken his position of leadership. By 1948 Chiang acknowledged much of the inefficiency and corruption, but half-hearted efforts to correct them were too little and too late. Ultimately, the Communists succeeded in winning over large numbers of followers by promising to eliminate all the shortcomings of the KMT, liberally and effectively using the claim of Chiang's corruption as a lynch pin of their propaganda campaign to seize power.

Chiang had good reason to predict that the rising power of the Communists, if not checked, would have grave consequences for China. A 1923 visit to the Soviet Union had opened Chiang's eyes to the truth of Communist ideology, and he was well aware what their takeover in China would portend for his country. Although he accepted the Communist offer to assist him in forming the Whampoa Military Academy in 1931, he was never taken in by their propaganda and bided his time until he could move against them. In 1941, after ten arduous years of confrontation, he said: "You think it is important that I have kept the Japanese from expanding during these years. . . . I tell you it is more important that I have kept the Communists from spreading. The Japanese are a disease of the skin; the Communists are a disease of the heart."[21]

Stilwell exerted tremendous pressure to get Chiang to unite the Communist and Nationalist armies to fight the Japanese, but this would have necessitated Chiang's approval to arm the Communists with Lend-Lease supplies, a policy he was loathe to endorse. It was not because he did not want to oust the Japanese from China. He always looked at the bigger picture and understandably saw the Communists as, in the long run, more dangerous. Chiang was hesitant to take the better equipped Japanese head-on in the belief that it would weaken his forces and lessen his chances to ultimately defeat the Chinese Communists. Stilwell, in characteristic fashion, bitterly and tactlessly disagreed with this view. Their ongoing disagreement was reported in an article by Samuel Lubell in the *Saturday Evening Post* on February 24, 1945 entitled, "Vinegar Joe and the Reluctant Dragon,"[22] wherein Stilwell is depicted as the courageous warrior thirsting for a chance to get his Chinese troops into battle and Chiang as the obstructionist. Walter Judd defended Chiang by pointing out that when the United States delayed its cross-channel invasion of France for a year, it was to save precious American lives, yet when the Generalissimo procrastinated in China for the same reason, he was labeled as a poor ally.

While Chiang's military and domestic methods had serious flaws, some reforms were instituted, including reducing the size of the army to allow for better feeding of the troops, installing a more efficient and honest system of paying soldiers, better sanitation procedures, and a more merit-based system of promotion, virtually all of this eventuating after Wedemeyer replaced Stilwell in October 1944.

There is ample evidence to support Chiang's desire for a more democratic regime. As early as 1936, just before the Japanese invasion, he sought to replace the "political tutelage" ordained by Sun Yat-sen with a more democratic system. As the prospects of defeating the Japanese improved, Chiang again turned his attention to how he could institute political reform, and by mid-1946 he had taken steps in this direction. General Marshall praised the new Chinese Constitution that was approved on Christmas Day 1946 as "democratic" and regarded the Communist rejection of it as unfortunate, since the document incorporated every major point the Communists had demanded.

The Communists and much of the Western press were continuously clamoring that corruption in the government be eliminated. The charge that this was the fatal, irremediable flaw in Chiang's government is inaccurate and unfair. Reminiscent of Abraham Lincoln's "house divided" speech ninety years earlier, Douglas MacArthur, in a March 4, 1948 cable to the House Foreign Affairs Committee, asserted:

> The international aspect of the Chinese problem, unfortunately, has become somewhat beclouded by demands for internal reform. Desirable as such reform may be, its importance is but secondary to the issue of civil strife now engulfing the land, and these two issues are as impossible of synchronization as it would be to alter the structural design of a house while the same was being consumed by flame . . . [T]he maintenance of China's integrity against destructive forces which threaten her engulfment is of infinitely more concern. For with the firm maintenance of such integrity, reform will gradually take place in the evolutionary processes of China's future.[23]

Walter Judd echoed these sentiments in an address before the Foreign Affairs Committee, after conferring with MacArthur during a 1947 trip to China and Japan:

> Our failure to help the Government of China effectively at the end of the war, with its otherwise insuperable problems, particularly the Communist rebellion, will turn out, I fear, to be the single greatest blunder in the history of the United States. For the first time in our relations with Asia, we confused the paramount strategic interests of the United States in that area with an internal purification problem in China.[24]

At Judd's request, MacArthur sent yet another cable to be read before a hearing of the House of Representatives being held to consider aid to China:

> I can say without the slightest hesitation that a free, independent, peaceful, and friendly China is of profound importance to the peace of the world and to the position of the United States. It is the fundamental keystone to the Pacific arch. Underlying all issues in China now is the military problem. Until it is resolved little progress can be expected toward internal rehabilitation, regardless of the extent of outside aid.

THE ROLE OF GEORGE MARSHALL

Some conservatives have laid a good measure of the blame for China's ultimately falling to the Communists upon George Marshall. The key provision of his December 1945 mission was an injunction to insist on an unachievable coalition between the Communists and the Nationalists as a condition for continued aid to Chiang Kai-shek. Marshall was not responsible for this directive in his instructions, though he can be held culpable for naïveté in believing that it had any prospect of success, at least after his first encounters with the Communists. Forest Pogue acknowledged that Truman's instructions made "the success of the mission ultimately impossible."[25]

Marshall's 1951 testimony before the United States Senate MacArthur hearings presented an entirely different picture from his position in 1945. Six years after his failed mission, he avowed that "when I got out to China and looked the ground over, from the very start, there was no doubt that the leadership of [the Chinese forces based in Yenan] were Marxist Communists, and they so stated in my presence."[26] If Marshall understood the ultimate motives of Communism in 1945, his actions certainly did not comport with it, as his efforts at mediation put far more pressure on Chiang Kai-shek to make concessions. Mao Zedong demanded three separate truces, all of which were granted by General Marshall, with all working to the enormous advantage of the Communists, allowing them, in one instance, to escape from a perilous position that threatened the annihilation of a substantial portion of their forces. Another allowed the Communists to regroup and rearm.

Marshall had the enormous leverage of Lend-Lease supplies to compel Chiang to come to terms, and he imposed an American arms embargo in July 1946 that effectively lasted for sixteen months. As testified to by Wedemeyer at the MacArthur hearings, it had fatal consequences for the fortunes of the Nationalist government. Vice Admiral Oscar C. Badger, who served in the area from December 1947 to October 1949, and Generals Claire Chennault and Francis Brink were of the same opinion.[27] In addition to hampering military efforts, the associated loss of morale further added to Chiang's difficulties.[28]

THE DIXIE MISSION

A huge propaganda coup for the Chinese Communists was achieved in the summer of 1944 when Chiang was obliged, over his objection and with great trepidation, to approve the "Dixie Mission," a visit to Communist head-quarters at Yenan by American State Department personnel that included John Stewart Service and members of the press. Chiang viewed the mission as an erosion of his leadership and the equivalent of *de-facto* recognition of the Communists as legitimate representatives of a portion of the Chinese population. The Communists used the mission to put on a propaganda show, arranging a visit to a "Potemkin Village," an idyllic representation of what life was like under Communist rule. A similar Communist fabrication of the truth had been staged in Siberia a few months earlier for Vice-President Henry Wallace's visit to the Soviet Gulag. During his trip to Kolyma in May 1944, the gullible Wallace never realized that he was visiting a prison and was served an elaborate banquet in his honor that had been carved out from the prisoner's rations. His speech shortly before his departure assured his hosts that their deception had worked:

> Both the Russians and the Americans, in their different ways, are groping for a way of life that will enable the common man every-where in the world to get the most good out of modern technology. There is nothing irreconcilable in our aims and purposes. Those who so proclaim are wittingly or unwittingly looking for war—and in my opinion, are criminal.[29]

There is no evidence that the stage managers for Wallace's fantasy trip were the same as the ones who put on the performance for the Dixie Mission, but the outcome was the same. Gunter Stein, in *The Challenge of Red China*, reported that the members of the delegation were delighted to observe an "active natural Yenan atmosphere . . . of cheerful, warm-hearted, practical Eighth Route Army men and their wives without lipstick and society manners."[30] John Service joined the love affair in his report to the State

Department on July 28, 1944, proclaiming, "There is everywhere an emphasis on democracy or unlimited relations with the common people." The trip was reported widely in the American press, and the ebullient endorsements of the Communists were afforded great weight in Washington.

THE INSTITUTE FOR PACIFIC RELATIONS

The Institute for Pacific Relations (IPR) was established in 1925 as a non-governmental international organization intended to provide a forum for discussion of problems and relations between nations of the Pacific Rim. Elite members of the business and academic communities lent their names in the belief that the policies and recommendations of the organization were in the best interests of and consistent with American policy. Funding came from philanthropic sources, including the Rockefeller and Carnegie Foundations, and the founders spoke in terms of Wilsonianism, an awareness of America's new role as a world power after World War I, with the conviction that liberal democracy should be promoted throughout the world.

The IPR sponsored conferences and research projects and issued publications designed to inform the American public about Pacific affairs, and in the 1930s and 1940s it became the most influential think tank for Asian affairs and American policy toward China. An IPR "resource packet" was adopted by 1,300 public school systems. The War Department purchased over three quarters of a million IPR pamphlets and, despite their blatantly pro-Communist tone, they became the principal source of information on the Far East for American service personnel serving in the Pacific theatre.

As the IPR gained influence, it became dominated by liberal thinkers, "fellow travelers" (a term coined by Leon Trotsky for those surreptitiously sympathetic to the Communist cause), and card-carrying Communists. Anthony Kubek assigned great weight to the IPR's role in facilitating the Communist takeover of China, noting: "For this achievement, the Communist manipulations of the IPR must be acknowledged a political masterpiece."[31]

As McCarthyism began to take hold in the early 1950s, the IPR finally came under investigation by the Senate Internal Security Subcommittee, which held hearings that lasted for over a year. Forty-six witnesses gave over five thousand pages of testimony, providing evidence that resulted in the identification of Communist sympathizers. The bi-partisan committee unanimously endorsed a 244-page report[32] that exposed the subversive practices of the IPR:

The Institute of Pacific Relations has not maintained the character of an objective, scholarly, research organization. The IPR has been considered by the American Communist Party and by Soviet officials as an instrument of Communist policy, propaganda and military intelligence. The IPR disseminated and sought to popularize false information including information originating from Soviet and Communist sources. A small core of officials and staff members carried the main burden of IPR activities and directed its administration and policies. Members of the small core of officials and staff members who controlled IPR were either Communist or pro-Communist.... Most members of the IPR, and most members of its Board of Trustees, were inactive and obviously without influence over the policies of the organization and the conduct of its affairs. IPR activities were made possible largely through the financial support of American industrialists, corporations, and foundations, the majority of whom were not familiar with the inner workings of the organization.... The names of eminent individuals were by design used as a respectable and impressive screen for the activities of the IPR inner core, and as a defense when such activities came under scrutiny.[33]

POPULAR BOOKS AND NEWS ARTICLES

A body of literature in the late 1930s portrayed Chiang and the Soong family in a negative light. *Man's Fate*, a novel by Marxist André Malraux, was set in Shanghai at the time of the bloody 1927 KMT coup. *The Tragedy of the Chinese Revolution*, by Trotskyite author Harold Isaacs, was considered at the time to be the most authoritarian work on the CCP/KMT split and the early life of Chiang.[34] A number of widely circulated books published in the 1940s also projected a candy-coated view of Chinese Communism. The most florid example was *Red Star Over China*, written by Edgar Snow, that recounted his highly propagandized experience as an embedded reporter with the CCP. Owen Lattimore, who was subsquently implicated in the leak of top-secret State Department documents to *Amerasia* magazine, penned *The Solution in Asia* which portrayed the Communists as democratic idealists who supported self-government and elected representatives. Theodore White, later acclaimed for his *The Making of the President* series, wrote *Thunder Out of China*, a Book Of The Month Club selection that depicted Chiang as a brutal dictator and Yenan as a haven of progressive thinking. White asserted that with Mao Zedongist Communism: "there is little likelihood of their returning to a policy of ruthless land confiscation or terror in the village except under the sharpest provocation."[35] All of these works were strongly endorsed by the IPR, and reviews in the press were invariably written by those recommended by their staff.

Likewise, Chiang Kai-shek and the Nationalists were undercut by prophets of doom such as Henry Wallace and Wendell Willkie,[36] whose reports upon their return from tours of China heaped abuse on the Nationalists as "corrupt reactionaries" and praised the Communists as "agrarian rebels" who were offering the only resistance to the armies of Japan.[37] In "The Tyrannous Decade," an article that appeared in Henry Luce's *Fortune* magazine, Herrymon Maurer summarized their influence:

> Even men once anxious to get supplies to China now thought complacently of Russian influence in China's Manchuria: it would be a token of U.S-Russian cooperation; it would encourage the Chinese to domestic reform. There was strong talk, *sotto voce*, from the State Department about forcing Chungking to terms with the Chinese Communists. There was wide agreement that China needed a Tito in the form of a Communist leader Mao Tse-tung, instead of a Mihailovich in the form of Chiang Kai-shek. There was a new force in the world, experts pointed out, and the world's future depended on warm Russian-American cooperation.[38]

HARRY DEXTER WHITE

Unlike the China Hands, there is little question about White's direct Communist ties, being identified by both Whitaker Chambers and Elizabeth Bentley as an agent active in espionage. White was a major proponent and collaborator in the formation of the notorious "Morgenthau Plan" to de-industrialize post-war Germany and convert it to a pastoral economy, a scenario that surely would have abetted the cause of Communist supremacy throughout Europe.

As assistant Secretary of the Treasury under Henry Morgenthau, White contributed significantly to the downfall of China's Nationalist government by preventing the delivery of desperately needed financial aid. After the United States had made a commitment to Chiang for two hundred million dollars in gold to stem the rampant inflation that was devastating the Chinese economy, White wrote Morgenthau on December 9, 1944 that: "We have stalled as much as we have dared and have succeeded in limiting gold shipments to 26 million this past year. We think it would be a serious mistake to permit further large shipments at this time."[39] White also endorsed the Dixie Mission and told Morgenthau that the "interests of the Chinese Communist Party does not run counter to those of the United States"[40]

White's defenders downplay his role in the demise of Nationalist China, claiming that Chiang received substantial economic aid from America during World War II but squandered it. In fact, for the entire war, China received approximately one-and-a-half billion dollars, a mere three percent of total Lend-Lease aid.[41]

White died of a heart attack in August 1948 as the investigations of the Senate Committee on Communism in America tightened the ring around him.

Some sources, including Elizabeth Bentley and Whitaker Chambers, tied White ideologically to Lauchlin Currie, a Canadian-born naturalized American economist who joined the Roosevelt administration in the early days of the New Deal as a junior member of the "brains trust." Currie's star-crossed career is still shrouded in mystery. While acting as Roosevelt's envoy to China, he sided with Chiang in his ongoing battle with Stilwell, and shortly after the war was a major player in American worldwide economic policy, yet later was intimated to be associated with those that "lost" China and was functionally exiled to Columbia after the renewal of his passport was refused.

THE TRUMAN DOCTRINE AND THE MARSHALL PLAN

By 1946, the Truman administration began to acknowledge the rising tide of Communism in Europe. While the die had already been cast in the Balkans, non-Communist governments were in place in Greece and Turkey, but seriously threatened by Communist agitation. The 1947 Truman Doctrine contained no geographical boundaries or limitations:

> I believe it must be the policy of the United States to support free peoples who are resisting subjugation by armed minorities or by outside pressures. I believe that we must assist free peoples to work out their own destinies in their own way.

Further communist expansion in Europe was something the framers of American foreign policy were willing take on, but they were horrified at the prospect that the President might have intended to fight Communism worldwide, particularly in China. George Kennan, whose career was launched with the "Containment Doctrine" that provided the philosophical underpinning of the Truman Doctrine, was chief among them. Kennan specifically and exclusively limited containment to the spread of Soviet Communist ideology in Europe. His highly influential remarks about limiting the Marshall Plan apply with equal force to the Truman Doctrine:

> Seen historically, from the perspective of two decades, this distinction between Europe's needs and those of other areas seems too obvious to be challenged. This was however, not the case at the time. Throughout the period of preparation of the legislation making possible American aid to Europe's recovery, and for years thereafter, those of us who had to do with the original Marshall Plan concept would be plagued with demands from the congressional side that we draw up or inspire similar programs for China, for the Middle East, or for Latin America.[42]

Kennan had little to be concerned about because the doctrine would not be used in Asia. President Truman's highly effective anti-Communist policies in Greece and Turkey in 1947 took the form of economic aid and a limited amount of military support with advisors, military equipment, and supplies. This would not be the case in Asia. Largely based on Kennan's treatise, the United States was deaf to recommendations contained in Wedemeyer's 1947 report and Congressman Walter Judd's admonitions to apply the same policies to China.

MAO'S PROPAGANDA CAMPAIGN AND THE INFLUENCE OF MOSCOW ON CHINESE COMMUNISM

As part of their ongoing, orchestrated propaganda campaign to seize control of China, the CCP strived to squelch any hint of connection to the Soviets, passing themselves off as a group of independent "agrarian reformers" who just happened to have a Communist political philosophy. The deception was largely successful in convincing a considerable body of liberal American diplomats and media. Their job was made considerably easier by the obvious flaws of Chiang and his Nationalist government, as well as a perfect storm of social, economic, and political factors.

Accordingly, the Chinese Communists made every effort to discount the connection between them and Moscow, passing themselves off as independent Chinese patriots simply out to "democratize" China and rid it of a corrupt regime. The writings of historian George Creel provided the strongest contemporary counterpoint to the CCP's program of deception:

> For years the American Communists, assisted by their army of "fellow travelers" and credulous "liberals" have worked untiringly to persuade the public that the Chinese party is a comparatively recent political manifestation, having no connection whatsoever with Moscow and the Third International, but a purely native movement born of a people's spontaneous revolt against the corrupt and oppressive dictatorship of Chiang Kai-shek. *All of which may be summed up as the Ultimate Lie.* An indisputable record proves that the Chinese Communist Party has been under Russia's control.[43] (emphasis added)

In 1948 Creel laid out how the CCP, then in its thirtieth year, had been organized and financed by Lenin and Trotsky and had been under Soviet control ever since, further noting that for reasons of expediency there had been intermittent cooperation with non-Communist opposition. But in each and every instance, secret assurances were given to rank and file party members that such moves were to be regarded as "tactical and temporary," and that the CCP made no bones about using falsehood and treachery to justify their fight to achieve power. He also cited American sales of scrap metal to the Japanese after 1937, inadequate Lend-Lease support, General Stilwell's enmity toward Chiang, the secret agreements between Roosevelt and Stalin at Yalta, and George Marshall's failure to establish a coalition government as additional factors that undercut the Nationalist government as well as the track record of failure in dealing with the Communists in Poland, Hungary, and Czechoslovakia.[44]

Proof of the impossibility of any binding coalition between the Nationalists and the Communists is given by Mao, whose 1940 "Red Bible" asserts that "the aid of the Soviet Union is an indispensable condition for the final victory."[45] In 1945, he flatly stated that a coalition would ultimately result in the defeat of both Chiang and "reactionary American imperialism."

Mao Zedong's propaganda campaign was wildly successful in bringing both the Foreign Service corps as well as General Stilwell to his way of thinking. It also succeeded in its goal of hiding the connections of the CCP with the Soviets. As time went on, the stated American policy of full support for

Chiang Kai-shek progressively eroded. Former Assistant Secretary of State Stanley K. Hornbeck,[46] in an exchange of letters with Dean Rusk, says the "tipping point" came in 1945, when the American government embarked on a course of conduct that ultimately undermined the Nationalists.[47] Shortly before the Communist takeover, *New York Times* reporter Hanson W. Baldwin reached the same conclusion:

> At this eleventh hour, as the United States gropes for a China policy, the American people are still being asked to believe what Max Eastman called last week, the "Moscow-manufactured hoax" that the Chinese Communists are not really Communists, but simply "agrarian reformers." He called it a myth ... yet myths die hard.... This same mistake has facilitated the Communist domination of nearly every country over which the Red tide has swept since the war.... The overwhelming evidence, therefore, is that the Chinese Communists are pursuing policies identical in aim with the policies of Moscow.[48]

CONGRESSMAN WALTER H. JUDD OF MINNESOTA

Along with Patrick Hurley, Minnesota Congressman Walter H. Judd struggled to counter what he contended was the corrosive influence of the China Hands. To an even greater degree than Wedemeyer, Judd's reputation as a crusader against Chinese Communism and Japanese expansion in the years before World War II has been marginalized. He surely was in a position to truly understand the mentality of the Chinese people. A physician, Judd went to China as a medical missionary in 1925, staying five years until a severe case of malaria forced his departure. In 1933 he returned to Fenchow, in the remote province of Shanxi, as a hospital superintendent, and was eventually captured by the Japanese, negotiating his release after five months of imprisonment. He spent the next two years touring the United States, heralding the dangers of Japanese military expansionism. In 1942, he was elected to the House of Representatives, where he served with distinction for twenty years, rising to become one of the most influential members of the House on foreign policy. Aside from the halls of Congress, Judd's crusade was promulgated in radio addresses, speeches to civic groups, and in newspaper and magazine articles.

Judd's consistent argument was that the American political establishment had a poor understanding of Asian culture and etiquette and consequently blundered continuously in its dealings in the area with tragic consequences. He asserted that the mistaken impression created in America about the history, psychology, and political aspirations of the Chinese was the result of an unprecedented propaganda campaign perpetrated by self-interested European imperialists, the CCP, abetted by Moscow, and by senior administration and State Department officials.

In his first major address to the House of Representatives on the subject of Asia, on February 25, 1943, Judd outlined how the United States mishandled its relations with the Japanese during the years leading up to Pearl Harbor, making grievous errors that contributed to the hardening of relations. He argued that American diplomats knew little about the Japanese mentality, and that our appeals to them were grounded on Western interests such as materialism, completely ignoring the important Asian concept of "saving face."[49]

In an address before the House on May 3, 1944, Congressman William J. Miller extensively quoted Judd's recent speech to a civic organization: "[America] will have to admit that we went into this war without the slightest understanding either of ourselves or of our enemies in the Pacific area."[50] Miller echoed Judd's praise for the courage of the Chinese during their 13-year struggle to hold the Japanese invaders at bay and expressed concern about the lukewarm American commitment and the impact it was having on the Chinese spirit, stating: "Only one thing could cause her to waver, a loss of expectation that out of her struggle she will eventually get full freedom and equal treatment among the nations of the world, a loss of confidence in the ultimate motives of her allies."

In a speech before the House on August 21, 1944, Judd cited a "good number" of articles, editorials and broadcasts about China that:

> Whether realized by their authors or not . . . are contributing to a systematic, organized, nation-wide propaganda campaign to discredit the central government of China and its leaders, especially Chiang Kai-shek, the Soong family and those western-educated Chinese who for several decades have influenced China profoundly in our direction. Some of these attacks have been thoroughly scurrilous, others merely a collection of vicious rumors and cheap gossip. In the most widely circulated collection I counted 14 statements that I personally know to be utterly false.[51]

Judd also charged that promises of assistance from Western democracies "which have not yet made good" were undermining confidence in Chiang's government and casting "doubt on the wisdom of his decisions." He praised Nobel laureate and Pulitzer Prize-winner Pearl Buck (who had grown-up in China as a daughter of a missionary and spent an extensive amount of time there subsequent to her marriage to an economist missionary), author of the best-selling novel *The Good Earth*, quoting her article in August 1944 for *Common Sense*, whereupon she condemned the erroneous information being disseminated by those who wrote about China with cultural blinders:

> Young journalists, inexperienced and without historical perspectives, judged a country thousands of years old by young American standards. China began to be condemned. Then, condemnation could not proceed swiftly enough. Indeed it was to the interest of those who were guiding our American foreign policies to encourage this condemnation. It provided reasons for not giving China swifter aid, the reasons, too, for not diverting anything from Europe to Asia . . . It has now been made clear . . . to the American people that China does not deserve aid from us because of her internal divisions and corruption.

While stressing that internal reform was necessary, Buck noted that the policy of Western condemnation of China has resulted in the "planting of a new hatred of the entire white race in millions of hearts."[52] She was also critical of the U.S. military leadership in China during the Stilwell period, acerbically noting that "the attitude of our American military men in China, with a few notable exceptions, has been insulting and arrogant toward the Chinese."[53]

On March 15, 1945, Judd invoked his authority by contrasting his years of work in China against "a flood of reports from people who do not have an adequate background of experience in Asia."[54] Although he did not specifically impugn the Allies' "Europe First" strategy, he decried the fact that America poured over ninety-eight percent of its supplies into Europe, with only one tenth of the remainder targeted for China, noting how the lack of support affected the morale of the population and how Chinese soldiers were left with grossly inadequate equipment, nutrition, and medical care. He placed the blame for massive Chinese inflation directly on the shoulders of the United States, who had flooded the country with paper money by flying

100,000 pounds of currency over the hump, resulting in the devaluing of Chinese currency by four-thousand percent,[55] and noted the pernicious effect of the profiteering and black market created in its wake.

Judd then charged that "the primary allegiance of the Chinese Communists is to Russia ... and their purpose is to make Russia overwhelmingly the strongest power in Asia as well as Europe,"[56] professing that:

[The CCP] adopted a great propaganda program to sell to the world the belief that they are merely downtrodden patriots, seeking to escape the tyranny and oppression of Chiang Kai-shek in order to get freedom and establish democracy—just like our forefathers were in 1776. By talking about freedom and democracy and unity ... and by calling all who disagree with them Fascists and Dictators, they have succeeded in selling to millions of Americans one of the greatest hoaxes any unsuspecting people ever bought in all history![57]

In response to President Roosevelt's analogy of a Chinese coalition government to taking a few Republicans into his Cabinet, Judd wryly pointed out, "We Republicans do not maintain a private army exercising arbitrary control over whole sections of the country ... the Communists do have a private army and a separate government. They are not just a political party. They are an armed rebellion."

Judd claimed that the propaganda directed against the Chinese Nationalist government was "approved, even inspired, by persons in our own War and State Departments,"[58] specifically focusing on the American demand for a consolidation of the KMT and the CCP.

Three years later, Judd read into the Congressional Record a series of fourteen articles about General Chennault by correspondent Clyde Farnsworth that documented a series of blunders committed by both General Stilwell and the State Department in its relations with China, and singled out China Hand John Paton Davies for his inaccurate and biased reports to the State Department that resulted in a deterioration of relations with Chiang Kai-shek. He also described how during the war years, American officers and officials in Chungking conducted forums of propaganda for the Chinese Reds, featuring unbridled criticism of the central government and contentions that the CCP "were not really Communists but just agrarian reformers," and that attendees were informed that this loose talk had been sanctioned by General Stilwell.[59]

In 1950, in a post-mortum of Chiang's fall and exile, Judd provided the nefarious details of the role of the American Communist Party in accelerating the American exit from China and ending assistance to the Nationalists, exposing how on November 18, 1945, party chairman William Z. Foster, instructed his members:

> On the international scale, the key task is to stop American intervention in China . . . On the question of China, which is our key concentration, we want to hold five hundred meetings all over the country to mobilize all the forces of the people that we can reach to put a stop to the intervention in China. Our party must use every ounce of its strength and skill and organizational ability to make these 500 meetings a success.[60]

To Foster, "American intervention" was analogous to assistance to Chiang's government. The instructions were immediately implemented. Two weeks later, the front page of the American Communist newspaper, the *Daily Worker*, was headlined "Quit China Drive Opens in Congress," over an article that reported the "democratic character of the great mass movement led by the Chinese Communists and to the dictatorial character of the Kuomintang clique led by Chiang Kai-shek." The subtitle pronounced "Protests forcing show-down on intervention in China—Representative DeLacy speaks up for an aroused Nation." Amazingly, the Communists had succeeded in enlisting the endorsement of six West Coast Congressmen: Hugh DeLacy, John Coffee, Charles Savage, Helen Gahagan Douglas,[61] Willis Patterson, and Ned Healy. This brilliant move by the Communists transformed members of the House of Representatives into unwitting accomplices to advance the Communist cause.

Judd then condemned the purge of a group of Far East experts from the State Department: "Mr. Chairman, I urge our Government to call back into emergency service statesmen like Grew, Hornbeck, Dooman, Berle—men who are real experts on Asia or on Communism, men whom the left wing boys pushed out of the Department."[62] Later, Judd recounted how he had been friendly with the "China Hand" Owen Lattimore in China, but after the party line changed, was treated "as if I had leprosy." He also bemoaned the influence of the reports of Lattimore and Alger Hiss, then a key man in the Far East Division of the State Department.[63]

A credible assessment of the reasons for the fall of the Nationalist government comes from Wedemeyer. His 1947 report to President Truman, published in *Wedemeyer Reports!* as Addendum VI, is a remarkably intellectual, prophetic and objective analysis of the situation in China prior to the Communist takeover that is best appreciated when read in its entirety. (See Appendix I.)

In 1949, Wedemeyer chose to be transferred to a stateside position in command of the Sixth Army at San Francisco, largely to avoid becoming embroiled in any controversy over America's China policy that he was so bitterly opposed to. His retrospective analysis was given at the MacArthur hearings in 1951, where he testified for three days and offered his opinion only in response to direct questions from members of the committee. While Wedemeyer was in agreement with MacArthur's aggressive strategy to defeat the Chinese Communists in Korea, he unequivocally defended President Truman's decision to recall him, reiterating his long-held philosophy that decisions of foreign policy, and ultimately military strategy, should be made by the President. As great intellects do, in areas where he did not deem himself authoritative, Wedemeyer offered his opinion yet was quite comfortable to defer to higher sources. When the subject of the fall of China was broached, there was no such reticence:

> The answer, in my judgment, is more [lack of] moral support than material support. His soldiers were lacking in spirit and enthusiasm for the job; and also, they began to lose confidence in their leader, Chiang Kai-shek. . . . Immediately after the war, propaganda from Yenan and Moscow repudiated the American objectives. . . . That propaganda, by pamphlets and by radio, was continuous and vociferous. I protested to the American Consul General . . . and it stopped for a while and then it continued vehemently and with increased action.
>
> After so many years of war, terrific dislocations, psychological, economic—that country was just tired of war. . . . All they wanted was food, shelter and peace. And the Communists exploited those basic, fundamental desires of the people; they exploited the corruption and the maladministrations that were present, to such a degree that Chiang Kai-shek was repudiated, the troops were dispirited and they didn't fight. [What went through their minds] was "Let's try this other ideology" . . . they were just so fed up they just stopped fighting.[64]

The other figure most qualified to offer an authoritative opinion was Walter Judd. Writing in the *Saturday Evening Post* in 1952, he blamed the demise of the Nationalist government on State Department policy:

> Truman's foreign policy has had a split-personality . . . following in Asia the opposite of what it advocated in Europe. For years its policy with respect to Communist aggression in Asia was based on inexcusable ignorance regarding communist objectives and wishful thinking about "agrarian reform." These were skillfully exploited by the Communist agents, sympathizers and fellow travelers who were permitted to infiltrate the State Department . . . The Administration, having closed its eyes to the dangers of Russian imperialism during the critical post war period, finally made a stand—in Greece against expanding communist aggression. . . . This was not because the Greek government was considered to be perfect, but because we knew that Greece had to be saved from Communism if we were, in the long run, to save ourselves. We gave vigorous moral and material support, including military advisers at the front, and it worked. Thus it was all the more incredible that, having plugged a gap in our security on the European front, that the Administration blandly and blindly opened the gates wide to the enemy on the Far Eastern front. In China it adopted a policy of defeatism and negativism. It not only abandoned our ally but publicly berated the Chiang Kai-shek regime, playing up its inevitable weaknesses after eight years of invasion and ignoring the importance of a free and friendly China.[65]

The opinions of Wedemeyer and Judd are not in any way discordant, and by amalgamating them, the most valid conclusion about the reason for China's fall into Communism can be surmised. Chiang's government fell under the weight of the panoply of social, economic, and political factors and the highly successful propaganda campaign waged against him. His ultimate military defeat by Mao Zedong was brought about by the half-hearted and belated support of an American government that eroded both the material ability and, more importantly, the spirit and morale of his army to prevail.

CHAPTER 13

WEDEMEYER IN RETIREMENT

Only the future is certain, the past continues to change.
Russian proverb—author unknown

Wedemeyer retired from the army in 1951 at the age of 52, several years short of the mandatory retirement age. He loved the Army, but the accumulation of disappointments and frustrations he experienced after the end of hostilities in August 1945, especially the suppression of his 1947 report on China and Korea, convinced him that his honor and integrity required him to speak out in opposition to the disastrous foreign policy decisions being formulated by America's civilian leadership. He was particularly disturbed and disappointed by the reversal of the initial enthusiastic endorsement his report received, at a time when Wedemeyer was convinced the situation in China could still be salvaged. In a letter to J. Leighton Stuart, American Ambassador in China, dated September 26, 1947, shortly after the completion of his report, he said he was " . . . highly gratified that both Truman and Marshall completely agreed with my recommendations. I now hope there will be no delay in implementing the courses of action I have suggested."[1]

Of course, there was no implementation. The report was suppressed, and Wedemeyer was convinced that this act further weakened the Nationalist government, aided the Communists, and ultimately contributed to circumstances leading up to the Korean War, which broke out in June of 1950. Only retirement from active service would allow him to remove the muzzle that constrains a military officer and permit him to speak his mind to the American public.

It was the Honor System instilled by his West Point experience, a code that he followed his entire life, that finally caused him to rebel at his inability to speak out while on active service. He mentioned this in an Oral History taken by Col Anthony S. Deskis in December 1972: "I think that the Honor System precluded sycophancy and the obfuscation between truth and a modified version of truth. And that was the big thing—I mentioned it earlier to you and it carried through all my service. *It was one of the reasons ultimately that I got out of the service."²* (emphasis added)

Before discussing Wedemeyer's civilian career in industry after retirement, it is necessary to mention his final significant military assignment, which was yet another instance where Wedemeyer's role in an important event has been underappreciated and even grossly misrepresented: the Allies' 1948 rescue of the Western enclave in Berlin.

THE BERLIN AIRLIFT

In 1948, Wedemeyer occupied the prestigious and powerful position of Chief of War Plans, an assignment which would naturally involve him intimately in any military crisis. In the early hours of June 24, 1948, Joseph Stalin ordered a halt to all traffic in and out of the divided city of Berlin, initiating a blockade that was to last for 328 days. Shortly after embarking from Washington on a proposed inspection tour of Berlin with Undersecretary of the Army General William H. Draper, Jr., Wedemeyer learned of the blockade. As Draper described it:

> I left early one morning (June 24th), with General (Albert C.) Wedemeyer, my chief planning officer at that time. We had our cables with us, that had accumulated during the night, and after we had breakfast on the plane, we read [them] and learned that the blockade was on. We were on our way to London. *On the way over we planned the airlift* (emphasis added). General Wedemeyer had had charge of the airlift over the hump in India earlier during the war, so he had a pretty good idea of what the different types of planes would carry in the way of tonnage, and how often a plane could land at an airport, through actual experience. I had negotiated in Berlin with the Russians for the feeding of Berlin some years before, for the British and American sectors, and later these included the French, so I knew the tonnage of food necessary on a ration level to feed the two and a half million people in those sectors of the city.³

In the same Oral History, Draper says he knew the number of planes available at that time and their capabilities. Wedemeyer and Draper met in London with Foreign Minister Ernest Bevin in order to initiate the plan. Bevin was very pessimistic about the ability of the Airlift to succeed but nonetheless agreed to cooperate and supplied some 25 planes. Later, Draper and Wedemeyer met with the French, who had no planes available to contribute but also agreed to do what they could to further the enterprise. The main contribution of France was to supply a number of airfields from which the planes could operate. Finally, in Berlin they met with General Lucius Clay, then Military Governor of Germany, who initially was not in favor of the airlift. Clay recommended a very aggressive armed convey to force their way through the Russian blockade. Wedemeyer, his superior, was aghast, and immediately vetoed that plan due to the vast superiority of Soviet forces and the real danger of provoking another war. After about one month, the airlift was floundering, and Wedemeyer again stepped in and was responsible for placing General William H. Tunner in full charge of the effort. Tunner had worked under Wedemeyer in China and had done a fine job supervising the "Hump" operation over the Himalayas from Aswan to Kunming. The installation of Tunner as operational head of the airlift proved to be the key to its success. Under his supervision, the operation immediately began to function efficiently, and his outstanding effort ultimately resulted in the Russians' removing the blockade. When the end of the airlift was approaching, Tunner and Wedemeyer exchanged a series of letters concerning the subject. On May 3, 1949, Tunner wrote to Wedemeyer:

> Now that rumors concerning the end of the blockade of Berlin are becoming stronger every day, I want to thank you for having brought about the opportunity for air transport to show its capabilities and potentialities to the world. None of us is sorry that the blockade is going to end. Indeed we only hope that rumors become fact without further delay. But we are grateful for the chance to show conclusively what air transport can do.[4]

Wedemeyer responded a week later, reflecting his pride at putting a small dent in Stalin's armor:

> Your good letter is deeply appreciated. It looks very much as if the technological skills and organizational ability of Americans may

have won a victory over the U.S.S.R. I am not naturally a suspicious soul, but I do hope that our policy-makers will be very cautious in the negotiations concerning future developments and commitments in Germany. At great sacrifice in lives, materiel and effort your gallant crowd has maintained better than an existing economy for over two million people. This is another epic making experience that one Bill Tunner can be proud of and I as an old friend congratulate you.[5]

Unfortunately, Wedemeyer's record involving the Berlin Airlift has suffered a fate similar to that rendered by most historians regarding his participation in the Victory Plan, his strategic vision relating to the cross-channel invasion, and his work in China. The most recent example of this continuing oversight is found in *Daring Young Men*[6] by Richard Reeves, a story of the Airlift published in 2010. Reeves acknowledged that while in China, Wedemeyer "played a major role" in the flying of supplies to Nationalist China's troops, and while Chief of Planning in 1948 consulted with the British; but, according to Reeves, Wedemeyer *advised against the airlift*. Proof of Reeves' error is contained in an article published in the *Washington Star* on January 3, 1979, which quoted a story about the Berlin Airlift that had recently appeared in the prestigious *London Guardian*, which a short time previously had obtained documents released after a thirty-year embargo:

In April 1948 the Soviet Union imposed a blockade on West Berlin and the *Guardian* said Churchill suggested to Prime Minister Clement Attlee that Russia be told to withdraw or face attack.

The records showed that Attlee's Labor government did not give the plan serious consideration and the U.S. Ambassador in London, Lewis Douglas, said it was full of 'practical infirmities' according to the Guardian.

Instead, when the Soviets set up the blockade the United States countered with a massive airlift.

The Guardian report said the idea of an airlift came from U.S. Army Gen. Albert C. Wedemeyer, who argued that a conventional land attack on Soviet forces in Eastern Europe would have meant destruction of the Western armies.

It said Wedemeyer's proposal was backed by Royal Air Force Chief Sir Charles Portal and approved by President Harry Truman and Attlee. The report concluded that although the British Cabinet approved the plan, they thought the airlift would fail.[7]

The Berlin Airlift was Wedemeyer's last military operation. After retirement from active service in 1951, Wedemeyer pursued a career in the private sector. He had received a number of job offers and finally accepted the position of Executive Vice President of AVCO,[8] a company that started in 1929 in the aviation industry but which, over the years, grew into a huge manufacturing conglomerate, concentrating on aviation products and equipment, with 22 plants throughout the country and thousands of employees. Wedemeyer was hired to deal with labor-management issues, starting at the then princely salary of $80,000 per year. He took an apartment in New York City, where he worked during the week and traveled to his Virginia farm on weekends. Wedemeyer knew that AVCO had numerous military contracts, including one very profitable one dealing with the production of proximity fuses, and he stipulated that his employment never require him to deal with the military, a self-imposed limitation that retiring military personnel now largely overlook, if not actually exploit.

He was dismayed to learn of the low—and, in his mind, inaccurate—regard that American industry had for the military, and he made a sincere effort to change it. The retired general had a very difficult time with the inherent conflict between the Honor Code that he revered at West Point and scrupulously followed his entire life, and the competitive, often less ethically grounded chase for the dollar in the capitalist environment.[9] After thirteen years, this tension ultimately resulted in his walking away from employment in industry altogether.

In 1975, he related some specific incidents where his code of honor conflicted with corporate culture. While at AVCO, Wedemeyer was charged with settling a "slow down" by workers at a Camden, New Jersey plant, and spent a few weeks investigating the cause. After interviewing many of the workers, he discovered a need for substantial improvement in working conditions, such as better toilet facilities, a movable "coffee cart" to facilitate hot drinks, snacks during break time, and installation of some safety features. The most important safety feature he recommended was the construction of a rail line from the factory to the docks so the very heavy metal plates that the workers were making could be handled with more efficiency and less risk. Upon concluding his investigation, he met privately with a few union officials who, from the sidelines, had been carefully observing the rapport he had established with the workers. Leadership of men in the army is little different from leadership in industry, and Wedemeyer's tact, honesty, sincerity, and directness had endeared him to the men. Wedemeyer was informed by the small group of union representatives that while his recommendations were worthy of implementation, the union wanted to take credit for them. They insisted that he announce that these improvements were a *union initiative* or otherwise they would completely block them. Wedemeyer was outraged since he knew that the union was continually disparaging the management, and one of his objectives was to improve the management/labor relationship. He knew that these management-initiated initiatives he had proposed would go a long way toward achieving this goal. He asked to meet with the entire union team and stipulated that he wanted the conversations recorded. Somewhat surprisingly, they agreed and he made his pitch to the union team but met the same objections. They wanted the credit. Wedemeyer returned to New York and played the tape to his astounded Board of Directors. While Wedemeyer's recommendations ultimately carried the day, his superiors were quite concerned about his unconventional labor/management methods.[10]

A few years later, he was assigned to deal with a strike at a plant in Indiana that had been going on for eleven months. Wedemeyer was dispatched to settle it. Again, he spent long hours talking to both management and workers and began to make substantial progress. He became very friendly with the chief union negotiator and often met with him socially. Eventually, there were only a few unresolved issues. They were close to a resolution of all but a few points, which despite prolonged efforts continued to stand in the way. Then, unexpectedly, top management dispatched a lawyer to the scene. The next day, when Wedemeyer tried to contact his union negotiator, his wife told him that her husband could not meet with him again, and that the strike had been settled. Astounded, Wedemeyer asked the reason why her husband could not talk to him, and she cryptically replied: "You know why!" Of course, Wedemeyer replied that he did not know why, but his ignorance was of short duration. He soon learned that the lawyer had been sent to Indiana with a $5,000 payoff for the union representative that eventually settled the strike. Wedemeyer immediately submitted his resignation.[11]

He then accepted a position as Chairman of the Board of the Academy Life Insurance Company. Under his leadership, the company expanded rapidly. Over time, as Wedemeyer acquainted himself with the nuances of state and federal insurance law, he discovered that, contrary to Federal and State statutes and regulations, the company was not maintaining adequate reserves and needed either an infusion of capital or a merger with a larger company in order to bring themselves into compliance. Unsuccessful in persuading the company to accept his recommendations, he submitted his resignation after three years of employment. This was Wedemeyer's last position in private industry. He later learned that his former associates were investigated and disciplined by the Securities and Exchange Commission.[12]

Wedemeyer then shifted his attention to politics, lecturing, traveling, and writing. It was his intention to write one more book. Parts of this unfinished work are at the Hoover Institution.

WEDEMEYER IN POLITICS 1951–1952

While living in New York during his employment at AVCO, Wedemeyer renewed his relationship with former President Herbert Hoover, whom he visited regularly at his residence in the Waldorf Towers in Manhattan. Wedemeyer's political affiliation was distinctly Republican, and he had no difficulty in accepting Hoover's request to support the candidacy of Senator Robert Taft for the Republican nomination for President in 1952. The two other prime contenders were Generals Dwight D. Eisenhower and Douglas MacArthur, with Ike clearly the frontrunner.

In 1947 and 1948, Eisenhower had been the military's Chief of Staff and Wedemeyer had many opportunities to meet with and develop admiration for him. Eisenhower then accepted the job as President of Columbia University and subsequently, in 1951, was appointed head of the newly created North Atlantic Treaty Organization [NATO] command in Europe. In several conversations with his former commander, Ike told Wedemeyer of the many solicitations for him to announce his candidacy for the Republican nomination and his unwillingness at the time to get involved in a partisan campaign. While Eisenhower vacillated, Ohio Senator Robert Taft's political fortunes were gathering momentum, and with Hoover's encouragement and guidance, Wedemeyer accepted the post of National Chairman of the Citizens for Taft. It is unclear as to whether Wedemeyer would have accepted the invitation had he known at the time that Eisenhower finally had made a decision to enter the race, because he never wanted his move to be interpreted as anti-Eisenhower. (Regrettably, it was so interpreted anyway.) Wedemeyer worked hard for Taft, meeting with state and local politicians throughout the country and coordinating the appointment of state chairmen and liaisons to professions and celebrities.

A few days before the convention, an event occurred that is now a mere footnote in the history of the Republican Party but at the time had the potential to change the course of American political history. Herbert Hoover was extremely active at the convention, and his opinion carried an enormous amount of weight in Republican circles. There were 1,200 voting delegates and 601 were required to win. The Credentials Committee had previously disallowed a substantial number of Southern delegates pledged to Taft and awarded them to Eisenhower, effectively nailing the coffin of the Taft candidacy, unless some miracle occurred. Before the first ballot, Eisenhower, with a total of 575 pledged delegates, was a bit short of the required number to win the nomination. In an effort to head off what seemed to be a certain win by Eisenhower, Hoover concluded that Taft, with a pledged total of 500 delegates, was not likely to acquire more unless something drastic happened. At a meeting of key Republican strategists called by Hoover at the Conrad Hilton Hotel in New York City,[13] a decision was made to consult with Taft, inform him of the current circumstances, and request that he swing his delegates to MacArthur. Although MacArthur had only 10 pledged delegates at that time, it was hoped that if Taft's 500 votes were added, it would only take a few defections to erode Ike's 575. Wedemeyer was designated to deliver the message, and the consensus of the group was that the combined Taft and MacArthur delegations, added to some defections, would be sufficient to nominate MacArthur, who was strongly preferred to Eisenhower. Taft agreed, but with the stipulation that he wanted to "test the waters" with the first vote. If, after that, it seemed unlikely that he was going to gain additional support, he would then switch his support to MacArthur and carry the day.

There was only one vote. Perhaps due to the fractionated first ballot opposition, Eisenhower won on the first ballot and the party unified behind the former hero of D-Day. Wedemeyer was active in the subsequent campaign. In Los Angeles, where he was introduced by John Wayne, he gave a 23-minute nationwide television and radio address in support of the Republican standard bearer. At the time it appeared that politics would be Wedemeyer's next arena of operation.

In 1954 Wedemeyer had a golden opportunity to move on to center stage in national politics when he had the chance to acquire a seat in the United States Senate without campaigning. He received a telephone call from the Governor of Nebraska informing him that sitting Senator Kenneth Wherry had unexpectedly died, and that the Governor wanted to appoint him as Senator for the unexpired two-year portion of the term, though with the stipulation that Wedemeyer agree not to run for re-election, since the Governor himself ultimately wanted the position. Under those conditions, Wedemeyer declined. He was not willing to be a "seat warmer" for another politician; the indirection or deception offended him. This decision effectively ended his short foray into politics. The remainder of his life would now be devoted to writing, traveling, and lecturing.

Many of Wedemeyer's later lectures and interviews focused on his life-long interest and passion for "Grand Strategy." In 1958, he published his *magnum opus, Wedemeyer Reports!*[14] He planned on writing another book on grand strategy and completed several chapters, although without finishing the whole.[15] He did, however, compose a comprehensive "Memorandum on a National Strategy Council" in 1983 that recommended the formation of a committee consisting of a select group of nationally prominent independent citizens as an advisory board.

From approximately 1963 to 1983, he and Mrs. Wedemeyer, the former Dade Embick, maintained Friends Advice, a country estate thirty miles south of Washington, DC. He wrote and published articles, gave hundreds of inter-views, frequently appeared on radio and television shows, delivered dozens of lectures, both in America and overseas, and maintained an active corre-spondence with historians, biographers, and the general public.

Before he died, he donated his personal records, papers, speeches, and other written material to the Hoover Institution at Stanford, California, where it is preserved in over a hundred and fifty boxes. The ephemera pro-vides a graphic record of his illustrious life: programs, menus, and place cards from dinners he attended, and business cards, visas, and passports, often from combat zones dating back over fifty years prior to his death. It is a wonder that he was able to preserve this vast cache of personal memorabilia while traveling all over the world. In addition, he saved countless documents, speeches, letters, and memoranda of historical and military significance that present a graphic and candid view of military history and those with whom he engaged, as well as an intimate record of his encounters with celebrities throughout the world.

Wedemeyer was a serious man who meticulously prepared his writings and speeches. Unlike many present-day public figures, his lecture career was not driven by a profit motive. He did not employ an agent, and there is no evidence he charged an exorbitant speaker's fee.[16] Atypically, yet character-istically for him, he rarely delivered a generic "canned" speech, so prevalent in today's lecture circuit assemblage but tailored the topic to the interests of the audience at hand. In one speech to veteran nurses who served in the

Burma theatre, Wedemeyer delivered a personal and touching tribute to their stamina, courage, and professionalism, mentioning and singling out for praise some individuals by name, including doctors, medics, field hospitals, and nurses with whom he had been personally acquainted.[17] Grand Strategy, Aid to China, and the proposed 1943 cross-channel invasion were favorite topics before Rotary Clubs, Veterans Associations, Chambers of Commerce, corporate and legislative groups, and college and university commencements.

Wedemeyer paid meticulous attention to answering correspondence and responded with care whether the communication was from top military or political leaders, former enlisted men under his command or their spouses, or from students and just plain ordinary citizens. This was the practice he had commenced while engaged in active duty and continued his entire life. He was as conscientious about responding to letters from the average person as he was with the illustrious. To give just one notable example of many culled from the hundreds of mundane letters contained in his records at the Hoover Institution: in November 1944 while in China, he received a letter from James A. Bowman, a seventh grade teacher in New Castle Pennsylvania, whose class was closely following the progress of the war with maps and in newspapers of the day. As a special project the class had decided to obtain signatures of world figures and place them on the wall of their class room. They sent Wedemeyer a 3-by-5 index card and, in a respectful letter, asked for his signature to add to their collection. At the time, the commanding General was heavily engaged in repulsing a renewed Japanese attack that threatened to capture the only remaining air supply depot in China. He could have been excused for not responding. Notwithstanding these pressing demands on his time, Wedemeyer promptly replied, and in his letter, with mock gravity, he noted that "War Department regulations preclude my signing the card," yet coyly mentioned, "of course my signature appears below."[18]

During his retirement, Wedemeyer received hundreds of requests for interviews. He answered promptly and in detail and rarely refused. He was most solicitous of young graduate students seeking information and assistance. He received a letter dated December 16, 1964 from Tong-Chin Rhee, a graduate student at Clark University, who was writing a doctoral dissertation on Sino-American Relations during the period 1944 to 1948, and inquired as to whether Wedemeyer would be available for an interview. Rhee lived in Washington, DC at the time, and Wedemeyer not only consented to the interview, but drove to Washington, picked up Rhee, drove him to his home in Virginia, submitted to a lengthy interview over a period of several hours, and then drove Rhee back. The interview covered aspects of Chinese history, American and Chinese relations during the period in question, and issues relating to the dispute between the Nationalists and the Communists. After digesting all the information obtained from the interview, Rhee mailed Wedemeyer an eight-page single-spaced summary and invited the general to make some brief general comments on the accuracy of the summation. Wedemeyer responded with his own six-page single-spaced critique that not only offered constructive point by point commentary but congratulated Rhee on his efforts and offered him suggestions for further study and reading.[19] Rhee's published dissertation[20] is a remarkable story of Chinese history during the war years up to and including the Communist takeover, in which he recognizes Wedemeyer as a pivotal figure in the struggle of the Nationalists to resist the Communists, and Rhee thanks him profusely for his efforts.

Wedemeyer remained consistent in later life with respect to critical positions he had advocated in earlier years. At age 86, he was interviewed by Darwin Olofson, a reporter for the Omaha *World Herald,* and was asked if he still believed the Allies should have invaded France in 1943. In the article entitled "Was a Year Too Late," Wedemeyer reaffirmed his earlier views and relates a fascinating story of a meeting in 1949 with former Prime Minister Churchill, King George VI, and a group of other British dignitaries in London a few years after the war.

Churchill had just completed his six-volume history of the Second World War, and naturally, a good deal of the discussion, no doubt liberally stimulated by Churchill's beverage of choice, centered on the war. Remembering Wedemeyer's resistance to his strategic vision, and no doubt hoping to catch his old nemesis off guard, the former First Lord of the Admiralty and Prime Minister coyly posed the question: "Do you still think we could have gotten across in 1943?" Wedemeyer unequivocally and emphatically replied "I do."[21]

No doubt the bulldog Churchill would have appreciated support for his own view, but the equally tenacious American maintained his position. The King was not only amused by the byplay but expressed keen interest in Wedemeyer's point of view. The contentious debate over a 1943 versus a 1944 cross-channel invasion was apparently not a subject the King was familiar with, having very likely received only the British version of how to conduct the European war, and he invited the now three-star General to expound at length upon it, no doubt to Churchill's chagrin. Wedemeyer surely enjoyed this opportunity for a reprieve of the incident at the White House in June of 1942, and he was delighted to playfully twist the Bulldog's tail once more, especially in the presence of the King. By this time the conventional wisdom was that the proper time for the invasion was 1944, and few disagreed with the decision. Even Eisenhower, an early proponent of the 1943 date, had done an about face on it in his own memoir, *Crusade in Europe*. Wedemeyer did not!

Wedemeyer was virtually the last surviving major figure of the Second World War. Until a few months of his death he was blessed with extraordinary health and vitality. He died on December 17, 1989 at the age of 92, and is buried in Arlington National Cemetery.

CHAPTER 14

CONCLUSIONS

You have to let the viewers come away with their own conclusions.
If you dictate what they should think, you've lost it.
—Maya Lin

When Albert C. Wedemeyer died in 1992, in his obituary in the *New York Times,* noted military historian John Keegan said the general was "one of the most intellectual and farsighted military minds America has ever produced." The December 20 obituary went on to praise Wedemeyer for his efforts as chief strategist in formulating an overall war plan for the United States shortly before America's entry into World War II, as well as his major role in planning for the Normandy invasion.[1] Keegan mentioned Wedemeyer's special assignment as an emissary for President Truman in 1947, when he was sent to China and Korea to make recommendations relating to the ongoing civil war between the Nationalist forces and the Communists. Keegan deplored the fact that Wedemeyer's report was suppressed and not released until after the Communists took over in 1949.

Keegan was correct in his assessment of Wedemeyer's contribution to the war effort, but his comments likely came as a surprise to those among the general public who probably best remembered him as having replaced the popular General "Vinegar Joe" Stilwell in the China-Burma-India theatre in 1944. Likewise they would have been unfamiliar with his role as a strategist, an effort to which he devoted his entire life. Indeed, the general public in 1992 probably was not even familiar with the influence of strategists and the important role played by them during World War II. Most of the public also knew little about Wedemeyer's service in Asia during the war. It was

Wedemeyer's fate to have his role in the Asian theatre diminished by Stilwell and his admirers, especially Barbara Tuchman, and later, his contribution as a major strategist of the war was overshadowed by such luminaries as Generals Marshall, Eisenhower, MacArthur, and others.

Wedemeyer learned to be a strategist by a process of lifelong study and travel to countless corners of the globe, including Washington, Berlin, London, Manila, New Delhi, and Chungking. He played important roles in both the Atlantic and Pacific areas and came into personal and sometimes sustained contact with war leaders on the highest level. Those leaders included President Roosevelt, Harry Hopkins, cabinet officers, the Chiefs of Staff, and senior field commanders. In Britain, he met frequently with Prime Minister Churchill as well as top members of the British government and military establishment. While in Asia, he met with Chiang Kai-shek, Chairman Mao Zedong, and Zhou Enlai. In Korea he met with Syngman Rhee. In Germany in 1937–38 he met with General Ludwig Beck and many other top ranking German military leaders while a student at the *Kriegsakademia*. Wedemeyer played a leading role in developing U.S. and Allied global strategy, including, as we have seen, plans for the invasion of Europe. Beginning in 1941, he attended conferences with the top warlords in Washington, London, Casablanca, Quebec, and Cairo. After Casablanca in 1943, President Roosevelt and the U.S. Joint Chiefs of Staff sent him eastward around the world to report results of the conference to Allied leaders in the Mediterranean area, the China-Burma-India region, and to General MacArthur in the Pacific. In all these travels and meetings with leaders of the military and political establishments, Wedemeyer enhanced his knowledge of strategy and its use in formulation of foreign policy in ways that would be useful to his government. He witnessed and participated in the changing role of the military in formulating foreign policy and observed the evolution from atop the crest of the wave as it coursed over the military/political establishment with events leading up to World War II and later during the Cold War.

His last official role as a strategist was following his service in World War II, when he was called on by President Truman in 1947 and asked to travel to China and Korea and to report on conditions and submit recommendations. Wedemeyer made his strategic recommendations for both China and Korea in his famous report, which President Truman immediately suppressed on very dubious grounds. His report contained recommendations for aid to Chiang Kai-shek and a "Guardianship" for Korea. The recommendations were ignored, and his report was not released until 1949, when it was appended to the thousand-page White Paper of Dean Acheson, by which time the Communists had already taken over. If Wedemeyer's recommendations had been adopted it could have resulted in the defeat of the Chinese Communists and would have obviated the artificial barrier in Korea at the 38th Parallel which kept the country divided. This was his last formal strategic recommendation which, had it been implemented, might well have avoided the Korean and the Vietnam Wars.

Many years after the end of World War II and aware of the inadequacy of national policy making to meet the threats of an increasingly turbulent world, Wedemeyer penned an article in 1983 titled "Memorandum on a National Strategy Council." He was addressing himself to our system of government in which often inexperienced officials come and go at frequent intervals. He raised the question of how our system can accommodate itself to the long-range imperatives of strategy. In this article, he recommended the creation of a small permanent "National Strategy Council" consisting of 11 distinguished citizens who would "devote their full time and talents to studying and formulating recommendations concerning national strategy in its broadest aspects." The body would have an advisory function only, comparable, as he said, to the Federal Reserve Board. The members would have access to all sources of official and unofficial information and strategic intelligence, and they would possess the experience, expertise, and time required to evaluate basic policy in the foreign and domestic fields. Wedemeyer concluded his essay by saying: "Never in my career have I written in greater concern for the future of our country, or with greater conviction of the need for reforms of the sort I have herein tried to describe."[2] Years later, he admitted that the concepts articulated in the article were idealistic and very likely would meet political roadblocks. Would entrenched politicians "cede" what they considered their domain? How could the political process be divorced from the appointment process? How likely would it be for a Chief Executive to look kindly on being "second guessed" by a group of unelected lifetime appointees? These were just some of the concerns Wedemeyer admitted as potential obstacles.[3] Further, he was addressing himself to only part of the problem, the inadequacy of the then-existing system. He could not have been expected to anticipate the special geopolitical challenges posed by modern-day terrorist activities.

THE HISTORY OF THE DEVELOPMENT OF NATIONAL STRATEGY

Strategy and the military's role in its formulation have had an uneven journey through United States foreign policy. Prior to World War II, the common understanding was that strategy and politics were entirely separate realms and that the military had no role in policy formulation. A United States Field Manual from 1930 set forth the then-official doctrine: "Politics and strategy are radically and fundamentally things apart. . . . Strategy begins where politics ends. All that soldiers ask is that once the policy is settled, strategy and command shall be regarded as being in a sphere apart from politics."[4] This limiting concept was to undergo a radical change during World War II, and Wedemeyer's background and experience, as well as his involvement in the creation of the Victory Plan, played a significant role in this change.

As war clouds loomed in early 1941, it was evident that changes had to be made in the role of the military in formulation of long-term strategy. The first noticeable step in the evolution of the military's enhanced importance in strategic planning during World War II occurred with the creation of the Joint Chiefs of Staff (JCS) shortly after Pearl Harbor. This was the first time that the heads of the various American military groups came together and met as one unit. As a key member of the War Plans Division, Wedemeyer interacted with the JCS on a regular basis. Early in the war, in order to coordinate strategy with Great Britain, the Chiefs of Staff of both America and Great Britain were joined to form a separate Combined Chiefs of Staff, a body through which all major strategic decisions were funneled. So powerful did the military voice become during World War II that only the President exercised a more decisive role in major foreign policy military/political decisions. After the war, the significant role of the military in strategic planning continued and even increased during the Cold War. In 1947, the military's expanded role was institutionalized with the passage that year of the National Security Act which made the JCS a permanent part of the foreign policy establishment.

The expanded role of the military, first during the Second World War and then during the Cold War, is easily understood. Both these wars had a "clarity" about them which lent themselves to military solutions. We had a particular enemy confined to a defined territorial location, and we knew a good deal about that enemy, its size, capabilities, and weaknesses, so we could chart the progress of the conflict in terms of success and failure by the battles won, enemies captured, territory recovered, and so on. In World War II, formal surrenders marked the cessation of hostilities, followed by occupation of the former enemies' homelands. In the Cold War we also had a defined "enemy," and the "war" ended with the collapse of the Soviet Union and a marked decrease in tensions between Russia and the United States.

However, the years following the Cold War witnessed a marked decrease in the influence of the military and a corresponding increase in civilian influence. The complexities of the Korean and Vietnam Wars, events in Somalia, Rwanda, and the Balkans, followed by Iraq, the war in Afghanistan, struggles with Iran, and most significantly, the war on terrorism, have all dramatically changed the landscape for strategic thinking and baffled the academics, as well as the political and military leaders who vainly sought to understand how the world's most powerful militaries failed to defeat what they disparaged as ragtag militias armed with the most basic of weapons. Add to this the additional challenges presented by terrorists like computer hackers, suicide bombers (female as well as male), and germ and chemical contamination warfare, and many political leaders concluded that old style long-term strategic planning no longer had a useful place. If this was true, the argument went, the military no longer had a significant place in strategic planning and was to be used only when political leaders made the decision to commit them in a combat role. This marked the commencement of the military's diminished role in overall strategic planning.

The lessened role of the military and its replacement by civilian authority turned out to be disastrous. Three articles in *Parameters*, the influential US Army's Senior Official Journal, the signal publication of the Army War College in Carlisle, PA, made an enormous impact, and were very influential in restoring the influence of the military in the formulation of long-term strategy.[5]

The earliest and perhaps most influential of the articles, General John R. Galvin's 1989 essay, stated right at the outset: "We need strategists. . . . We need senior generals and admirals who can provide solid military advice to our political leadership, and we need young officers who can provide solid military advice—options, details, the results of analysis—to the generals and admirals."[6] Galvin was sounding the alarm. He recognized strategists as very special people, the best individuals who are "uniquely qualified by aptitude, experience, and education in the formulation and articulation of military strategy . . . " Galvin's definition of strategy is taken directly from the US Department of Defense Dictionary of Military and Associated Terms:

> . . . the art and science of developing and using the *political, economic, and psychological* powers of a nation, together with its armed forces, during peace and war, to secure national objectives.[7] (emphasis supplied)

This definition is almost a verbatim copy of Wedemeyer's, and although Galvin does not mention Wedemeyer by name, he lists as examples of superb strategists Generals Marshall, Eisenhower, and Bradley, a citation which surely, by implication, incorporates Wedemeyer, if not in this particular section of the article then certainly later when Galvin, in describing what the ideal strategists should look like, paints a portrait of what he conceives should be the ideal strategist and in every respect parallels Wedemeyer's career. According to Galvin, a strategist should have a comprehensive background in the history of nations and of warfare and their political processes. He must have a curious mind, a belief in continued education in both military and civilian schools, and a mind nourished by continuous lifetime study. He goes on to emphasize this last: " ... the development of capabilities as a strategist is a matter of *continuing personal application* more than anything else.[8] The strategist should be exposed to all levels of military command in all of the services, and possess a "strong and comprehensive knowledge of military history."[9] With regard to instruction presently given in the military schools, the faculty should be one with low turnover, and they should avoid the practice of placing prior years' graduates on the staff, a criticism Wedemeyer leveled at Leavenworth.[10] Galvin goes on to make a number of other sensible recommendations, all of which were in line with Wedemeyer's view on how to promote independent thinking, such as small classes and avoiding the common practice of requiring the "party line" or "school solution" to problems presented in the military academies. One point emphasized over and over is that a competent strategist is the product of "continuing personal application more than anything else," something that could have come straight from Wedemeyer's mouth. Galvin is probably the first to recommend that strategists not be limited in their education to military schools: " ... [W]e must afford the promising strategist the opportunity, through such avenues as civilian education or fellowships, to expand his horizons and connect the knowledge he gains in units to the wider world."[11] With the exception of Wedemeyer's never having had the experience of attending a civilian educational institution, he is recommending the career path precisely followed by Wedemeyer himself. One could almost guess that Galvin had read Wedemeyer's book before he penned the article. Chapter IV of *Wedemeyer Reports!* entitled "Education of A Strategist" contains Wedemeyer's checklist of critical items important to the development of a strategist: (1) a great interest in history; (2) a serious approach to life; (3) a lifelong curiosity;[12] and (4) experience, all of which precisely mirror Galvin's catalog of requirements.

Galvin's 1989 article had an immediate impact. Two decades later, Lt. Colonel Charles P. Moore, Director of the Basic Strategic Arts Program at the US Army War College, a strategist since 2002, singled out Galvin in the second article in *Parameters* in 2009, and the title "What's the Matter with Being a Strategist (Now)?" could just as well have ended with an exclamation as a question mark. Moore credits Galvin with the vision to understand the disastrous implications of the United States' engaging in limited wars without competent strategic advisors. The debacle in Iraq is cited as the most egregious example. He could have added the Korean and Vietnam Wars, as well as events in Somalia, Rwanda, the Balkans, Iran, Iraq, and the current war in Afghanistan. Moore quotes Barry D. Watts, noted defense analyst who, in commenting on the Iraq war said, "US performance in Iraq provides ample evidence that it [United States strategic competence] has been declining for some time."[13] Watt's comment would apply with equal force to the other conflicts. Moore adds that Galvin's recommendations have had a decidedly positive effect, and as a result, "A reversal of that trend [to ignore the use of military strategists] is taking place, one that has gone unnoticed and will likely remain underappreciated for years to come—the return of the Army strategist."[14] After reviewing the history of the importance of strategic intelligence in war, Moore identifies the high point of US Army Strategic influence during World War II. He cites the importance of strategists like Wedemeyer and the unfortunate decline in their utilization by the political establishment after World War II:

> Marshall recognized General Dwight D. Eisenhower's abilities and appointed him as Chief of the War Plans Division in the War Department [the command post for World War II]. It was here that Eisenhower, with the aid of a number of highly talented subordinates such as Leonard T. Gerow and Albert C. Wedemeyer, devised the strategy for a global war . . . and eventually provided Marshall with "the first specific plan for a cross-channel invasion" of Europe. These officers played a critical role in developing and implementing military strategy in support of national objectives, facilitating Presidents Franklin D. Roosevelt and Harry S. Truman's ability to prosecute a successful global war. Army strategists were essential to Allied victory; their contributions reflected the zenith of American operational and strategic art during this critical period in world history. Unfortunately, this was an ascent that would too quickly decline.[15]

The 9/11 attacks made Galvin's recommendations even more critical. Shortly after 9/11, Deputy Secretary of Defense Paul Wolfowitz, picking up and expanding on Galvin's recommendations, assembled a team of scholars, Middle Eastern experts, and analysts to help identify and deal with the problems that allowed the attack to occur. In a pointed criticism of the current US government policies, he said to author Bob Woodward: "The US government, especially the Pentagon, is incapable of producing the kinds of ideas and strategy needed to deal with a crisis of the magnitude of 9/11"[16] Wolfowitz posed important questions, such as who are the terrorists, where did this attack come from, how does it relate to Islamic history, the history of the Middle East, and contemporary Middle East tensions? As he said: "What are we up against here?"[17] These are not the kinds of issues that faced the World War II planners, and it was obvious that a new approach was necessary, which demanded bringing the military back into the picture, not relying solely on the political process as the sole method of dealing with the crisis. He was advocating a new method, which would include military strategists, but with a far different sort of training from that of their predecessors.

The process of properly training strategists, a direct result of Galvin's recommendations, commenced almost immediately. These new strategists are now schooled and qualified in a formal way by the US Army War College. The curriculum is entitled Basic Strategic Art Program (BSAP). In 2001, a workshop that included defense and strategic education experts from the US Military Academy, US War College, National Defense University, Joint Force Staff College, and a number of civilian institutions devised a comprehensive curriculum designed to meet current needs. It continues to evolve in order to meet ever-changing circumstances. The course expanded from a seven student program in 2003 to three fifteen student sessions in 2008.[18] The curriculum is flexible and proceeds along no set path; rather, the students " . . . benefit from a range of experiences that provide a balance of military schools, civilian education, and developmental jobs as they mature."[19] By the winter of 2009, BSAP, initiated on Galvin's recommendation, had graduated 180 military strategists.[20] Because it stresses the importance of study in civilian institutions, especially in the area of international affairs, history, and economics, many of the students return to a variety of universities and pursue doctoral degrees. In stressing the critical need for continuous lifelong self-improvement as a key ingredient of a good strategist, Moore again singles out Wedemeyer as perhaps the best example:

The life of General Albert C. Wedemeyer, one of Eisenhower's key war planners and author of the comprehensive Victory Plan of 1941, suggests that the cumulative effect of education, experience, and a curious mind placed him on firm strategic ground at the outset of World War II. Typical of an interwar officer, General Wedemeyer attended multiple staff colleges and overseas assignments, even graduating from Germany's *Kriegsakademie* in 1938. Equally important, he continued the reading habits established in his youth. . . . It is to his reading, rather than to external influences, that one must turn to understand the intellectual preparation that Albert Wedemeyer brought with him to his job on the General Staff in 1941.[21]

This is high praise for Wedemeyer, and Moore, in paying tribute to him as a "key war planner," the author of the Victory Plan, citing the impact of the "cumulative effect of education, experience," and most importantly, "a curious mind," has encapsulated in one sentence the entire career of Albert Cody Wedemeyer.

The third and concluding article on strategy from *Parameters*, published in the spring of 2010 by Bart Schuurman, traces its evolution through history, with particular emphasis on its present-day role in the changed nature of warfare.[22] Schuurman, a researcher in the Department of Art History at Utrecht University, The Netherlands, faults what he calls the "New Wars" strategists for suggesting that the failure of Western armed forces to prepare for and deal with present-day limited warfare is due to their failure to entirely dismiss what they call the "outmoded theories" of Carl von Clausewitz.[23] Schuurman takes a hard look at the arguments of New War theorists. He agrees that they are correct when they say that the nature of armed conflict has drastically changed, and Western nations must decisively alter the way they currently think about and prepare for armed conflict:

The "new wars" school of thought has contributed significantly to understanding why conventional military superiority has limited value in civil wars or counterinsurgencies. Victory in such conflicts no longer rests on the ability to inflict massive destruction but on the ability to wrestle popular support away from one's opponents, isolating the insurgent or the terrorist from the things he needs most. New war theorists have shown that western armed forces have to decisively alter the way in which they think about and prepare for armed conflict.

He departs from the the latest school of strategists, however, when they claim that the theories enunciated by Clausewitz over 150 years ago are no longer useful and should be discarded. According to Schuurman, the New War strategists fall into error when they attack Clausewitz and dismiss his theories on the sole ground that Clausewitz conceived of war entirely as contests between *states*, and did not anticipate the kind of present-day conflict nations are compelled to deal with. The New Wars writers contend that since most modern conflicts are not between *states*, Clausewitz's theories no longer work. Schuurman says this is a total misreading and credits Clausewitz scholar Christopher Bassford for pointing out that the Prussian's argument must be carefully studied and understood as a subtle dialectic, which makes sense when carefully examined. Bassford reviews Clausewitz and makes the point that misreading him is the result of believing that his theories apply only to formal *states*. As he put it:

> Part of the confusion ... arises from the Prussian's use of a dialectical method of presentation. As such, Clausewitz's musings about war as an abstract phenomenon removed from reality should not be examined independently but should be seen as the first part of a larger argument. He posits war's tendency to extremes as the thesis to which his most famous statement that "[war] is merely the continuation of policy by other means" is the antithesis.[24]

This distinction is critical to not only validating Clausewitz, but, since Wedemeyer is a Clausewitz advocate, also to understanding the utility of Wedemeyer's concepts on strategy. It is the emphasis on *war as the continuation of policy by other means* that is crucial, and both Clausewitz and Wedemeyer stress the fact that *policy* is set by the state, not the military. Like Clausewitz, Wedemeyer was no advocate of the use of unlimited force, nor are their ideas on strategy of no utility in analyzing conflicts where actors other than *states* participate. As M.L.R. Smith points out: "Call it what you will—new war, ethnic war, guerrilla war, low-intensity war, terrorism, or the war on terrorism—in the end, there is only one meaningful category of war, and that is war itself."[25]

Wedemeyer would agree with Schuurman that Clausewitz's theories still apply. He would argue that despite the change in circumstances and the nature of the threat, the same bedrock principles hold. What has to be modified is the training of the strategists and employment of new methods of attack. New threats simply call for different training and use of strategists in dealing with terrorism. For example, Wedemeyer's definition of "strategy" was simple and still useful:

> The art and science of developing and employing all the *political*, *economic*, and *psychological* resources of a nation together with its armed forces in the ongoing struggle to insure the security and well-being of the people. (emphasis added)[26]

That definition of "strategy" is as useful today as it was when Wedemeyer first articulated it over 65 years ago, but the relative importance of its three components have changed drastically. While he always stressed the importance of the psychological aspect, he would have elevated it to far greater significance in today's employment of strategy. He learned the importance of winning the "hearts and minds" of the populace when he was in China in 1944–45 and witnessed firsthand the impact that Communist propaganda had on the Chinese people. He also witnessed the impact of propaganda when he was in Germany in 1936–38. He sympathized with the isolationist view prior to Pearl Harbor, based on his extensive reading about use of false propaganda deliberately disseminated during the First World War to induce the United States to enter it. Wedemeyer also knew of the public relations battle that went on in the United States to elevate Mao and discredit Chiang Kai-shek in the minds of Americans.

Today's new strategists face unique problems. They must learn how to *anticipate* threats that their predecessors would not have imagined, and regretfully, to date, have been largely misunderstood and unexpected. Current world tensions include the fantasy notion of abolishing nuclear weapons, as well as "resetting" relations with Russia, reconciling the irreconcilable in the Middle East, achieving rapprochement with Islam, and winding down the conflicts in Iraq and Afghanistan, just to mention the major ones. Regrettably, the approach has too often been responsive, not pro-active. For example, when the planes hit the World Trade Towers, we installed screening to detect weapons, insulated the pilots from hijackers breaking into their cabins, and allocated millions of dollars to screen passengers and open a "terrorist no-fly list." When the "shoe-bomber" tried to blow up a plane, we required passengers to remove shoes for inspection; when the "underwear bomber" unsuccessfully tried to set off his concealed explosives, we spent millions on more sophisticated x-ray machines, and enhanced "pat-downs" derisively called "scope or grope." We protect our soldiers from the devastating impact of Improvised Explosive Devices [IED's] with reinforced armored vehicles which must be constantly made stronger to protect against stronger explosives. This is a *reactive* instead of a *proactive* approach to the problem, not the way Wedemeyer would have approached it, and not the way the new strategists discussed by Moore are trained to react.

This reactive approach, which seemingly is how we are now targeting terrorists and dealing with world tensions, assumes that the next attack will follow the previous pattern, and therefore millions of dollars, and countless man hours are directed in an effort to defeat that particular effort, when the focus ought to be on anticipating the nature of the next attack, a completely different experience. Like those now being trained, Wedemeyer would have anticipated that these new terrorists are not likely to repeat the same procedure in the next attack and instead, would come up with new and novel ways to harm us, and that is exactly what they have done. Just as these new strategists are being trained, Wedemeyer would have carefully examined the "political, economic, and psychological" aspects of his definition of strategy. For example, recent developments such as global communication networks and the international financial market provide terrorist organizations like al-Qaeda with the ability to threaten their opponents in hitherto unforeseen ways that demand new approaches. And why should this be surprising? It is only logical that the materially inferior actor will pursue strategies that seek to surprise and bypass the superiority of their opponents. Indeed, the strategy of al Qaeda is not designed to defeat military forces, but *to destroy our will to resist*.

These new strategists, trained as Wedemeyer was, and that Moore and Schuurman describe, are being taught to think ahead and not limit their strategies to defending against the last attack. We can hope there are a number of nascent Wedemeyers among them who will be up to the task. Further, we hope that the lessons of the 1930s and the post-World War II Cold War will not be forgotten, but taken into account by these new strategists; namely, that despite the risks involved, we must not appease aggression. Finally, we hope we have learned that aggressors keep pushing until they encounter resistance. And by the time that happens, it may be too late to prevent the damage.

APPENDIX I

DIRECTIVE TO LIEUTENANT GENERAL WEDEMEYER

You will proceed to China without delay for the purpose of making an appraisal of the political, economic, psychological and military situations—current and projected. In the course of your survey you will maintain liaison with American diplomatic and military officials in the area. In your discussions with Chinese officials and leaders in positions of responsibility you will make it clear that you are on a fact-finding mission and that the United States Government can consider assistance in a program of rehabilitation only if the Chinese Government presents satisfactory evidence of effective measures looking towards Chinese recovery and provided further that any aid which may be made available shall be subject to the supervision of representatives the United States Government.

In making your appraisal it is desired that you proceed with detachment from any feeling of prior obligation to support or to further official Chinese programs which do not conform to sound American policy with regard to China. In presenting the findings of your mission you should endeavor to state as concisely as possible your estimate of the character, extent, and probable consequences of assistance which you may recommend, and the probable consequences in the event that assistance is not given.

When your mission in China is completed you will proceed on a brief trip to Korea to make an appraisal of the situation there with particular reference to an economic aid program in Korea and its relation to general political and economic conditions throughout the country. Before going to Korea you will communicate with General MacArthur to ascertain whether he desires you to proceed via Tokyo.

You will take with you such experts, advisers and assistants as you deem necessary to the effectiveness of your mission.

APPROVED
S/ HARRY S. TRUMAN
JULY 9, 1947

APPENDIX II

REPORT TO THE PRESIDENT, 1947, PARTS I–V
19 SEPTEMBER 1947
MEMORANDUM FOR THE PRESIDENT:

My dear Mr. President:
In compliance with your directive to me of 9 July 1947, the attached "REPORT ON CHINA-KOREA" is respectfully submitted.

In consonance with your instructions, advisers from State, Treasury, War and Navy Departments accompanied me on a two months fact-finding mission in the Far East. The principal cities and some rural areas in China and Korea were visited. Successful efforts were made to reach all categories of people as measured by economic position, intellectual attainment and divergent political viewpoints. Conferences were held with public officials and with private citizens in all walks of life. Approximately 1,200 memoranda from individuals and groups were received and considered.

The report includes pertinent data in appendices which may be of interest and assistance to appropriate government departments and agencies. The report presents against a global background my estimates of the situations, current and projected, in both China and Korea, and recommends what I deem to be sound courses of action for achievement of United States objectives in the Far East.
RESPECTFULLY YOURS,

S/ A.C. WEDEMEYER
C. WEDEMEYER,
LIEUTENANT GENERAL, U.S. ARMY.
461

MEMBERS OF MISSION
16 July-18 September 1947

Captain James J. Boyle . . . . Aide-de-Camp-Secretary,
War Department
Captain Horace Eng . . . . Aide-de-Camp-Interpreter,
War Department
Lt. Colonel Claire E. Hutchin, Jr. . . . . Military Advisor,
War Department
Mr. David R. Jenkins . . . . Fiscal Advisor
Mr. Philip D. Sprouse . . . . Political Advisor,
State Department
Rear Admiral Carl A. Trexel . . . . Engineering Advisor,
Navy Department.
Mr. Melville H. Walker . . . . .Economic Advisor,
State Department
Mr. Mark S. Watson . . . . Press and Public Affairs Advisor,
Baltimore Sun, Baltimore, Md.
Lt. General A.C. Wedemeye . . . . Special Representative
of the President of the United States.

CHINA-KOREA
Part I-*General Statement*

China's history is replete with examples of encroachment, arbitrary action, special privilege, exploitation, and usurpation of territory on the part of foreign powers. Continued foreign infiltration, penetration or efforts to obtain spheres of influence in China, including Manchuria and Taiwan (Formosa), could be interpreted only as a direct infringement and violation of China's sovereignty and a contravention of the principles of the Charter of the United Nations. It is mandatory that the United States and those other nations subscribing to the principles of the Charter of the United Nations should combine their efforts to insure the unimpeded march of all peoples toward goals that recognize the dignity of man and his civil rights and, further, definitely provide the opportunity to express freely how and by whom they will be governed.

Those goals and the lofty aims of freedom-loving peoples are jeopardized today by forces as sinister as those that operated in Europe and Asia during the ten years leading to World War II. The pattern is familiar—employment of subversive agents; infiltration tactics; incitement of disorder and chaos to disrupt normal economy and thereby to undermine popular confidence in government and leaders; seizure of authority without reference to the will of the people—all the techniques skillfully designed and ruthlessly implemented in order to create favorable conditions for the imposition of totalitarian ideologies. This pattern is present in the Far East, particularly in the areas contiguous to Siberia.

If the United Nations is to have real effect in establishing economic stability and in maintaining world peace, these developments merit high priority on the United Nations' agenda for study and action. Events of the past two years demonstrate the futility of appeasement based on the hope that the strongly consolidated forces of the Soviet Union will adopt either a conciliatory or a cooperative attitude, except as tactical expedients. Soviet practice in the countries already occupied or dominated completes the mosaic of aggressive expansion through ruthless secret police methods and through an increasing political and economic enslavement of peoples. Soviet literature, confirmed repeatedly by Communist leaders, reveals a definite plan for expansion far exceeding that of Nazism in its ambitious scope and dangerous implications. Therefore in attempting a solution to the problem presented in the Far East, as well as in other troubled areas of the world, every possible opportunity must be used to seize the initiative in order to create and maintain bulwarks of freedom.

Notwithstanding all the corruption and incompetence that one notes in China, it is a certainty that the bulk of the people are not disposed to a Communist political and economic structure. Some have become affiliated with Communism in indignant protest against oppressive police measures, corrupt practices and maladministration of National Government officials. Some have lost all hope for China under existing leadership and turn to the Communists in despair. Some accept a new leadership by mere inertia.

Indirectly, the United States facilitated the Soviet program in the Far East by agreeing at the Yalta Conference to Russian re-entry into Manchuria, and later by withholding aid from the National Government. There were justifiable reasons for these policies. In the one case we were concentrating maximum Allied strength against the Japanese in order to accelerate crushing defeat and thus save Allied lives. In the other, we were withholding unqualified support from a government within which corruption and incompetence were so prevalent that it was losing the support of its own people. Further, the United States had not yet realized that the Soviet Union would fail to cooperate in the accomplishment of world-wide plans for post-war rehabilitation. Our own participation in those plans has already afforded assistance to other nations and peoples, friends and former foes alike, to a degree unparalleled in humanitarian history.

Gradually it has become apparent that the World War II objectives for which we and others made tremendous sacrifices are not being fully attained, and that there remains in the world a force presenting even greater dangers to world peace than did the Nazi militarists and the Japanese jingoists. Consequently the United States made the decision in the Spring of 1947 to assist Greece and Turkey with a view to protecting their sovereignties, which were threatened by the direct or inspired activities of the Soviet Union. Charges of unilateral action and circumvention of the United Nations were made by members of that organization. In the light of its purposes and principles such criticisms seemed plausible. The United States promptly declared its intention of referring the matter to the United Nations when that organization would be ready to assume responsibility.

It follows that the United Nations should be informed of contemplated action with regard to China. If the recommendations of this report are approved, the United States should suggest to China that she inform the United Nations officially of her request to the United States for material assistance and advisory aid in order to facilitate China's post-war rehabilitation and economic recovery. This will demonstrate that the United Nations is not being circumvented, and that the United States is not infringing upon China's sovereignty, but contrariwise is cooperating constructively in the interest of peace and stability in the Far East, concomitantly in the world.

The situation in Manchuria has deteriorated to such a degree that prompt action is necessary to prevent that area from becoming a Soviet satellite. The Chinese Communists may soon gain military control of Manchuria and announce the establishment of a government. Outer Mongolia, already a Soviet satellite, may then recognize Manchuria and conclude a "mutual support agreement" with a *de facto* Manchurian government of the Chinese Communists. In that event, the Soviet Union might accomplish a mutual support agreement with Communist-dominated Manchuria, because of her current similar agreement with Outer Mongolia. This would create a difficult situation for China, the United States and the United Nations. Ultimately it could lead to a Communist-dominated China.

The United Nations might take immediate action to bring about cessation of hostilities in Manchuria as a prelude to the establishment of a Guardianship or Trusteeship. The Guardianship might consist of China, Soviet Russia, the United States, Great Britain and France. This should be attempted *promptly* and could be initiated only by China. Should one of the nations refuse to participate in Manchurian Guardianship, China might then request the General Assembly of the United Nations to establish a Trusteeship, under the provisions of the Charter.

Initially China might interpret Guardianship or Trusteeship as an infringement upon her sovereignty. But the urgency of the matter should encourage a realistic view of the situation. If these steps are not taken by China, Manchuria may be drawn into the Soviet orbit, despite United States aid, and lost, perhaps permanently, to China.

The economic deterioration and the incompetence and corruption in the political and military organizations in China should be considered against all-inclusive background lest there be disproportionate emphasis upon defects. Comity requires that cognizance be taken of the following:

Unlike other Powers since V-J Day, China has never been free to devote full attention to internal problems that were greatly confounded by eight years of war. The current civil war has imposed an overwhelming financial and economic burden at a time when resources and energies have been dissipated and when, in any event, they would have been strained to the utmost to meet the problems of recovery.

The National Government has consistently, since 1927, opposed Communism. Today the same political leader and same civil and military officials are determined to prevent their country from becoming a Communist-dominated State or Soviet satellite.

Although the Japanese offered increasingly favorable surrender terms during the course of the war, China elected to remain steadfast with the Allies. If China had accepted surrender terms, approximately a million Japanese would have been released for employment against American forces in the Pacific.

I was assured by the Generalissimo that China would support to the limit of her ability an American program for the stabilization of the Far East. He stated categorically that, regardless of moral encouragement or material aid received from the United States, he is determined to oppose Communism and to create a democratic form of government in consonance with Doctor Sun Yat-Sen's principles. He stated that some progress has been made along these lines but, with spiraling inflation, economic distress and civil war, it has been difficult to accomplish fully these objectives. He emphasized that, when the Communist problem is solved, he could drastically reduce the Army and concentrate upon political and economic reforms. I retain the conviction that the Generalissimo is sincere I his desire to attain these objectives. I am not certain that he has today sufficient determination to do so if this requires absolute overruling of the political and military cliques surrounding him. Yet, if realistic United States aid is to prove effective in stabilizing the situation in China and in coping with the dangerous expansion of Communism, that determination must be established.

Adoption by the United States of a policy motivated solely toward stopping the expansion of Communism without regard to the continued existence of an unpopular repressive government would render any aid ineffective. Further, United States prestige in the Far East would suffer heavily, and wavering elements might turn away from the existing government to Communism.

In China and Korea, the political, economic and psychological problems are inextricably mingled. All of them are complex and are becoming increasingly difficult of solution. Each will be discussed in the course of this report. However, it is recognized that a continued global appraisal is mandatory in order to preclude disproportionate or untimely assistance to any specific area.

The following three postulates of United States foreign policy are pertinent to indicate the background of my investigations, analyses and report:

The United States will continue support of the United Nations in the attainment of its lofty aims, accepting the possible development that the Soviet Union or other nations may not actively participate.

Moral support will be given to nations and peoples that have established political and economic structures compatible with our own, or that give convincing evidence of their desire to do so.

Material aid may be given to those same nations and peoples in order to accelerate post-war rehabilitation and to develop economic stability, provided:

That such aid shall be used for the purposes intended.

That there is continuing evidence that they are taking effective steps to help themselves, or are firmly committed to do so.

That such aid shall not jeopardize the American economy and shall conform to an integrated program that involves other international commitments and contributes to the attainment of political, economic and psychological objectives of the United States.

Part II-China
POLITICAL

Although the Chinese people are unanimous in their desire for peace at almost any cost, there seems to be no possibility of its realization under existing circumstances. On one side is the Kuomintang, whose reactionary leadership, repression and corruption have caused a loss of popular faith in the Government. On the other side, bound ideologically to the Soviet Union, are the Chinese Communists, whose eventual aim is admittedly a Communist state in China. Some reports indicate that Communist measures of land reform have gained for them the support of the majority of peasants in areas under their control, while others indicate that their ruthless tactics of land distribution and terrorism have alienated the majority of such peasants. They have, however, successfully organized many rural areas against the National Government. Moderate groups are caught between Kuomintang misrule and repression and ruthless Communist totalitarianism. Minority parties lack dynamic leadership and sizable following. Neither the moderates, many of whom are in the Kuomintang, nor the minority parties are able to make their influence felt because of National Government repression. Existing provincial opposition leading to possible separatist movements would probably crystallize only if collapse of the Government were imminent.

Soviet actions, contrary to the letter and spirit of the Sino-Soviet Treaty of

1945 and its related documents, have strengthened the Chinese Communist position in Manchuria, with political, economic and military repercussions on the National Government's position both in Manchuria and in China proper, and have made more difficult peace and stability in China. The present trend points toward a gradual disintegration of the National Government's control with the ultimate possibility of a Communist-dominated China.

Steps taken by the Chinese Government toward governmental reorganization in mid-April 1947 aroused hopes of improvement in the political situation. However, the reorganization resulted in little change. Reactionary influences continue to mold important policies even though the Generalissimo remains the principal determinative force in the government. Since the April reorganization, the most significant change has been the appointment of General Chen Cheng to head the civil and military administration in Manchuria. Projected stops include elections in the Fall for the formation of a constitutional government, but, under present conditions, they are not expected to result in a government more representative than the present regime.

ECONOMIC

Under the impact of civil strife and inflation, the Chinese economy is disintegrating. The most probable outcome of present trends would be, not sudden collapse but a continued and creeping paralysis and consequent decline in the authority and power of the National Government. The past ten years of war have caused serious deterioration of transportation and communication facilities, mines, utilities and industries. Notwithstanding some commendable efforts and large amounts of economic aid, their overall capabilities are scarcely half those of the pre-war period. With disruption of transportation facilities and the loss of much of North China and Manchuria, important resources of those rich areas are no longer available for the rehabilitation and support of Chinas' economy.

Inflation in China has been diffused slowly through an enormous population without causing the immediate dislocation which would have occurred in a highly industrialized economy. The rural people, 80 per cent of the total Chinese population of 450 million, barter foodstuffs for local handicraft products without suffering a drastic cut in living standards. Thus, local economics exist in many parts of China, largely insulated from the disruption of urban industry. Some local economics are under the control of Communists, and some are loosely under the control of provincial authorities.

The principal cause of the hyper-inflation is the long-continued deficit in the national budget. Present revenue collections, plus the profits of nationalized enterprises, cover only one-third of governmental expenditures, which are approximately 70 per cent military, and an increasing proportion of the budget is financed by the issuance of new currency. In the first six months of 1947 note-issue was tripled but rice prices increased seven-fold. Thus prices and governmental expenditures spiral upwards, with price increases occurring faster than new currency can be printed. With further price increases, budget revisions will undoubtedly be necessary. The most urgent economic need of Nationalist China is a reduction of the military budget.

China's external official assets amounted to $327 million (US) on July 30, 1947. Privately-held foreign exchange assets are at least $600 million and may total $1500 million, but no serious attempt has been made to mobilize these private resources for rehabilitation purposes. Private Chinese assets located in China include probably $200 million in gold, and about $75 million in U.S. currency notes. Although China has not exhausted her foreign official assets, and probably will not do so at the present rates of imports and exports until early 1949, the continuing deficit in her external balance of payments is a serious problem.

Disparity between the prices of export goods in China and in world markets at unrealistic official exchange rates has greatly penalized exports, as have disproportionate increases in wages and other costs. Despite rigorous trade and exchange controls, imports have greatly exceeded exports, and there consistently has been a heavy adverse trade balance.

China's food harvests this year are expected to be significantly larger than last year's fairly good returns. This moderately encouraging situation with regard to crops is among the few favorable factors which can be found in China's current economic situation.

Under inflationary conditions, long-term investment is unattractive for both Chinese and foreign capital. Private Chinese funds tend to go into short-term advances, hoarding of commodities, and capital flight. The entire psychology is speculative and inflationary, preventing ordinary business planning and handicapping industrial recovery.

Foreign business enterprises in China are adversely affected by the inefficient and corrupt administration of exchange and import controls, discriminatory application of tax laws, the increasing role of government trading agencies and the trend towards state ownership of industries. The Chinese Government has taken some steps toward improvement but generally has been apathetic in its efforts. Between 1944 and 1947, the anti-inflationary measure on which the Chinese Government placed most reliance was the public sale of gold borrowed from the United States. The intention was to absorb paper currency, and thus reduce the effective demand for goods. Under the circumstance of continued large deficits, however, the only effect of the gold sales program was to retard slightly the price inflation and dissipate dollar assets.

A program to stabilize the economic situation was undertaken in February

1947. The measures included a wage freeze, a system of limited rationing to essential workers in a few cities, and the sale of government bonds. The effect of this program has been slight, and the wage freeze has been abandoned. In August 1947, the unrealistic official rate of exchange was replaced, for proceeds of exports and remittances, by a free market in foreign exchange. This step is expected to stimulate exports, but it is too early to determine whether it will be effective.

The issuance of a new silver currency has been proposed as a future measure to combat inflation. If the government continued to finance budgetary deficits by unbacked note issue, the silver would probably go into hoards and the price inflation would continue. The effect would be no more than that of the gold sales in 1944-1947, namely, a slight and temporary retardation of the inflationary spiral. The proposal could be carried out, moreover, only through a loan from the United States of at least $200 million in silver.

In the construction field, China has prepared expansive plans for reconstruction of communications, mines and industries. Some progress has been made in implementing them, notably in the partial rehabilitation of certain railroads and in the textile industry. Constructive results have been handicapped by a lack of funds, equipment and experienced management, supervisory and technical personnel.

On August 1, 1947, the State Council approved a "Plan for Economic Reform." This appears to be an omnibus of plans covering all phases of Chinese economic reconstruction but its effectiveness cannot yet be determined.

Public education has been one of the chief victims of war and social and economic disruption. Schoolhouses, textbooks and other equipment have been destroyed and the cost of replacing any considerable portion cannot now be met. Teachers, like other public servants, have seen the purchasing power of a month's salary shrink to the market value of a few days' rice ration. This applies to the entire educational system, from primary schools, which provide a medium to combat the nation's grievous illiteracy, to universities, from which must come the nation's professional men, technicians and administrators. The universities have suffered in an additional and no less serious respect-traditional academic freedom. Students participating in protest demonstrations have been severely and at times brutally punished by National Government agents without pretense of trial or public evidence of the sedition charged. Faculty members have often been dismissed or refused employment with no evidence of professional unfitness, patently because they were politically objectionable to government officials. Somewhat similarly, periodicals have been closed down "for reasons of military security: without stated charges, and permitted to reopen only after new managements have been imposed." Resumption of educational and other public welfare activities on anything like the desired scale can be accomplished only by restraint of officialdom's abuses, and when the nation's economy is stabilized sufficiently to defray the cost of vital activities.

MILITARY

The overall military position of the National Government has deteriorated in the past several months and the current military situation favors Communist forces. The Generalissimo has never wavered in his contention that he is fighting for national independence against forces of an armed rebellion nor has he been completely convinced that the Communist problem can be resolved except by force of arms. Although the Nationalist Army has a preponderance of force, the tactical initiative rests with the Communists. Their hit-and-run tactics, adapted to their mission of destruction at points or in areas of their own selection, give them a decided advantage over Nationalists, who must defend many critical areas including connecting lines of communication. Obviously large numbers of Nationalist troops involved in such defensive roles are immobilized whereas Communist tactics permit almost complete freedom of action. The Nationalists' position is precarious in Manchuria, where they occupy only a slender finger of territory. Their control is strongly disputed in Shantung and Hopei Provinces where the Communists make frequent dislocating attacks against isolated garrisons.

In order to improve materially the current military situation, the Nationalist forces must first stabilize the fronts and then regain the initiative. Further, since the Government is supporting the civil war with approximately seventy per cent of its national budget, it is evident that steps taken to alleviate the situation must point toward an improvement in the effectiveness of the armed forces with a concomitant program of social, political and economic reforms, including a decrease in the size of the political and economic reforms, including a decrease in the size of the military establishment. Whereas some rather ineffective steps have been taken to reorganize and revitalize the command structure, and more sweeping reforms are projected, the effectiveness of the Nationalist Army requires a sound program of equipment and improved logistical support. The present industrial potential of china is inadequate to support military forces effectively. Chinese forces under present conditions cannot cope successfully with internal strife or fulfill China's obligations as a member of the family of nations. Hence outside aid, in the form of munitions (most urgently ammunition) and technical assistance, is essential before any plan of operations can be undertaken with a reasonable prospect of success. Military advice is now available to the Nationalists on a General Staff level through American military advisory groups. The Generalissimo expressed to me repeatedly a strong desire to have this advice and supervision extended in scope to include field forces, training centers and particularly logistical agencies.

Extension of military aid by the United States to the National Government might possibly be followed by similar aid from the Soviet Union to the Chinese Communists, either openly or covertly-the latter course seems more likely. An area of conflicting ideologies might be created as seems more likely. An arena of conflicting ideologies might be created as in 1935 in Spain. There is always the possibility that such developments in this area, as in Europe and the Middle East, might precipitate a third world war.

Part III-Korea
POLITICAL

The major political problem in Korea is that of carrying out the Moscow Agreement of December 1945 for the formation of a Provisional Korean Government to be followed by a Four-Power Trusteeship over Korea. The United States-Soviet Joint Commission, established in accordance with that Agreement, reached a deadlock in 1946 in the effort to implement the Moscow Agreement due to Soviet opposition to consultations with the Commission by all Korean democratic parties and social organizations, as provided for in that Agreement. Soviet motives have been to eliminate to eliminate the extreme rightist groups in the United States zone from consultations and subsequently from participation in the new government, thus ensuring a Communist-dominated government in Korea. Soviet objections to such consultations have been based on the rightist groups; openly expressed opposition to trusteeship, while the United States has taken the position that to disqualify these groups would deprive a large section of the Korean people of an opportunity to express views regarding their government.

A resumption of the Joint Commission meetings in May 1947, following an exchange of notes between Secretary Marshall and Foreign Minister Molotov, resulted in a further deadlock on the same issue, although these notes had established a formula which would have permitted participation in consultation by the rightist groups in question. After the Soviet Government failed to reply to Secretary Marshall's note of August 12 requesting the submission by the Commission of a joint status report or separate reports by each Delegation, the United States Delegation on August 20 transmitted a unilateral report to Washington. An American proposal then made to China, the United Kingdom and the Soviet Union for a Four-Power conference to discuss Korea has been agreed to by China and the United Kingdom but has been rejected by the Soviet Union.

Internally, the Korean problem has been complicated by the Soviet establishment of a Communist regime in North Korea and by the machinations in South Korea of Communist groups, openly hostile to the United States. The terrorist activities of extreme rightists, who have strongly opposed trusteeship, have continually obstructed the efforts of United States authorities. The latter, in accordance with their Directives, are endeavoring to turn over to Koreans as rapidly as possible full administrative responsibility in governmental departments. In consonance with this plan they have organized an interim Korean legislative assembly and in general, are striving to carry out a policy of "Koreanization" of government in South Korea.

ECONOMIC

South Korea, basically an agricultural area, does not have the overall economic resources to sustain its economy without external assistance. The soil is depleted, and imports of food as well as fertilizer are required. The latter has normally come from North Korea, as have most of the electric power, timber, anthracite and other basic products.

The economic dependence of South Korea upon North Korea, and of Korea as a whole, in pre-war years, upon trade with Japan and Manchuria, cannot be too strongly emphasized. Division of the country at the 38" North parallel and prevention of all except smuggling trade between North and South Korea have reduced the Korean economy to its lowest level in many years. Prospects for developing sizable exports are slight. Food exports cannot be anticipated on any scale for several years, and then only with increased use of artificial fertilizer. South Korea's few manufacturing industries, which have been operating at possibly 20 per cent of pre-war production, are now reducing their output or closing down. In part this is a natural result of ten years of deferred maintenance and war-time abuse, but lack of raw materials and essential repair parts, and a gross deficiency of competent management and technical personnel are the principal factors.

A runaway inflation has not yet occurred in South Korea, because the Military Government has restrained the issuance of currency by keeping governmental expenditures and local occupation costs at reasonable levels; because cannibalization and the use of Japanese stocks have kept some industries going; and because the forcible collection of rice at harvest time has brought in sufficient food to maintain—with imports provided by the United States—an adequate official ration in the cities. Highly inflationary factors such as the exhaustion of raw material stocks, cumulative breakdowns in public services and transportation, and the cutting of power supply from the North might occur simultaneously. The South Korean economic outlook is, therefore, most grave.

A five-year rehabilitation program starting in July 1948, and requiring United States financing at a cost of $647 million, has been proposed by the Military Government. A review of preliminary estimates indicates that the proposed annual rehabilitation cost would be substantially greater than the relief program of $137 million which was tentatively approved for fiscal 1948 but later reduced to $92.7 million. These preliminary estimates of costs and the merits of individual projects need careful review. It is not considered feasible to make South Korea self-sustaining. If the United States elects to remain in South Korea support of that area should be on a relief basis.

SOCIAL-CULTURAL

Since the Japanese were expelled, the Korean people have vehemently and unceasingly pressed for restoration of their ancient culture. There is particular zeal for public education. Individual and collective efforts to reduce illiteracy have produced results meeting the praise of American Military Government officials. There will be materially better results when there are more school buildings, more trained teachers and advisors, and many more textbooks in the Korean language. Current American activities aim at adult visual education on a modest but reasonably effective scale. South Korea's health and public welfare work are at present fully as effective as under Japanese administration and considerably more so in the prevention of serious diseases. Even the Koreans' eagerness for improvement cannot immediately overcome the unquestionable need for large funds for social betterment.

MILITARY

The military situation in Korea, stemming from political and economic disputes which in turn are accentuated by the artificial barrier along the 38 degree North parallel, is potentially dangerous to United States strategic interests. Large scale Communist inspired or abetted riots and revolutionary activities in the South are a constant threat. However, American forces supplemented by quasi-military Korean units are adequate to cope with such trouble or disorder except in the currently improbably event of an outright Soviet-controlled invasion. Whereas American and Soviet forces engaged in occupation duties in South Korea and North Korea respectively are approximately equal, each comprising less than 50,000 troops, the Soviet-equipped and trained North Korean People's (Communist) Army of approximately 125,000 is vastly superior to the United States-organized Constabulary of 16,000 Koreans equipped with Japanese small arms. The North Korean People's Army constitutes a potential military threat to South Korea, since there is strong possibility that the Soviets will withdraw their occupation forces, and thus induce our own withdrawal. This probably will take place just as soon as they can be sure that the North Korean puppet government and its armed forces, which they have created, are strong enough and sufficiently well indoctrinated to be relied upon to carry out Soviet objectives without the actual presence of Soviet troops.

It appears advisable that the United States organize, equip and train a South Korean Scout Force, similar to the former Philippine Scouts. This force should be under the control of the United States military commander and initially should be officered throughout by Americans, with a program for replacement by Korean officers. It should be of sufficient strength to cope with the threat from the North. It would counteract in large measure the North Korean People's Army when American and Soviet forces are withdrawn from Korea, possibly preclude the forcible establishment of a Communist government, and thus contribute toward a free and independent Korea.

Part IV-Conclusions

The peaceful aims of freedom-loving peoples in the world are jeopardized today by developments as portentous as those leading to World War II.

The Soviet Union and her satellites give no evidence of a conciliatory or cooperative attitude in these developments. The United States is compelled, therefore, to initiate realistic lines of action in order to create and maintain bulwarks of freedom, and to protect United States strategic interests.

The bulk of the Chinese and Korean peoples are not disposed to Communism and they are not concerned with ideologies. They desire food, shelter and the opportunity to live in peace.

CHINA

The spreading internecine struggle within China threatens world peace. Repeated Amerian efforts to mediate have proved unavailing. It is apparent that positive steps are required to end hostilities immediately. The most logical approach to this very complex and ominous situation would be to *refer the matter to the United Nations.*

A China dominated by Chinese Communists would be inimical to the interests of the United States, in view of their openly expressed hostility and active opposition to those principles which the United States regards as vital to the peace of the world.

The Communists have the tactical initiative in the overall military situation. The Nationalist position in Manchuria is precarious, and in Shantung and Hopei Provinces strongly disputed. Continued deterioration of the situation may result in the early establishment of a Soviet satellite government in Manchuria and ultimately in the evolution of a Communist-dominated China.

China is suffering increasingly from disintegration. Her requirements for rehabilitation are large. Her most urgent needs include governmental reorganization and reforms, reduction of the military budget and external assistance.

A program of aid, if effectively employed, would bolster opposition to Communist expansion, and would contribute to gradual development of stability in China.

Due to excesses and oppressions by government police agencies, basic freedoms of the people are being jeopardized. Maladministration and corruption cause a loss of confidence in the Government. Until drastic political and economic reforms are undertaken United States aid cannot accomplish its purpose.

Even so, criticism of results achieved by the National Government in efforts for improvement should be tempered by a recognition of the handicaps imposed on China by eight years of war, the burden of heroic opposition to Communism, and her sacrifices for the Allied cause.

A United States program of assistance could best be implemented under the supervision of American advisors in specified economic and military fields. Such a program can be undertaken only if China requests advisory aid as well as material assistance.

KOREA

The situation in Korea, in its political, economic and psychological aspects, is strongly and adversely influenced by the artificial barrier of the 38 degrees North parallel separating agricultural South Korea from the more industrialized North Korea.

The South Korean economic position is grave. Agriculture is debilitated and there are few other resources.

The establishment of a self-sustaining economy in South Korea is not feasible. Accordingly, United States aid should include a minimum of capital investment and should consist chiefly of items required for support on a relief basis.

Korean Communist agents are creating unrest and fomenting disorder in South Korea. The terrorist and obstructive activities of extreme rightist groups are further aggravating this situation.

Since the United States-Soviet Joint Commission meetings have twice ended in deadlock, and offer no real hope of success, the United Nations now seems to be the appropriate medium through which a Provisional Korean Government, functioning under a Four-Power Trusteeship, can be established.

The United States may be confronted with a situation requiring decisions concerning continued occupation in South Korea should the Soviet Union withdraw her occupation forces. This could reasonably be expected to occur when the Soviet-created puppet government and its armed forces are sufficiently well established to carry out Communist objectives without the presence of Soviet troops.

The creation of an American controlled and officered Korean Scout Force, sufficient in strength to cope with the threat from the North, is required to prevent the forcible establishment of a Communist government after the United States and Soviet Union withdraw their occupation forces.

Part V-Recommendations
IT IS RECOMMENDED:
That the United States Government provide as early as practicable moral, advisory,

and material support to China and South Korea in order to contribute to the early establishment of peace in the world in consonance with the enunciated principles of the United Nations, and concomitantly to protect United States strategic interests against militant forces which now threaten them.

That United States policies and actions suggested in this report be thoroughly integrated by appropriate government agencies with other international commitments. It is recognized that any foreign assistance extended must avoid jeopardizing the American economy.

CHINA

That China be advised that the United States is favorably disposed to continue aid designed to protect China's territorial integrity and to facilitate her recovery, under agreements to be negotiated by representatives of the two governments, with the following stipulations:

That China inform the United Nations promptly of her request to the United States for increased material and advisory assistance.

That China request the United Nations to take immediate action to bring about a cessation of hostilities in Manchuria and request that Manchuria be placed under a Five-Power Guardianship or, failing that, under a Trusteeship in accordance with the United Nations Charter.

That China make effective use of her own resources in a program for economic reconstruction and initiate sound fiscal policies leading to reduction of budgetary deficits.

That China give continuing evidence that the urgently required political and military reforms are being implemented.

That China accept American advisors as responsible representatives of the United States Government in specified military and economic fields to assist China in utilizing United States aid in the manner for which it is intended.

KOREA

That the United States continue efforts for the early establishment of a Provisional Korean Government in consonance with the Moscow Agreement and meanwhile provide necessary support of the political, economic and military position of South Korea.

It is recommended that:

United States withdrawal from Korea be based upon agreements with the Soviet Union to effect proportional withdrawals, with as many guarantees as possible to safeguard Korean freedom and independence.

Military aid be furnished to South Korea which would support the achievement of such adequate safeguards and which would envisage:

Continuing to furnish arms and equipment to Korean National Police and Korean Coast Guard.

The creation of an American-officered Korean Scout Force to replace the present Constabulary of sufficient strength to cope with the threat from the North.

Continued interim occupation by United States Army forces in Korea.

Advice in training of technical specialists and tactical units.

APPENDIX III

ORREN L. JONES
SUITE 418
815 CONNECTICUT AVENUE, N.W.
WASHINGTON, D. C. 20006

AREA CODE 202
298-7365

27 December 1968
General Albert C. Wedemeyer, USA(Ret.)
Boyds, Maryland 20720

Dear General Wedemeyer:

During the period 1943-45 I was assigned as the Alternate Air Force Member of the Joint Logistics Committee of the Joint Chiefs of Staff and the Combined Administrative Committee (US-UK) of the Combined Chiefs of Staff.

I was, as such, Chief of the Office within the Army Air Corps Headquarters having jurisdiction over matters pertaining to the Chiefs of Staff. When I took over the job I had a safe and two or three classified papers; and when I left the Air Force in 1945 there were approximately 30,000 Top Secret Document in my office, including such operations as OVERLORD.

My office selected Officers to serve on Committees charged with the preparation of logistical data and processed such documents through all necessary Staff Agencies within the Headquarters before submission to the Joint or Combined Chiefs of Staff for consideration.

I approved or disapproved such papers before submission to the Chiefs of Staff

241

for final determination. When approved by the Chiefs, Admiral Leahy signed the outgoing directives as the Chief of Staff to the Commander-in-Chief, Franklin D. Roosevelt.

Because almost every project or operation had logistical implications if followed, therefore, that my office, of necessity, had to receive all the papers emanating from the organizations of the Chiefs of Staff, such as, the Joint and Combined Military Transportation Committees, the Joint and Combined Communications Committees, the Joint Strategic Survey Committee, the Joint Staff Planners, the Army-Navy Petroleum Board, the Joint and Combined Intelligence Committees, and so and so on. These papers dealt with the overall management and conduct of the Global War and touched every field of human endeavor. These Committees prepared the Agenda for all the Conferences from Casablanca to Yalta and Potsdam; and maintained relations on a day-to-day basis between the Leaders of State during the time when they were not in conference.

I had the opportunity of working with many of the leaders connected with the Joint and Combined Chiefs of Staff. I personally attended the Conference at Cairo between the President and Prime Minister. During this period of time I became well acquainted with Brig. General Patrick Tansey (Deputy Director of the C.I.A. until a few years ago). General Tansey was then the Army Member of the Joint Logistics Committee, with his primary job being the Chief of the Logistical Division of the Operation Division of the War Department General Staff.

I became interested in the personalities of World War II Theatre Commanders; how they got their jobs; and a host of other questions as to their training and ability.

General Tansey would frequently call for me to discuss many sensitive and important items on the Agenda of the Joint Logistics Committee. He was generally opposed to giving anything and everything we had away to Great Britain, and particularly of trying to build up their post-war economy at our expense during war time. He told me that General Wedemeyer was one of the few officers on duty who was well versed in the politics of many nations of the world, spoke many languages, and was always a threat to the British because of his vast knowledge as to their methods of operations and intent.

General Tansy told me that Sir John Dill and Lt. General Freddie Morgan (of the British Government stationed here) were intent on getting General Wedemeyer out of Washington, and into a place where he could have little impact upon the operations and objectives of the British.

The American Military were opposed to the release of General Wedemeyer and had great plans for his future, but once General Morgan discovered this attitude he immediately advised the Prime Minister, who, in turn, on a political level, appealed to Roosevelt for a special assignment for General Wedemeyer as deputy to Lord Louis Mountbatten, who had just been assigned as Commander to the S.E. Asia Command.

This eliminated General Wedemeyer from pursuing his job here, and it also took him out of circulation until late in the war; consequently, he did not emerge a full General until he took over as Commander of the China Theatre.

I gathered from General Tansey that your future as a Commander was most certainly delayed and that the American military had lost a valuable and a highly trained leader during the build up of our forces in both the E.T.O. and the Pacific.

I may also add that you would have possibly emerged to one of the few top positions during the early part of the war had the British not sold a bill of goods to Mr. Roosevelt. It would be easy for me to believe that a lot of our history books would read quite differently today had this trick of fate not entered in your career.

I wrote this same type of letter to you several (10 or so) years ago, but at that time in greater detail. I am putting it to print now for such use as you may give it in your next book or for other historical purposes.

I did not know you until a few years ago, but since I have made your acquaintance everything that General Tansy told me has been confirmed with the strong feeling that the hand of destiny was on your shoulder; but the politicians had their way.

With highest personal regards and best wishes.

Sincerely and faithfully,

Orren L. Jones
OLJ/mj   Colonel, USAF Res. (Ret.)

APPENDIX IV

Dear Orren:

The letter that you wrote to me dated December 27th is sincerely appreciated. I had an inkling that the developments as you outlined them so cogently were taking place and it was just a matter of time before the British could, without being personally disagreeable to me, remove me from the scene. Because of my background, experience, knowledge, interest, observation and travels, as well as attendance at a foreign school in Europe, I was prepared, primarily at the expense of the American taxpayer, to contribute constructively to the formulation of policy and strategy. It is an indictment of our system when a foreign power—friend, neutral or foe—can influence the assignment of Americans to posts of responsibility.

This happened to me also in 1946 when General Marshall asked me to accept the post of Ambassador in relief of Pat Hurley who had resigned out in China. I agreed to do so for one year, indicating that I felt my experience was primarily in strategy and the military. Of course he did not have the final say so but wielded a great deal of power, so he asked President Truman to appoint me. This information leaked and the Chinese Communists protested violently. After the China Theatre closed, I was ordered home and was awaiting in the spring of 1946 for my orders to return as American Ambassador. Out of the blue a message came from Marshall asking the President to appoint Dr. Leighton Stuart, a Presbyterian minister of many years' service in China as American Ambassador to China instead of General Wedemeyer. This action was precipitated by the Communist reaction. Dean Ache-

244

son, at that time Undersecretary of State, asked me to drop by his office and showed me the telegram. He said he was sorry about it. I replied, "I did not ask for the appointment and really did not want it, and most everyone in the State Department knew this." I did comment that I had purchased about $800 worth of clothes that an Ambassador is supposed to wear—striped trousers etc. Dean Acheson suggested that the State Department pick up the tab for that. Then I added just before I departed that I thought it was most unfortunate that any foreign power, particularly a Communist group, could interfere and block the appointment of any individual to a position of responsibility in our government.

In closing, I should emphasize to you, Orren—perhaps you already realize this because of our recent close contacts—that I am humble and deeply grateful for all of the opportunities that my government has given me to serve our nation, the Army, and God.

This note that you sent to me is a wonderful demonstration of loyalty to principle as well as to friend and I shall never forget your expression of friendship manifested in so many ways.

Sincere good wishes to you and your loved ones for health and happiness.

As ever,

A. C. WEDEMEYER
General, U. S. Army (Ret.)

Mr. Orren L. Jones
815 Connecticut Avenue, N. W., Suite 418
Washington, D. C, 20008

cc: Major General Patrick H. Tansey

APPENDIX V

A. C. WEDEMEYER
GENERAL UNITED STATES ARMY, RETIRED
FRIENDS ADVICE
BOYDS, MARYLAND
20720

JULY 15, 1977

Dear President Chang:

I am deeply moved to learn that you, and the Council of the China Academy, have conferred upon me the honorary degree of Doctor of Philosophy. Your good letter of June 24th has arrived, as have the impressive embossed citation and the academic cap and gown. I accept this high honor with profound gratitude, and with mixed feelings of pride and humility.

I am proud, in the first instance, that my career and achievements, such as they have been, should earn generous recognition from the political and intellectual leaders of the Republic of China. I have been privileged to know and work with many of those leaders in the past, and have formed the highest regard for their character and abilities. They are worthy representatives of the great people and traditions of China. History has placed in their hands, not only the task of preserving what is good and useful in the ancient Chinese culture, but also that of building on Taiwan a new and modern Republic which stands as a beacon of progress and civilization in the Orient. These tasks are being well performed.

I am proud, too, and pleased, that the honorary doctorate you have bestowed upon me is a degree in Philosophy. That fine old word suggests much more to me than a specialized academic discipline. It suggests a search for first principles, for broad understanding, for the ways of wisdom. Whatever degree of wisdom I may have achieved, future generations will have to judge. I do know that that search has always been a challenge to me, and that I have done my best through the years to pursue it.

During my formal schooling, the curricula invariably emphasized military subjects. In spite of this somewhat narrow focus, there were continued opportunities for broader reading in the exciting world of Plato, Aristotle, Confucius, Kant, Voltaire, Locke, William James and countless other notable figures of history, science and philosophy. I accompanied these great minds on their various quests for wisdom through the portals of intellectual and moral disciplines. The impact of these experiences on my life and habits of thought was deep and lasting.

As a professional military man with a philosophic interest, I have necessarily been concerned with such issues as the proper societal role of soldiers and the purpose of war. In these matters, Plato and Aristotle were influential teachers. Although they assigned important and useful roles to soldiers, both insisted that peace and harmony were the ideal conditions of mankind toward which statesmen ought always to strive. Military institutions were not, therefore, ends in themselves, nor could armed conflict be considered praiseworthy under any and all circumstances. "War must be for the sake of peace," Aristotle declared, "business for the sake of leisure, things necessary and useful for the sake of things noble . . ." Not all ages or nations, of course, have shared these attitudes. There were times in China's history, for instance, when the military were neither respected nor admired. In Sparta, on the other hand, military institutions and values were accorded undue emphasis.

The balanced views of the ancient Athenians nonetheless survived into the modern world, and I for one remained attached to them. This attachment led me into eventual conflict with prevailing concepts of strategy. Throughout history the term "strategy" has assumed an almost exclusively military connotation. By World War II, the inadequacy of so narrow a concept had been brought home to me time and again. And yet, in World War II, the thoughts and acts of Allied leaders continued to focus on the clash of arms and the physical destruction of nations. The political goals for which the war was allegedly being fought, and the employment of the many non-military means which were available for advancing these goals, were pushed into the background of our consciousness. We had largely forgotten not only the ancient Greek philosophers as well as Sun Tze and Clausewitz, but the American General, William T. Sherman, as well. "The legitimate object of war," Sherman's once famous words on his memorial in Washington remind us, "is a more perfect peace." The development since 1945 of horrendous weapons of mass destruction, and of delivery systems of previously unimagined capabilities, seem to me to place a vastly greater urgency than ever before on the search for non-violent methods of settling human disputes.

In the years immediately following World War II, I had the opportunity of expounding these ideas more fully to students at the National War College in Washington. I proposed and advocated a more comprehensive definition of strategy, to wit: "Strategy is the art and science of employing all of a nation's resources to accomplish objectives defined by national policies." I categorized the available resources, or "instruments of policy," as political, economic, psycho-social, and military. Among the political instruments I included diplomatic persuasion and the use of alliances; among the economic, reciprocal trade agreements as well as boycotts and the denial of war-making resources to potential enemies; among the psycho-social, cultural exchanges and various motivated forms of overt and covert propaganda. If the first three of these categories are employed in a timely and intelligent manner, I argued, the chances that the fourth—naked military force—would have to be invoked would be significantly reduced. Progress would be made at the same time toward a more stable, peaceful, and prosperous world order. Time has only heightened, in my judgment, the soundness of this analysis.

On July 9th of this year, I had the good fortune of becoming an octogenarian. As shadows lengthen, my greatest disappointment undoubtedly lies in the fact that the free people of the earth have not yet taken the concerted actions–political, economic, psycho-social, and military–necessary to defend themselves against totalitarian aggression. Too often solemn commitments have not been honored by members of international organizations. I continue to believe that free nations having compatible aims and objectives must unite and cooperate realistically if they are to survive.

Despite disappointments, however, I am convinced that I have been, and remain a very fortunate mortal. I have had many challenging opportunities to serve my fellow man in an environment of freedom. Of these opportunities, none was more satisfying than that presented in my association with the Chinese in the struggle against a common enemy during World War II. I count myself greatly favored, too, in the possession of a devoted family and many loyal friends. Last but not least, the good opinion and approbation of contemporaries—as evidenced by the honorary degree you have recently so generously bestowed upon me—makes me feel rich indeed. My heartfelt thanks go out to you, president Chang, and to the distinguished Council of the China Academy.

Sincerely,

A. C. WEDEMEYER
General, U. S. Army (Ret.)

Dr. Chang Chi-yun
President, The China Academy
Hwa Kang, Yang-ming-shan
Taiwan
Republic of China

APPENDIX VI

MARCH 24, 1945.

Dear George,

I have read your letter of March 21st to my daughter Anna and I have noted with concern your plan to publicize your unfavorable opinion of one of our allies at the very time when such a publication from a former emissary of mine might do irreparable harm to our war effort. As you say, you have held important positions of trust under your Government. To publish information obtained in those positions without proper authority would be all the greater betrayal. You say you will publish unless you are told before March 28th that I do not wish you to do so. I not only do not wish it but I specifically forbid you to publish any information or opinion about an ally that you may have acquired while in office or in the service of the United States Navy.

In view of your wish for continued active service, I shall withdraw any previous understanding that you are serving as an emissary of mine and I shall direct the Navy Department to continue your employment wherever they can make use of your services.

I am sorry that pressure of affairs prevented me from seeing you on Monday. I value our old association and I hope that time and circumstance may some day permit a renewal of our good understanding.

Sincerely yours,
s/Franklin D. Roosevelt

Commander George H. Earle, U. S. N.,
The Racquet Club,
Philadelphia, Pa.

NOTES

PREFACE

1. Forest C. Pogue. *George C. Marshall: Ordeal and Hope,* New York: The Viking Press, 1965, p. 122. [hereafter *Ordeal*]
2. Field Marshall The Right Hon. Alan Francis Brooke, was senior commander in the British Army, Chief of the Imperial General Staff. In 1946 after retirement from the Army he was known as Alanbrooke, and we will use that title throughout this book.
3. John Keegan. *Six Armies In Normandy,* New York: The Viking Press, 1982, p. 30. [hereafter *Six Armies*]
4. Keegan. *Six Armies*, p. 34; The "Victory Program," of which Wedemeyer was the chief author was a document created by the War Plans Division of the United States Army during the hectic pre-war period in the spring of 1941. It was the American response to the question of how to build up our armed forces, how to mobilize industry to a wartime level, and how to fight the Nazis. It is discussed in detail in Chapter III.
5. The author thought that John Keegan might have some clue as to why Wedemeyer was not used in the Normandy campaign. In response to a letter sent to him, Keegan said he had not contemplated the idea. Letter to John J. McLaughlin Sept. 12, 2006. Keegan's response spurred the author on to investigate this point further.
6. Richard Reeves. *Daring Young Men—The Heroism and Triumph of the Berlin Airlift,* New York: Simon & Schuster, 2010. [hereafter *Daring*]

INTRODUCTION

1. I find it curious that, to my knowledge, this fascinating incident is not noted by any of the many historians who knew of the White House meeting. Even Wedemeyer does not mention it in 1958 when he published *Wedemeyer Reports!* However, he does allude to it in a general way in 1986 when he commented on an article written by John Colville in *Commentary* September 1985, "How the West Lost the Peace in 1945." [hereafter "How the West Lost"] Wedemeyer Papers Hoover Institution Stanford, California. Box 23. file 17 p. 4. [hereafter ACW Hoover] Wedemeyer makes a direct reference to the incident in a letter April 16, 1985 to a "Mr. Matthews" [no address or first name] which *inter alia* says: "...I had the sobering task of defending the American plans in the presence of President Roosevelt and the Combined Chiefs of Staff, after the Prime Minister had eloquently and persuasively presented his own radically different ideas." ACW Hoover box 23 file 14; Wedemeyer again refers to the meeting in the June 1987 issue of the *American Legion Magazine*, p. 14–38. [hereafter *Legion*]; Wedemeyer talks at

length about the White House meeting and his presentation that evening June 21st 1942 in the Deskis Oral History Interview taken in 1973. Deskis Interview. Sec 4. [hereafter Deskis]

2. It would not be the only time that Roosevelt put Churchill in such an uncomfortable position. At Teheran, in November/December 1943, he frequently chided Churchill as a ploy to gain the favor of Joseph Stalin.

3. Going past Gibraltar was a truly risky proposition. Franco's Spain, though neutral, was friendly to the Nazis who assisted them in the recent revolution and American planners feared the Nazis would invade Spain and easily overwhelm Gibraltar from the north. This would have blocked the Mediterranean completely. If this had occurred the event would have been more than a mere footnote to history; it had the potential of being a complete chapter if not a book!

4. Albert C. Wedemeyer. *Wedemeyer Reports!* New York: Henry Holt & Company, 1958, p. 369. [hereafter *WR!*]

5. *WR!*, p. ix.

6. *WR!*, p. 433.

CHAPTER ONE—BEGINNINGS

1. While this may be true, research by biographer Keith Eiler failed to establish a connection. Deskis. sec. 1, page 1.3; Deskis. sec. 1, page 2.4; A Catholic Jesuit Priest at Creighton, Father Ignatius Riley, expressed disappointment that the young man he so respected had slowly inclined toward religious beliefs different from orthodox Roman Catholicism. Deskis, sec.1. p. 6.5; Deskis. sec. 1, p. 46; Deskis. sec. 1, p. 21.

7. Deskis. sec. 1, p. 17.

8. *WR!*, p. 44.

9. Deskis. sec. 1, p. 11.

10. *WR!*, p. 45.

11. Deskis. sec. 1.

12. Deskis. sec 1, p. 13–14.

13. Deskis. sec 1, p. 32.

14. Deskis. sec. 1, p. 38.

15. Deskis. sec. 1, p. 1.

16. Deskis. sec. 1, p. 38.

17. Deskis. sec. 1, p. 29.

18. Deskis. sec. 2, p. 9.

19. Deskis. sec. 1, p. 30.

CHAPTER TWO—THE EDUCATION OF A STRATEGIST

1. Of necessity, most of the material on Wedemeyer's two years at the German Command and General Staff school comes from only two sources: Wedemeyer's own book *Wedemeyer Reports!* published in 1958, and Keith E. Eiler who interviewed Wedemeyer in 1983 at age 86, and printed the interview in *American Heritage* October/November 1983 under the title "The Man Who Planned the Victory." [hereafter "Eiler Victory"]. Eiler's later reflections on Wedemeyer, "An Uncommon Soldier," was published in 2001 in the *Hoover Digest*, #4. [hereafter "Soldier"]

2. Eiler. "Victory," p. 38.

3. Eiler. "Soldier," p. 4; Germany had similar arrangements with other countries.

4. *WR!*, p. 54.

5. *WR!*, p.54–57.

6. *WR!*, p. 61.
7. *WR!*, p. 57.
8. *WR!*, p. 52.
9. Eiler. "Victory," p. 43.
10. *WR!*, p. 49.
11. *WR!*, p. 61.
12. *WR!*, p. 52.
13. *WR!*, p. 53.
14. *WR!*, p. 39.
15. Karl-Heinz Frieser. "Blitzkrieg Legende, Der Westfeldzug 1940, Operationen des Zweiten Weltkrieges. München: R. Oldenbourg.
16. *WR!*, p. 48; As Andrew Roberts said, the Germans were fighting their fifth war of aggression in seventy-five years and were very good at it. It took the Allies "half a war" to catch up. *The Storm of War*. New York: Harper Collins, 2011, p. 24. [hereafter *Storm*]
17. Kent Roberts Greenfield, military historian and general editor of the U.S. Army in World War II describes tragic scenes early in the war of United States troops shooting down American planes, and US airmen dropping bombs on their own troops, all due to confusion and total lack of coordination. In the early days of the war some generals actually refused to allow "air cover." It was not until the later stages of the war that these early problems were overcome. *American Strategy in World War II: A Reconsideration*, Baltimore: Johns Hopkins Press, 1963, p. 102–104. [hereafter *American Strategy*]
18. *WR!*, p. 61.
19. Charles E. Kirpatrick. *An Unknown Future and a Doubtful Present*, Honolulu Hawaii: University Press of the Pacific, p. 11. [hereafter *Unknown Future*]
20. This was true, not only with respect to military reports from American officers attending schools but other reports as well. In March 1941 a full report on the capabilities of the Japanese Zero aircraft that was so effective against the United States in the early years of the war was forwarded by military intelligence to Washington. The report detailed its maneuverability, range and engine power, information which would have been immensely useful to our airmen in the early stages of the war. This report was promptly filed away without examination by appropriate "experts." Theodore H. White. *Thunder Out of China*, New York: William Sloane Associates, Inc., 1946, p. 83. [hereafter *Thunder*]
21. Kirpatrick. *Unknown Future*, p. 11; *WR!*, p. 11.
22. *WR!*, p. 62.
23. *WR!*, p. 62.
24. While doing research at the Marshall Library, Lexington, VA, the author asked Paul B. Baron, Director of the Marshall Library and Archives about this famous "Black Book" and he confirmed the widely held belief that Marshall did maintain such a book, and he has frequently been asked about it, but it has never been uncovered.
25. Wedemeyer was the first person from his West Point class to receive both a first star and then a forth star. Interview with Wedemeyer by Tong-Chin Rhee January 14, 1965. ACW Hoover Box 20, File 4. [hereafter *Rhee Interview*]
26. Eiler. "Victory," p. 45.
27. *WR!*, p. 434.
28. John D. Eisenhower. *Allies Pearl Harbor to D-Day*, New York: Doubleday & Company, 1982, p. 62. [hereafter *Allies*]
29. *WR!*, p. 92.
30. See the excellent essay by Russell F. Weigley "The American Military and the Principle of Civilian Control from McClellan to Powell." *The Journal of Military History*. Vol. 57,

No. 5. October 1993. pp. 27–58. [hereafter "Civilian Control"]. In perhaps the most important Anglo-American strategic decision of World War II, the decision to postpone the cross-channel invasion scheduled for 1943 in favor of the North African campaign, the political pressure on the American military strategists was immense, and as Weigley says, the American military establishment thought it a grave mistake; certainly Wedemeyer did. See: Weigley, p. 46.

31. *WR!,* pp. 53–53; See: Chapter 14, Conclusion, which reviews the uneven course of strategy prior to World War II and thereafter.

32. "Heartland Theory," *Wikipedia*, p. 1. A review of the principles of MacKinder. [hereafter "Heartland"]

33. *WR!,* pp. 130, 131; Keegan. *Six Armies*. p. 39.

34. Churchill's first speech as Prime Minister to the House of Commons, May 10, 1940.

35. Sir John Kennedy. *The Business of War—The War Narrative Of Major-General Sir John Kennedy*, London: Hutchinson of London, 1957, p. 305. [hereafter *Business of War*]

36. *WR!,* p. 64.

37. Walter Scott Dunn Jr. *Second Front Now—1943*, University of Alabama Press 1980. [hereafter *Second Front*]; John Grigg. *1943 The Victory That Never Was*, New York: Hill and Wang, A Division of Farrar, Straus and Giroux, 1980. [hereafter *The Victory*]

38. Tuvia Ben-Moshe. "Winston Churchill and the 'Second Front'; A Reappraisal" *The Journal of Modern History*, Vol. 62, No. 3. (Sept., 1990), pp. 503–537. [hereafter "Second Front"]. This writer argues convincingly that Churchill was opposed to the cross-channel plan from the beginning, that his statements in his own 6-volume history of the war, to the contrary, are not persuasive, and that Churchill, a master writer, positioned himself in such a fashion, that had the invasion been a failure, he would have been able, to "prove" with his great writing skill, and documents, some of which he withheld from his 6-volume work, that he was against it all along, and only gave in under extreme pressure to the demands of Allied planners.

39. March 5, 1946.

40. *WR!,* p. 91.

41. Kennan, who wrote the "X" article anonymously in *Foreign Affairs*, was quickly identified as the author and it vaulted him into immediate prominence as the originator of the "Containment Doctrine."

42. George F. Kennan. *Memoirs 1925–1950*, Boston: Little Brown and Company, 1967, pp. 307–309. [hereafter *Memoirs*]; the growth of the War College, and its current impact on American strategic interests is covered at length in Chapter 14, Conclusion.

43. Quoted in Kirpatrick. *Unknown Future*, p. 22.

44. Kennan. *Memoirs*, p. 185.

45. *WR!,* p. 90.

CHAPTER THREE—WRITING THE VICTORY PROGRAM

1. William L. Langer and S. Everett Gleason. *The Undeclared War 1940–1941*, New York: Harper & Brothers, 1953, Chapter VII Defense Demands and Campaign Promises. [hereafter *Undeclared War*]

2. Maurice Matloff and Edwin M. Snell. *Strategic Planning For Coalition Warfare 1941–1942*, Office of the Chief of Military History Department of the Army Washington, D.C. ,1953 Green Book Series, Chapter I. [hereafter *Strategic Planning*]

3. Henry G. Gole. *The Road to Rainbow Army Planning For Global War, 1934–1940*, Annapolis, MD: Naval Institute Press, 2003, p. xii.

4. There had been an earlier meeting between the two years before when Roosevelt was

Assistant Secretary of the Navy in the Wilson administration.

5. On May 23, 1941, Charles A. Lindbergh and U.S. Senator Burton K. Wheeler addressed an overflow crowd of 22,000 at Madison Square Garden in New York City. *New York Times*, May 24, 1941.

6. Matloff and Snell. *Strategic Planning*, Chapter I, The War Plans.

7. Langer and Gleason. *The Undeclared War*, p. 239.

8. Matloff and Snell. *Strategic Planning*, Chapter I, and Chapter II.

9. Matloff and Snell. *Strategic Planning*, Chapter III British-American Plans. January–November 1941, pp. 31–37.

10. Robert E. Sherwood. Roo*sevelt & Hopkins—An Intimate History*, New York: Harper & Brothers, 1948, p. 273, 274. [hereafter *Roosevelt & Hopkins*]

11. Sherwood. *Roosevelt & Hopkins*, p. 272.

12. Sherwood. *Roosevelt & Hopkins*, p. 273; Sherwood on p. 274 quotes respected historian Charles A. Beard who wrote a searing indictment of the President's secret pre-war dealings with England, labeling them totally "unconstitutional."

13. Pogue. *Ordeal*, pp. 158–159.

14. Sherwood. *Roosevelt & Hopkins*, p. 273.

15. The Lend Lease Bill was passed March 11, 1941.

16. Sherwood notes the irony that had the knowledge of the meetings and the plans formulated fallen into the hands of the Germans or the Japanese no great harm would have occurred; but, on the other hand, had the knowledge come to the attention of the press or the Congressmen then debating the Lend-Lease Bill, American preparations for war would likely have been ruined. *Roosevelt & Hopkins*, pp. 273–274.

17. Pogue. *Ordeal*, p. 39, 56; See reports of public opinion polls made by the American Institute of Public Opinion, *Fortune*, and the Office of Public Opinion Research on the question of U.S. neutrality, in Hadley Cantril, ed. *Public Opinion, 1935–1946*, Princeton: Princeton University Press, 1951, p. 956 ff.

18. *New York Times*, May 23, 1941.

19. Lend-Lease was the major United States aid program to the allies between 1941–1945 which enabled the United States of America to supply England, Russia, China and other countries with vast amounts of war material. The supplies were given with no requirement of repayment. The program commenced in March of 1941 and ended soon after V-J day, on September 2, 1945.

20. Eisenhower, John. *Allies*, 1982, p. xx.

21. Matloff and Snell. *Strategic Planning*, p. 59.

22. An indication of the lack of preparedness of the country was noted by *Fortune* August 1941 on pages 42–43 when it reported that ". . . the United States is not merely falling short, it is failing spectacularly, in nine different ways and nine different places." See also: Pogue. *Ordeal*, Chapter VII.

23. Kirpatrick. *Unknown Future*, p. 51.

24. Kirpatrick. *Unknown Future*, pp. 51–53.

25. "Overall Production Requirements" was ultimately shortened to "The Victory Program."

26. Langer and Gleason. *Undeclared War*, p. 738; Mark S. Watson, Chief of Staff: *Prewar Plans and Preparations, The United States Army in World War II*. Department of the Army 1950, pp. 338–339. [hereafter *Plans and Preparations*]

27. Pogue acknowledges the "assignment" to Wedemeyer of writing the Victory Program and cites *Wedemeyer Reports!* uncritically throughout *Ordeal*, but does not lavish any praise on him, same being reserved for Marshall, Eisenhower and Roosevelt, with Wedemeyer seemingly a mere scrivener.

28. The Pentagon was not completed until January 1943.
29. Richard M. Leighton and Robert W. Coakley. *Global Logistics and Strategy 1940–1943*, Office of the Chief of Military History Department of the Army Washington, D.C., 1955 (Green Book Series), pp. 129–132. [hereafter *Global Logistics*]
30. *WR!*, p. 69.
31. Eiler. "Victory," p. 40.
32. Dunn. *Second Front*; Grigg. *The Victory*.
33. *WR!*, Chapter V. "The Victory Program," pp. 63–76.
34. *WR!*, pp. 74, 75.
35. One factor that Wedemeyer failed to take into account was that in the Second World War approximately 70% of the armed forces were service personnel never intended for actual combat. This is uniquely American, and Wedemeyer erred when he used the ratio of service personnel to fighting forces from the First World War. No other country had anywhere near this high a percentage of service support staff. Kent Roberts Greenfield. *The Historian and the Army*. New Brunswick: Rutgers University Press. 1954. pp. 66–67. [hereafter *Historian*] One unforeseen consequence of this phenomenon was that in the last stages of the war (The Battle of the Bulge) the army was critically short of combat troops. Many untrained cooks, clerks, truck drivers and other service personnel were rushed into combat without adequate training.
36. Sherwood. *Roosevelt & Hopkins*, Chapter III. "1942—The Narrow Margin," pp. 439–478.
37. *WR!*, pp. 65–71.
38. Andrew Roberts. *Masters and Commanders*, New York: Harper Collins, 2009, p. 50. [hereafter *Masters*]
39. Kirpatrick. *Unknown Future*, p. 60.
40. Kirpatrick. *Unknown Future*, pp. 59–72.
41. Eiler. "Victory," p. 40.
42. Kirpatrick. *Unknown Future*, p. 62–63.
43. Kirpatrick. *Unknown Future*, p. 63.
44. Letter to Graduate student Tong-Chin Rhee January 26, 1965. ACW Hoover. Box 20. File 4. [Wedemeyer notes in this letter that his concerns were mostly greeted with "pooh-pooh," although some who did agree, "were reluctant to develop the thought."]
45. *WR!*, p.74.
46. Letter dated March 12, 1958 from Wedemeyer to Colonel William P. Scobey. Eiler Records, Hoover Institution, Box 3. [hereafter Eiler Hoover]
47. Eisenhower, J. *Allies:*, p. 63.
48. Matloff and Snell. *Strategic Planning*, p. 61
49. Matloff and Snell. *Strategic Planning*, p. 61.
50. *WR!*, p. 15.
51. Keith Eiler. *Wedemeyer on War and Peace*, Stanford CA: Hoover Institution Press, 1987, p. 13. [hereafter *War*]
52. Thomas Fleming. *The New Dealers' War F.D.R And The War Within World War II*, New York: Basic Books, A Member of the Perseus Books Group, 2001, p. 26. [hereafter *New Dealers*]
53. Letter March 2, 1942 from Henry L. Stimson to President Roosevelt, FDR Library. Stimson file.
54. Mark Perry. *Partners in Command*, New York: The Penguin Press, 2007, p. 60. [hereafter *Partners*]
55. Perry. *Partners*, p. 74.

56. Memorandum on a National Strategy Council. Written 1983. ACW Hoover. Box 23, file 2.

57. Colville. "How the West Lost" pp. 41–47.

58. Hanson W. Baldwin. *Great Mistakes of the War*, New York: Harper & Brothers,1950, p. 33. [hereafter *Great Mistakes*]; Fleet Admiral William D. Leahy, who became Roosevelt's Personal Chief of Staff, agreed with this assessment. *I Was There*. New York: McGraw-Hill Book Company, Inc., 1950, p. 110. [hereafter *I Was There*]

59. Dunn. *Second Front*, Foreword to book.

60. Grigg. *The Victory*; Dunn, *Second Front*.

61. Eiler. "Victory," p. 42; Letter from Wedemeyer to author Charles B. MacDonald, March 2, 1978. ACW Hoover, Box 49, folder 4.

62. B. H. Liddell Hart. *The German Generals Talk*. New York: Berkley Publishing Corp., 1948, p. 191. eighth edition, p. 191.

63. Von Runstedt was later replaced by Field Marshal von Kluge who held the post till the collapse came, and shortly after swallowed a dose of poison in despair.

64. Hart. *German Generals* , p. 201.

65. Eiler. "Soldier," p. 2.

66. Langer and Gleason. *Undeclared, War*, p. 741.

67. Letter Marshall to Wedemeyer. December 23, 1942. George G. Marshall Library. Pentagon Office 1938–1951. Box 90, Wedemeyer.

68. In fact, he spends more time praising General Patton for ". . . his outstanding perform- ance" in pre-war maneuvers held in Louisiana and Texas in late August 1941, for which shortly thereafter Patton, then a Colonel ". . . was to be promoted to brigadier general." *Ordeal*, p. 163.

69. One exception is Keith E. Eiler with his *Wedemeyer on War and Peace*, and his superb article "An Uncommon Soldier" In fairness to Pogue it must be mentioned that Pogue had to rely on information supplied by Marshall, and although Pogue, an experienced and respected military historian who had for several years sought to interview Marshall, it was not until 1956 that Marshall consented to be interviewed for his biography. The interviews did not commence until February 1957, 2 years before Marshall's death. In his later years, Marshall, although still holding enormous respect for Wedemeyer, had somewhat soured on what he termed Wedemeyer's political views, at one point saying that Wedemeyer's recommendations to beat the Russians to the East had be- come an "obsession." George G. Marshall Interviews, Larry L. Bland (ed.). George G. Marshall Foundation, Lexington, VA, 1996, p. 602. [hereafter Pogue-Marshall Inter- view]

70. Perry. *Partners*, p. 60; Stanley Weintraub. *15 Stars—Eisenhower, MacArthur, Marshall*, New York: Free Press, 2007.

71. An even greater irony is that the plan that contributed so greatly to the defeat of Germany was formulated by a man whose political philosophy was much more in line with the Germans than the British.

72. Keegan. *Six Armies*, pp. 31, 34.

73. Tuvia Ben-Moshe. *Churchill-Strategy and History*, Boulder Colorado: Lynne Rienner Publishers, Inc. 1992.

74. Kirpatrick. *Unknown Future*, pp. 2–3.

75. Mark A. Stoler. *Allies and Adversaries*, Chapel Hill, North Carolina: University of North Carolina Press, pp. 48–51.

76. Leighton and Coakley in their contribution to the history of World War II, *Global Logistics and Strategy*, note Wedemeyer's contribution as "principal author" but question

the method he used to calculate the size of the army necessary. p. 130–131; 132; 651.

77. Eiler. "Soldier," p. 9.

CHAPTER FOUR—UNDERMINING THE VICTORY PROGRAM

1. The "Victory Program" as authored by Wedemeyer came before the Joint Chiefs of Staff and was incorporated into over all plans which some called the "Joint Board Estimate of United States Overall Production Requirements." Over time, for a variety of reasons, Wedemeyer's name was not associated with the program with the same closeness as the names of Eisenhower and Marshall.

2. Sherwood. *Roosevelt & Hopkins*, p. 232.

3. Sherwood. *Roosevelt & Hopkins*, p. 243.

4. Sherwood. *Roosevelt & Hopkins*, p. 239.

5. Sherwood. *Roosevelt & Hopkins*, p. 262.

6. Pogue. *Ordeal*, p. 144.

7. Churchill, in his six volume history of the war, which he rushed into print, immediately after the conclusion of hostilities, denied that he was opposed to a cross-channel invasion; it was only the "timing" that he questioned; these claims, when stacked up against his prior verbal and written record are less than convincing.

8. December 22, 1941 to January 14, 1942. Actually the conference consumed 14 full days, since Churchill made one trip to Canada and took a short Florida vacation before returning to England.

9. This was a justifiable concern and precisely what the isolationist press was urging. Sherwood. *Roosevelt & Hopkins*. p. 445; this tends to confirm Roosevelt's concern that had not Hitler taken the first step and declared war on the United States, he would not have had an easy time convincing Congress to declare war on Germany.

10. Sherwood. *Roosevelt & Hopkins*, p. 440.

11. Roberts. *Masters*, p. 71.

12. Roberts. *Masters*, p. 72.

13. Roberts. *Masters*, p. 72.

14. David Bercuson & Holger Herwig. *One Christmas in Washington*, Woodstock and New York: The Overlook Press, 2005, p. 100. [hereafter *Christmas*]

15. Bercuson & Holger. *Christmas*, p. 99.

16. Sherwood disagrees. He says that the President "immediately agreed" to meet with Churchill. *Roosevelt & Hopkins*, p. 439.

17. Pogue. *Ordeal*, p. 262.

18. Use of the word "invasion" was deliberately vague, and never specified any "cross-channel" attack. Undoubtedly this was his first version of the "soft underbelly" approach.

19. Arthur Bryant. *The Turn of the Tide*, Garden City NY: Doubleday & Company, 1957. p. 225. [hereafter *Tide*]

20. Perry. *Partners*, p. 31.

21. Major General J.F.C. Fuller. *The Conduct of War 1789–1961*, New Brunswick, New Jersey: Rutgers University Press, 1961, p. 273. [hereafter *War*]

22. Winston S. Churchill. vol. 2. *The Second World War—Their Finest Hour*, p. 21.

23. Pogue. *Ordeal*, p. 304.

24. Pogue. *Ordeal*, p. 305; Matloff and Snell. *Strategic Planning*, p. 177.

25. Eisenhower, J. *Allies*, p. 63.

26. Dieppe resulted in sixty percent of the 6,000-man force being either killed, wounded or captured, and not a single strategic objective was achieved.

27. According to Roberts it was held on March 24th. *Masters*, p. 128.

28. Ranking member of the British war council in America; It was anticipated that if the plan was submitted earlier to the British representatives in Washington it would have been bogged down in endless debate. Norman Gelb. *Desperate Venture—The Story of Operation Torch*, New York: William Morrow and Company, 1992, p. 53. [hereafter *Venture*]; Roberts. *Masters*, p. 128.

29. Roberts. *Masters*, p. 128.

30. Roberts. *Masters*, p. 132; According to Roberts, Marshall was willing to consider a North African operation on the condition that Vichy France would "invite" the Americans to invade their territories. Of course this never happened, but at no time did American endorsement of a North African campaign include approval of extended operations, i.e. Sicily, and then Italy. Roberts. *Masters*, p. 70.

31. Paul Fussell. *Wartime-Understanding and Behavior in the Second World War*, New York: Oxford University Press, 1989, p. 138.

32. Rick Atkinson. *An Army At Dawn*, New York: Henry Holt & Company, 2002, p. 283, 284, 288. [hereafter *Army*]; many historians remark about these famous red leather dispatch cases, which Sherwood says ". . . make British officials look really official." Sherwood. *Roosevelt & Hopkins*, p. 442.

33. Atkinson. *Army*, p. 288.

34. Atkinson. *Army*, p. 284.

35. Pogue. *Ordeal*, p. 266.

36. Joseph L. Strange. "The British Rejection of Operation SLEDGEHAMMER, an Alternative Motive" *Military Affairs*, Vol. 46, No. 1. (Feb. 1982), pp. 6–14. [hereafter "British Rejection"]

37. Sherwood. *Roosevelt & Hopkins*, p. 393.

38. Like many controversial issues, the evidence is not always solely in one direction. Roberts cites evidence suggesting that Churchill was not unalterably opposed to a cross-channel invasion, including his recommendation for construction of many LST'S [Landing Ship Tanks] and other invasion craft, which would be used in a cross-channel attack. However, Churchill, ever the word master, hedged his comments with the cautionary "when the time is ripe." *Masters*, p. 38, 52.

39. One author disagrees: Norman Gelb says the Prime Minister ". . . responded with unqualified approval to" [the American proposals for a 1943 cross-channel invasion]. *Venture*, p 70.

40. Roberts. *Masters*, p. 151.

41. Matloff and Snell. *Strategic Planning*, p. 188.

42. Roberts. *Masters*, p. 157.

43. Roberts. *Masters*, p. 157.

44. Matloff and Snell. *Strategic Planning*, p. 189.

45. Leighton and Coakley make the interesting observation that the British "approval"of the American plans might have been a very clever strategic deception, suggesting that, perhaps, the initial approval was done for the single purpose of insuring that the Americans would keep their main emphasis in Europe and not the Pacific. That would account for what he describes as their ". . . quick and even enthusiastic" endorsement. Global Logistics, p. 360; Matloff and Snell agree that Churchill's "acceptance" of the American plan was a deception designed to head off American efforts to concentrate on the Pacific. U.S. Army in World War II. *Strategic Planning 1941–1942*," p. 189.

46. Roberts. *Masters*, p. 158.

47. General Mark W. Clark. *Calculated Risk*, New York: Enigma Books, 2007, p. 25.

48. When Mountbatten returned to England, the first thing he did was to send Roosevelt a message voicing his "concerns" about the cross-channel plan and reiterate the British

interest in North Africa. Sherwood. *Roosevelt & Hopkins*, p. 582, 583.
49. A document titled "DIVERSION," undated and unsigned, but very likely written by Wedemeyer years after the war, bears out the American contention that an adequate amount of equipment, supplies, and landing craft would have been available in England in June 1943 if they were not diverted to other operations, especially the Mediterranean. ACW Hoover, Box 75. file 1.
50. Andrew Roberts comes close to admitting this. *Masters*, p. 169.
51. Gordon A. Harrison. *Cross Channel Attack-European Theatre of Operations*, BDD Special Editions 1951, p. 28. [hereafter *Cross Channel*]
52. Leighton and Coakley, *Global Logistics 1940–1943*, p. 385; Sherwood. *Roosevelt & Hopkins*, p. 604.
53. Sherwood. *Roosevelt & Hopkins*, p. 605.
54. Leighton and Coakley. *Global Logistics 1940–1943*, p. 385; Secretary Stimson agreed that the coupling of SLEDGEHAMMER and BOLERO was the cause of the abandonment of the 1943 cross-channel invasion. *Henry L. Stimson* by McGeorge Bundy. New York: Harper and Brothers, 1947, p. 418. [hereafter *Stimson*]
55. Roberts. *Masters*, p. 158.
56. Roberts. *Masters*, p. 158.
57. Ben-Moshe. "Second Front," p. 514.
58. A thorough search of the President's personal records at the Hyde Park Museum did not turn up any records of the many communications. The records of Harry Hopkins are also located at Hyde Park and they also contain little information relating to these many communications between Roosevelt and Churchill.
59. *WR!*, p. 170.
60. Roberts. *Masters*, p. 412.
61. Quoted in Fleming, *The New Dealers' War*, p. 135; the victories of the navy at Midway and the Coral Sea were significant but not seen at the time as important as they proved to be in the future.
62. Eiler. "Victory," pp. 42–43.
63. Mountbatten had been given explicit instructions from Churchill, and he confirmed his understanding of the points in a memorandum he sent to Roosevelt a week after the meeting. Eisenhower, J. *Allies*, p. 91.
64. Roberts. *Masters*, p. 212; Pogue relates how Roosevelt, in good humor, evidently accepted the short delay due to logistical difficulties; not so, according to Stephen Early, the president's press secretary who stormed at Marshall a few days later: "You almost lost us control of Congress . . ." Pogue. *Marshall Interviews*. p. 15.
65. This author combed the records of the President and Hopkins at Hyde Park in a vain effort to find any information concerning these two critical meetings. None was found. Andrew Roberts says that Roosevelt and Churchill agreed at the Hyde Park meeting that no attack on France would take place in the year 1942, and though no authority is cited in support of this statement, it is certainly consistent with everything that transpired the following day in Washington. Roberts. *Masters*, p. 5.
66. Shortly after America entered the war the Chiefs of Staff of each country, Army, Navy, and Air Force were combined to create an enlarged board named "Combined Chiefs of Staff." Each country maintained their own "Chief's of Staff" in addition.
67. Sherwood devotes a good deal of attention to that important late Sunday evening meeting at the White House on June 21, 1942, but says that the opposition to the Prime Minister's proposals were made by Hopkins and Marshall. There is no mention of Wedemeyer. *Roosevelt & Hopkins*, p. 592.
68. *New York Times*, June 23, 1942, p. 1.

69. Leighton and Coakley. *Global Logistics 1940–1943*, p. 669; The Allies were indeed fortunate that Germany did not invade Spain and take over Gibraltar. That this was seriously contemplated by the Nazis was a very real concern, expressed early and often. The Americans knew of this danger. In May 1941 Roosevelt had been advised by Admiral Leahy in Vichy France that Marshal Petain "expects an early advance of German troops through Spain with the purpose of either taking Gibraltar or occupying some place on the coast from which the Straits can be controlled by gunfire and from which troops can be sent to Spanish Morocco." Sherwood. *Roosevelt & Hopkins*, p. 296. Evidence surfaced after the war that Generalissimo Franco was indeed willing to let the Nazis through Spain for the purpose of seizing Gibraltar, and the only thing that intervened was that Hitler was not willing to pay the steep economic and political price demanded. William Henry Chamberlin. *America's Second Crusade*, Henry Regnery Company, 1950, p. 85. [hereafter *Crusade*]

70. Bundy. *Stimson*, p. 427.

71. Roberts. *Masters*, p. 90.

72. Roberts. *Masters*, p. 312.

73. Leighton and Coakley. *Global Logistics . . . 1940–1943*, p. 673.

74. Sherwood. *Roosevelt & Hopkins*, p. 591.

75. Sherwood. *Roosevelt & Hopkins*, p. 594.

76. Churchill. *Second World War: The Hinge of Fate*, p. 651.

77. Leighton and Coakley. *Global Logistics . . . 1940–1943*, p. 665–667.

78. *WR!*, p. 191.

79. Leighton and Coakley. *Global Logistics . . . 1940–1943*, p. 664.

80. Leighton and Coakley. *Global Logistics . . . 1940–1943*, p. 664.

81. Leighton and Coakley. *Global Logistics . . . 1940–1943*, p. 666.

82. Sherwood. *Roosevelt & Hopkins*, p. 305; Beaverbrook attended the Moscow conference with Stalin in September 1941. On his return he dictated a lengthy memo opposing military diversions and pressed for a Second Front while the Germans were heavily engaged in the Russian front. A copy of his memorandum was given to Harry Hopkins. Sherwood. *Roosevelt & Hopkins*, p. 393. On other occasions Breaverbrook proclaimed himself both publicly as well as privately as a vigorous, uncompromising advocate of the Second Front. Indeed, he resigned from his government post in February 1942 to pursue his campaign for a Second Front. Roberts. *Masters*, p. 118.

83. Leighton and Coakley. *Global Logistics, 1940–1943*, p. 686.

84. Dwight Eisenhower. *Crusade in Europe*, New York: Doubleday & Company, 1948, p. 53–54. The American Joint Chiefs of Staff, on the other hand, never changed their mind with regard to their opposition to further ventures in the Mediterranean. Leighton and Coakley. *Global Logistics . . . 1940–1943*, p. 665.

85. Interview conducted by Darwin Olofson on June 4, 1984. ACW HOOVER, Box 23 file 11.

86. Ben-Moshe. "Second Front," f/n 15.

87. Sir Martin Gilbert. "Churchill and D-Day," *Finest Hour* #122. Autumn 2001.

88. Roberts. *Masters*, p. 418–419.

89. Roberts. *Masters*, p. 479.

90. Churchill. *The Second World War: Closing the Ring*, p. 154. The Italian campaign lasted 608 days, cost 321,000 Allied casualties, and 23,501 American lives. This is not what one would call a "brief and spirited" campaign.

91. The North African campaign commenced November 8, 1942; Rome was not entered until June 5, 1944, the day prior to D-Day.

92. Wedemeyer comments on the Colville Article. ACW HOOVER, Box 23, folder 17.
93. ACW HOOVER, Box 6, file 28.
94. *WR!*, p. 140.

CHAPTER FIVE—WESTERN INFLUENCE ON CHINA

1. Michael Schaller. *The United States and China in the Twentieth Century*, New York: Oxford University Press, 1979, p. vi. [hereafter *US and China*]
2. "Quarantine" Speech in Chicago, October 5, 1937.
3. There were, of course, other commercial interests. One that deserves mention is that of Amasa Delano, who passed the family fortune and interest in China to his grandson, Franklin Delano Roosevelt.
4. Schaller. *US and China*, p. 14.
5. Schaller. *US and China*, p. 11.
6. Schaller. *US and China*, p. 12.
7. "Perpetuity" in this case was until 1997 when China took it back. It was one of Mao Zedong's first acts to accomplish this recovery.
8. Schaller. *US and China*, p.13. To the enormous credit of Secretary of State Hull he was instrumental in encouraging and stewarding through the Senate a law abrogating this 100-year old travesty which was approved unanimously by the Senate on January 11, 1943. The British and Chinese governments signed a similar treaty on the same day.
9. Shaller. *US and China*, p. 16.
10. Shaller. *US and China*, p. 14.
11. While all the other nations accepted reparations, the United States returned it's share to China to build a great university where over 4,600 Chinese students in the next 40 years were educated. Speech of Walter H. Judd, part of the Congressional Record, May 3, 1944, p. A2256.
12. White. *Thunder*, p. 126.

CHAPTER SIX—STILWELL'S WAR

1. Donovan Webster. *The Burma Road,* New York: Farrar, Straus and Giroux, 2003, p. 29. [hereafter *Burma*]
2. Webster. *Burma*, p. 221.
3. Eisenhower, J. *Allies*, p.51; Stilwell's selection was not pleasing to Chiang-Kai-shek. The last person he wanted was a so called "China expert." Michael Schaller. *The U.S. Crusade in China, 1938-1945*, New York: Columbia University Press, 1979, p. 75. [hereafter *Crusade*]
4. Drum was ultimately assigned a minor stateside command and entered mandatory retirement in 1943.
5. Hans van de Ven. *War and Nationalism in China 1925–1945*, London and New York: Routledge Curzon, 2003. [hereafter *War*]
6. Herbert Feis. *The China Tangle*, Princeton: Princeton University Press, 1953, p. 15. [hereafter *Tangle*]
7. The ARCADIA conference went from December 22, 1941 to January 14, 1942. Sherwood. *Roosevelt & Hopkins*, p. 444.
8. This Board was one of the most important of the war, and it's composition provoked more heated arguments than any other during the conference. Decisions of the Board regarding distribution of supplies vitally affected the implementation of strategy in the theatres of war affected, and protests over its decisions were frequent. Sherwood. *Roosevelt & Hopkins*. p. 470, 471. President Roosevelt was the one who made the final

decisions, regarding it's structure and in the process served notice early on in the war that in vital areas of decision, his view was final. Roosevelt accepted General Marshall's strong recommendation that the Munitions Assignment Board was to be under the direction and control of the Combined Chiefs of Staff. Harry Hopkins was designated as a sub-committee of one under the Combined Chiefs as Administrator. Sherwood. *Roosevelt & Hopkins*, p. 472.

9. Schaller. *Crusade*, pp. 93–94.
10. "Chief of Staff" to Chiang was the one assignment of all that really rankled Stilwell; at the first meeting between Stilwell and Chiang, Stilwell was asked by Chiang to "describe his responsibilities." Stilwell went through the entire list but failed to mention Chief of Staff. Chiang asked him "Are you my Chief of Staff or not?" and Stilwell was compelled to say that he was. Jay Taylor. *The Generalissimo*, Cambridge: Harvard University Press, 2009, p. 196, 197. [hereafter *Generalissimo*]
11. The Ledo Road, a 478 mile roadway was started in late 1942 and took 27 months to complete. During construction, 1100 Americans died from Japanese snipers, accidents or disease.
12. Schaller. *Crusade*, p. 101.
13. Barbara W. Tuchman. *Stilwell and the American Experience in China 1911–45*, New York: The MacMillan Company, 1970, p. 270. [hereafter *Stilwell*]
14. Churchill. Vol. 4, "The Hinge of Fate." Book 2, Chapter 20.
15. van de Ven. *War*, p. 19.
16. Webster. *Burma*, p. 129, 130.
17. Webster. *Burma*, Chapter 1.
18. Quoted in Christopher Thorne. Allies *of a Kind—The United States, Britain, and the War Against Japan, 1941–1945*, New York: Oxford University Press, 1978. p. 187. [hereafter *Allies*]
19. As is so often true with regard to these issues, a different version is related by Louis Allen in *Burma The Longest War 1941–45*, New York: St. Martin's Press, 1984. p. 71; this version suggests the arrival of the Chinese forces were too little and too late to have made any difference. [hereafter *Longest War*]
20. Schaller. *Crusade*, p. 97. Enforced conscription by brutal means was another. 104.
21. Schaller. *Crusade*, p. 102–103.
22. Newly named China's foreign minister, but more importantly Chiang's brother in law.
23. Jack Belden. *Retreat With Stilwell*, Garden City, New York: Blue Ribbon Books, 1944, p. 69. [hereafter *Retreat*]
24. Schaller. *Crusade*, p. 104.
25. Feis. *Tangle*, p. 74.
26. Feis. *Tangle*, p. 31.
27. Webster. *Burma*, p. 36.
28. Theodore H. White (ed.) *The Stilwell Papers*, New York: William Sloane Associates, Inc. 1948, p. 53. [hereafter *Stilwell Papers*]
29. Charles F. Romanus and Riley Sunderland. *United States Army in World War II China-Burma-India Theater*, "Stilwell's Mission," Office of the Chief of Military History Department, (Green Book Series), pp. 138–39.
30. van de Ven. *War*, p. 32.
31. Taylor. *Generalissimo*, p. 197–197.
32. Taylor. *Generalissimo*, p. 204.
33. Webster. *Burma*, p. 14.
34. Eisenhower, J. *Allies*, p.51.

35. Tuchman. *Stilwell*, p. 295.
36. Webster. *Burma*, p. 44.
37. The best account of this fascinating story is *Retreat With Stilwell*, by Jack Belden a *Time* reporter who also refused to fly out and marched every step of the way alongside Stilwell.
38. Belden. *Retreat With Stilwell*, p. 368.
39. Webster. *Burma*, p. 44–45.
40. Schaller. *Crusade*, p. 103
41. Schaller. *Crusade*, p. 104.
42. Schaller. *Crusade*, p. 110.
43. Churchill never wavered in his opposition to the Burma campaign. At one point he sarcastically described it as "... the future right to toil through the swamps and jungles of Burma...." Feis. *Tangle*, p. 71.
44. White. *Stilwell Papers* quoted in Schaller, *Crusade*, p. 121.
45. Tragically, Wingate was killed in a plane crash on March 24th, 1944.
46. Taylor. *Generalissiomo*, p. 267.
47. Webster. *Burma*, p. 148.
48. F.F. Liu. "Stilwell and Wedemeyer Missions in China" parts reprinted in Ex *CBI* Roundup June 1957, p. 8; Chennault, perhaps, in what does not seem to be a compliment, says he was "... a fine field commander, one of the best divisional commanders the United States ever produced." *New York World Telegram*, March 27, 1943 quoted by Hon. Walter H. Judd, extension of remarks at speech in House of Representative. The British, on the other hand, who were the least complimentary sniped that Stilwell had become *"the best three-star company commander in the United States Army."* (emphasis added) Webster. *Burma*, p. 156.
49. White. *Stilwell Papers*, p. 200.
50. Schaller. *Crusade*, p. 110.
51. Hanna Pakula. *The Last Empress*, New York: Simon & Schuster, 2009, p. 448. [hereafter *Empress*]
52. Joseph and Stuart Alsop. "The Feud Between Stilwell and Chiang," *Saturday Evening Post*, January 7, 1950.
53. *New York World Telegram*. March 23, 1948. Cited in Speech of Hon. Walter H. Judd. Speech before House of Representatives June 19, 1948. p. 6.
54. *New York World Telegram*. March 24, 1948. Quoted by Hon. Walter H. Judd as extended remarks to House of Representatives in speech delivered June 19, 1948.
55. The reason for "explicit" was the belief, probably justified, that Chiang's subordinates knew that translated messages that contained unpleasant information were not welcome, and they were often softened in tone.
56. To this day the precise text of the telegram has not been revealed. White. *Stilwell Papers*, p. 333.
57. Hurley's motivation for urging the recall of Stilwell is a mystery. Stilwell thought he was a supporter but the opposite was actually the case. Giving Hurley the benefit of the doubt one would have to suppose that he actually thought it imperative that Chiang remain in power. Schaller. *Crusade*, p. 170.
58. Feis. *Tangle*, p. 200.
59. Brooks Atkinson. *New York Times*, October 31, 1944.
60. Schaller. *Crusade*, p. 175.
61. Stilwell report to the War Department. p. 70.
62. Schaller. *Crusade*, p. 152, 153; Frank Dorn. *Walkout With Stilwell in Burma*, New York: Thomas Y. Crowell Company, 1971. [hereafter *Walkout*]

63. Dorn. *Walkout*, p. 75, 76.
64. Dorn. *Walkout*, p. 78.
65. It would seem from Dorn's account that these "instructions from higher authority" were actual orders which if confirmed would have been carried out. This episode is a frightening reminder of the defense of "Superior Orders" interposed at the Nuremberg trials following World War II. Interestingly, the "defense" which actually existed for several centuries was anticipated by the Allies and declared illegal prior to the trials by the International Criminal Court, clearly in anticipation of the interposition by the defense. Of course that declaration itself raises the interesting question of the legality of what was clearly was an "ex post facto" law.
66. M. Stanton Evans. *Blacklisted by History—The Untold Story of Senator Joe McCarthy,* New York: 2007, pp. 420, 421; *Chicago Tribune*, December 20, 1985; The plot, attributed to Roosevelt, is further mentioned by historian Frederick W. Marks, III in his highly readable and well documented *Wind Over Sand*. Athens, GA: University of Georgia Press, 1988, p. 182.
67. Allen. *Longest War*, p. 72
68. Reagan E. Schaupp. Major, USAF. "A Research Report Submitted to the Faculty in Partial Fulfillment of the Graduation Requirements." Maxwell Air Force Base, Alabama, April 2006.
69. Speech. Hon. Walter Judd. House of Representatives. June 19, 1948.
70. Eisenhower, J. *Allies*, p. 51.

CHAPTER SEVEN—EASED OUT TO ASIA

1. Morgan had held this position since Casablanca in January 1943.
2. *WR!*, p. 246.
3. General George S. Patton. *War As I Knew It*, New York: Mariner Books, 1995, p. 63.
4. Drew Pearson. "Washington Merry-Go-Round," *Washington Post*, January 25, 1965.
5. *WR!*, p. 249.
6. William Stueck. *The Wedemeyer Mission*, Athens GA: the University of Georgia Press, 1984, p. 22.
7. *WR!*, p. 249.
8. *WR!*, p. 250.
9. *WR!*, p. 248.
10. Ronald Schaffer. "General Stanley D. Embick: Military Dissenter" *Military Affairs*, vol. 37. Oct. 1973, pp. 89–95.
11. Wedemeyer and Embick were not the only American planners to hold pre-war isolationistic views. Many American policymakers agreed with them. It should be recalled that the 1940 extension of the draft act, was passed in the House of Representatives by a single vote! In 1937 there was strong support for the "Ludlow Resolution" a measure to amend the Constitution to provide that no declaration of war, except in the case of a direct attack, could be declared without the sanction of a national referendum. The measure failed by only a narrow margin.
12. Fleming. *New Dealers*, p. 137.
13. See for example Chamberlin. *Crusade*, p. 15, which details such things as "banning Beethoven," changing the name of Sauerkraut to "liberty cabbage," "Four-minute men," rushing about the country selling war bonds and hate with equal vigor and much more; little known and less reported in history is the existence during the same pre war period of large groups representing vocal opposition to America's entry of the war demonstrating in public venues. The "Fight for Freedom" and "Committee to Defend America"

purchased numerous adds in national newspapers and periodicals, many depicting Nazi atrocities. Chamberlin. *Crusade,* p. 114; *New York Times.* October 19, 1941; See: Susan A. Brewer. *To Win the Peace: British Propaganda in the United States during World War II,* Ithaca, NY: Cornell University Press, 1997.

14. Wedemeyer most certainly must have been unaware that in some circles Lindbergh was suspected to be a spy, but for whom? The United States or Germany? Lindbergh's double life with a wife and family in the United States and a number of secret alliances in Europe, fathering several children, fueled speculation as to who was the true Lindbergh.

15. Pogue. *Ordeal,* p. 133.

16. Stoler. *Allies,* p. 10, 11.

17. Pogue. *Ordeal,* pp. 130–133.

18. Wedemeyer testimony. Hearings Before the Committee on Armed Services and the Committee on Foreign Relations United States Senate 82nd Congress 1951, p. 2477. [hereafter *Military Situation in the Far East*]

19. Franklin D. Roosevelt Library Hyde Park. PSF War Department, folder 82 [hereafter FDRL]

20. FDRL, PSF War Department, folder 82.

21. Anthony Kubek. *How the Far East Was Lost,* Chicago: Henry Regnery Company, 1963, p. 35. [hereafter *Far East*]

22 Sherwood. *Roosevelt & Hopkins,* p. 641.

23. Fleming. *New Dealers,* Chapter 12.

24. Sherwood. *Roosevelt and Churchill,* p. 478.

25. Laurence Rees. *Behind Closed Doors,* BBC Books, 2008, pp. 249–251.

26. Tyler Kent. "The Roosevelt Legacy and the Kent Case" *Journal of Historical Review.* vol. 21 2002.

27. Peter Rand notes that President Roosevelt was also a master at getting rid of people who "got into his hair," and in the autumn of 1944, Roosevelt, in an effort to persuade Chiang Kai-shek to place General Stillwell in charge of all Chinese troops, sent Ambassador Patrick Hurley to negotiate with Chiang Kai-shek. Donald Nelson, recently deposed as head of the War Production Board was sent also, just to be rid of him. This tactic was well known to Churchill. PeterRand. *China Hands,* New York: Simon & Schuster, 1995, p. 243.

28. *WR!* was an enormous success, receiving almost universal high praise in every major literary review and newspaper throughout the country; not surprisingly less so in England, considering the severe criticism of British Planners, their political motivation, and especially the severe critique of Churchill's overblown self importance as a military expert.

29. *WR!,* p. 272.

30. *New York Times,* October 30, 1944.

31. Capt. Alexander H. Von Plinsky, III USA. "General Albert C. Wedemeyer's Missions in China, 1944–1947: An Attempt to Achieve the Impossible"; A Thesis in partial fulfillment of the requirements for the degree of Master of Military Art and Science. Fort Leavenworth, Kansas, 1991.

32. Wedemeyer Oral History. Herbert Hoover Presidential Library, West Branch IA Winter 1969–70 pp. 3–4. Interesting that President Roosevelt would want to keep Hoover advised of war plans and strategy, but never had the same concern for Vice President Truman who was virtually shut out of any top level discussions.

33. Col. Yeaton was an intimate friend and advisor to Wedemeyer in China, and remained a close associate his entire life. While in China Wedemeyer posted Yeaton to Yenan as his personal advisor on Communist activities.

34. Interview Wedemeyer with Tong-Chin Rhee. January 1965. ACW Hoover.
35. Wedemeyer Oral history to Raymond Henle, Director of the Herbert Hoover Library.
36. Eiler. "Victory," pp. 35–46.
37. *WR!*, p. 273.
38. Letter Orren Jones to Wedemeyer December 27, 1968 (Appendix III); Wedemeyer reply to Jones January 7, 1969. Hoover Institution, Eiler Records, "The Victory Plan Leak." The author engaged a researcher at Kings College London where the records of Dill and Morgan are located but no documentation was located indicating that Dill or Morgan ever committed these thoughts in a writing.
39. Green to Wedemeyer, July 2, 1971. Eiler papers, Hoover Institution.
40. Eiler. Hoover, Box 14, "Victory Plan Leak."
41. It was essential to keep China in the war. About 1,000,000 Japanese troops were tied up in China, who would have been otherwise available in the Pacific. The Japanese controlled the entire coast of China and there was no port open for delivery of material. The only two routes open to the Americans for supply to the Chinese were the air route over the dangerous "Hump" or the Burma Road.
42. Churchill. *Second World War.* 1952, p. 650.
43. Mountbatten praises Wedemeyer for the brilliance of his plan ["Axiom"] for the amphibious part of the planned spring 1944 operation to retake Burma. This feature of the operation was opposed by the British and ultimately not put into operation. Feis. *Tangle*, p. 128.
44. Many years after the war in a speech to the American Association for Chinese Studies, Wedemeyer vividly recalled Chiang's bitter disappointment at this turn of events and added that neither the American government nor the American people fully appreciated how China's resistance to the Japanese tied up well over a million Japanese troops who would otherwise have been moved to other battle sites, with potentially disastrous implications in the Pacific war. In retrospect, it is difficult to minimize the sacrifices Chiang endured as a consequence of his loyalty to his allies and determination to fight the Japanese. Aside from the massive civilian and military casualties, it forced him to compromise his internal struggle against the rival Communists. The list of potential scenarios had Chiang capitulated to the Japanese at various junctures is mind-boggling. For instance, had he made peace with Japan prior to America's entry into the war, enough troops would likely have been available to follow Pearl Harbor with a land invasion that would easily have succeeded in capturing the defenseless Hawaiian Islands.
45. Schaller. *Crusade*, p. 164.
46. White. *Stilwell Papers*, June 22, 1944.
47. *WR!*, p. 272.
48. FDRL. PSF Great Britain, Box 36.
49. FDRL. PSF Great Britain, Box 36.

CHAPTER EIGHT—CHINA COMMANDER

1. *WR!*, p. 277.
2. Rand. *Hands*, p. 245.
3. *WR!*, p. 270.
4. Rand. *Hands*, p. 247.
5. *New York Times*, October 31, 1944, p. 1.
6. Tillman Durdin, a columnist for the *New York Times* was imprudent enough to venture off the carefully controlled Communist compound to look around for himself. He received some pretty rough treatment from his hosts, but the experience gave him a

glimpse of some things that the Communists were not eager for him and his colleagues to see. Rand. *Hands*, p. 238.

7. Edgar R. Snow. *Red Star Over China*, New York: Grove Atlantic, 1977. Snow's reprehensible reporting has been compared to the equally appalling fictitious account of Walter Duranty in the *New York Times* in his reporting on the Ukrainian famine of 1923, deliberately induced by Stalin, which resulted in the starvation of eight million Ukrainians. Snow's original edition was republished several times, in each instance removing passages that approached criticism of the Communists per "instructions" from his Communist friends.

8. Agnes Smedley. *China's Red Army Marches*, New York: Hyperion Press, 1977.

9. Chambers was the famous accuser of Alger Hiss in one of the most famous perjury trials in American history, which resulted in the conviction and imprisonment of Hiss. The trial and the publicity launched the career of the then obscure Congressman Richard Nixon.

10. Whittaker Chambers. "Crisis," an essay in *Time*, November 13, 1944. As was the then custom, the essays were unsigned, but it was not long before Chambers was identified as the author.

11. Thomas Johnson and Gretta Palmer. "Wedemeyer's Outstretched Hand," *The New Leader*, August 31, 1946, p. 9–10.

12. Johnson and Palmer. "Outstretched Hand," p. 10; It must be pointed out in fairness that Stilwell also rejected pomp and ceremony. Upon his arrival in China he refused to live in a lavish villa prepared for him by the Chinese. Schaller. *Crusade* p. 102.

13. *WR!*, p. 282.

14. *WR!*, p. 284.

15. *WR!*, p. 284

16. *WR!*, p. 294; Romanus and Sunderland "Time Runs out in the CBI" Chapter 2; letter to General Embick June 11, 1944.

17. Romanus and Sunderland report that Stilwell did, indeed, have plans for an offensive operation to retake some coastal port cities and eventually move up to Manchuria, but these plans were never given to Wedemeyer. *The United States Army in World War II. The China-Burma-India Theatre* "Stilwell's Command Problems" p. 449; to the contrary see: General Chennault's contention that the only planning Stilwell ever did was for the Burma campaign, and in the Stilwell's staff there was no theatre planning for China. Extension of remarks of Walter H. Judd in speech to House of Representatives June 19, 1948 in which he extends the remarks to include Chennault's article in the *New York World Telegram*, March 30, 1948.

18. *WR!*, p. 303, 304; *The U.S. Army in World War II*, "Stilwell's Command Problems" p. 470; Wedemeyer never forgave Stilwell for this breach of military protocol. In a letter to Colonel Star at the Hoover Institution dated July 22, 1974 he mentioned it. Eiler records. Hoover Institution Box 14, "Stilwell"; Again in 1980, at the age of 82, the bitter memory remained. Wedemeyer mentions it again in an interview he gave to Kam Tai Lee. Wedemeyer papers. Hoover Institution. Box 22, file 25.

19. Testimony of General MacArthur. May 3, 1951. *Military Situation in the Far East*, Vol. 1, p. 26.

20. ACW Hoover. Box 81, file 14; Wedemeyer waited for three months to write this letter because he did not want to make these comments until he was sure that he could dictate them to a trusted secretary.

21. Letter Wedemeyer to Yeaton August 9, 1972. ACW Hoover Box 70 file 1. Colonel Yeaton, who had Wedemeyer's complete trust and confidence, was appointed by him to

head the American Observers group at Communist headquarters in Yenan.

22. *WR!*, p. 271.
23. Mentioned in a Top Secret Report and Recommendation dated December 10, 1944 Wedemeyer to General Marshall. ACW. Hoover. Box 82, File 33.
24. Feis. *Tangle*, pp. 209–10.
25. *WR!*, p. 295.
26. *WR!*, p. 295.
27. Schaller. *Crusade*, p. 202.
28. Wedemeyer letter to General Marshall dated December 10, 1944. ACW Hoover, Box 82, file 33.
29. Leonard Mosley. *Marshall-Hero For Our Times*, New York: Hearst Books, 1982, p. 363.
30. White. *Thunder*, p. 125.
31. Wedemeyer speech November 5, 1976. "Relations with Wartime China: A Reminiscence" *Asian Affairs: An American Review*. Vol. 4, No. 3, 1977, p. 198.
32. White. *Thunder*, p. 132.
33. White. *Thunder*, p. 133.
34. *WR!*, pp. 297–299; fairness compels acknowledging that Stilwell had basically the same idea, to train and equip 30 divisions to fight the Japanese. *The Stilwell Papers*, October 5, 1942; Feis. *Tangle*, p. 46 However Stilwell's friction with Chiang Kai-shek and disputes over authority never allowed his proposal to go into operation. There is no evidence that Wedemeyer was ever aware of Stilwell's plan. He left nothing in writing when he departed. It could be argued that he was not hoping that Wedemeyer had any success in his command. Furthermore, Stilwell's plan did not incorporate any of the unique recommendations for solving command disagreement problems. Stilwell's notes [*The Stilwell Papers*, published 1948] which contained his vision of concentrating on 30 divisions like Wedemeyer's plan were personal papers which he took with him and later appeared in the *Stilwell Papers* which were not published until after his death.
35. Larry L. Bland, (ed.) *George C. Marshall's Mediation Mission*, Marshall Foundation, Lexington VA. 1998, p. 97.
36. Webster. *Burma*, p. 201; *WR!*, p. 288.
37. *WR!*, p. 289.
38. *WR!*, p. 285; see also Naval Academy historian Maochun Yu who observes that tales of Communists' "valiant fighting" masked a policy of outright collaboration between Yenan and the Japanese. Yu. *OSS In China—Prelude to Cold War*, Yale University Press, 1966, pp. 221–22. p. 107; Evans. *Blacklisted* and also Jung Chang and Jon Halliday. *Mao. The Unknown Story*. New York: Alfred A. Knopf, 2005, pp. 204–205. [hereafter *Mao*]
39. Chang. *Mao*, p. 204.
40. Bob Kadel, ed. *Where I Came In: China-Burma-India*, Paducah, KY: Turner Publishing Company, 1986, p. 22; The recommendation was based on the recapture of the critical Burma city of Myitkyina which at the time Wedemeyer had reason to believe was directly the result of Stilwell's efforts. Later Wedemeyer learned that the credit should have been given to Colonel Charles N. Hunter, and Wedemeyer seems to have regretted his decision. Letter of Wedemeyer to Colonel Richard F. Staar, Associate Director of Hoover Institution, dated July 22, 1974. Eiler Hoover. Box 14, "Stilwell File"; see also: Letter Wedemeyer to Jessie Stearns, in which he recites that he recommended Stilwell for the fourth star, and Stilwell never knew about it. Eiler Hoover, Box 14.
41. Kadel. *Where I Came In*, p. 22.
42. The author was fortunate to obtain a copy of this rare and wonderful book from Kent

Kadel, son of Colonel Robert J. Kadel who was tracked down in, Indiana.

43. Top Secret letter Wedemeyer to General Stanley D. Embick December 7, 1944. ACW Hoover. Box 81 file 7; Interview of General Wedemeyer by Tong-Chin Rhee December 16, 1964. ACW Hoover. Box 20. file 14.

44. *WR!*, p. 285.

45. Schaller. *Crusade*, p. 269.

46. Chang. *Mao*, p. 286; Over time the "John Birch Society" has acquired an unfortunate reputation as a radical right wing extremist group, and John Birch, himself a true American hero has been demonized. This is unfortunate. For an accurate account of John Birch's life, and the true story of how he died based on the testimony of one of the soldiers that was with him and also shot and left for dead, but survived, see *The Life of John Birch*. Robert H. W. Welch, Jr. Boston: Western Islands Publishers. 1954.

47. Quoted in *WR!*, pp. 316–7.

48. Mao Tse-tung directive of October 1937 to his followers, quoted in part in *WR!*, p. 283.

49. Mosley. *Hero*, p. 363.

50. In 2005 while doing research in Chunking, this author had occasion to visit the "Stilwell Museum" which contains at least 75 large pictures of a smiling Stilwell shaking hands with and drinking toasts to Mao and Chou en Lai. This was Stilwell's headquarters for two years, and then Wedemeyer's for one year. There is not a single reference to, or a picture of Wedemeyer.

51. Tuchman. *Stilwell*, p. 429.

52. Taylor. *Generalissimo*, p, 248

53. Schaller. *Crusade*, p. 264.

54. Sir Adrian Carton de Wiart, quoted in Feis. *Tangle*, p. 411.

55. *WR!*, p. 348.

56. Kubek. *Far East*, p. 386.

57. Schaller. *Crusade*, p. 262, 263; the CCP responded by announcing that they did not intend to be bound by this edict, and in fact did in numerous instances arrange for Japanese surrender, reoccupy territory formerly held by the Japanese, and in the process acquired huge stores of Japanese arms and equipment.

58. Schaller. *Crusade*, p. 263.

59. To quote exactly: "The Crimea Conference was a successful effort by the three leading Nations to find a common ground for peace. It ought to spell the end of the system of unilateral action, the exclusive alliances, the spheres of influence, the balances of power, and all the other expedients that have been tried for centuries—and have always failed."

60. Schaller. *Crusade*, p. 264.

61. Feis. *Tangle*, p. 355.

62. The Communists let loose at end of war with tremendous propaganda effort, including a live radio broadcast denouncing Chiang on August 14, 1945.

CHAPTER NINE—GENERAL MARSHALL'S FAILED MISSION IN CHINA

1. Wedemeyer, well versed in the historical documents which set the principles for which the United States went to war (and promptly forgot), wistfully remembered President Roosevelt's famous Birthday Speech of February 22, 1942, when he told the American people in one of his fireside chats: "We of the United Nations are agreed on certain broad principles in the kind of peace we seek. The Atlantic Charter applies not only to the parts of the world that border the Atlantic but to the whole world; disarmament of aggressors, self-determination of nations and peoples, and . . . freedom of speech, freedom of religion, freedom from want, and freedom from fear."

2. Events disclosed that Hurley was justified in his lack of confidence in Service. Congressman Walter Judd on October 19, 1949, on the floor of the House of Representatives, charged that Service was guilty of secretly "conniving" against the recognized government of China back in 1944 when he was a State Department representative in Chungking. Judd produced a secret memorandum written by Service to General Stilwell recommending use of the Chinese Communist forces. Judd was angered that this important memorandum was omitted from the Acheson China "White Paper." *New York Times*, October 20, 1949.

3. Keith E. Eiler. "Devotion and Dissent Albert Wedemeyer, George Marshall, and China" an essay in *George C. Marshall's Mediation Mission to China*. (ed.) Larry I. Bland. p. 94; Kubek. *How the Far East Was Lost*, p. 319.

4. Langer and Gleason. *Undeclared War,* Chapter XX; Schaller. *US and China*, chapter 3. "From the Marco Polo Bridge to Pearl Harbor"; It was not until about July of 1941 when the United States placed restrictions, then a blockade on high grade steel, petroleum, and aviation fuel.

5. Bland, George C. *Mediation Mission*, p. 92.

6. Kubek. *Far East*, p. 323.

7. Bland. *Mediation Mission*, p. 91.

8. Bland. *Mediation Mission*, p. 91.

9. Pogue, Marshall's official biographer in his most prestigious four volume life history of Marshall aptly entitled volume three George C. Marshall "Organizer of Victory, 1943–1945."

10. Mark A. Stoler. "Why George Marshall?" Essay in Bland. *Mediation Mission*, p. 3.

11. Mosley. *Hero*, p. 365.

12. Bland. *Mediation Mission*, p. 92.

13. *WR!*, p. 370.

14. Mosley. *Hero*, p. 365; Much later Wedemeyer said that he regretted this harsh assessment of Marshall: Eiler. "Devotion and Dissent: Albert Wedemeyer, George Marshall and China." Bland. *Mediation Mission*. p. 114.

15. Message. Wedemeyer to WARCOS August 15, 1945. Quoted in Bland. *Mediation Mission* p. 95].

16. Message Wedemeyer to WARCOS, August 15, 1945, Bland. *Mediation Mission,* p 95.

17. Walter H. Judd. Speech House of Representatives, July 18, 1950.

18. The Cathay Hotel is where in prewar days, the rich Chinese and their ladies, the arms dealers, and warlords used to gather. It is still elegant, and the author had tea in the famous lobby tea room in January 2005 while doing research for this book.

19. Bland. *Mediation Mission*, p. 92.

20. Mosley. *Hero*, p. 353.

21. Mosley. *Hero*, p. 364.

22. Mosley. *Hero*, p. 366.

23. Mosley. *Hero*, p. 364.

25. Bland. *Mediation Mission*, p. 92.

24. Mosley. *Hero*, p. 367; *WR!*, p. 363.

26. "Consultation with General Albert C. Wedemeyer." Committee on Un-American Activities House of Representatives eighty-fifth Congress (second session) January 21, 1958, p. 2.

27. Mosley. *Hero*, p. 360; Wedemeyer sharply criticized his old boss in *Wedemeyer Reports!*, p. 369–70 for what seemed to him lack of vision in his strategic outlook on China. Wedemeyer never changed his substantive opinion on how to deal with the Nationalists vs. Communists civil war and the political dispute, but regretted the harsh tone of his

criticism of Marshall in the book. Bland. Marshall's *Mediation Mission*, p. 114.

28. Bland. *Mediation Mission*, p. 93.
29. Bland. *Mediation Mission*, p. 93.
30. Although General Marshall had previously taken Wedemeyer on many of his prior missions to London, Casablanca, Quebec, Cairo, and other conferences, he did not take him to the first meeting with the Chinese Communists, because Wedemeyer was not popular in Yenan. Bland. *Mediation Mission,* p. 93.
31. Bland. *Mediation Mission*, p. 98.
32. Zang Suchu, a Chinese historian believes that the initial success, especially the cease fire was due only to both sides wanted to gain time to improve their position. Bland. *Mediation Mission*, p. 46.
33. Mosley. *Hero*, p. 375; Bland. *Mediation Mission*, p. 98.
34. Bland. *Mediation Mission,* p. 17.
35. Bland. *Mediation Mission*, p. 100.
36. Suzanne Pepper. "The KMT-CCP Conflict, 1945–1949," The Nationalist Era in China 1927–1949. New York: Cambridge University Press, 1991, p. 299.
37. Bland. *Mediation Mission*, p. 101.
38. Bland. *Mediation Mission*, p. 101.
39. Mosley. *Hero*, p. 377.
40. Bland. *Mediation Mission*, p. 508.
41. Mosley. *Hero*, p. 377.
42. Bland. *Mediation Mission*, p. 107.
43. Chang. *Mao*, p. 294.
44. Kubek. *Far East*, p. 328.
45. *WR!*, p. 370.
46. *WR!*, p. 370.
47. Bland. *Mediation Mission*, p. 114.
48. Chang. *Mao*, p. 294.
49. Bland. *Mediation Mission*, p. 107.
50. Wedemeyer Memorandum: "Chinese Problem," August 10, 1946, ACW Hoover, Box 90.
51. Letter Wedemeyer to Colonel C.E. Hutchin, August 10, 1946. ACW Hoover, Box 81.
52. "Statement by the President, United States Policy Toward China," December 15, 1945, Bland. *Mediation Mission*, p. 504.

CHAPTER TEN—WEDEMEYER'S 1947 MISSION TO CHINA

1. Bland. *Mediation Mission*, p. 98; Mosley. *Hero*, p. 375.
2. Mosley. *Hero*, p. 380.
3. *WR!*, p. 364, 365; Mosley's statement that Wedemeyer was highly pleased at the offer of an Ambassadorship is not accurate. *Hero*, p. 380.
4. Mosley. *Hero*, p. 376.
5. *WR!*, p. 366.
6. *WR!*, p. 368.
7. *WR!*, p. 368.
9. *WR!*, p. 371.
10. *WR!*, pp. 371–2.
11. *WR!*, p. 373.
12. *WR!*, p. 380.
13. *WR!*, p. 380.
14. Kubek. *Far East*, p. 385.

15. The directive is reproduced in full in Appendix V of *Wedemeyer Reports!*
16. Kubek. *Far East*, p. 387; if there need be any proof of how much Wedemeyer was hated by the Communists, one need look no further than a reading of the sworn testimony of Louis Budenz, former editor of the Daily Worker, who said that Wedemeyer was on the Communist blacklist and was ". . . scheduled to be removed from the scene. . . ." Hearings before the Subcommittee to Investigate the Administration of the Internal Security Laws of Committee on the Judiciary. United States Senate. 82nd Congress, 2nd Session. 1952. Part 2, p. 623. [hereafter IPR Hearings]
17. *WR!*, p. 386.
18. Wedemeyer letter to Henry Luce, July 8, 1946. ACW Hoover. box 93.
19. Wedemeyer letter to Henry Luce, July 14, 1947. ACW Hoover box 93.
20. Kubek. *Far East*, p. 387.
21. *WR!*, p. 387.
22. "United States Relations With China," The China White Paper pp. 255–256.
23. A complete copy of the report is in Appendix VI of *Wedemeyer Reports!;* the portions of the report relating to Korea will not be addressed.
24. *WR!*, p. 391.
25. *WR!*, p. 396.
26. *WR!*, p. 397; Kubek. *Far East*, p. 390.
27. *WR!*, p. 398; Wedemeyer's report was subsequently published in Dean Acheson's famous 1,000-plus page "White Paper" "United States Relations With China, published 1949 along with numerous other documents.
28. *WR!*, p. 396.
29. Kubek. *Far East*, p. 391.
30. *New York Times*, December 18, 1947.
31. Wedemeyer appeared before the Senate Committee on Appropriations on December 17, 1947 and he was asked if he had his report with him. He replied that Secretary Marshall "admonished" him and asked him not to discuss the report. Later when Marshall himself appeared before the committee and was asked why he "joined in the suppression" of the report, he replied curtly "I did not join in the suppression of the report. I personally suppressed it." Kubek. *Far East*, p. 391.
32. *Military Situation in the Far East*, Part 1, p. 32; Kubek, *Far East*, p. 408.

CHAPTER 11—THE ROLE OF THE RUSSIAN BEAR

1. See the following web site which has the entire series of letters: http://www.gwu.edu/~nsarchiv/coldwar/documents/episode-1/fdr-ml.htm.
2. Chamberlin. *Crusade*, p. 94.
3. ACW Hoover. Box 20, folder 20.
4. ACW Hoover. Box 20, folder 20.
5. Keenan. *Memoirs*, pp. 83–85; Charles E. Bohlen. *Witness to History,* New York: W.W Norton & Company, Inc., 1973, pp. 41–44; *New Dealers' War*, p. 284.
6. Walter H. Judd. Speech to the House of Representatives, July 18, 1950.
7. Chamberlin. *Crusade*, p. 185.
8. Sherwood. *Roosevelt & Hopkins*, pp. 748–9.
9. Sherwood. *Roosevelt & Hopkins*, pp. 748–9.
10. John R. Dean. *The Strange Alliance*, New York: Viking Press, 1946, pp. 97–98; Wedemeyer reported the same experience in the projected, but never published, book, parts of which are at the Hoover Institution.
11. *Life*, August 30, 1948.

12. Francis Perkins. *The Roosevelt I Knew*, New York: Viking Press, 1946, p. 78.
13. *New York Times*, November 19, 1943; *Memoirs of Cordell Hull*, vol. 21, p. 1315.
14. James F, Byrnes. *Speaking Frankly*, New York: Harper & Brothers, 1947, p. 23.
15. Sherwood. *Roosevelt & Hopkins*, p. 870.
16. *WR!*, p. 340.
17. Sherwood. *Roosevelt & Hopkins*, Chapter XXXIII, "The Yalta Conference."
18. John V. Fleming. *Anti Communist Manifesto*, New York: S.W. Norton & Company, 2009, p. 209.
19. Warren F. Kimball. Diplomatic History, "Thirty Years After, or the Two Musketeers," Spring 1994.

CHAPTER TWELVE—HOW THE COMMUNISTS TOOK CHINA

1. Tuchman. *Stilwell*, p. 531.
2. Brian Crozier. *The Man Who Lost China*, New York, Charles Scribner's Sons, 1976.
3. Rand. *Hands*, p. 238; in footnote 141 of this page Rand cites a September 27, 1989 PBS Documentary "China in Revolution" in which Davies essentially repeats what he said to Leonard Gross in the *Look* article of 1969.
4. E. J. Kahn, Jr. *The China Hands—America's Foreign Service Officers and What Befell Them*. New York: the Viking Press, 1972.
5. Taylor. *Generalissimo*, p. 220.
6. Kubek. *Far East*, Chapter X, lists myriad instances of questionable conduct bv the Foreign Service Officers.
7. David Halberstan. *The Best and the Brightest*, New York: Random House, 1972, p. 114.
8. Kubek. *Far East*, p. 229.
9. E.J. Kahn. *The China Hands*, p. 97.
10. E.J. Kahn. *The China Hands*, p. 118.
11. E.J. Kahn. *The China Hands*, p.118.
12. Quoted in full and made an exhibit #247, IPR Hearings. Part 3 p. 785.
13. George Creel. *Russia's Race for Asia*, New York: The Bobs-Merrill Company, p. 143. [hereafter *Russia's Race*]
14. IPR Hearings, pp. 200, 201.
15. Leonard Gross. "John Paton Davies, Jr. Quiet End To A Shabby Era." *Look* March 4, 1969, p. 82; Davies was investigated and cleared by eight loyalty-security board and then found by the ninth to have shown "lack of judgment, discretion and reliability" and was dismissed from the Foreign Service by Secretary of State John Foster Dulles. Nine years later Under Secretary of State Nicholas de B Katzenbach issued a memorandum clearing him, in what, perhaps, was the most astonishing reversal of opinion. *The Washington Post* commencing on January 21, 1952 printed a series of 6 articles by columnist Richard C. Hottelet detailing a extraordinary interview he had with Russian Foreign Minister Maxim Litvinov in 1946. Hottelet was obliged to withhold publishing the interview until after Litvinov's death, which occurred January 2, 1952. In the 1946 interview, Litvinov, who was clearly upset that he was about to be removed from his position of influence, told Hottelet that the "Soviet Union can't be trusted or appeased." *Washington Post*, January 21, 22, 23, 24, 24, 1952.
16. Chiang was betrayed by one of his own generals in 1937 when he visited the Chinese city of Sian. He was turned over to the Chinese Communists who likely would have assassinated him, but for the intervention of Stalin, who, ever fearful of the Japanese and a potential attack through Manchuria, compelled Mao to release Chiang on condition that the Nationalists and Chinese Communists form what was the first of a

tenuous "United Front" against the Japanese. Stalin knew that Chiang was the only Chinese leader at that time with sufficient power to lead the country.

17. That pledge was disregarded after the second atomic bomb hit Japan.
18. Taylor. *The Generalissimo*, Chapter 6.
19. One was New York Times reporter Tillman Durdin who was complimented by historian Creel for exposing the fraud. *Russia's Race,* p. 189.
20. Creel. *Russia's Race,* p. 221.
21. White. *Thunder,* p. 129.
22. Samuel Lubell. "Vinegar Joe and the Reluctant Dragon," *Saturday Evening Post,* February 24, 1945, p. 9–38.
23. Quoted in Creel. *Russia's Race,* p. 13, 14.
24. Congressman Judd speech in the House of Representatives July 18, 1950 quoting MacArthur.
25. Pogue. *George C. Marshall: Statesman 1945–1949,* New York: Viking, 1987, p. 63.
26. *Military Situation in the Far East,* p. 377.
27. *Military Situation in the Far East,* pp. 2025, 2745, 2749.
28. *Military Situation in the Far East,* pps. 2317, 18, 2329.
29. Ann Applebaum. *Gulag, A History,* New York: First Anchor Books, 2004, p. 441–444.
30. Kubek. *Far East,* p. 228.
31. Kubek. *Far East,* p. 361.
32. Report of the Committee on the Judiciary Eighty-Second Congress second session July 2, 1952. Report No. 2050.
33. Final Report, p. 223.
34. Taylor, *Generalissimo,* p. 221
35. White. *Thunder,* pp. 234, 236.
36. Willkie's traveling partner, Gardner Cowles, editor of *Look* later revealed that the notorious womanizer Willkie and Madame Chiang's friendship may have been peppered with moments of sexual intimacy; see: Taylor. *Generalissimo,* pp 216–220.
37. Creel. *Russia's Race,* p. 102.
38. Herrymon Maurer. "The Tyrannous Decade." *Fortune,* February 1948.
39. David Reese. "Harry Dexter White—A Study in Paradox," New York: Coward, McCann & Geoghegan, 1973, p. 89.
40. Kubek. *Far East,* p. 199.
41. Reese. *Dexter White,* p. 164.
42. Kennan. *Memoirs,* 1967.
43. Creel. *Russia's Race,* p. 9; see the powerful article by Max Eastman and J.B. Powell in the June 1945 issue of *Readers Digest,* "The Fate of the World is at Stake in China," exposing in detail the myths about the Chinese Communists and their claims that the CCP was not directed from Moscow. The subject matter contained in the article inflamed the Institute of Pacific Relations.
44. Creel. *Russia's Race,* p. 11.
45. Creel. *Russia's Race,* p. 177.
46. Stanley K. Hornbeck served officially in connection with Far Eastern matters during most of the years from 1918 to 1944. He was chief of the Division of Far Eastern Affairs of the Department of State from 1928 to 1937; he was an advisor on political relations from 1937 to 1944, an Assistant to the Secretary of State in 1944.
47. The correspondence between Dr. Hornbeck and Dean Acheson is described in full in the Senate Report number 2050 on page 202.
48. *New York Times,* November 21, 1948.

49. This lack of cultural awareness applied with equal force to the Chinese later in the decade. It was also largely ignored with disastrous consequences in the late 1970's in our dealings with Iran, and applies even more urgently to our present day dealings with the followers of Islam!

50. Miller speech to the House of Representatives, May 3, 1944 incorporating Judd's speech to Wethersfield Businessmen and Civic Association, April 27, 1944.

51. Judd speech to the House of Representatives, August 21, 1944.

52. Extension of remarks of Congressman Judd in quoting sections of Pearl Buck's article "Our Last Chance in China," House of Representatives, August 21, 1944.

53. Judd extension of remarks to the House of Representatives, August 21, 1944.

54. Judd speech to the House of Representatives, March 15, 1945.

55. Specifically, he noted that the equivalent of a Chinese one hundred dollar bill was worth an American twenty-three cents.

56. Judd speech to the House of Representatives, March 15, 1945.

57. Judd speech to the House of Representatives, March 15, 1945.

58. Judd speech to the House of Representatives, March 15, 1945.

59. Extension of remarks of Congressman Judd before the House of Representatives, June 19, 1948.

60. Judd speech to the House of Representatives, July 18, 1950.

61. Congresswoman Douglas paid a heavy price for her unwitting support of the Communist cause. Her next congressional opponent, Richard Nixon, distributed her voting record printed on red paper during the campaign and succeeded in defeating her. Nixon's red-baiting strategy was the catalyst of his rapid ascendency in Republican circles.

62. Judd speech to the House of Representatives, July 18, 1950.

63. Oral Histories. Walter H. Judd, August 1960, April 1969, December 1970. OH-196 Eisenhower Library, Abeline KS, pp. 47–49.

64. *Military Situation in The Far East,* pp. 2317–2318.

65. Judd. *Saturday Evening Post,* October 11, 1952.

CHAPTER THIRTEEN—WEDEMEYER IN RETIREMENT

1. ACW Hoover, Box 94, file 7.

2. Deskis Tape 1, side 1, p. 14.

3. General William H. Draper, Jr. Oral History, Truman Library, pp. 64–66.

4. Letter of Tunner to Wedemeyer, May 3, 1949. Eiler, Hoover, Box 1. "Berlin Airlift."

5. Letter of Wedemeyer to Tunner, May 10, 1949. Eiler, Hoover, Box 1. "Berlin Airlift."

6. Reeves. *Daring,* p. 37.

7. *Washington Star,* January 3, 1979. Eiler, Hoover, Box 1. "Berlin Air Lift."

8. AVCO has gone through many corporate name changes and reorganizations. In 1985 AVCO was acquired by Textron, and currently is part of the family of McDonnell Douglas.

9. Wedemeyer, in 1975, comments ruefully on the change in the "Honor Code" as he knew it and accepted it at West Point, and the manner in which it is applied today. As a Presidential appointee to review procedures at West Point, he learned that the strict interpretation of the code has been eroded; he was dismayed to learn that the attitude now seemed to be "What Can I Get Away With," and Wedemeyer saw little difference between ethics and morals at the Academy and in industry. [Deskis sec. 7]

10. Deskis, sec. 7, pp. 46–48.

11. Deskis, 1975 sec. 7, pp 50–52.

12. Deskis, sec. 7, pp. 50–52.

13. Also present were Richard Berlin, President of Hearst Publications, columnist George Sokolsky, Lewis Strauss, Lawrence Richey and several other notable personages including Wedemeyer.
14. *Wedemeyer Reports!* was on the Best Seller list for about one year. Then it suddenly dropped off the list and little was heard about it in the press. Wedemeyer was told by a friend who had many years of experience in the publishing field that "word had gone out" that the merits of the book should be played down. Undated interview with Wedemeyer. ACW Hoover, Box 6 File 3.
15. ACW Hoover, Box 20, File 20.
16. This impression was reinforced in a telephone conversation between the author and granddaughter Pamela Wedemeyer November 11, 2007. The Wedemeyer website, General-Wedemeyer.com has enabled the author to locate and communicate with all of the living relatives of General Wedemeyer.
17. ACW Hoover, Box 110, File 4.
18. ACW Hoover, Box 80, File 8.
19. ACW Hoover, Box 20, File 4. The author is impressed with the concern Wedemeyer showed for this kind of inquiry, particularly since his own experience in sending dozens of letters to authors, historians and others while writing his dissertation was met in many cases with silence.
20. Rhee. "Sino American Relations From 1942 Through 1949: A Study of Efforts to Settle The China Problem," Clark University, Worcester MA, 1967. The author made an effort to contact Rhee, but sadly he had passed away.
21. *World Herald*, June 4, 1984. ACW Hoover, Box 23, File 11.

CHAPTER FOURTEEN—CONCLUSIONS
1. *New York Times*, December 20, 1992.
2. Albert C. Wedemeyer. "Memorandum on A National Strategy Council." Hoover Institution, Box 23, File 2.
3. Letter Wedemeyer to Joseph D. Douglas Jr., May 13, 1987. ACW Hoover, Box 23, file 3.
4. Eiler. *Wedemeyer,* p. xx.
5. John R. Galvin. "What's The Matter With Being A Strategist?" *Parameters*, March 1989, vol. XIX pp. 5–19; Charles P. Moore. "What's the Matter With Being a Strategist (Now)?" Parameters, Winter 2009, pp. 5–19; Bart Schuurman. "Clausewitz and the "New Wars' Scholars," Parameters, Spring 2010, Vol. XXX, pp. 89–100.
6. Galvin. "Strategist," p. 2.
7. US Department of Defense, Dictionary of Military and Associated Terms, JCS Pub 1 (Washington: GPO, 1 June 1987).
8. Galvin. "Strategist," p. 8.
9. Galvin. "Strategist," p. 9.
10. *WR!*, p. 50.
11. Galvin. "Strategist," p. 10.
12. At age 74 in an oral history General Wedemeyer discounts the value of paper degrees, often awarded to people who may seldom pursue serious intellectual endeavors after graduation; he emphasizes the importance of a "philosophy of life, a purpose, or goal . . . and a curiosity about life . . ." Deskis, Section 2, p. 13.
13. Moore. "Strategist Now," p. 5.
14. Moore. "Strategist Now," p. 6.
15. Moore. "Strategist Now," p. 7.

16. Bob Woodward. *State of Denial,* New York: Simon & Schuster, 2006, p. 83.
17. Woodward. *Denial,* p. 83.
18. Moore. "Strategist Now," p. 12.
19. Moore. "Strategist Now," p. 13.
20. Moore. "Strategist Now," p. 16.
21. Moore. "Strategist Now," p. 14.
22. Schuurman. "New Wars' Scholars."
23. Carl von Clausewitz. *On War,* ed. and translated by Michael Howard and Peter Paret. New York: Everyman's Library, 1993.
24. Schuurman. "New Wars," p. 93.
25. M.L.R. Smith. "Strategy in the Age of Low Intensity Warfare: Why Clausewitz is Still More Relevant than His Critics," Isabelle Duyvesteyn and Jan Angstrom (eds.) *Rethinkng The Nature of War.* East Sussex: England, p. 52.

BIBLIOGRAPHY

BOOKS

ATKINSON, Rick. *An Army At Dawn—The War in North Africa, 1942–1943.* New York: Henry Holt and Company. 2002.

_____. *The Day of Battle—The War in Sicily and Italy, 1943–1944.* New York: Henry Holt and Company. 2007.

BALDWIN, Hanson W. *Great Mistakes of the War.* New York: Harper and Brothers. 1949.

BELDEN, Jack. *Retreat With Stilwell.* Garden City, New York: Blue Ribbon Books. 1944.

_____. *China Shakes the World.* New York and London: Monthly Review Press. 1949.

_____. *Still Time to Die.* Philadelphia: The Blakiston Company. 1943.

BEN-MOSHE, Tuvia. *Churchill—Strategy and History.* Boulder Colorado: Lynne Rienner Publisher, Inc. 1992.

BERCUSON, David and HOLGERHERWIG, Holger. *One Christmas in Washington.* New York and Woodstock: The Overlook Press. 2005.

BLUMENSON, Martin. *The Battle of the Generals. The Untold Story of the Falaise Pocket: The Campaign That Should Have Won World War II.* New York: William Morrow. 1993.

BOHLEN, Charles E. *Witness to History 1929–1969.* New York: W. W. Norton & Company, Inc. 1973.

BRADLEY, Omar N. *A General's Life.* An Autobiography [with Clair Blair] New York: Simon and Schuster. 1983.

BROWN, Elizabeth Churchill. *The Enemy At His Back.* New York: Free Enterprise. 1956.

BRYANT, Arthur. *The Turn of The Tide.* Garden City, NY: Doubleday & Company, Inc. 1957.

BUDENZ, Louis Francis. *This is My Story.* New York: McGraw-Hill Book Company, Inc. 1947.

BUHITE, Russell D. *Nelson T. Johnson and American Foreign Policy Toward China 1925–1941.* East Lansing Michigan: Michigan State University Press 1968.

_____. *Patrick J. Hurley and American Foreign Policy.* Ithaca, NY: Cornell University Press. 1973.

BULLITT, Orville H. (ed.) *For the President Personal & Secret.* w/introduction by George F. Kennan. Boston: Houghton Mifflin Company. 1972.

BURNS, James MacGregor. *Roosevelt: The Soldier of Freedom 1940–1945.* New York: Francis Parkman Prize Collection. History Book Club. 1970.

BUTCHER, Harry C. Capt. *My Three Years With Eisenhower 1942–1945.* New York: Simon And Schuster, 1946.

BYRD, Martha. *Chennault Giving Wings to the Tiger.* Tuscaloosa, Alabama: The University of Alabama Press. 1987.

BYRNES, James F. *Speaking Frankly.* New York and London: Harper & Brothers. 1947. New Haven: Yale University Press. 2005.

_____. *All In One Lifetime.* London: Museum Press Limited. 1960.

BYRON, John and PACK, Robert. *The Claws of the Dragon. Kang Sheng—the Evil Genius Behind Mao.* New York: Simon & Schuster 1992.

CHAMBERLIN, William Henry. *America's Second Crusade.* Chicago: Henry Regnery Company. 1950.

CHANG, Carsun. *The Third Force in China.* New York: Bookman Associates. 1952.

CHANG, Jung and HALLIDAY, Jon. *Mao: The Unknown Story.* New York: Alfred A. Knopf. 2005.

CHENNAULT, Claire Lee. *Way of a Fighter.* New York: G.P. Putnam's Sons. 1949.

CHURCHILL, Winston, S. *The Second World War.* (6 vols) New York: Houghton Mifflin Company. 1953.

CLARK, General Mark. W. *From the Danube to the Yalta.* New York: Harper and Brothers 1944.

CLARK, General Mark W. *Calculated Risk.* New York: Enigma Books. 2007.

CLINE, Ray S. *Secrets Spies and Scholars: Blueprint of the Essential CIA.* Washington D.C: Acropolis Books Ltd. 2009.

_____. *Washington Command Post: The Operations Division.* Office of the Chief of Military History United States Army. Washington, D.C. 1951.

COAKLEY, Robert W. and LEIGHTON, Richard M. *Global Logistics and Strategy 1943–1945.* Office of the Chief of Military History. United States Army. Washington, D.C. 1968.

COHEN, Warren I. *America's Response to China—An Interpretative History of Sino-*

American Relations. New York: John Wiley & Sons, Inc. 1971.

———. *The Chinese Connection and American-East Asian Relations.* New York: Columbia University Press. 1978.

COLVILLE, John. *Winston Churchill and His Inner Circle.* New York: Wyndham Books. 1981.

———. *The Fringes of Power—10 Downing Street Diaries 1939–1955.* New York: W.W. Norton & Company. 1985.

CRANKSHAW, Edward. *The New Cold War—Moscow v Peking.* Baltimore: Penguin Books, Ltd. 1963.

CREEL, George. *Rebel At Large.* New York: G. P. Putnam's Sons. 1947.

———. *Russia's Race for Asia.* New York: The Bobs-Merrill Company. 1949.

CROSWELL, D.K.R. *Beetle—The Life of General Walter Bedell Smith.* Lexington Ky.: The University of Kentucky Press. 2010.

CROZIER, Brian. *The Man Who Lost China.* New York: Charles Scribner's Sons. 1976.

DALLEK, Robert. *Franklin D. Roosevelt and American Foreign Policy 1932–1945.* New York: Oxford University Press. 1979.

———. *Harry S. Truman.* New York: Henry Holt and Company 2008.

———. *The Lost Peace—Leadership in a Time of Horror and Hope, 1945–1953.* New York: Harper Collins Publishers. 2010.

DALLIN, David J. *Russia & Postwar Europe.* New Haven: Yale University Press. 1943.

———. *The Real Soviet Russia.* New Haven: Yale University Press. 1944.

———. *The Big Three—United States, Great Britain, Russia.* New Haven: Yale University Press. 1945.

———. *Soviet Russia and the Far East.* New Haven: Yale University Press. 1948.

———. *The Rise of Russia In Asia.* New Haven: Yale University Press. 1949.

DAVIES, Joseph E. *Mission to Moscow.* Garden City New York: Garden City Publishing Co. Inc. 1943.

DEAN, John R. *The Strange Alliance.* New York: The Viking Press. 1946.

DE TOLEDANO, Ralph and LASKY, Victor. *Seeds of Treason: The True Story of the Hiss-Chambers Tragedy.* New York: Funk & Wagnalls Company 1950.

DE TOLEDANO, Ralph and BARNES, Harry Elmer. (ed.). *Perpetual War For Perpetual Peace. A Collection of Essays Appraising the Foreign Policy of Roosevelt.* Caldwell, Idaho: The Claxton Printers, Ltd. 1953.

DE TOLEDANO, Ralph. *Spies, Dupes & Diplomats.* New Rochelle, New York: Arlington House. 1967.

DEANE, John R. *The Strange Alliance—The Story of Our Efforts At Wartime Co-Operation With Russia.* New York: The Viking Press. 1946.

D'ESTE, Carlo. *Decision in Normandy.* New York: E. P. Hutton, Inc.1938.

DORN, Frank. *Walkout With Stilwell in Burma.* New York: Thomas Crowell Company. 1971.

DULLES, John Foster. *War or Peace*. New York: The MacMillan Company 1950.

DUNN, Walter Scott, Jr. *Second Front Now—1943*. University of Alabama Press 1980.

EASTMAN, Lloyd E; CH'EN, Jerome; PEPPER, Suzanne and VAN SLYKE, Lyman. *The Nationalist Era in China 1927–1949*.

EILER, Keith E. *Wedemeyer on War and Peace*. Hoover Institution. Stanford CA 1987.

_____. *Mobilizing America—Robert Paterson and the War Effort 1940–1945*. Ithaca New York: Cornell University Press. 1997.

EISENHOWER, Dwight D. *Crusade in Europe*. New York: Doubleday & Company 1948.

EISENHOWER, John S.D. *Allies—Pearl Harbor to D-Day*. Garden City New York: Doubleday & Company. 1982.

EVANS, M. Stanton. *Blacklisted by History—The Untold Story of Senator Joe McCarthy and His Fight Against America's Enemies*. New York: Crown Forum. 2007.

FEIS, Herbert. *The China Tangle—The American Effort in China From Pearl Harbor to the Marshall Mission*. Princeton NJ: Princeton University Press. 1953.

_____. *Churchill-Roosevelt-Stalin. The War They Waged and the Peace They Sought*. Princeton, NJ: Princeton University Press. 1957.

_____. *From Trust to Terror—the Onset of the Cold War*. New York: W. W. Norton & Company 1970.

FLEMING, John V. *The Anti-Communist Manifestos—Four Books That Shaped the Cold War*. New York: W.W. Norton Co. 2009.

FLEMING, Thomas. *The New Dealer's War—FDR and the War Within World War II*. New York: Basic Books. 2001.

FLYNN, John T. *Country Squire In The White House*. New York: Doubleday, Doran and Company, Inc. 1940.

_____. *The Roosevelt Myth—A Critical Account of the New Deal and Its Creator*. New York: The Devin-Adair Company. 1948.

_____. *While You Slept. Our Tragedy in Asia and Who Made It*. New York: The Devin-Adair Company. 1951.

_____. *The Lattimore Story. The Full Story of the Most Incredible Conspiracy of Our Time*. New York: The Devin-Adair Company. 1962.

_____. *Forgotten Lessons—Selected Essays of John T. Flynn*. Gregory P. Pavlik (ed.) The Foundation for Economic Education, Inc. Irvington-On-Hudson, New York. 1996.

FORRESTAL, James. *The Forrestal Diaries*. Walter Millis (ed.) New York: The Viking Press 1951.

FOSTER, William Z. *Toward Soviet America*. New York: International Publishers. 1970

FREELAND, Richard M. *The Truman Doctrine and the Origins of McCarthyism*.

New York: Schocken Books. 1974.

FULLER, J.F.C. Major General. *The Second World War. 1939–1945*. New York: Meredith Press. 1948.

_____. *The Conduct of War 1789–1961*. New Brunswick, NJ: Rutgers University Press. 1961.

FUNK, Arthur Layton. *The Politics of Torch—The Allied Landings and the Algiers Putsch*. Lawrence Kansas: The University Press of Kansas. 1974.

FUSSELL, Paul. *Thank God For The Atom Bomb and Other Essays*. New York: Summit Books. 1988.

_____. *Wartime. Understanding and Behavior in the Second World War*. New York: Oxford University Press. 1989.

_____. *Doing Battle—The Making of a Skeptic*. Boston: Little Brown and Company. 1996.

_____. *The Boys' Crusade—The American Infantry in Northwestern Europe, 1944–1945*. New York: The Modern Library. 2003.

GADDIS, John Lewis. *The United States and the Origins of the Cold War 1941–1947*. New York: Columbia University Press. 1972.

_____. *The Cold War—A New History*. New York: The Penguin Press 2005.

GELB, Norman. *Desperate Venture—The Story of Operation Torch*. New York: William Morrow and Company, Inc. 1992. Naperville, IL: Sourcebooks Media Fusion 2009.

GILBERT, Martin. *Road To Victory—Winston Churchill 1941–1945*. London: William Heinemann Ltd. 1986.

GOLE, Henry G. *The Road To Raimbow—Army Planning For Global War 1934–1940*. Annapolis, MD: Naval Institute Press. 2003.

GREENFIELD, Kent Roberts. *The Historian and the Army. An Historians Account of How the History of World War II is Being Written*. New Brunswick, NJ: Rutgers University Press. 1954.

_____. *American Strategy in World War II—A Reconsideration*. Baltimore: The Johns Hopkins Press. 1963.

GREENFIELD, Kent Roberts (ed.) *Command Decisions. 20 Crucial Command Decisions That Decided the Outcome of World War II*. London: Methuen & Co. Ltd. 1960.

GREW, Joseph C. *Turbulent Era. A Diplomatic Record of Forty Years—1904–1945*. (Vol. 2) Boston: Houghton Mifflin Company. 1952.

GRIFFITH, Robert and THEOHARIS, Athan. (eds.) *The Specter. Original Essays on the Cold War and the Origins of McCarthyism*. New York: New Viewpoints. A Division of Franklin Watts, Inc. 1974.

GRIGG, John. *1943 The Victory That Never Was*. New York: Hill and Wang—A Division of Farrar, Straus and Giroux. 1980.

GRIGGS, Thurston. *Americans in China: Some Chinese Views*. Washington, D.C.: Foundations for Foreign Affairs. 1948.

GWYER, J.M.A. and BUTLER, J.R. M. *Grand Strategy Volume III*. London: Her Majesty's Stationery Office. 1964.

HARPER, John Lamberton. *American Visions of Europe—Franklin D. Roosevelt, George F. Kennan, and Dean G. Acheson*. Cambridge UK: Cambridge University Press. 1996.

HARRIMAN, W. Averell. With ABEL, Elie. *Special Envoy to Churchill and Stalin 1941–1946*. New York: Random House. 1975.

HARRISON, Gordon A. *Cross Channel Attack*. New York: BDD Promotional Book. 1951.

HART, H. Liddell. *The German Generals Talk*. New York: William Morrow & Company. 1948.

HASTINGS, Max. *Overlord. D-Day, June 6, 1944*. New York: Simon and Schuster. 1984.

_____. *Retribution—The Battle for Japan, 1944–45*. New York: Alfred A. Knopf. 2008.

_____. *Winston's War—Churchill 1940–1945*. New York: Alfred A. Knopf. 2010.

HIGGINS, Trumbull. *Soft Underbelly—The Anglo American Controversy Over the Italian Campaign 1939–1945*. New York: The MacMillan Company. 1968.

HORNBECK, Stanley K. *The United States and the Far East: Certain Fundamentals of Policy*. World Peace Foundation. 1942.

HULL, Cordell. *The Memoirs of Cordell Hull*. New York: The Macmillan Company 1948. 2 Volumes.

HUNTER, Robert with DAVIS, Forrest. *The Red China Lobby*. New York: Fleet Publishing Corporation. 1963.

ISAACS, Harold R. *No Peace For Asia*. Cambridge MA: The M.I.T. Press. 1947.

ISAACSON, Walter and Evan THOMAS. *The Wise Men: Six Friends and the World They Made*. New York: Simon and Schuster. 1986.

JENKINS, Roy. *Churchill. A Biography*. New York: Farrar, Straus and Giroux. 2001.

JONES, Joseph M. *The Fifteen Weeks*. New York: The Viking Press. 1955.

JORDAN, George Racey. *From Major Jordan's Diaries*. New York: Harcourt, Brace and Company 1952.

JORDAN, Jonathan W. *Brothers—Rivals—Victors. Eisenhower, Patton, Bradley, and the Partnership that Drove the Allied Conquest in Europe*. New York: NAL Caliber, a Division of Pengiun Group. 2011.

JUDD, Walter H. *Walter H. Judd: Chronicles of A Statesman*. With preface by Edward J. Rozek (ed.) Denver, Colorado: Grier & Company. 1982.

KAHN, E. J. Jr. *The China Hands—America's Foreign Service Officers and What Befell Them*. New York: The Viking Press. 1972.

KAI-SHEK. Chiang. *Soviet Russia in China*. New York: Farrar, Straus and Giroux. 1965.

KEEGAN, John. *Six Armies in Normandy*. New York: The Viking Press. 1982.

KEELEY, Joseph. *The China Lobby Man—The Story of Alfred Kohlberg*. New

Rochelle, New York: Arlington House. 1969.

KENNAN, George E. *Memoirs 1925–1950*. New York: Little Brown and Company. 1967.

KENNEDY, Sir. John. *The Business of War—The War Narrative of Major-General Sir John Kennedy*. London: Hutchinson of London. 1957.

KERSHAW, Ian. *Fateful Choices—Ten Decisions That Changed The World 1940–1941*. New York: The Penguin Press. 2007.

KIMBALL, Warren F. *The Juggler—Franklin Roosevelt as Wartime Statesman*. Princeton NJ: Princeton University Press. 1991.

_____. *Forged in War—Roosevelt, Churchill, and the Second World War*. New York: William Morrow and Company, Inc. 1997.

KIRPATRICK, Charles E. *An Unknown Future and A Doubtful Present—Writing the Victory Program*. Honolulu, Hawaii: University Press of the Pacific. 2005.

KUBEK, Anthony. *How The Far East Was Lost. American Policy and the Creation of Communist China, 1941–1949*. Chicago: Henry Regnery Company 1963.

_____. *The Red China Papers—What Americans Deserve to Know About U.S.-Chinese Relations*. New Rochelle, New York: Arlington House Publishers. 1975.

LA FEBER, Walter. *America, Russia, and the Cold War, 1945–1966*. New York: McGraw-Hill Publishing Companies, Inc. (8th ed. 1996).

LANE, Arthur Bliss. *I Saw Poland Betrayed—An American Ambassador Report To The American People*. Boston-Los Angeles: The Americanist Library. 1948.

LANGER, William L. and GLEASON, Everett. *The Undeclared War 1940–1941*. New York: Harper and Brothers. 1953.

LARRABEE, Eric. *Commander in Chief. Franklin Delano Roosevelt, His Lieutenants & Their War*. New York: Harper & Roe. 1987.

LASH, Joseph P. *Roosevelt and Churchill 1939–1941—The Partnership That Saved The West*. New York: W. W. Norton & Company. 1976.

LATTIMORE, OWEN. *Solution in Asia*. Boston: Little Brown and Company. 1945.

LEAHY, William D. Fleet Admiral. *I Was There—The Personal Story of the Chief of Staff to Presidents Roosevelt and Truman*. New York: McGraw-Hill Book Company, Inc. 1950.

LEIGHTON, Richard M. and COAKLEY, Robert W. *Global Logistics and Strategy 1940–1943*. Office of the Chief of Military History. Department of the Army. Washington, D.C. 1955.

LIANG, Chin-tung. *General Stilwell in China, 1942–1944: The Full Story*. New York: St. John's University Press. 1972.

LOHBECK, Don. *Patrick J. Hurley An American*. Chicago: Henry Regnery Company. 1956.

LOMAZOW, Stephen. and FETTMAN, Eric. *FDR's Deadly Secret*. New York: Peresues Books Group. 2010

LOWENHEIM, Francis L., LANGLEY, Harold D. and JONAS, Manfred (eds.)

Roosevelt and Churchill Their Secret Wartime Correspondence. New York: Saturday Reviews Press/ E.P. Dutton & Co. Inc. 1975.

LYONS, Eugene. *The Red Decade. The Classic Work on Communism in America During the Thirties.* New Rochelle New York: Arlington House. 1941.

MARKS, Frederick W. *Wind Over Sand—The Diplomacy of Franklin Roosevelt.* Athens GA: The University of Georgia Press 1988.

MARSHALL, George C. *George C. Marshall's Mediation Mission to China.* (ed. Larry I. Bland) Lexington, VA: George C. Marshall Foundation. 1998.

MARSHALL, George Catlett. *The Papers of George Catlett Marshall. vol. 5 "The Finest Soldier" January 1, 1945–January 7, 1947.* (eds.) Larry I. Bland and Sharon Ritenour Stevens. Baltimore: The Johns Hopkins University Press 2003.

MATLOFF, Maurice and SNELL, Edwin M. *Strategic Planning For Coalition Warfare 1941–1942.* Office of the Chief of Military History Department of the Army Washington, D.C. 1953.

McCARTHY, Senator Joseph R. *America's Retreat From Victory—The Story of George Catlett Marshall.* New York: The Devin Adair Company. 1952.

McLELLAN, David. S. *Dean Acheson—The State Department Years.* New York: Dodd, Mead & Company. 1976.

MEACHAM, Jon. *Franklin and Winston—An Intimate Portrait of an Epic Friendship.* New York: Random House 2003.

MINER, Steven Merritt. *Between Churchill and Stalin The Soviet Union, Great Britain, and the Origins of the Grand Alliance.* Chapel Hill: North Carolina Press 1988.

MOORAD, George. *Lost Peace in China.* New York: E. P. Dutton & Co. 1949.

MORAN, Lord. *Churchill—Taken From The Diaries of Lord Moran—The Struggle For Survival.* Boston: Houghton Mifflin Company. 1966.

MORGAN, Ted. *Churchill—Young Man In A Hurry 1874–1915.* New York: Simon And Schuster. 1982.

_____. *FDR—A Biography.* New York: Simon and Schuster. 1985.

MORRIS, Robert. *No Wonder We Are Losing.* New York: The Bookmailer. 1958.

MOSLEY, Leonard. *Marshall Hero For Our Times.* New York: Hearst Books. 1982.

MORTON, Louis. *Strategy and Command The First Two Years.* Center of Military History United States Army Washington D.C. 1989. New Haven: Yale University Press. 1999.

MOWRER, Edgar Ansel. *The Nightmare of American Foreign Policy.* New York: Alfred A. Knopf. 1948.

OFFNER, Arnold A. *Another Such Victory—President Truman and the Cold War 1945–1953.* Stanford CA: Stanford University Press 2002.

O'NEILL, James E. and KRAUSKOPH, Robert W. (eds.) *World War II an Account of Its Documents.* Washington, D.C.: Howard University Press. 1976.

OVERY, Richard. *Why The Allies Won.* New York: W.W. Norton & Co. 1995.

PARRISH, *Thomas. Roosevelt and Marshal—Partners in Politics and War—the Personal Story.* New York: William Morrow and Company, Inc. 1989.

PAYNE, Stanley G. *Franco and Hitler. Spain, Germany, and World War II.* New Haven: Yale University Press. 2008.

PERKINS, Francis. *The Roosevelt I Knew.* New York: The Viking Press. 1946.

PERRY, Mark. *Partners in Command.* New York: The Penguin Press. 2007.

POGUE, Forrest C. *George C. Marshal: Ordeal and Hope 1939–1942.* New York: The Viking Press. 1966.

———. *George C. Marshall: Organizer of Victory 1943–1945.* New York: The Viking Press. 1973.

———. *George C. Marshall Statesman 1945–1959.* New York: The Viking Press. 1987.

———. *George C. Marshall Interviews and Reminiscences.* Lexington VA. George C. Marshall Foundation. 1996.

RAND, Peter. *China Hands.* New York: Simon & Schuster. 1995.

REES, Laurence. *Behind Closed Doors—Stalin, The Nazis, and The West.* BBC Books. 2008.

REEVES, Richard. *Daring Young Men—The Heroism and Triumph of The Berlin Airlift.* New York: Simon & Schuster. 2010.

ROBERTS, Andrew. *Masters and Commander—the Military Geniuses Who Led the West to Victory in WWII.* London: Penguin Books. 2009.

ROMANUS, Charles F. and SUNDERLAN, Riley. 3 volumes: *Stilwell's Mission to China; China-Burma-India Stilwell's Command Problems; and China-Burma-India Time Runs Out in CBI.* Center of Military History United States Army.

RUSHER, William A. *Special Counsel—An Inside Report On The Senate Investigations Into Communism.* New Rochelle, New York: Arlington House. 1968.

SAMSON, Jack. *The Flying Tiger—The True Story of General Claire Chennault and the U.S. 14th Air Force in China.* Guilford, Conn: The Lyons Press. 1968.

SCHALLER, Michael. *The U.S. Crusade in China, 1938–1945.* New York: Columbia University Press. 1979.

———. *The United States and China in the Twentieth Century.* New York: Oxford University Press. 1979.

SCHMITDZ, David. F. *Henry L. Stimson. The First Wise Man.* Wilmington DE: SR Books. 2001.

SERVICE, John S. *Lost Chance in China.* (Joseph W. Esherick) The World War II Dispatches of John S. Service. New York: Random House 1974.

SHERWOOD, Robert E. *Roosevelt and Hopkins An Intimate History.* New York: Harper & Brothers. 1948.

———. *The White House Papers of Harry L. Hopkins.* London: Eyre & Spottiswoode. 1949 [2 volumes].

SMITH, Gaddis. *American Diplomacy During the Second World War.* New York: Alfred A. Knopf. 2nd Edition. 1985.

SNOW, Edgar. *Edgar Snow's China—A Personal Account of the Chinese Revolution Compiled From the Writings of Edgar Snow.* New York: Random House. 1981.

STANDLEY, William H. Admiral, and AGETON, Arthur A. Rear Admiral. *Admiral Ambassador to Russia.* Chicago: Henry Regnery Company. 1955.

STETTINIUS, Edward R. *Lend-Lease—Weapon For Victory.* New York: The MacMillan Company. 1944.

STETTINIUS, Edward R. Jr. *Roosevelt and the Russians: The Yalta Conference.* Garden City New York: Doubleday & Company. 1949.

_____. *The Diaries of Edward R. Stettinius, Jr.* [eds. Thomas M. Campbell and George C. Herring] New York: New Viewpoints—A Division of Franklin Watts, Inc. 1975.

STIMSON, Henry L. & BUNDY, McGeorge. *On Active Service in Peace and War.* New York: Harper & Brothers. 1947.

STOLER, Mark A. *George C. Marshall Soldier Statesman of the American Century.* New York: Twayne Publishers. 1989.

STOLER, Mark A. *Allies and Adversaries—The Joint Chiefs of Staff, the Grand Alliance, and U.S. Strategy in World War II.* Chapel Hill NC: The University of North Carolina Press. 2000.

_____. *Allies In War. Britain and America Against the Axis Powers 1940–1945.* London: Hodder Arnold. 2005.

STUECK, William. *The Wedemeyer Mission. American Politics and Foreign Policy During the Cold War.* Athens, GA: The University of Georgia Press. 1984.

TAYLOR, Jay. *The Generalissimo Chiang Kai-Shek and The Struggle for Modern China.* Cambridge, Mass. The Belknap Press of Harvard University Press. 2009.

THOMAS, John N. *The Institute of Pacific Relations. Asian Scholars and American Politics.* Seattle: University of Washington Press. 1974.

THORNE, Christopher. *Allies of a Kind. The United States, Britain, and the War Against Japan.* New York: Oxford University Press. 1978.

TSOU, Tang. *America's Failure in China 1941–50.* [two vols.] Chicago: University of Chicago Press. 1963.

TUCHMAN, Barbara W. *Stilwell and the American Experience in China 1911–1945.* New York: The Macmillan Company. 1970.

_____. *Notes From China.* New York: Collier Books. 1972.

UTLEY, Freda. *Last Chance In China.* New York: The Bobbs Merrill Company. 1947.

_____. *The China Story.* Chicago: Henry Regnery Company. 1951.

VANDENBERG, *Arthur H. Senator—The Private Papers of Senator Vandenberg.*(ed.) Arthur H. Vandenberg, Jr. New York: Houghton Mifflin Company. 1952.

VAN DE VEN, Hans. *War and Nationalism in China 1925–1945.* London and New York: Routgeledge Curzon. 2003.

WATSON, Mark Skinner. *Chief of Staff: Prewar Plans and Preparations.* Historical

Division Department of the Army Washington, D.C. 1950.

WEBSTER, Donovan. *The Burma Road. The Epic Story of the China-Burma-India Theatre in World War II.* New York: Farrar, Straus and Giroux 2003.

WEDEMEYER, General Albert C. *Wedemeyer Reports!* New York: Henry Holt & Company 1958.

WEIL, Martin. *A Pretty Good Club. The Founding Fathers of the U.S. Foreign Services.* New York: W.W. Norton & Company. 1978.

WELCH. Robert. *Again, May God Forgive Us.* Chicago, Ill. Henry Regnery Company 1952.

WELCH, Robert H.W. *The Life of John Birch.* Boston and Los Angeles: Western Islands Publishers. 1960.

WELLS, Sumner. *Where Are We Heading?* New York: Harper & Brothers. 1946.

WEST, Bing. *The Wrong War—Grit Strategy, and the Way Out of Afghanistan.* New York: Random House. 2011.

WHITE, Theodore H. and Annalee Jacoby. *Thunder Out of China.* New York: William Sloane Associates, Inc. 1946.

WHITE, Theodore H. (ed.) *The Stilwell Papers.* New York: William Sloane Associates, Inc. 1948.

WILLOUGHBY, Charles A. *Shanghai Conspiracy—The Sorge Spy Ring.* New York: E. P. Dutton & Company, Inc. 1952.

ZACHARIAS, Capt. Ellis M. USN. *Secret Missions. The Story of an Intelligence Officer.* New York: G. P. Putnam's Sons 1946.

_____. *Behind Closed Doors. The Secret History of the Cold War.* New York: G. P. Putnam's Sons 1950.

MISCELLANEOUS BOOKS

A DECADE OF AMERICAN FOREIGN POLICY. Basic Documents 1941–1949 [Revised Edition] Department of State Washington 1985.

BUTLER, Susan. (ed.) *My Dear Mr. Stalin.* Complete Correspondence/FDR and Stalin. 1997.

COLD WAR, THE. *A Conflict of Ideology and Power.* (2nd edition) and with introduction by Norman A. Graebner. Lexington MA: D. C. Heath and Company. 1976.

CONSERVATIVE PAPER, THE. [a collection of essays with intro by Melvin R. Laird] Garden City NY: Anchor Books 1964.

SINO-AMERICAN RELATIONS 1945–1955 A JOINT REASSESMENT OF A CRITICAL DECADE. Harry Harding and Yuan Ming Editors. Wilmington Delaware: SR Books. 1989.

ARTICLES

ALSOP, Joseph and Stewart. From *Saturday Evening Post.* April 30, 1949. "How Our Foreign Policy is Made."

_____. "The Lesson of Korea" *Saturday Evening Post*. September 2, 1950.

ALSOP, Joseph. "The Feud Between Stilwell and Chiang" *Saturday Evening Post*. January 7, 1950.

_____."We Opened the Door for The Communists" *Saturday Evening Post*. January 14, 1950.

_____. "The Foredoomed Mission of General Marshall" *Saturday Evening Post*. January 21, 1950.

_____. "Will China Stay Red?" *Saturday Evening Post*. October 30, 1954.

_____. "Wallace's Policy Defended by Alsop" *New York Times*. October 19, 1951.

ATKINSON, Rick. "Ten Things Every American Student Should Know About Our Army in World War 2" http://www.fpri.org/footnotes/1415.200905. atkinson.usarmywwii.html

BALDWIN, Hanson. W. "U.S. Cannot Longer Accept Myth that Reds Are 'Agrarian Reformers,' it is Held" *New York Times*. November 21, 1948.

_____. "Behind the Removal of General Stilwell" *New York Times*. October 30, 1944.

BEAVERBROOK, Lord "Beaverbrook Asks 2nd Front in Europe to Bolster Russia" *New York Times*. April 24, 1942.

BEN-MOSHE, Tuvia. "Winston Churchill and the 'Second Front': A Reappraisal" *The Journal of Modern History*. Sept 1990.

BESS, Demaree. "What Does Russia Want?" *The Saturday Evening Post*. March 20, 1943.

_____. "Gambling With Peace" *The Saturday Evening Post*. April 8, 1939. p. 25.

_____. "The Cost of Roosevelt's 'Great Design'" *The Saturday Evening Post*. May 27, 1944.

BLUMENSON, Martin. "Can Official History Be Honest History?" *Military Affairs*. 1962.

BRADEN, Spruille. "Turmoil in State Department" *U.S. News and World Report*. April 9, 1954.

BUCK, Pearl. S. "Our Last Chance in China" *Common Sense*. August 1944. p. 265.

_____. "Our Dangerous Myths About China" *New York Times*. Oct. 23, 1949. [BOOK 1]

BUDENZ, Louis. "How The Reds Snatched Henry Wallace" *Colliers*. September 18, 1948.

BUDENZ, Louis Francis. "How the Communists Hoodwinked FDR" *The American Mercury*. October 1954. p. 5–14.

BUHITE, Russell "D. Patrick J. Hurley and the Yalta Far Eastern Agreement" *The Pacific Historical Review*. Vol. 37, No. 3. (Aug., 1968), pp. 343–353.

BULLITT, William C. "Can Truman Avoid World War III?" *The American Mercury*. June 1947.

_____. "How We Won the War and Lost the Peace" *Life*, Aug 30, 1948.

BUNTING, Josiah. "Marshall, Stimson, Roosevelt: Strategic Decisions, 1940–

1945" a Speech delivered 2005 at Johns Hopkins. http://www.sais-jhu.edu/merrillcenter-original/BuntingPaper.pdf

BYRNES, James F. "Sect of State Disputes Hurley Charges" *New York Times*. December 8, 1945.

CARROLL, Ann W. "Who Lost China?" An excellent essay. http://www.ewtn.com/library/HOMELIBR/FR89102.TXT

CHAMBERLIN, William Henry. "How Franklin Roosevelt Lied America Into War" *The Journal of Historical Review*. Nov–Dec 1944

———. "Information, *Please* About Russia" *Harper's Magazine*. April 1944.

———. "The Sources of Russia's Strength" *Harper's Magazine* March 1943.

CHENNAULT, General. Three News Reports *New York Times*. (1) July 16, 1945 "Critics of China 'Shock' Chennault. He praises Chiang. (2) July 17, 1945. "Chennault Hailed by Chinese Press." (3) July 20, 1945. "Chennault 'Ouster'is Reported Denied.

COHEN, Warren I. Review of three books by Warren L. Cohen [All Relate to the Cold War]: (1) *The Committee of One Million: "China Lobby" Politics, 1953–1971* by Stanley D. Bachrack; (2) *The Origins of the Cold War in Asia.* by Yonosuke Nagai and Akira Iriye, (eds.) 1977; (3) *Harry Truman's China Policy: McCarthyism and the Diplomacy of Hysteria*, 1947–1951 by Lewis McCarroll Purifoy. 1976. Some good language on why Kennan and Acheson as advisors to Truman applied the "Truman Doctrine" to Europe and Middle East, but not to Asia. http://www.jstor.org/stable/2701290.

———. Review of: [1] *The China Lobby in American Politics.* Au: KOEN, Ross and KAGAN, Richard C. [2] *Lost Chance in China: The World War II Despatches of John S. Service.* Au: John S. Service; [3] *The Institute of Pacific Relations: Asian Scholars and American Politics.* Au: John N. Thomas. Located: http://www.jstor.org/stable/2700997.

COLVILLE, John. "How the West Lost the Peace in 1945" *Commentary*. September, 1985.

CREEL, George. "The President's Health" *Colliers*. March 3, 1945. p. 15.

CRIBBS, John M. LTC. "President Roosevelt's Recall of General Stilwell from China: A Military Casualty of Bureaucratic Politics" National War College Essay. 1994.

DALLEK, Robert. "Franklin Roosevelt as World Leader" *The American Historical Review*, vol. 76, No. 5 (December 1971).

DANDHEV, Alex. "Very Special Relationship: Field Marshall Sir John Dill and General George Marshall." An Essay from the Web. http://handle.dtic.mil/100.2/ADA440887

DAVIS, Elmer. "U.S. Is Loosing the War of Words" *Life* Magazine. March 22, 1943.

DAVIS, Forrest. "The January Promise" (two parts) *Saturday Evening Post*. Feb. 20, and Feb 27, 1943

_____. "Roosevelt's World Blueprint" *Saturday Evening Post*. April 10, 1943.

_____. "What Really Happened at Teheran" (part 1) *Saturday Evening Post*. May 13, 1944.

_____. "What Really Happened at Teheran" (part 2). *Saturday Evening Post*. May 20, 1943.

DEVINE, Michael J. Book Review of *From Roosevelt to Truman: Potsdam, Hiroshima and the Cold War*. Au: Wilson D. Miscamble. *Diplomatic History*. Vol. 32, No. 1 January 2008.

DURDIN, Tillman. "Basic Issues in China Unchanged in 20 Years" *New York Times*. December 2, 1945

_____. "China Reds boast Broad Land Shift—Confiscation in Third Phase . . . " *New York Times*. February 4, 1947.

_____. "China Reds Get Manchuria, Leaders in Chunking Fear" *New York Times*. November 15, 1945.

_____. "China Reds Offer Division of Power" *New York Times*. September 12, 1945.

_____. Six *New York Times* articles. (1) December 23, 1945. "Chungking Rivals Greet Marshall, Welcome him to Chungking"; (2) December 24, 1945. "Marshall Confers With Chinese Reds to Hear Their Case"; (3) January 2, 1946. "Marshall and Red Study China's War"; (4) January 5, 1946. "Marshall Parley With Chinese Near"; (5) January 7, 1946 "Marshall to Meet Opposing Chinese at Session Today"; (6) January 10, 1946. "Chinese Services Believed Merging"

_____. "China's Civil War Officially At End" *New York Times*. January 14, 1946.

_____. "Marshall's Task in China Delicate and Intricate" *New York Times*. December 16, 1945.

_____. "Marshall's Views Spur New Efforts in China" *New York Times*. January 12, 1947.

_____. "Peace Accord in China Due Today As Marshall Mediation Succeeds" *New York Times*. January 9, 1946.

_____. "Talks Said to Go Smoothly" *New York Times*. September 2, 1945.

_____. "The Basic Issues in China" *New York Times*. September 29, 1946.

_____. "U.S. Army to Shun Any Strife in China" *New York Times*. August 31, 1945.

_____. "Wedemeyer Near End of Task of Surveying China For Truman" *New York Times*. August 22, 1947.

EARLE, George H. "FDR'S Tragic Mistake" *Confidential* magazine. August 1958. p. 14.

EILER, Keith E. "An Uncommon Soldier" *Hoover Digest*. 2001, No. 4.

_____. "The Man Who Planned The Victory: An Interview with General Albert C. Wedemeyer by Keith E. Eiler" *Hoover Digest*. No. 4, 2001.

EMERSON, William. "Franklin Roosevelt as Commander-in-Chief in World

War II" *Military Affairs*. Vol 22 Winter 1958–59.

FLEMING, Thomas. "The Big Leak" Disclosure of FDR's War Plans, The Victory Plan. *American Heritage Magazine*. December 1987.

GADDIS, John Lewis. "Was The Truman Doctrine a Real Turning Point?" *Foreign Affairs*. January 1974. pp. 386–402.

_____. "Korea in American Politics, Strategy, and Diplomacy, 1945–50" in *The Origins of the Cold War in Asia*. Akira IRIYE, ed. New York: Columbia University Press. 1977

GITTINGS, John. "If Mao Had Met Roosevelt: An Alternative View of US-China Relations" An essay. In *President Gore . . . And Other Things That Never Happened*. (ed) Duncan Brack. London, Politico's 2006, pp. 171–183.

GREAVES, Percy L. Jr. "Admission of MAGIC Demolishes FDR's Claim of Surprise" From *The Real Infamy of Pearl Harbor*. *Journal of Historical Review*, 2001.

GREY, Jeffrey (ed.) *Essays on Official History in the United States and British Commonwealth*. One selected: "Change Becomes Continuity: The Start of the U.S. Army's 'Green Book' Series. By Edward J. Drea.

HARBUTT, Fraser. "Churchill, Hopkins, and the 'Other' Americans An Alternative Perspective on Anglo-American relations, 1941–1945" *The International History Review*. May 1986.

HAUSER, Maj. Peter F. "Lessons From the Kriegsakademie" *Air Power Journal*. 1966. Co Authors Maj John C. Orndorff and Lt. Col. John C. Rawls.

HAVEMANN, Ernest. "Close Up of A Ghost—Harry Dexter White Turns Out To Be Arrogant, Diligent Man Who Kept Going To Movies" *Life*. November 23, 1953 pp. 29–35.

HILL AND KNOLTON, INC. "Finding the Facts" *Newsweek*. August 4, 1947 on Wedemeyer and his 1947 Fact Finding Trip to China/Korea.

HOPKINS, Harry. "The Inside Story of My Meeting With Stalin" *The American Magazine*. December 1941 p. 14.

HORNBECK, Stanley K. "China and American Foreign Policy" *Annals of the American Academy of Political and Social Science*. Vol 138 (Jul 1928) pp. 26–37.

_____. "The Attitude and Policy of the United States Toward China" *Annals of the American Academy of Political and Social Science*. Vol 132. (Jul 1927) pp. 48–51.

_____. His review of *The Manchurian Crisis. 1931–1932: A Tragedy in International Relations*. Au: Sara R. Smith. *The American Historical Review*. Vol. 54, No. 2 (Jan 1949) pp. 363–364.

_____. A review of his book *The United States and the Far East: Certain Fundamentals of Policy*. Review by Esther B. Chu. *Far Eastern Survey*. Vol 12, No. 17 (August 25, 1943).

_____. A review of his book *Contemporary Politics in the Far East*. Reviewed by Payson J. Treat in *The American Historical Review*. Vol. 22, No 3 (apr. 1917)

HURLEY, Patrick. "China is Unconquerable" Press Release in *New York Times*. December 16, 1944

_____. "Hurley Sees Big 3 Agreed on China" *New York Times*. April 29, 1945.

_____. "Hurley Reported About to Resign" *New York Times*. September 16, 1945.

HURLEY, Patrick J. Report of his Resignation. Truman promises China Policy to be revealed in toto. Congressional investigation of resignation assured. *New York Times*. November 30, 1945.

_____. Two *New York Times* articles. (1) December 6, 1945. "Hurley Accuses 5 Officials of Sabotaging Chinese Policy; Says 2 Sought Chiang's Ruin" (2) December 7, 1945. "Mr. Hurley on The Stand."

_____. *New York Times* article. December 7, 1945. "Hurley Contends Acheson Defeated Our Policy in Iran."

HURLEY, Patrick. Text of Hurley's address of resignation from *New York Times* November 28, 1945.

_____. Short article, from *Foreign Relations* on Hurley resignation and the controversy.

JACOBIUS, Arnold J. List of References to ACW in books published between 1943 and 1953. 2 Parts.

JAFFA. Harry V. "Churchill's Relevance to the Challenges of the Present" From The Churchill Center.

JOHNSON, Thomas and PALMER, Gretta. "Wedemeyer's Outstretched Hand— A General Who Made A Reality of American-Chinese Friendship" *The New Leader*. August 1946. Also published in *Reader's Digest* same year Oct.

JUDD, Walter H. "The Case For the Republicans" *The Saturday Evening Post*. October 11, 1952.

_____. "Remarks on the State Department White Paper" undated. Hoover Institution. Hornbeck File Box 263, Judd.

KAMP, Joseph P. "America Betrayed." Article on the tragic consequences of Reds on the Government Payroll. Constitutional Educational League, 342 Madison Avenue New York, New York. 1950

KEENAN, George F. The Famous "X" Article in *Foreign Affairs*. Winter 1947

KENT, Tyler. "The Roosevelt Legacy and The Kent Case" *Journal of Historical Review*. Vol 21 2002. The story of the 5-year imprisonment of a State Department code clerk in London in 1940 who accumulated information on FDR and the Prime Minister which compromised FDR's claim of neutrality. Kent's diplomatic immunity waived by USA and he stayed in British prison the entire war.

KIMBALL, Warren F. "The Cold War Warmed Over" *The American Historical Review*. A review of 3 books. (1) *The United States and the Origins of the Cold War, 1941–1947* by John Lewis Gaddis; (2) *The Limits of Power: The World and the United States Foreign Policy, 1945–1954* by Joyce Kolko and Gabriel Kolko. (3) *The New Left and the Origins of the Cold War* by Robert James Maddox.

_____. "Thirty Years After, or The Two Musketeers" Presidential Address. *Diplomatic History*. 18, No. 2 Spring 1994.

_____. "The Incredible Shrinking War: The Second World War, Not (Just) the Origins of the Cold War." *Diplomatic History*. Vol. 25. No. 3 (Sumer 2001).

KIRPATRICK, Major Charles E. "Computing the Requirements for War—the Logic of the Victory Plan of 1941" Contemporary History [undated] web site: http://www.history.navy.mil/colloquia/cch5c.htm

KROCK, Arthur. "President Rebukes OWI for Broadcast on Regime In Italy" *New York Times*. July 28, 1943

_____. Report on Yalta Conference "Two Reporters of the Yalta Conference" *New York Times*. March 1, 1945.

_____. "Hopkins War Role" *New York Times*. July 4, 1945. Tribute to Hopkins from President Truman on resignation of Hopkins.

_____. "Behind Mr. Vandenberg's Broad Phrases. *New York Times*. March 1, 1946.

_____. "Republicans Launch Foreign Policy Attack" *New York Times*. June 26, 1949. Vandenberg Joins in GOP Criticism—China and Spain the Issues.

_____. "Chiang Kai-shek and Our Post-War Policy" *New York Times*. February 10, 1956.

KUBEK, Anthony. "The Morgenthau Plan and the Problem of Policy Perversion" *Journal of Historical Review*. Summer 1989. Vol. 9 # 3.P. 287.

_____. "Communism At Pearl Harbor" A 22-page article on Internet: www.geocities.com/Pentagon/6315/comatph.html?20083.

_____. "The Amerasia Papers: A Clue To the Catastrophe of China" The Introduction to the Two volume Hearings, a duplicate. Subcommittee to Investigate the Administration of the Internal Security Act and Other Internal Security Laws of the Committee on the Judiciary United States Senate. January 26, 1970.

LaFEBER, Walter. "Roosevelt, Churchill and Indochina: 1942–45" *The American Historical Review*. December 1975.

_____. Review by him of *American-East Asian Relations: A Survey*. Au: Ernest R. May, and James C. Thompson, Jr. "The Journal of East-Asian Relations." Vol. 32, 1973.[Book 9]

_____. "Roosevelt, Churchill and Indochina: 1942–1945" *American Historical Review*. 80 December 1975 pp. 1277–1295.

_____. "American Policy-Makers, Public Opinion, and the Outbreak of the Cold War, 1945–1950. *The Origins of the Cold War in Asia*. Akira *Iriye* ed.

LANIUS, Charles. "Spain, Next Step For Hitler?" *The Saturday Evening Post*. February 27, 1943.

LASKY, Victor. "The Case Against Dean Acheson" (Combined With) Article by HUIE, William Bradford. "The Untold Facts in the Forrestal Case" from *The New American Mercury*. Reprinted from Congressional Record of December

6, 1950 as inserted by Senator Joseph McCarthy.

LAWRENCE, W.H. "Byrnes Disputes Hurley's Charges in Senate Inquiry" Says no evidence produced. Asserts policy is to Broaden Chiang's Regime to Include Reds and other factions. *New York Times*. December 8, 1945

LEIGHTON, Richard M. "Overlord Revisited: An Interpretation of American Strategy in the European War, 1942–1944" *The American Historical Review*. 1963.

LEVINE, Steven I. "A New Look at American Mediation in the Chinese Civil War: The Marshall Mission in Manchuria" *Diplomatic History*. Fall 1979. Issue 4. pp. 349–376.

LIPPMAN, Walter. "Mr. Hurley and Mr. Wheeler" *Washington Post*. November 29, 1945

LIU, F.F. "Stwilwell and Wedemeyer Missions in China" [extract from book *A Military History of China*—1924–1949. Princeton University Press] Ex CBI Roundup June 1957. pp. 6–15.

LOWRY, Dr. Charles W. Article in *The Pilot Southern Pines* August 11, 1986. On Wedemeyer reply to Colville.

LUBELL, Samuel. "Vinegar Joe and the Reluctant Dragon" *The Saturday Evening Post*. February 24, 1945.

LUCE, Clare Booth. "U.S. General Stilwell Commands Chinese on Burma Front" from *Life*. April 27, 1942.

_____. "Burma Mission—*Life* Reports on U. S. General Stilwell and Staff.

_____. *Essay on General Stilwell*. "U.S. General Stilwell Commands Chinese on Burma Front" *Life*. April 27, 1942. "Just Before they Took A Hell of A Beating" *Life*. June 15, 1942. p. 94.

LUCE, Henry R. "The American Century" *Diplomatic History*. Spring 1999.

LUNDESTAD, Geir. "American Grand Strategy since 1940" *Diplomatic History*. September 2007.

MACLEAN, Elizabeth Kimball. "Joseph E. Davies and Soviet American Relations, 1941–1943. *Diplomatic History*. Winter 1980, Issue 4. pp. 73–93.

MACDONALD, Douglas J. "Communist Bloc Expansion in the Early Cold War: Challenging Realism, Refuting Revisionism" *International Security*. Vol. 20, No. 3 Winter, 1995–1996 pp. 152–188.

MANLEY, Chesley. Interview with Manley by FBI February 8. 1942 following leak of Victory Plan. [National Archives Legal Folder # 1] R.G. 319 Army Intelligence File 1941–1948. Box 051.

MARSHALL, General George. Statement January 7, 1947 on American Views on Situation in China. www.fordham.edu/halsall/mod/1947-marshall-china.html

MARSHALL, General. Statement and report in *New York Times,* January 12, 1947, that he is disappointed CCP will not participate in Constitutional Convention.

MATLOFF, Maurice. "Grand Strategy and the Washington High Command" Chapter 21 from *American Military History.*

_____. "The American Approach to War" Essays from book *The Theory and Practice of War.* London: Cassell. 1965. Essays Presented to Captain B. H. Liddell Hart (ed.) Michael Howard. Essay 10.

MATTHEWS, Herbert L. *New York Times* article October 10, 1948. Churchill quoted as saying only the Atomic Bomb lies between Freedom and Russian domination. Fears possible of another war.

MAURER, Herrymon. "The Tyrannous Decade" *Fortune* magazine February 1948.

MacARTHUR, Hearings. *New York Times* article June 17, 1951. Reviews the testimony, with criticism of discrepancies.

McCARRAN, Pat. Senator. "Charges Acheson Gave 'Misleading' Information on China. Sees 'Softness' on China." News Release: *New York Times*. April 17, 1949.

McFARLAND, Keith D. "Shooting Star" *Diplomatic History.* June 2007.

McNAUGHTON, Frank. "Mme. Chiang in the U.S. Capitol." *Life* Magazine. March 8, 1943. p. 11.

MORGENTHAU, Henry, Jr. "How FDR Fought the Axis" Part III. *Colliers.* October 11, 1947. The third of three part series.

MOORE, Charles P. "What's the Matter With Being a Strategist (Now)?" *Parameters.* December 22, 2009.

MOORE, Harriet. "Soviet Far Eastern Policy" *Far Eastern Survey.* March 12, 1941.

_____. "Silence of Understanding" *Far Eastern Survey.* March 8, 1943.

MOORE, Harriet. "Soviet Far Eastern Relations Since 1941" *Pacific Affairs.* Sept 1944.

MOUNTBATTEN, Lord Louis. Feature article in *Life.* August 17, 1942. p. 63.

MULSHINE, Paul. Article Ledger May 5, 2011 on Counter Insurgency Warfare. Mentions President Kennedy and several opponents, who favor instead Special Forces.

MURPHY, Charles J.F. "Crisis in China" The Yenan Communists have not come up to their advance billing. A Sure American policy could bring the peace China and, apparently, Russia want. *Life.* December 17, 1945 p. 106.

NOBLE, Harold. J. "Our Most Dangerous Boundry" [Korea] *Saturday Evening Post.* August 31, 1946.

OLOFSON, Darwin. A reporter interviewed General Wedemeyer and wrote story June 4, 1984 for *World-Herald Bureau.* He reports Churchill, post war asked ACW if he still thought a 1943 cross channel attack was the best time. He answered yes.

OSGOOD, Col. John (ret) "The Three Major Strategic Considerations That Shaped 'Europe First Strategy' During World War II" Essay source. web: http://www.juris99.com/mil/wc11.htm

PARRISH, Michael E. "Soviet Espionage and the Cold War" *Diplomatic History.*

Winter 2001.

PEARSON, Drew. "U.S. Would Qualify 'Slave Labor'" *The Washington Post.* May 20, 1945. p. 5B.

_____. Article in *Washington Post* June 15, 1945. Faults the criticism of the Foreign Service Officers.

PERLOFF, James. "China Betrayed Into Communism" July 24, 2009. Essay. *The New American.com.*

_____. "Pearl Harbor: Hawaii Was Surprised; FDR Was Not" *The New American* December 4, 2008. (Interesting details on Marshall and FDR that they had a good deal of prior knowledge about attack on Pearl Harbor and withheld it from Kimmel and Short)

PICKLER, Gordon K. "Antithetic American Experiences in China: Stilwell and Chennault" *Air University Review.* January 1972.

PLETCHER, David M. "The United States and Extraterritoriality" *Diplomatic History.* June 2003.

PULESTON, Capt. W. D, USN Ret. "Blunders of World War 2" *U.S. News and World Report.* February 4, 1955.

RAACK, R.C. "Stalin's Plans for World War II" *Journal of Contemporary History.* April 1991.

_____. "Stalin's Role in the Coming of World War II" 2 items *World Affairs.* Spring 1996, and Fall 1996.

RAICO, Ralph. "Rethinking Churchill" A debunking of the Churchill Myth. A five part essay. Chapter 12 from *The Costs of War.* Au: John V. Denson (book contains a lot of fine essays).

RESIS, Albert. "The Churchill-Stalin Secret 'Percentages' Agreement on the Balkans, Moscow, October 1944" *The American Historical Review.* Vol. 83, No. 2 Apr., 1978 pp. 368–387.

RESTON, James B. "Soviet Moderation in U.N. Inspires Hopes, Suspicions" *New York Times.* September 21, 1950.

_____. "Wheeler Lays Stimson Attack to 'Plot' for War" Intent to terrify people. *New York Times.* July 29, 1941.

_____. "Bewildered Congress Faces World Leadership Decision" [Need to decide whether to come to aid of Greece—Truman Doctrine Aid to Greece and Turkey]

_____. "China Recognition Issue Is Complex One For Us" *New York Times.* November 27, 1949.

_____. "U.S. Will Now Follow Hands-Off Policy In China" *New York Times.* April 24, 1949.

_____. Two articles from *New York Times.* [1] May 1, 1959 "U.S. Stays Skeptical in Negotiating With Russia"; [2] "Big Three Would Withdraw To Ports in North Under Proposal" [Kennan's Plan "A"] Having to do with Berlin Blockade and efforts to resolve.

_____. *New York Times.* January 1, 1951. Wedemeyer's purchase of diplomatic wardrobe. Acheson's telling ACW his "appointment" had been rescinded.

_____. "New Secretary of State Takes Over at Critical Period at Home and Abroad" *New York Times.* January 12, 1947.

_____. "Discrepancies Dot Major Testimony in McArthur Study" *New York Times.* June 11, 1951.

ROBERTSON, Walter S. "A Top Diplomat's Story of How the Reds Took China" *U.S. News and World Report.* June 29, 1959. p. 72–73.

SALISBURY, Laurence E. "Changes In China" *Far Eastern Survey.* January 31, 1945.

_____. "New Aid to China" *Far Eastern Survey.* April 21, 1948.

_____. "Our China Policy" *Far Eastern Survey.* April 25, 1945.

_____. "Personnel and Far Eastern Policy" *Far Eastern Survey.* December 19, 1945.

_____. "Report on China" *Far Eastern Survey.* November 15, 1944.

_____. "Support of the Status Quo" *Far Eastern Survey.* October 24, 1945.

SANDERS, Donald B. "Stalin Plotted a Separate Peace" *The American Mercury.* November 1947.

SCHUURMAN, Bart. "Clausewitz and the 'New Wars' Scholars" *Parameters.* Spring 2010 pp. 89–100.

SCHAFFER, Ronald. "General Stanley D. Embick: Military Dissenter" *Military Affairs,* Vol 37, (October 1973).

SHALETT, Sidney. *New York Times* article November 11, 1945 "Stability by Evolution in U.S. Far East Policy" Aim to Prevent the Rise of New Aggressor in Orient.

SHERWOOD, Robert E. "The Secret Papers of Harry L. Hopkins" *Colliers.* July 17, 1948.

SCHRECKER, E. "Soviet Espionage on American TV" *Diplomatic History.* April 2003.

SHERWOOD, Robert E. "The Secret Papers of Harry L. Hopkins" *Collier's.* May 29, 1948.

SIDEY, Hugh. "A Prescient Soldier Looks Back" *Time* Magazine. March 7, 1983. Very complimentary article about Wedemeyer's background, war planning, endorsement of a 1943 invasion, his run-ins with Churchill who had other strategic ideas.

SMALL, Melvin. "How We Learned to Love the Russians: American Media and the Soviet Union During World War II" *The Historian.* May 1974 pp. 455–78.

SMITH, Beverley. "Why We Went to War in Korea" The White House Story. *Saturday Evening Post.* November 10, 1951.

SMITH, Leo. "How Red Agents Operated Inside the White House" *The National Police Gazette.* [March 1954] p. 5–9.

SMITH, M. Brewster. "The Personal Setting of Public Opinions: a Study of Attitudes Toward Russia" *Public Opinion Quarterly* XI (Winter 1947) Opinion Poll on Russia. 1947–1948.

SNOW, Edgar. "Asia Saved Our Bacon" *The Saturday Evening Post*. February 27, 1943.

_____. "Must China Go Red?" *The Saturday Evening Post*. May 12, 1945.

_____. "Sixty Million Lost Allies" *The Saturday Evening Post*. June 18, 1944.

SOMMERS, Martin. "Why Russia Got The Drop On US" *The Saturday Evening Post*. February 8, 1947.

STEELE, Richard W. "Franklin D. Roosevelt and His Foreign Policy Critics." *Political Science Quarterly*. Vol. 943, No. 1 (Spring, 1979) pp. 15–32.

STEPHANSON, Anders. "War and Diplomatic History" *Diplomatic History*. Summer, 2001.

SWEWART, Maxwell. "Wedemeyer's Report on China." *The Nation*. September 20, 1947.

STIMSON, Henry L. "The Decision To Use The Atom Bomb" *Harper's*. February 1947.

STOLER, Mark A. "Avoiding entry Into World War II" *Diplomatic History*. April 2003.

_____. "From Continentalism to Globalism: General Stanley D. Embick, the Joint Strategic Survey Committee, and the Military View of American National Policy During the Second World War" *Diplomatic History*. Summer 1982. Issue 3, pp. 303–320.

_____. "Shooting Star" *Diplomatic History*. June 2007.

_____. "The 'Second Front' and American Fear of Soviet Expansion, 1941–1943" *Military Affairs*. (October 1975).

_____. "The Second World War in U.S. History and Memory" *Diplomatic History*. Summer 2001.

_____. "War and Diplomacy: Or Clausewitz for Diplomatic Historians" *Diplomatic History*. January 2005.

_____. "What a Long, Strange Trip It's Been" *Diplomatic History*. June 2007.

_____. "A Half Century of Conflict: Interpretations of U.S. World War II Diplomacy" Historiography and Bibliography. *Diplomatic History*. Vol 25 No. 3 (Summer 2001).

STRANGE, Joseph L. "The British Rejection of Operation Sledgehammer, An Alternative Motive" *Military Affairs*. Vol. 46 February 1982.

SULZBERGER, C.L. "Litvinov a Lonely Jeremiah Who foresaw the 'Cold War'" *New York Times*. January 3, 1952.

THEOHARIS, Athan. "James F. Byrnes: Unwitting Yalta Myth-Maker" *Political Science Quarterly*. Vol. 81. (December 1966).

_____. "Roosevelt and Truman on Yalta: The Origins of the Cold War" *Political Science Quarterly*. Vol. 87, (June 1972).

THOMPSON, Dorothy. "Roosevelt, Churchill and Hitler" *Look* Magazine. January 14, 1941. p. 8.

THOMPSON, James C. "Dragon Under Glass: Time For A New China Policy" *The Atlantic.* October 1967.

TONG, Hollington . "Why Red China Won't Break" *The Reader's Digest.* July 1957. pp. 97–100.

TRUMAN, Harry. His statement on U.S. Policy on China delivered December 15, 1945. *New York Times.*

_____. *New York Times* article. October 28, 1952. Text of Truman Statement Disputing Eisenhower Speech on Korea.

_____. "Yalta ... China ... Hiss ... Korea ... MacArthur ... The Campaign They All Get in the News When Truman Speaks Out." *U.S. News and World Report.* Sept. 14, 1956. pp. 118–123.

TUCHMAN, Barbara. "If Mao Had Come to Washington: An Essay in Alternatives" *Foreign Affairs.* October 1972. p. 44–64.

VANDENBERG, Senator Arthur H. *New York Times* article February 28, 1946 by C.P. Trussel. "What is Russia Up to? Urges Open Clear Policy."

WALLACE, Henry. *New York Times* article September 22, 1946 on the rift between Truman and Wallace as a result of Wallace "go soft" on Russia speech which resulted in Truman demanding Wallace resignation.

_____. *New York Times.* Dec. 9, 1949. "Wallace Cut Off From Atomic Data" per General Groves.

WEBER, Mark. "Was Hiroshima Necessary?" *Journal of Historical Review.* June 1997.

WEDEMEYER, General. "Let's Draw the Line Now" *Collier's* Magazine. November 17, 1951

_____. *Newsweek* article August 1947 on his fact-finding trip.

_____. Interview. *U.S. News & World Report.* "Korea True Will not Last" September 14, 1951.

_____. *New York Times* article. December 23, 1953, citing Wedemeyer and another general who say Soviet has Superiority in Europe.

_____. "General Wedemeyer's Plan For Future World Policy of U.S." *U.S. News and World Report.* June 22, 1951.

WILLKIE, Wendell. *Life* Magazine. April 26, 1943. p. 73. report on the success of his book *One World.*

WITTMER, Felix. "Freedom's Case Against Dean Acheson" *American Mercury.* April 1952. p. 3. Devastating indictment of Acheson; long string of pro commie steps and activities of Acheson; cover ups, defense of commi cronies in high places, ignoring of warnings, including a Senate appropriations committee with FBI information on commi in State Dept. General Marshall ignored the report. A whole lot of ammunition. *New York Times* article November 15, 1945: Address of Dean Acheson at Madison Square rally auspices of American Soviet Friendship. Statement of Acheson to effect that never had the interests of USA and USSR clashed! Long string of Acheson statements praising USSR, proposing pro Communist positions, and indicating no threat whatsoever from CCP (immediately follows the *American Mercury* article).

WEIGLEY, Russell F. "The American Military and the Principle of Civilian Control From McCellan to Powell" *The Journal of Military History*. October 1993.

WEINBERG, Gerhard L. "Comments on the Roundtable" *Diplomatic History*. Summer 2001.

WELLER, George. "Let's Quit Kidding Ourselves About China" *Saturday Evening Post*. June 7, 1947. p. 111.

WELLES, Benjamin. *New York Times* article. July 19, 1947. "Chinese Promise to Improve Army." Changes based on U.S. experience.

WHITE, Theodore H. "Life Looks At China" *Life* magazine. May 1, 1944. p. 99.

WHITE, Theodore H. and JACOBY, Annalee. "Zero Hour in China" *Harper's Magazine*. September 1946.

WHITE, William S. "Nazi Tactics Laid to McCarthy Foes" A Charge by Senator Ferguson. *New York Times*. July 25, 1950.

_____. *New York Times* article. January 10, 1951. General MacArthur denies testimony by Acheson that he ever urged a Coalition government in China. Also he charges that the Marshall Mission to China was a Blunder.

_____. "Marshall Says U.S. Must Never Yield on Entry of Communist China to U.N.; Denies any Soft Policy Toward Reds. *New York Times*. May 11, 1951

_____. *New York Times* article. May 2, 1951. "Wedemeyer in '47 Bade U.S. Army Korea to Avert Invasion." General's advice Ignored. Report Freed by President Shows.

_____. *New York Times* article. June 13, 1951. "Wedemeyer Says McArthur Denied Manchrian Troops." He says we must Draw Line and Tell Kremlin "No More."

WHITE, Thomas D. "Strategy and the Defense Intellectuals" *Saturday Evening Post*. May 4, 1963.

WILEY, Bell Irvin. "Kent Roberts Greenfield: An Appreciation" *Military Affairs*. winter 1958.

WILLOUGHBY, Maj. General Charles. Memorandum on The Chinese Communist Party. May 1, 1947 Military Intelligence Section.

WILTZ, John Edward. "The MacArthur Hearings of 1951: The Secret Testimony" *Military Affairs*. Vol. 39, December 1975.

YOUNG, Kenneth Ray. "The Stilwell Controversey: A Bibliographical Review" *Military Affairs*. April 1975. "The Stilwell Controversy: A Bibliographical Review" *Military Affairs*. 1975.

ZACHARIAS, Ellis, M. Real Admiral. "We Did Not Need to Drop the Bomb" *Look* magazine. May 23, 1950

_____. "How We Bungled the Japanese Surrender" *Look* magazine. June 6, 1950. [A Photocopy in Book 10]

ZUBOK, Vladislav. "Stalin's Plans and Russian Archives" *Diplomatic History.* 21. Spring 1997. pp. 295–305.

MISCELLANEOUS

APPLEBY, Simon. Web Site for Casablanca Conference, and some history and general information.

AMERICAN FOREIGN POLICY. *New York Times* article. March 1, 1946. Discussion of views of Secretary Byrnes and Senator Vandenberg.

ATOMIC WAR. "Threat of Atomic War-Basis of Misunderstanding With Soviet." *New York Times.* November 15, 1945.

CHINESE TINDER BOX. Article in *New York Times.* November 10, 1945.

COMMITTEE ON UN-AMERICAN ARTICITIES. Annual Report 1957. February 3, 1958. House Report 1350.

DIXIE MISSION, THE. A website article on the mission, which was told by Jack Klein. http://dixiemission.org/story.html

FORT LEAVENWORTH. Feature article in Life. August 17, 1942. p. 69. *"Get Tough with Russia"* Article from *New Republic.* March 18, 1946.

"HEADLINES AND WHAT'S BEHIND THEM." (ed) Joseph P. Kamp. Vol. III No. 1. February 1, 1951. A series of articles about Secretary of State Dean Acheson.

HEARTLAND THEORY. Web article.http://en.wikipedia.org/wiki/The_Nazis _Strike

INSTITUTE OF PACIFIC RELATIONS. In 15 Parts Plus Senate Report. Report of the Committee on the Judiciary Eighty-Second Congress Second Session pursuant to S. Res. 366. Hearings Held July 25, 1951–June 20, 1952 By the Internal Security Subcommittee.

McGOVERN, William M. His testimony before House Committee on Foreign Affairs. 80th Congress November 22, 1947.

SPECIAL MATERIAL RELATING TO CONGRESSMAN WALTER H, JUDD

JUDD, Hon Walter H. March 15, 1945 [3 Hoover 1 [e] Remarks in H. Representatives. "What Is The Truth About China?"

April 27, 1944 Wethersfield Businessman Speech "Our Job in The Pacific" [Cong Record May 3, 1944].

August 21, 1944 House of Rep. Speech "Our Last Chance in China" [extension of remarks of Pearl S. Buck in Common Sense August 1944] August 21, 1944.

House of Rep. Speech August 21, 1944 "Our Last Chance in China" [extension of remarks of Pearl S. Buck in Common Sense August 1944].

JUDD, Hon Walter H. March 15, 1945 Remarks in H. Representatives. "What Is The Truth About China?"

JUDD, Walter H,"How and Why Did We Get Into War In Korea?" Remarks by Judd in House of Rep. July 18, 1950.

JUDD, Hon. Walter H. Chair "Special Study Mission to Southeast Asia and the Pacific" July 2, 1954 House Committee on Foreign Affairs.

ORAL HISTORIES & INTERVIEWS

BYROADE, Henry. Oral History from Harry S. Truman Library. [Military Attache to General Marshall on China Mission]

CHENNAULT, Mrs. Clair L. Oral History of Mrs. Chennault taken November 21, 1966 by Raymond Henle, Director of Herbert Hoover Presidential Library.

HANDY, General Thomas. Oral History from Eisenhower Library. [PDF File].

JUDD, Walter H. Three Oral Histories. [1] from Eisenhower Library. Paul Hooper interview (3 sessions) August 1968, April 1969, and December 1970; [2] By Jerry Hess. April 13, 1970 From President Harry S. Truman Library [3]. Taken at Judd's Residence_in Washington D.C. January 26, 1976 by Charles T. Morrissey.

KIMMEL, Admiral. Interview. Relating to Pearl Harbor. Condemns FDR talks about his own and General Short's version. Gives citations to other articles/books. *Pacific Affairs*. September 1938.

MELBY, John F. Oral History Interview. Foreign Service Officer Chunking 1945–1945.

Harry S. Truman Library. November 7, 14, 21 & 28, 1972.

MORRIS, Robert. Ph.D. Oral History of Mr. Morris (on his dealings with former President Herbert Hoover) taken January 9, 1970 by Raymond Henle, Director of Herbert Hoover Presidential Library.

ROBERTSON, Walter S. Oral History of Mr. Robertson taken December 1, 1969 by Raymond Henle, Director of Herbert Hoover Presidential Library.

_____. The Reminiscences of Walter S. Robertson. Eisenhower Administration Project. Oral History Research Office. Columbia University 1970.

SERVICE, John S. Oral History With John. S. Service, March 28, April 6 and April 28, 1977. Harry S. Truman Library & Museum.

WEDEMEYER, General. Oral History taken by Forrest Pogue, February 1, 1958.

_____. Oral History taken by Col. Anthony Deskis December 1972.

_____. Oral History, taken by Raymond Henle director of Herbert Hoover Library. Winter 1969–70.

_____. Interview by Colonel Don H. Hampton on "Mobilization Planning" 1984.

_____. Very good interview by Kam Tai Lee of December 29, 1980. Wide ranging discussion of KMT and CCP what were reasons for loss of war? Reasons CKS against Guardianship for Manchuria; his 1947 report; Rightness of Stilwell's Burma campaign? Critical comments on Burma Road ACW opposed to it; it did not pay dividends; critical of Marshall for not supporting KMT.

THESES AND DISSERTATIONS

FELZER, Alan. "Congress and China, 1941–1950." A Dissertation 1960. Michigan State University.

JOHNSON. Erik L. "Never Never Land: Lieutenant General Albert C. Wedemeyer in China, October 1944 to August 1945" Graduate Thesis on General Wedemeyer's tour in China October 1944–August 1945.

MAGAW, Eugene Milo. "Lieutenant General Albert C. Wedemeyer and China 1944–1947." A Dissertation.

RHEE, Tong-Chin. Dissertation: *Sino-American Relations From 1942 Through 1949: A Study of Efforts to Settle the China Problem*. Clark University. 1976.

SCHIMMEL, Lee Ann. "The Evolution of an Interventionist—Senator Arthur T. Vandenberg. 1945–1949." A Master's Thesis.

SPEIGHTS, Duris, Jr. "The Wedemeyer Mission and the China Policy" A Master's Degree Thesis 1962.

VON PLINSKY, Alexander H. Capt. "General Albert C. Wedemeyer's Missions in China, 1944–1947: An Attempt to Achieve the Impossible" A Thesis presented at the Command And General Staff School for Master's Degree.

CHRONOLOGY

1901, September 7, "Boxer Protocol," p. 82
1919, June 28, Treaty of Versailles, p. 18
1933, November 16, Maxim Litvinov letter to Roosevelt, p. 163
1937, July 7, Japanese stage incident at the Marco Polo Bridge, p. 78
1937, October 5, Roosevelt's quarantine of Japan, p. 79
1940, June 22, Fall of France, p. 35
1941, January 29th–March 29th, ABC-1 staff conference, p. 35
1941, February 9, Churchill's "Give us the tools" speech, p. 50–51
1941, May 22. U.S. isolationist rally, p. 36
1941, June 22, Germany invades the Soviet Union, p. 164
1941, July 9, Roosevelt orders preparation of a mobilization plan, p. 37
1941, December 7, Pearl Harbor attack, p. 58
1941, December 12, Eisenhower reassigned, p. 44
1941 December 22, US-British ARCADIA Conference, p. 51
1942, February 15, British surrender at Singapore, p. 91
1942, February 26, Roosevelt letter to Secretary Stimson, p. 113
1942, March 2, Wedemeyer letter to Roosevelt, p. 44
1942, March 25, Eisenhower endorses the Victory Plan, p. 45
1942, April 4, MODICUM Conference in London, p. 58–59
1942, April 29, Japanese take Lashio, cut the Burma Road, p. 105
1942, June 2, Mountbatten White House meeting, p. 68
1942, November 8, Operation TORCH begins, p. 69–70
1942, December 23, Marshall's letter of gratitude to Wedemeyer, p. 47
1943, March 29, *Life* magazine's "Special USSR Issue," p. 170
1943, April 1, Marshall and Roosevelt discuss cross-channel attack, p. 56
1943, November 7, General Hurley arrives in China, p. 89
1944, April 10, Lend-lease conditional cut, p. 99
1944, April 18, Churchill expresses doubts on OVERLORD, p. 74
1944, May 3, Congressman Miller speech before the House, p. 192
1944, June 5, Allied forces enter Rome, p. 72
1944, August 21, Congressman Judd speech before House, p. 192
1944, September 19, Roosevelt sends sharp telegram to Chiang, p. 102

INDEX